THE PERSISTENCE OF

THE SACRED IN

MODERN THOUGHT

· · · · · · · · · · · · · · · · · · · ·

THE PERSISTENCE OF

THE SACRED IN

MODERN THOUGHT

Edited by

CHRIS L. FIRESTONE

and

NATHAN A. JACOBS

·

University of Notre Dame Press

Notre Dame, Indiana

Copyright © 2012 by University of Notre Dame
Notre Dame, Indiana 46556
www.undpress.nd.edu
Manufactured in the United States of America

All Rights Reserved

Library of Congress Cataloging-in-Publication Data

The persistence of the sacred in modern thought /
edited by Chris L. Firestone and Nathan A. Jacobs.
p. cm.
Includes index.
ISBN-13: 978-0-268-02906-7 (pbk. : alk. paper)
ISBN-10: 0-268-02906-7 (pbk. : alk. paper)
E-ISBN: 978-0-268-07974-1
1. God. 2. Philosophy and religion. 3. Philosophy, Modern.
I. Firestone, Chris L., 1957– II. Jacobs, Nathan.
BL473.P46   2012
210—dc23
2012015583

∞ *The paper in this book meets the guidelines for permanence and durability of the Committee on Production Guidelines for Book Longevity of the Council on Library Resources.*

. . . .

To

STEVEN R. POINTER

First-Rate Administrator, Historian, Mentor, and Friend

Contents

Introduction

CHRIS L. FIRESTONE & NATHAN A. JACOBS

The collection of essays to follow looks at the role of God in the work of major thinkers in modernity. The philosophers of this period are, by and large, not orthodox theists; they are freethinkers, emancipated by an age no longer tethered to the authority of church and state. This side of the story, which portrays the great minds of Western thought as cutting ties with the sacred and moving increasingly toward the secular, has received ample attention in classrooms and throughout the literature. The essays in this volume, however, are united around the belief that this is only one side of an even more complex and diverse story (or, more exactly, collection of stories), and that treating this side as the whole story, as is often done, hopelessly distorts the truth of the matter. The flipside of the story is about theologically astute, enlightened philosophers, bent not on removing God from philosophy but on putting faith and reason on more sure footing in light of advancements in science and a felt need to rethink the relationship between God and world. This book is focused on this oft-ignored side of the story—that is, the theologically affirmative dimensions of major philosophical figures stretching from René Descartes to Søren Kierkegaard. Our purpose is to help halt and indeed reverse the slow secularization of the respective philosophical positions in modernity, a secularization that has been mounting over the last two hundred years.

Before we begin unpacking the specific nature and aims of the essays to follow, a word about our use of terms is in order. In employing the cluster of terms *modern, modernity,* and *modern thought* to describe the period covered in this book, we are intentionally using broad brushstrokes as we strive to capture an overarching understanding of a key interval in Western thought. What we do not claim to offer is any kind of precise social or political history. In other words, this volume is directed more toward the history of ideas and the specific "thought-world" of each individual philosopher than toward any sort of empirical history of philosophy or philosophical movements. The terms *modernity* and *modern thought,* as we will use them, thus cover not only the seventeenth and eighteenth centuries but also large chunks of the centuries just before and after them. In other words, we use the terms *modernity* and *modern thought* to refer to the entire "Age of Reason," or the period of thought from roughly Descartes, Hobbes, and Pascal all the way to Fichte, Schelling, and Hegel. More will be said regarding the beginning and ending of this period below. For now, it will suffice to say that this period is singularly significant in the history of ideas for its wealth of freethinking individuals, its epoch-making philosophical systems, and its initiation of a comprehensive set of challenges to orthodox standards.

Another cluster of terms that will attract a large share of our attention throughout are *secular, secularism,* and *secularization.* Harvey Cox is quite right in noting that "the word 'secularization' retains vague and fuzzy overtones. Despite its usefulness as a 'hinge category,' opening a door for discussion among theologians, sociologists, literary critics, historians, and others, the word often seems slippery and imprecise."[1] The term s*ecularization* has been used to indicate everything from mere modernization to antireligious modernization and has been applied to an even wider range of cultural and intellectual human activities.[2] While a *sacred/secular* distinction can be used to indicate a profound difference in how peoples approach the world, as it does in Mircea Eliade's *The Sacred and the Profane,*[3] *secular* need not connote "contrary or opposed to the sacred." In the wide or generic sense, it may merely indicate something outside the religious sphere.[4] The contributors to this volume acknowledge this point. Be that as it may, *secular* in the academy in general and philosophy in specific often means something more than merely the mundane or nonreligious. And this more restrictive definition of *secular* or *secularization* will be used in this book.

Many of the thinkers covered in this volume, though by no means all of them, can be described as secular in the wide or generic sense. Most, for example, stand somewhere outside the standard orthodox conceptions of Christianity (or, in the case of Baruch de Spinoza, Judaism). What is at issue is not whether one or another of these thinkers is an orthodox religious adherent—most were not—but whether it is possible or desirable to understand the respective philosophy outside of the religiously and theologically affirmative position each philosopher maintains. In other words, the term *secularization,* as we will be using it, signifies the tendency of interpreters after the modern period to downplay, extract, hinder, or otherwise work contrary to the religious and theological dimensions of modern thinkers, regardless of the significance of such dimensions for a proper understanding of these thinkers. *Secularization,* in this sense, is a revisionist approach to the history of ideas, where philosophers are recast and repackaged as agnostics, skeptics, or atheists, antithetical to religion and theology, regardless of whether this portrait captures the actual contours of the given figure's visage.

Understood in the above way, the phenomenon of secularization is no chimera. As a movement, it is traceable to an assemblage of post-Hegel academics who made the removal of God and metaphysics a seminal part of their public agenda. The works of Friedrich Nietzsche, Ludwig Feuerbach, and Karl Marx are well-known examples. Nietzsche, capitalizing on the work of Schopenhauer, rejected the idea that anything lies behind the physical world other than the "will to power"; Feuerbach reasoned that the very notion of God is nothing more than a projection of human characteristics and desires; and Marx's take on religion completed the movement toward a secularized *Weltanschauung,* begun by Nietzsche and Feuerbach. Such left-Hegelians, as Peter Hodgson puts it, "anthropologize[d] the synthesis [of nature and spirit in Hegel], transferring it from *Geist* to man—to man not as an individual but as a species essence *(Gattungswesen)*."[5]

The secularization push is not restricted to philosophy, however. We find in the wider academic sphere persons such as F. W. Newman and George Jacob Holyoake. Newman writes in his essay "Programme of Freethought Societies" that "secularism accepts no authority but that of Nature, adopts no methods but those of science and philosophy, and respects in practice no rule but that of the conscience, illustrated by the common sense of mankind." For him, "[Secularism] utterly disowns tradition as the ground of belief, whether miracles and supernaturalism be claimed or not claimed on its side. No sacred scripture or ancient church can be made the basis of belief."[6] Holyoake puts flesh on Newman's position by methodically presenting the principles of secularization. According to Holyoake, "The leading ideas of Secularism are humanism, moralism, materialism, [and] utilitarian unity: Humanism, the physical perfection of this life—Moralism, founded on the laws of Nature, as the guidance of this life—Materialism, as the means of Nature for the Secular improvement of this life—Unity of thought and action upon these practical grounds."[7] Holyoake takes the "distinctive peculiarity" of the secularist to be the conviction that this program constitutes "a religiousness to which the idea of God is not essential, nor the denial of the idea necessary."[8] God may not be known to be dead in this brand of secularism, but he is hopelessly irrelevant in the academic arena.

Perhaps the most extreme brand of secularization, however, appears in the work of Leo Strauss (and his followers). Strauss's form of secularization employs a hermeneutic of suspicion, which presumes that Descartes and Kant merely started the ball rolling, as it were, with regard to their respective shifts away from the settled religious orthodoxies and orthopraxis of their day. Thus, if we are to read them rightly, we must presume that all theological or religious talk found in their work is either lingering European bias toward Christianity; juvenile inability to shake watchful specters and angels looming overhead since catechesis; or merely an evasive maneuver meant to throw off censors in an effort to get their views published. We can be certain, however, that all the while they proceeded in faith that those who followed after them would take these thoughts down the slippery slope they intended toward agnosticism, skepticism, and atheism. We cannot therefore proceed with historical business as usual when reading such figures, argues Strauss, but must employ an esoteric reading of philosophical texts, recognizing that the given philosopher's true position is always between the lines and contrary to the orthodoxies of the day. As Strauss puts it:

> If it is true that there is a necessary correlation between persecution and writing between the lines, then there is a necessary negative criterion: that the book in question must have been composed in an era of persecution, that is, at a time when some political or other orthodoxy was enforced by law or custom. One positive criterion is this: if an able writer who has a clear mind and a perfect knowledge of the orthodox view and all its ramifications, contradicts surreptitiously and as it were in passing one of its necessary presuppositions or consequences which he explicitly recognizes and maintains everywhere else, we can reasonably suspect that he was opposed to the orthodox system as such and—we must study his whole book all over again, with much greater care and much less naïveté than ever before. In some cases, we possess even explicit evidence proving that the author has indicated his views on the most important subjects only between the lines.[9]

In the case of Strauss, this hermeneutic of suspicion should never stop with modernity but should work backwards through the whole of philosophical history. For "a glance at the biographies of Anaxagoras, Protagoras, Socrates, Plato, Xenophon, Aristotle, Avicenna, Averroes, Maimonides, Grotius, Descartes, Hobbes, Spinoza, Locke, Bayle, Wolff, Montesquieu, Voltaire, Rousseau, Lessing and Kant, and in some cases even a glance at the title pages of their books, is sufficient to show that they witnessed or suffered, during at least part of their lifetimes, a kind of persecution which was more tangible than social ostracism."[10] In the end, charity bids us not to take the claims of such thinkers at face value but to trust that the philosophical giants of Western thought were far too advanced in their thinking to truly embrace the opiate of the masses.

The current volume is meant to push back the secularization of modern thought, embodied in figures such as Strauss, a secularization that has been advancing ever since the great works of modernity were first written. By highlighting and, in many cases, defending the theologically affirmative dimensions of thinkers such as Thomas Hobbes, Gottfried Leibniz, John Locke, Immanuel Kant, F. W. J. Schelling, and G. W. F. Hegel, in the face of contemporary understandings with needlessly negative emphases, this book presents a substantial counterbalance to the secularizing trend and a timely correction of deeply held misperceptions about this crucial period of Western thought. Many, if not most, of these thinkers drink deeply from the well of Judeo-Christian thought and indeed hold a measurable array of religious convictions that inform and, at times, dictate the rest of their work.

To be sure, our collective concern here is not to defend Christianity or any other historical faith through the figures discussed in this volume. Nor is our concern to commend these thinkers' respective theologies or personal religious outlooks. Moreover, in suggesting that the figures discussed in this collection are more theologically affirmative than typically supposed, we are not suggesting that the types of theology they affirm are in anyway faithful to a certain historical orthodoxy—be it Christian or otherwise. No doubt the respective theologies represented in this collection are, in most cases, innovative. What we do intend to demonstrate, however, is that the very significant theological dimensions discussed in this volume, whether orthodox or heterodox, are of great importance to the figures discussed here, and that if these theological dimensions are downplayed, ignored, or otherwise removed, then a proper understanding of these figures has been lost. Hence, this collection presents an array of essays from top scholars in their respective fields of research, united by the conviction that the increasingly secular portrayals of the patriarchs of modernity—portrayals that seek to downplay or remove theologically affirmative elements—are in desperate need of revision.

The field of Kant studies, from which the editors came to approach this volume, provides an excellent example of both the secularizing tendency in the study of modern thought with which this book takes issue and the positive developments that can occur when these secularizing tendencies are resisted. *Kant and the New Philosophy of Religion* (2006) makes the case that there are essentially two interpretive trends regarding Kant's philosophy of religion in the field of Kant studies.[11] One trend is principally negative toward religion and theology, while the other affirms the religious and theological dimensions of Kant's thought. For ease of reference, the editors of *Kant and the New Philosophy of Religion* call these two trends "traditional" interpretations and "affirmative" interpretations.

Interpretations designated "traditional" are primarily negative in their assessment of the prospects of grounding religion and theology in the Kantian paradigm. Traditional interpreters have a wide range of positions on the place of God in Kant's philosophy. Some, such as Allen Wood and Denis Savage, argue that Kant's philosophy is deistic;[12] others, including Keith Ward and Don Cupitt, think it is most amenable to theological nonrealism;[13] and still others, such as Matthew Alun Ray and Yirmiahu Yovel, argue that it supports either agnosticism or atheism but nothing more.[14] Despite differences on the exact nuances, all these interpreters agree that Kant's philosophy works decidedly against those who would seek to gain a foothold for religion and theology in reason. And, at the end of the day, these interpreters conclude that Kant's philosophy of religion offers no real help in overcoming the essentially negative thrust of his theoretical philosophy. Kant understood traditionally is a thoroughly secular Kant. He is an agnostic, atheist, deist, or nonrealist, and, so the argument goes, to suggest anything more is to go beyond the parameters of what his "central" corpus will allow.[15]

Contrary to their negative counterparts, theologically affirmative interpretations of Kant typically hold that Kant's philosophy provides a rationale for God-talk and religious faith. But the case cannot be made without looking beyond the *Critique of Pure Reason,* and sometimes to Kant's writings both before and after 1781. Affirmative readers usually make it a point to capture a sense of the whole of Kant's philosophical enterprise — something that is lost when too strong an emphasis is placed on the first half of the *Critique of Pure Reason* and those aspects of Kant's writings that support its chastening of theology.

The arguments articulated and defended by these theologically affirmative interpreters vary greatly, but all within this camp agree that theological affirmation, though diverse in substance and form, is the real legacy of Kant. Ronald Green, Ann Loades, Stephen Palmquist,

Adina Davidovich, John Hare, Elizabeth Galbraith, and others have therefore argued that traditional interpretive approaches to Kant on religion and theology are wholly inadequate.[16] To the extent that the affirmative camp is right, traditional interpretations are either short-sighted or negligent. They miss either the plethora of positive resources in Kant's philosophy for grounding religion and theology or the opportunities for understanding these resources as genuine contributions to the critical philosophy.

The conclusion in *Kant and the New Philosophy of Religion* regarding these interpretive trends is that these traditional renderings of Kant constitute the "largest unified minority report" on how to interpret Kant's philosophy of religion but that, when all relevant data are considered, these renderings represent neither the majority in the field of Kant studies nor the most accurate interpretation of Kant on religion and theology. Thus the hermeneutic superstructure of the traditional interpretation is in need of renovation, and the basis for an affirmative grounding of religion and theology in Kant's philosophy needs to be more adequately articulated.

In Defense of Kant's Religion (2008) is the attempt by the editors of this book to follow up on the strides taken in *Kant and the New Philosophy of Religion*.[17] There we argue that a careful and charitable understanding of Kant's critical philosophy unlocks his main text on religion, *Religion within the Boundaries of Mere Reason*. Set in the context of a civil trial that considers arguments from both traditional and affirmative camps, we call forward witnesses from each side in order to draw out the best evidence for and against the cogency of Kant's philosophy of religion. In dialogue with expert testimony, we develop an interpretation that sheds new light on Kant's *Religion* and, in so doing, seek to exonerate the text from the charges of incoherence leveled by its critics.

Among Kant's chief critics is Nicholas Wolterstorff. In essays such as "Conundrums in Kant's Rational Religion" and "Is it Possible or Desirable for Theologians to Recover from Kant?," Wolterstorff is highly critical of Kant's philosophy of religion and equally skeptical of its usefulness for the theological enterprise. In writing *In Defense of Kant's* Religion, we approached Wolterstorff with the thesis that Kant's thought had been unduly secularized and that a more careful reading of the relevant texts would show his work to be not only coherent but more positive toward religion and theology than typically supposed. Although skeptical, Wolterstorff read the finished manuscript and committed to writing its foreword. He was convinced that the research had merit, solved most, if not all, the conundrums in the text, and offered the best available reading in the literature.[18]

What emerges in the process of our exposition is a Kant very different from the secular one presented by the traditional camp. To use Wolterstorff's words, this Kant is "more metaphysical, more willing to engage in speculative theology, less dismissive of actual religion."[19] Although the verdict is still out on exactly how best to understand Kant's philosophy of religion and its relationship to theology, the theologically negative trend in Kant studies, both through our study and through numerous others emerging in the field, is beginning to be undone. Patent acceptance of the secularized standard is waning, and, with it, the stigma formerly associated with interpreters who take religion and theology to be of central importance to getting Kant right. Kant's philosophy of religion is now taken seriously in a way that it was not formerly. Reading Kant well, for a growing number of scholars, means having a clear picture of how Kant's philosophy of religion and religious convictions fit in with his philosophical system as a whole.

What is clear from the above account is that scholars are beginning to notice what has been lost in the traditional or religiously and theologically negative understanding of Kant's thought. The whole thrust of Kant's work in denying the dogmatist and skeptic is to put faith in better, more rational light, not worse. The fact that his position is difficult or undesirable to some is no reason to dismiss it, downplay it, or otherwise circumvent it when trying to understand him. Without question, more work needs to be done, but certainly over the last thirty-five years a "new wave" of Kant interpretation has been building and is having a considerable impact on Kant studies today.[20]

In view of these developments in Kant studies, the editors of this volume took up the question: *Is Kant the only philosopher of the period who has been subject to the relentless effect of the secularizing trend?* With this question in hand, we began to approach top scholars in the various fields within the study of modern thought. Among the first approached was Wolterstorff. Convinced that the Straussians in particular had damaged the common understanding of John Locke's philosophy, Wolterstoff agreed to contribute an essay on Locke. He then encouraged us to continue pursuing this question of secularization with notable scholars focusing on other modern figures. As we approached these scholars, we found resounding agreement that the current project was a necessary and timely one.

Soon, there was a chorus of desecularizing voices that now echo throughout this volume. We were delighted to hear this resonance from such top scholars as Peter Hodgson (in reference to Hegel) and John Cottingham (in reference to Descartes), both of whom were contacted early on in the project and immediately agreed to contribute. The manifold support came so swiftly that within one month's time we had the full fifteen contributors. In fact, we had to decide early on to limit the number of contributions to fifteen, as there had been such interest that the collection threatened to grow to nearly twenty-five essays. The collective understanding of these fifteen contributors is that each figure discussed in this volume has been, in a word, secularized. Put bluntly, the significance of God to modern thought has gone missing in action, and what these contributors have done on behalf of their respective fields is raise the flag of awareness by writing groundbreaking new essays that demonstrate persuasively the persistence of the sacred in modern thought.

As a work in the history of ideas, this volume is organized around a figure-based approach. Authors have sought to assess the state of their respective fields under the theme of secularization and to make an argument for the significance of God to a proper understanding of the figure in question. There is no attempt on the part of contributors to override in a comprehensive fashion the effects of secularization in their subject areas. Instead, each essay represents an argument meant to stake a significant claim counter to the secularizing trend described above and to do so in such a way as to offer a genuine contribution to the given field of study. These two features—staking a claim counter to the secularized reading and making a genuine contribution to the given field—were indeed the litmus test for inclusion in this volume.

Essays have been ordered more or less chronologically rather than thematically. But we have stepped outside the bounds of convention in at least one way that requires some explanation: we have decided to include Søren Kierkegaard in this collection. The reason is this. One prominent way of thinking about philosophy after modernity is to see it as dividing into two streams—one secular and antimetaphysical and the other theistic and metaphysical (in the distinctly post-Kantian sense of these terms). The existentialists, Nietzsche and Kierkegaard, are the two fountainheads—one atheistic and one Christian—of these *post*-modernist movements. But the secularized rendering of modern thought does not stop with Hegel; it proceeds, rather remarkably, in an effort to devour the Great Dane of nineteenth-century Christendom. Thus Myron Penner's essay on Kierkegaard is included as a concluding unscientific, indeed antisecularist, postscript that addresses this secular push.

Now, the theologically affirmative dimensions drawn out in this volume are varied and in no way uniform. Cottingham (on Descartes) and Hodgson (on Hegel) argue that God is so central to their respective figures' thought that to remove or bracket this feature is to do systematic violence to their respective philosophies; Firestone (on Kant) and Mariña (on Schleiermacher) contend that to treat the theistic component of these respective thinkers' thought along nonrealist lines is at odds with a careful reading of their respective arguments; Clayton (on Spinoza) and Hardy (on Hume) demonstrate that these so-called atheists retain a certain belief in God, even if they reject theologies with greater likeness to Christian orthodoxy; Jacobs (on Leibniz) and Adams (on Schelling) suggest that the lack of theological depth on the part of most philosophical interpreters is in many ways to blame for the distorted and theologically truncated readings of these respective figures; Martinich (on Hobbes) and Snobelen (on Newton) dispel common antitheistic myths regarding these respective figures via careful scrutiny of primary sources; and Wolterstorff (on Locke) and Bost (on Bayle) demonstrate that the apparent dissonance between these respective figures' theological profession and philosophical treatises is better explained by their respective methods than by a hermeneutic of suspicion along Straussian lines.

It would be too cumbersome to review the details of each argument leveled in this volume. Nevertheless, in the course of compiling the research contained here, a number of preliminary conclusions have come to the fore regarding modern thought and its secularization. The following list is not exhaustive, but it does represent eight major themes found throughout the fifteen essays that are especially significant for the desecularizing process and may help lay the groundwork for demonstrating the persistence of the sacred in modern thought:

1. There are in fact no atheists among the modern figures discussed in this volume; those accused of such positions are either heterodox or thin moral theists.

2. The disciplinary rift between philosophy and theology, and the secularizing of the former, have contributed to an increasingly distorted understanding of modern figures who did not divorce these spheres and indeed knew each far better than many specialists do today.

3. Contemporary academics are prone toward specialization, which enables them to compartmentalize their thinking in a way that the systematizing and unifying thinkers of modernity did not.

4. Modern philosophers thought it possible to respect the disciplinary limitations placed on the philosophical sphere without abandoning personal faith commitments that rest on things outside that sphere.

5. Because labels are often given by opponents of a given thinker, not—or at least not initially—by historians proper, these polemical labels can often stick and ultimately distort the actual intent of the given thinker.

6. As terms and presuppositions change and are combined with the polemical aims of new movements, the potential for misinterpretation based on "standard" labels increases exponentially.

7. Secularizing readings are often agenda-driven revisionist histories that retroactively interpret the aims of a figure on the basis of the significance of his thought to where his followers have taken it, rather than on detailed analysis of the philosopher himself.

8. In light of the potential for agenda-driven misinterpretation, past or present, careful textual analysis is required so as to avoid perpetual misreading.

Certainly these overarching conclusions are not the whole of what is discussed within this volume. The secularization of each figure has a narrative all its own. However, the above eight conclusions represent a common thread found to run through the discussions of several of the figures treated here and thus offer some common themes to their respective secularizing narratives. Our hope is that, in identifying and discrediting these common disservices to some of the main figures of modernity, we will demonstrate the persistence of the sacred in modern thought.

Notes

1. Harvey Cox, foreword to *Secularization and the University,* by Harry E. Smith (Richmond, VA: John Knox Press, 1968), 9.
2. See, e.g., *Rethinking Secularization: Reformed Reactions to Modernity,* ed. Gerard Dekker, Donald A. Luidens, and Rodger R. Rice (Lanham, MD: University Press of America, 1997), 1–2.
3. Mircea Eliade, *The Sacred and the Profane: The Nature of Religion,* trans. Willard R. Trask (Orlando, FL: Harcourt Brace Jovanovich, 1987), 10.
4. Cf., e.g., Alvin Plantinga, "Science and Religion: Why Does the Debate Continue?," in *The Religion and Science Debate: Why Does It Continue?,* ed. Harold W. Attridge (New Haven: Yale University Press, 2009), 94.
5. See chapter 14 of this book, Peter C. Hodgson's "Hegel and Secularization."
6. F. W. Newman, "Programme of Freethought Societies," *Reasoner,* no. 388, n.d., n.p., quoted in George Jacob Holyoake's *The Principles of Secularism Illustrated,* 3rd ed. (London: Book Store, 1871), 15.
7. Holyoake, *Principles,* 28.
8. Holyoake, *Principles,* 12.
9. Leo Strauss, *Persecution and the Art of Writing* (Glencoe, IL: Free Press, 1952), 31–32.
10. Strauss, *Persecution,* 33.
11. *Kant and the New Philosophy of Religion,* ed. Chris L. Firestone and Stephen R. Palmquist (Indianapolis: Indiana University Press, 2006).

12. See Allen W. Wood, "Kant's Deism," and Denis Savage, "Kant's Rejection of Divine Revelation and His Theory of Radical Evil," both in *Kant's Philosophy of Religion Reconsidered,* ed. Philip J. Rossi and Michael W. Wreen (Bloomington: Indiana University Press, 1991), 1–20 and 54–76, respectively.

13. See Keith Ward, *The Development of Kant's View of Ethics* (Oxford: Basil Blackwell, 1972), and Don Cupitt, "Kant and the Negative Theology," in *The Philosophical Frontiers of Christian Theology: Essays Presented to D. M. MacKinnon,* ed. Brian Hebblethwaite and Stewart Sutherland (Cambridge: Cambridge University Press, 1982), 55–67.

14. See Matthew Alun Rayn, *Subjectivity and Irreligion: Atheism and Agnosticism in Kant, Schopenhauer, and Nietzsche* (Aldershot: Ashgate, 2003). See also Yirmiahu Yovel, *Kant and the Philosophy of History* (Princeton: Princeton University Press, 1980).

15. For a thorough summary of these theological positions in the realm of Kant studies, see Chris L. Firestone, *Kant and Theology at the Boundaries of Reason* (Aldershot: Ashgate, 2009).

16. Adina Davidovich, *Religion as a Province of Meaning: The Kantian Foundations of Modern Theology* (Minneapolis, MN: Fortress Press, 1993); Elizabeth Cameron Galbraith, *Kant and Theology: Was Kant a Closet Theologian?* (San Francisco: International Scholars Publications, 1996); Ronald M. Green, *Religious Reason: The Rational and Moral Basis of Religious Belief* (New York: Oxford University Press, 1978) and *Religion and Moral Reason: A New Method for Comparative Study* (New York: Oxford University Press, 1988); John E. Hare, *The Moral Gap: Kantian Ethics, Human Limits, and God's Assistance* (Oxford: Clarendon Press, 1996); Ann L. Loades, *Kant and Job's Comforters* (Newcastle upon Tyne: Avero Publications, 1985); and Stephen R. Palmquist, *Kant's System of Perspectives* (Lanham, MD: University Press of America, 1993) and *Kant's Critical Religion* (Aldershot: Ashgate, 2000).

17. Chris L. Firestone and Nathan Jacobs, *In Defense of Kant's* Religion (Indianapolis: Indiana University Press, 2008).

18. See Nicholas Wolterstorff, foreword to Firestone and Jacobs, *In Defense,* xi–xii.

19. Wolterstorff, foreword, xii.

20. Talk of a "new wave" of Kant interpretation is drawn from Keith Yandell, who uses this term when identifying interpreters of these stripes as "new wavers." See Keith Yandell, "Who Is the True Kant?," *Philosophia Christi* 9, no. 1 (2007): 81–97.

Chapter 1

The Desecularization of Descartes

JOHN COTTINGHAM

It is striking that Descartes is not generally treated in the anglophone academy as a Christian philosopher, in the manner of Augustine, say, or Thomas Aquinas; indeed, he is generally presented in textbooks in a way that systematically downplays the religious dimension of his thought. Descartes, as the cliché has it, was the "father of *modern* philosophy"; and modern philosophy, as we all know, is a secular subject, long since emancipated from its medieval servitude to theology. Most modern analytic philosophers steer clear of God, and many are committed to an explicitly naturalistic outlook. Descartes is principally studied, in countless Introduction to Philosophy courses, for what he has to say about topics of interest to modern "mainstream" philosophy, such as the basis of knowledge, the nature of the mind, the structure of science, language and meaning; and should his writings from time to time include reference to God, this tends to be regarded as cumbersome baggage that his philosophical outlook would really be better off jettisoning, if it could only manage to do so, rather than as the vital and indispensable core of the system.[1] Of course, most students who have studied Descartes know that he provides "proofs" for God's existence, and as part of their work they may be expected to expound and criticize his arguments in the Third and Fifth Meditations. But such texts are often treated as little more than target practice (offering the chance to show how great philosophers can produce flawed reasoning). They may be required reading for an exam designed to test knowledge of the *Meditations,* but they are apt to be taught as something that can be forgotten with relief when one comes to what are taken to be the more important and philosophically interesting questions in the *Meditations,* such as the dreaming argument, the logic of the *Cogito,* or the relation between mind and body.

There is, perhaps, nothing intrinsically wrong with such selectivity in the teaching of the history of philosophy. It is understandable that an instructor, in expounding any great canonical philosopher of the past, would wish to give special attention to the arguments and theses that seem most relevant to current concerns. But there are dangers. Filleting a fish can make it more presentable for the dinner table, but it also involves discarding the very structure that once gave strength, shape, and stability to the living organism. Most philosophers, I think, would concede that to attempt to teach Aquinas's philosophy without attending to the centrality of God in his thought would create impossible distortions. In this paper, I want to explore the various ways in which this is also true of Descartes. I shall begin by looking at the role of God in Descartes's scientific work and shall then move on to a more general exploration of the way in which Descartes's theism pervades his entire philosophical outlook.

Science, Systematicity, and Completeness

A striking feature of Cartesian thought sets it apart from a great deal of current philosophy, namely, its systematicity and unity. The hyperspecialization of modern academic philosophy has involved a greater and greater fragmenting of the subject into separate compartments,[2] so that the practitioner of philosophy of mind, say, is so involved in technical debates in his or her special area that he or she has little time or inclination to attend a seminar on, say, ethics or the philosophy of science. Such compartmentalization would have been anathema to Descartes. Indeed, it is plausible that, were he alive today, he would see today's philosophical scene as a reversion to the scholasticism that he regarded as his life's work to combat. When he promoted his own vision of philosophy as an organic unity, he was partly reacting against the scholastic conception of knowledge as a series of specialities, each with its own methods and standards.[3] In his famous arboreal metaphor, he sees the whole of his scientific system (which includes medicine, mechanics, and morals) as a series of branches growing out of the single trunk of physics.[4] This implies, for Descartes, that the kind of understanding involved in each case is ultimately based on a uniform mathematical template involving "order and measure," as he explains in his early work, the *Regulae:* "I came to see that the exclusive concern of mathematics is with questions or order of measure, and that it is irrelevant whether the measure in question involves numbers, shapes, stars, sounds, or any other object whatever. This made me realize that there must be a general science which explains all the points that can be raised concerning order and measure irrespective of the subject-matter, and that this science should be called *mathesis universalis*—a venerable term with a well-established meaning, for it covers everything that entitles these other sciences to be called branches of mathematics."[5] Cartesian science, then, is unified, insofar as it operates with formal, in principle mathematically describable, proportions and ratios. So here is a first level of unification. But there is a deeper level of organic unity, which Descartes goes on to express by saying that the unified trunk of physics itself grows out of metaphysical roots. What precisely does this mean, and why does it involve God?

A standard answer would be that Descartes's mathematically based science involves "clear and distinct ideas"—for example, ideas of quantity and extension and motion—and that Descartes wanted to provide metaphysical foundations for this science by showing that our grasp of these fundamental building blocks of science is reliable. To establish this, he was obliged to venture into the murky domain of theism, eventually wheeling in God as the guarantor of our clear and distinct ideas. This was the view, for example, of the great Cartesian editor Charles Adam,[6] and it more or less corresponds to how most modern anglophone philosophers read Descartes's *Meditations*.[7] The idea, put crudely, is that when Descartes came to write the *Meditations,* having already devised a new scientific system based on mathematical principles, he now wanted to validate it by showing that it met traditional standards of deductive certainty (of the kind his scholastic predecessors and rivals were committed to), and that in order to achieve that end he tried, after the event, as it were, to bolt a dubious metaphysical undercarriage onto the scientific machinery he had previously developed.

Together with this interpretation goes an implicit critique of the Cartesian project so described—first, that it was doomed to failure, and second, that it was unnecessary to begin with. It was doomed, so runs the story, because in order to wheel in God, Descartes was obliged to develop the theistic proofs in the Third and Fifth Meditations, which unfortunately do not work (either because the premises are flawed or because they cannot be established without circularity); and it is unnecessary because science does not require such transcendent underpinning. Instead (so runs the argument), what science really needs is to become wholly naturalized and autonomous, aiming to provide the simplest and most elegant mathematical descriptions of the cosmos that are consistent with the data and abandoning any confused aspirations for some absolute divine guarantee that the answers so produced are the right ones. So the overall evaluation of Descartes, on this view, is that he took us only partway toward our self-sufficient modern world (appropriately enough for one who was a pioneer on the threshold of modernity). He took us to the modern ideal of a unified mathematical physics (the ideal now entrenched in the goal of modern science to achieve a grand "theory of everything"), but he unfortunately remained mired in a medieval cosmology that was stuck with supposing it needed a divine guarantor. And once we have appreciated this (so the story concludes), we can salvage what is valuable about Descartes by giving him credit for helping to design the modern scientific machinery, while politely ignoring the obsolete theistic undercarriage.

Like much of what has aptly been called the "shadow history" of philosophy, this account of the Cartesian project has a normative as well as a descriptive component.[8] Descriptively, it is supposed to match, more or less, Descartes's actual intentions and objectives: the idea is that he cobbled together some metaphysics merely to bolster his main scientific aims.[9] The additional normative element is an implicit value judgment to the effect that Descartes's impressive program for science failed to take the desirable final step that would have made it wholly autonomous and independent of any supernaturalist elements.

I want to argue that both elements of this account are unsustainable. First, it is highly implausible to suggest that Descartes's work in metaphysics was merely instrumental, some kind of philosophical afterthought aimed at merely providing support for his scientific ambitions. And second, the supposedly desirable goal of a complete and fully autonomous science turns out on examination to be incoherent, irrespective of whether it is couched in the philosophical language of the seventeenth century or of our own time.

With regard to the first point, although Descartes's preoccupations with mathematics and science go back to his early career, his interest in theistic metaphysics was certainly no afterthought. It is important to remember that he was, all his life, a devout Catholic, and one who had been educated by the Jesuits. This of course does not in itself prove that he had a strong interest in philosophical questions about God, but it makes it certain that he was exposed to such questions from an early age. References to God are prominent in Descartes's early notebooks written during his travels in Germany in his midtwenties, when he had the famous dreams of founding a new scientific system.[10] And in his early thirties, when he was occupied with working on optics and planning what was to become his early treatise on physics, *Le monde,* he did not allow his pressing scientific concerns wholly to eclipse his continuing metaphysical interests, as he explained in a letter to his mentor, Marin Mersenne: "I may some day complete a little treatise of Metaphysics, which I began when in Friesland, in which I set out principally to prove the existence of God and of our souls when they are separate from the body, from which their immortality follows. I am enraged when I see that there are people in the world so bold and so impudent as to fight against God."[11] Much later, in the dedicatory letter to his masterpiece, the *Meditations,* the first work to be published under his own name, he picked up on the earlier ambitions recorded in the Mersenne letter, observing that he had always regarded the topics of God and the soul as prime examples of subjects suitable for demonstrative philosophical proof.[12]

There is no reason to doubt the genuineness and sincerity of these enduring professions of interest in theistic metaphysics. More important, they connect up in a very direct and integral way with Descartes's scientific methodology. The cosmology developed in *Le monde* does, it is true, go a certain distance toward the idea of a self-sufficient physics.[13] In describing the workings of "nature," Descartes tells us, he is referring, not to "some goddess or any other sort of imaginary power," but merely to "matter itself," operating in accordance with what are later called the "ordinary laws" of motion.[14] Yet these laws, Descartes goes on to make clear, are themselves a direct function of the initial motion that God imparts to the particles of matter when he creates them, coupled with the conserving power by which he keeps them in existence. It is not a matter of his intervening, or really of his acting like some kind of cosmic "manipulator" (as some interpreters of Cartesian physics have suggested);[15] rather, the "ordinary laws of motion," the principles that govern all material interactions, are a single, immutable, divinely decreed framework, kept permanently in operation by God's eternal creative and conserving will.[16]

Physics and metaphysics are thus, for Descartes, interconnected in the closest possible way. Physics can never be wholly autonomous because, to Descartes's way of thinking, the very operation of the mathematically describable laws of motion presupposes the divine creator and conserver who is their "primary cause." As Descartes declares in his later and more polished presentation of his cosmology, the *Principles of Philosophy,* "In the beginning God created matter along with its motion and rest; and now, merely by his regular concurrence, he preserves the same amount of motion and rest in the material universe as he put there in the beginning."[17]

But is this metaphysical "grounding" of Cartesian science something that its author would have done better to leave out? This brings us to our second point, namely, the matter of whether the modern ideal of a wholly autonomous physics is coherent. Such a question of course raises philosophical issues of great complexity, but for present purposes this much at least can be said. Suppose, following the general Cartesian program for the mathematicization of science, scientists one day manage to develop a fully comprehensive model of the cosmos, based on the best mathematical covering laws (whatever those turn out to be); suppose, that is, that we jump way past Descartes, leave behind Newton, go beyond Einstein, and envisage the future formulation of the unifying set of equations that is the holy grail of contemporary physicists—the final "theory of everything" (TOE).[18] Could such a theory in principle constitute an autonomous physics—that is to say, a complete, self-sufficient system, which indeed explained everything? The answer, it seems clear, must be No. For the assertion that the cosmos, so described, is "closed," that there is nothing further to be sought by way of rational explanation of its existence and nature, would not itself be a piece of physics, or any kind of natural science, but would be an additional, metaphysical claim.

For all the brilliance of our modern physicists, we should not be overawed into taking seriously their ambitions to bring a terminus to all inquiry, as, for example, when Stephen Hawking speculates that if physicists could manage to formulate a grand unified theory of everything it "might be so compelling that it brings about its own existence."[19] Logically, there seem to be only three possible options in cosmology. The first, in effect followed by Descartes, is the religious view that these ultimate mathematical laws are grounded in a transcendent reality that, in the words of Aquinas, "all men call God."[20] The second is the skeptical position that there may be some final explanation of these laws but that we humans are unable to know what it is—that the "ultimate springs and principles" of nature are, in the words of David Hume, "totally shut up from human curiosity and inquiry."[21] And the third is what may be called the "quietist" stance, that we simply have to accept the operation of these laws as a brute fact, utterly resistant in principle to any rational explanation.[22] It is tempting, but mistaken, to think that any actual or future advance in science could somehow make this cosmological trilemma disappear or could provide us with a "complete" scientific theory that sidesteps the need to address it.

None of this, of course, has any tendency to show that the Cartesian option of a theistic underpinning for science is necessarily correct—nor is it meant to. What it *is* meant to show is that completely secularizing Descartes's science, retaining his mathematico-physical trunk but chopping it off from its theistic metaphysical roots, would not—in the way the secularizers often seem to assume—thereby automatically provide something improved or more coherent from the philosophical point of view. The boot is on the other foot. What is incoherent is the modernist assumption of Hawking and others that science *qua* science could somehow progress so far as to be self-contained and complete, that is, to be somehow able to dispense with metaphysics entirely. Secularizing Descartes foists on him the dangerous fantasy of complete scientific autonomy. Desecularizing him at least makes his approach consistent with a truth we have good reason to accept, namely, that physics, however far it progresses, can never be cosmologically complete.

Cartesian Cognition and God

The argument of the previous section opened by referring to a fairly standard picture of Descartes as wheeling in God merely to provide some epistemic backing for the foundations of his scientific system. This picture is but one manifestation of what may be called an "epistemological bias" in the modern interpretation of Descartes—the idea that his overwhelming preoccupation in metaphysics is with knowledge and its validation. To be sure, Descartes is interested in providing stable foundations for science—he says so explicitly at the start of the First Meditation; and to help in this task he uses a sifting procedure, the winnowing fan of doubt. But the widespread idea that his principal concerns are those of the modern academic "epistemologist," directing his main efforts to the defeat of someone called "the skeptic," leads to a serious distortion of his actual aims. The title of the First Meditation is significant here: "On What May Be Called into Doubt." To call something into doubt *(in dubium revocare)* is not to claim that it is in fact, in the normal sense of that term, doubtful or that it cannot reasonably be believed. In introducing the *Meditations,* Descartes explicitly states that the purpose of his reasoning is *not* to prove "that there really is a world, and that human beings have bodies and so on—*since no sane person has ever seriously doubted these things.*"[23]

The "epistemological bias" may also lead to more fundamental misunderstandings about the structure of Descartes's system. Although he follows an "order of discovery" that starts by escaping from doubt into the indubitable self-awareness of the individual meditator, we should beware of supposing that Descartes's philosophical perspective is a wholly "private" or subjective one, or that his philosophy is ultimately an autocentric or individualistic system that, in the words of one critic, would "bring all reality within the ambit of the Cogito."[24] Descartes does indeed invite us to follow him on an individual journey toward truth and knowledge, but it is a fundamental error to think that the order of the steps in the journey reflects Descartes's conception of what is logically prior in the order of reality itself.

In his Synopsis to the *Meditations,* Descartes, far from insisting on the absolute primacy of the thinking subject, emphasizes not one but two equally ranked items that enjoy the utmost certainty and self-evidence: the mind's awareness of itself and its awareness of God. The point of my procedure, says Descartes, is not to prove that, for example, there is an external world (something no sane man has doubted) but to help us to realize "that these reasonings *[rationes]* are not as solid and transparent as those whereby we reach awareness *[cognitio]* of our own minds and of God."[25]

The two Latin terms just highlighted deserve a brief comment, since attending to their connotations will help us interpret this passage properly. First, though Descartes's word *rationes* is often appropriately translated by the English word *arguments,* to render it in this way here can be misleading, since it may suggest an inferential process or proof and hence may immediately incline us to view Descartes's project in what Alvin Plantinga has called "evidentialist" terms.[26] Evidentialism is Plantinga's name for the doctrine that justified belief in a given proposition must always be based on supporting evidence of some kind—that is, by showing how it is based on other beliefs we hold (for example, by being either inferred or logically deduced from those beliefs). The evidentialist, in other words, always insists on an explicit or implicit argument: whether it is based on empirical data or demonstrative proof, there is always some kind of movement from premises to conclusion. Yet it is far from clear that this is Descartes's model in the case of his most certain and evident truths. The Latin word *rationes* (the plural of *ratio,* "reason") actually has a much wider scope than that of "arguments" and can mean something more like "reasons" or "reasonings" or "rational reflections." And some rational reflections can be very direct and immediate in the way they apprehend the truth of a belief. The Cartesian *Cogito* is a paradigm case of this. Descartes himself insisted that it was not the conclusion of a syllogism but was "recognized as self-evident by a simple intuition of the mind."[27] Although generally known by the tag Descartes gave it, *Cogito ergo sum* ("I am thinking, *therefore* I exist"), the "reasoning" is not so much a movement from premise to conclusion as a direct, self-evident realization that nothing could possibly make me not exist so long as I am entertaining the thought that I exist. So, the *ergo,* implying an inference from thought to existence, convenient as it is for a summary label of the famous Cartesian process, turns out (as several commentators have observed) to be in a certain sense dispensable.[28] Indeed, Descartes himself dispenses with it. In his definitive presentation of the reasoning of the meditating subject in reaching self-awareness, there is no *ergo*—nor indeed is *cogito* ("I think") even cited as a premise. Descartes simply says: "I am, I exist, is certain so long as it is put forward by me or conceived in my mind."[29]

The second piece of Latin vocabulary needed to understand our passage correctly is the term *cognitio* ("awareness" or, literally, "cognition"). This is an important quasi-technical term in Descartes, often employed to convey a direct and isolated mental apprehension that does not require to be supported by evidence, or deduced, from other propositions.[30] So it is an entirely appropriate term for him to use concerning the famous "reasoning" whereby the meditator becomes directly and transparently aware of his own existence. *Cognitio* ("awareness") and *ratio* ("reason") thus dovetail nicely to convey the kind of direct and immediate rational perception involved.

And now we come to the nub. *Just exactly that kind of direct awareness is, for Descartes, involved in our apprehension of God.* The mind's awareness *(cognitio)* of God is, as we have just seen, ranked equally by Descartes, alongside the mind's self-awareness, as one of the two items listed in the Synopsis as most certain and evident. It is secured by rational reflection with a self-evidence equal to that enjoyed in the meditator's awareness of his own consciousness.

Although exhibited in the Third Meditation as the conclusion of an argument, the process whereby the meditator comes to acknowledge the author of his being is actually very swift and direct. God is in many ways more like a kind of immediate presence that is felt, more or less strongly, from the very outset of the *Meditations* and that guides and informs every step of the journey. Even in the First Meditation, in the morass of systematic doubt, God is automatically and almost by intuitive mental reflex acknowledged as "supremely good and the source of truth."[31] Could this be a mere piece of caution—designed to protect the writer against the theologians who were always ready to portray his method of doubt as subversive of the faith? Granted, we know that in the seventeenth century serious risks were run by any-one who gave the slightest appearance of seeming to question God, and Descartes was very concerned about being misunderstood or ma-liciously attacked.[32] But in fact the idea of God as source of truth is no mere cautious concession to prying theologians; it is the very center of gravity of Cartesian thought, exerting a decisive pull throughout the reasoning of the *Meditations*. God, glimpsed at the outset of the inquiry, and never effectively eclipsed by the extremity of doubt, is recognized and adored as the "immense light" in the Third Meditation, declared in the Fourth to be the fountain of "wisdom and the sciences," up-held in the Fifth as the perfect bestower of all we need to avoid error, and finally, in the Sixth, vindicated as the creative power of "immea-surable goodness," who secures our human well-being.[33]

We have to remember that Descartes, in writing about God, was steeped in a meditative and contemplative tradition stretching from Augustine (in his *Confessions*), through Anselm (in the *Proslogion*), through Bonaventure (in his *Journey of the Mind toward God*), a tradition that intermingles philosophical reasoning with humble praise and wor-ship.[34] The two elements may seem incompatible to the modern ana-lytic mind, but they coexist happily in the tradition. It is noticeable, for example (though to modern readers perhaps baffling), that Anselm actually *addresses* God, humbly prays to him, at the very moment he is about to embark on trying to prove his existence by deploying the famous ontological argument: "I will not attempt, Lord, to reach your height, for my understanding falls so far short of it. But I desire to understand your truth just a little, the truth that my heart believes and loves."[35] The thought is an Augustinian one: God could never be brought wholly within the grasp of our human comprehension, for that would be the best indication that what was so grasped was not God: *[Deus] non est, si comprehendisti*—if you claim to have grasped him, what you have grasped is not God.[36] Like Augustine and Anselm before him, Descartes stresses in many of his writings how far the human mind falls short in its grasp of the infinite. God, he says, is like a mountain that we can somehow touch in our thought but can never encompass.[37] And in a passage in the *Meditations,* whose style and tone is such that it could easily have come from Augustine or Anselm, Descartes expresses the longing "to gaze with wonder and adoration on the beauty of this immense light, so far as the eye of my darkened intellect can bear it."[38] This is hardly the tone of the dispassionate analytic philosopher, engaged for purely instrumental reasons on the epistemic project of validating the edifice of science. Rather, it is the voice of the worshipper, one for whom philosophy and science would make no sense without the divine source of truth and goodness that irradiates it from start to finish.

Admittedly the passage just quoted comes at the end of Descartes's reasoning to support God's existence in the Third Meditation, whereas Anselm is prepared to pray, and to adore, before even embarking on his own reasoning. But such differences may not be quite as significant as they initially appear. In the light of the point just explored about Descartes's "reasoning," and his "cognition" of the two fundamental truths of his system, self-awareness and awareness of God, we should be ready to consider the idea that Descartes's acknowledging of his creator's existence may actually hinge on a very basic and straightforward intuition. To be sure, he does take some time to elaborate his reasoning in the Third Meditation,[39] just as, for that matter, Anselm does for his own very different reasoning in the *Proslogion,* but in both cases the basic insights explored are fundamentally very simple ones. To repeat: one's awareness of God's existence is ranked by Descartes right alongside the mind's awareness of itself. In the case of God, the rational intuition involved can be compressed to a single nugget of cognition, what Descartes encapsulated in his earlier writings by means of a tag that deserves to be much better known, *Sum, ergo Deus est*—"I am, therefore God exists."[40]

The key to how this simplicity and immediacy works is Descartes's awareness of his own creaturely imperfection, which plays a pivotal role in his reaching for God. "How could I understand that I doubted or desired—that is, lacked something—and that I was not wholly perfect, unless there were in me some idea of a more perfect being which enabled me to recognize my own defects by comparison?"[41] Descartes's conception of God is a conception of something infinitely beyond him, the understanding of which is intimately linked to awareness of his own weakness and finitude. Or, as St. Bonaventure put it in the thirteenth century, in phrasing that is uncannily close to that later used by Descartes: "How would the intellect know that it was a defective and incomplete being, if it had no awareness of a being free from every defect?"[42] The "awareness" of my finite and imperfect self, in short, carries with it, for Descartes, an implicit and immediate awareness of something other than myself, which necessarily eludes my mental grasp. This crucial point is very aptly seized on in the interpretation of the Cartesian "reasoning" for God offered by Emmanuel Levinas. On Levinas's view, "What Descartes is reporting is not a step in a deductive reasoning, but a profound religious experience, an experience which might be described as the experience of a *fissure,* of a confrontation with something that disrupted all his categories. On this reading, Descartes is not so much proving something as *acknowledging* something, acknowledging a Reality that he could not have constructed, a Reality which proves its own existence by the very fact that its presence in my mind turns out to be a phenomenological impossibility."[43]

What the Levinas reading in effect succeeds in uncovering is a kind of luminous paradox at the heart of the Cartesian cognition of God. On the one hand the Cartesian program cannot proceed unless the meditator has a "clear and distinct" idea of God—the need for such clarity and distinctness is the chief slogan of Cartesian philosophy, the very hallmark of the system. But on the other hand, it is crucial to the apprehension of that idea of God as authentic that it exceeds the complete grasp of the human mind, that it cannot be fully encompassed by my finite intellect.[44] It thus turns out that Descartes's so-called trademark argument hinges in one crucial respect on a mode of reflection very similar to that which we find in Anselm's ontological argument, namely, reflection on what happens when the finite creature attempts to confront its infinite creator—when, as Anselm put it, the "wretched mind" is "stirred up to contemplation of God."[45] Crucially,

God is for Anselm *not* the "greatest conceivable being" (as inaccurate sketches of his reasoning sometimes put it) but instead *id quo nihil maius cogitari potest*—"that than which nothing greater can be thought." Like a necessarily receding horizon, God eludes the limits of our thought, so that any claim to bring him fully within the horizon of our cognition would be self-refuting: the purported achievement would be the best possible evidence that what had been brought within the horizon was not God but some lesser being.

It may perhaps begin to be clear from this why talk of a "profound religious experience" is far from inappropriate as a description of what is recorded in Descartes's reasoning for God's existence. This does not mean that the reasoning is not elaborated in ways that can properly engage the attention of the analytic philosopher;[46] nor does it mean that, when we read Descartes's text, logic and critical analysis are supposed to be swept away in some irrational flow of devotion or adoration. Just as with Augustine, Anselm, and Bonaventure, indeed in many respects more than with any of these three cases, Descartes's reflections wear a robust philosophical clothing in a way that repays close and careful scrutiny. But beneath that clothing, or, to change the metaphor, at the core of the reasoning, is, I am arguing, a religious encounter: the sense of creatureliness, which the finite human mind is forced to acknowledge when it comes up against something that it can clearly glimpse but knows it can never fully encompass. At the very center of Descartes's thinking is a kind of submission to the higher and the greater, an implicit withdrawal from the claim to self-sufficiency and autonomy that is the hallmark of the modern secular mind.

Coda: Descartes, Modernity, and the Fantasy of Autonomy

What is the purpose of "desecularizing" Descartes? Part of the point may be historical: to gain a more nuanced and accurate account of the character of his thought, in the light of the tradition he inherited and the intellectual climate that shaped him. Connected with this is the scholarly matter of doing justice to the internal logic of his actual writings on science and on metaphysics. But however fruitful such approaches may be, the point of studying a seminal thinker such as Descartes can never, in my view, be simply historical or scholarly. There is always the further philosophical aim of seeing what light his ideas shed on our own contemporary worldview, and how, in turn, our modern outlook tends, if we are not careful, to be retrojected back onto the way we interpret his views.

If we think of the "modernity" that Descartes is standardly represented as having inaugurated, the feature that comes to mind more than any other is the championing of self-sufficient reason against inherited authority. And this is indeed an authentic strand in Descartes's thinking. The manifesto he presented in his first published work proclaims the value of individual "good sense," the "best distributed thing in the world," and upholds the weapon of clear and precise reasoning and careful critical reflection against the stifling authority and obfuscation of the Schools.[47]

If this is what is meant by autonomy and self-sufficiency, then we have good reason both to admire Descartes's advocacy of these values and to applaud their entrenchment within our modern intellectual culture. But there is another, more suspect, conception of autonomy, sometimes associated with the secularization of our culture, that would do no credit to Descartes were it laid at his door. This is the fantasy of humanity as somehow "self-creating," in the sense that we are supposed to be able to generate our own values by an act of will. In this fantasy, there are no objective values, merely projections by human beings of their own tastes and preferences. Friedrich Nietzsche, who is perhaps the most significant promoter of this idea, seems to have supposed that humans (of an exalted type) could somehow create meaning and value for themselves by a grand volitional act—a notion that involves serious confusion. I cannot, of course, make something valuable by choosing or willing it (as if I could make cardboard nutritious by deciding to eat it); indeed, this idea precisely puts the cart before the horse, since it is hard to see how my choices or acts of will can be worthwhile unless their objects already have independent value.[48] Going back a century or so to the Enlightenment, the Kantian notion of autonomy is sometimes seen as foreshadowing this "creationist" account of value, on the grounds that Kant speaks of autonomy, "the basis of the dignity of human nature and of every rational nature," as that aspect of our will whereby it must be considered as *selbstgesetz-gebend* ("giving the law to itself").[49] It may, however, be possible to give a more benign interpretation of the Kantian ideal of autonomy, according to which what is important about the autonomous being is the ability to make decisions independently of the arbitrary will of another, acting in the full light of reason, free from internal or external interference with one's rational processes. Hence, to be autonomous I must be free from external tyranny (my dignity as a rational agent must be respected) and also from internal interference, such as arises from the contingencies of appetite and mere inclination.[50]

Whatever the correct interpretation of Kant (a subject for a different paper), it seems clear in the case of Descartes that if he is an advocate of autonomy his idea of it falls very much closer to the "benign" model, sketched in the previous paragraph, than it does to the "self-creationist" model. Nothing in the Cartesian corpus seems remotely close to a promotion of the idea that humans could generate their own value system or determine the conditions for a worthwhile life by a voluntary act of choice. On the contrary, Descartes's model of free and rational action is very much a matter of our orienting ourselves toward objective truth and objective value that is not in any sense the creation of our own will. Both in our pursuit of truth and in our pursuit of the good, we human beings are free insofar as our intellects grasp the clear and distinct ideas that generate spontaneous assent. From a great light in the intellect, says Descartes in the Fourth Meditation, there follows a great inclination of the will; and the more I incline in a given direction, either because reasons of truth and goodness point that way or because of divinely produced disposition of my inmost thought, the freer is my choice.[51]

Descartes is often called a "rationalist"—a label that has long been recognized as misleading if it is rigidly contrasted with "empiricist" and taken to imply a disdain for observation and experiment; for Descartes was a rationalist who believed in innate ideas, while also acknowledging the vital role of sensory experience in scientific inquiry.[52] But Descartes was also a rationalist in a broader sense, namely, one whose philosophy is founded on a fundamental belief in the power of reason—the ability of the human mind to discern the truth without any help from the received wisdom of established authority and to distinguish what is clear and coherent from what is obscure and confused.[53] But it is vital to add that for Descartes, the true, desecularized Descartes, we are not the authors of truth or the creators of value. Reason is our greatest human gift, but it is a gift we did not construct for ourselves, and it is an instrument we must learn to use properly by directing it toward the "immense light" of truth and goodness, which we did not create. That kind of rationalism still has much to teach us.

Notes

I am grateful for helpful comments received when I presented earlier versions of this paper at Claremont Graduate University, Notre Dame University, University of Southampton, Yale University, and Oxford University. I am also grateful for helpful comments by two anonymous referees for the University of Notre Dame Press. The section of the paper entitled "Cartesian Cognition and God" incorporates material from my article "Sceptical Detachment or Loving Submission to the Good: Reason, Faith and the Passions in Descartes," which appeared in *Faith and Philosophy* 28, no. 1 (January 2011): 44–53, and is included here by kind permission of the editor.

Abbreviations used in these notes for works by Descartes are as follows: AT, the standard Franco-Latin edition of Descartes by Charles Adam and Paul Tannery, *Oeuvres de Descartes,* 12 vols., rev. ed. (Paris: Vrin/CNRS, 1964–76), cited with volume number (or number-letter) and page number; CSM, *The Philosophical Writings of Descartes,* vols. 1 and 2, trans. John Cottingham, Robert Stoothoff, and Dugald Murdoch (Cambridge: Cambridge University Press, 1985), cited with volume number and page number; CSMK, *The Philosophical Writings of Descartes,* vol. 3, trans. John Cottingham, Robert Stoothoff, Dugald Murdoch, and Anhony Kenny (Cambridge: Cambridge University Press, 1991), cited with page number.

1. Margaret Wilson was one of the first to sound a warning about this secularizing tendency, observing that the Dreaming Argument and the Cogito "have both been almost consistently 'interpreted' by English-speaking analytical philosophers, as if they were self-standing arguments," to be understood in isolation from Descartes's own stated objectives in writing the *Meditations,* where he "repeatedly insists on the great importance of . . . God." Margaret Wilson, *Descartes* (London: Routledge, 1978), 3–4.

2. There are many philosophers, I suspect, who for professional reasons go along with this compartmentalizing tendency but harbor a sneaking anxiety that the subject they are locked into bears little relation to what originally inspired them to pursue a philosophical career. For some of the issues involved here, see John Cottingham, "What Is Humane Philosophy and Why Is It at Risk?," *Philosophy,* suppl. 65 (2009): 1–23; and Anthony O'Hear, ed., *Conceptions of Philosophy,* Royal Institute of Philosophy Series (Cambridge: Cambridge University Press, 2009).

3. This is a conception partly derived from Aristotle; see, for example, *Nicomachean Ethics* [ca. 325 BC] 1.3.

4. "The whole of philosophy is like a tree. The roots are metaphysics, the trunk is physics, and the branches emerging from the trunk are all the other sciences, which may be reduce to three principal ones, namely medicine, mechanics and morals." René Descartes, preface to the 1647 French translation, by Claude Picot under Descartes's direction, of the *Principles of Philosophy [Principes de philosophie],* AT IXB 14 and CSM I 186.

5. René Descartes, *Rules for the Direction of Our Native Intelligence [Regulae ad directionem ingenii,* ca. 1628], rule 4 (AT X 376–78 and CSM I 18–19).

6. "Descartes ne demande à la métaphysique qu'une chose, de fournir un appui solide à la vérité scientifique" (AT XII 143).

7. For a not untypical example, see Tom Sorell, *Descartes,* in the Oxford "Past Masters" series (Oxford: Oxford University Press, 1987), where the main emphasis is on epistemological and scientific aspects of the Cartesian system, and the "religious aura" of the *Meditations* is presented as something "contrived" by Descartes to conceal the unorthodox nature of his science (57).

8. See Richard A. Watson, "Shadow History in Philosophy," *Journal of the History of Philosophy* 31 (1993): 95–109.

9. A view I must confess to having been tempted by in earlier work; see John Cottingham, "A New Start? Cartesian Metaphysics and the Emergence of Modern Philosophy" (1992), repr. as ch. 2 in John Cottingham, *Cartesian Reflections* (Oxford: Oxford University Press, 2008).

10. The night of dreams when he glimpsed the "foundations of a wonderful science" was November 10, 1619, after which Descartes made a vow of thanksgiving to visit the shrine of the Virgin at Loretto. Inscribed in the first section of his early notebooks dating from this time was the motto from the Psalms (111, or 110 in the Vulgate), "Initium sapientiae timor Domini" (The fear of the Lord is the beginning of wisdom). See AT X 213 ff. and CSM I 1 ff., and Cottingham, *Cartesian Reflections,* ch. 14.

11. Descartes to Marin Mersenne, November 25, 1630, AT I 181 and CSMK 29.

12. René Descartes, "Dedicatory Letter to the Theology Faculty of the Sorbonne," in *Meditationes de prima philosophia* (1641), AT VII 1 and CSM II 3.

The *Discourse on the Method* [*Discours de la méthode*] and accompanying scientific essays (*Optics, Meteorology,* and *Geometry*) were published anonymously, four years earlier.

13. But it goes this distance only a certain way. I now think I tended to exaggerate the extent of this in my "Plato's Sun and Descartes's Stove: Contemplation and Control in Cartesian Philosophy," in *Rationalism, Platonism and God,* ed. Michael Ayers, Proceedings of the British Academy 149 (London: Oxford University Press, 2007), 15–34, repr. as ch. 15 of Cottingham, *Cartesian Reflections.*

14. René Descartes, *Le monde* [ca. 1633], ch. 7 (AT XI 37 and CSM I 92) and ch. 6 (AT XI 34 and CSM I 91).

15. According to Daniel Garber, Descartes replaces the scholastic picture of individual substances animated by "tiny souls," with a picture of "one great soul, God, who . . . manipulates the bodies of the inanimate world as we manipulate ours." *Descartes's Metaphysical Physics* (Chicago: University of Chicago Press, 1992), 116. The image is rather too anthropomorphic to convey what Descartes has in mind and also seems too suggestive of a sequence of actions in time, rather than an eternally decreed dynamic ordinance.

16. Creation and conservation are, for Descartes, only conceptually, not really, distinct. Third Meditation, AT VII 49 and CSM II 33.

17. René Descartes, *Principles of Philosophy* [*Principia philosophiae,* 1644], pt. 2, art. 36. Descartes goes on to describe the "secondary" laws of motion, but these are not really additional principles generating movement, merely mathematical descriptions of the *way* things are moved by God's immutable creative and conserving power—namely, so that the overall "quantity of motion" remains (a) unaltered unless externally impinged on (the principle of inertia); (b) in a straight line; and (c) with invariant and precisely specifiable alterations of direction or motion in the case of collision (pt. 2, arts. 37–40).

18. For an accessible account of the quest for a TOE, see Brian Greene, *The Elegant Universe* (London: Jonathan Cape, 1999).

19. Stephen Hawking, *A Brief History of Time* (London: Bantam Press, 1988), 192–93.

20. The "Five Ways" of Aquinas all end with some such phrase as "and this everyone calls God" (*quod omnes dicunt Deum*). *Summa theologiae* [1266–73], I, q. 2, art. 3.

21. David Hume, *An Enquiry concerning Human Understanding* [1748], sec. 4, pt. 1, para. 12, ed. T. Beauchamp (Oxford: Oxford University Press, 1999). The Beauchamp edition provides numbered paragraphs within each part, allowing references to be located by those using other editions.

22. I chose the relatively neutral label of *quietist* (as opposed to, say, "absurdist" or "irrationalist") to avoid begging any questions. Compare the following famous exchange between Frederick Copleston and Bertrand Russell. "COPLESTON: Then you would agree with Sartre that the universe is what he

calls 'gratuitous'? Russell: Well, the word 'gratuitous' suggests that it might be something else. I should say that the universe is just there, and that's all." Debate broadcast by the BBC in 1948, reprinted in Bertrand Russell, *Why I Am Not a Christian* (London: Allen and Unwin, 1957), 152.

Some cosmologists suggest that "bruteness" can be avoided by the idea of a multiverse: ours is but one of an indefinite number of island universes, each instantiating different fundamental physical laws. A further step sometimes made is that all these other putative universes might turn out under scrutiny to involve some kind of incoherence, so that the actual universe we have is somehow "inevitable." Brian Greene, *The Elegant Universe: Superstrings, Hidden Dimensions, and the Quest for the Ultimate Theory* (New York: Norton, 1999), ch. 12. However, from the fact that the existence of x with properties other than F is impossible, it clearly does not follow that the actual existence of x is inevitable.

23. *Meditations,* Synopsis, AT VII 15–16 and CSM II 11 (emphasis supplied).

24. "God as fully self-sufficient being *(Ens subsistens)* was considered [by Aquinas and his successors] as the indispensable support . . . for every created being, and hence for man. The *cogito ergo sum* carried within it a rupture with this line of thought. . . . After Descartes, philosophy became a science of pure thought: all that is *being*—the created world, and even the Creator, is situated within the ambit of the Cogito, as contents of human consciousness." John Paul II, *Memory and Identity* (London: Orion, 2005), 9. For more discussion of the problems in this way of construing the Cartesian perspective, see John Cottingham, "The Role of God in Descartes's Philosophy," ch. 17 in *A Companion to Descartes,* ed. Janet Broughton and John Carriero (Oxford: Blackwell, 2006), 287–301, repr. as ch. 13 of Cottingham, *Cartesian Reflections.*

25. *Meditations,* Synopsis, AT VII 16 and CSM II 11.

26. Alvin Plantinga, *Warranted Christian Belief* (Oxford: Oxford University Press, 2000), ch. 3.

27. *Meditations,* Second Set of Replies to Objections, AT VIII 140 and CSM II 100.

28. The first in the line was Jaakko Hintikka, who argued that the Cogito was better construed as a kind of performance than as an inference. "Cogito, ergo sum: Inference or Performance?," *Philosophical Review* 71 (1962): 3–32.

29. Second Meditation, AT VII 25 and CSM II 17.

30. Descartes thus contrasts *cognitio* ("awareness") with *scientia* ("knowledge")—the latter implying a connected and systematic cognitive structure, as opposed to an isolated and immediate cognition; see Second Replies, AT VII 141 and CSM II 101 n. 2.

31. AT VII 22 and CSM II 15.

32. See, for example, Descartes to Princess Elizabeth of Bohemia, May 10, 1647, AT V 16 and CSMK 317.

33. AT VII 52 and CSM II 36 (Third Meditation); AT VII 53 and CSM II 37 (Fourth); AT VII 43 and CSM II 62 (Fifth); AT VII 88 and CSM II 61 (Sixth).

34. Augustine, *Confessiones* [397–401]; Anselm of Canterbury, *Proslogion* [1077–78]; Bonaventure, *Itinerarium mentis in Deum* [1259].

35. Anselm of Canterbury, *Proslogion,* ch 1, translated in John Cottingham, ed., *Western Philosophy,* 2nd ed. (Oxford: Blackwell, 2008), 346. All subsequent quotations from this work are taken from this edition.

36. "Quid ergo dicamus, fratres, de deo? si enim quod vis dicere, si cepisti, non est deus: si comprehendere potuisti, aliud pro deo comprehendisti. si quasi comprehendere potuisti, cogitatione tua te decepisti. hoc ergo non est, si comprehendisti: si autem hoc est, non comprehendisti." (What then shall we say, brothers, of God? Whatever you say, if you have grasped it, that is not God. For if you have been able to grasp it, what you have grasped is something other than God. If you have been capable in any way of grasping him in your thought, then by your thought you have deceived yourself. So if you have grasped him, it is not God, and if it is God, you have not grasped him.) Augustine, *Sermones* [early fifth cent.] 52.16.

37. "I say that I know [that God is the author of everything, including the eternal truths], not that I conceive it or grasp it; because it is possible to know that God is infinite and all powerful although our soul, being finite, cannot grasp or conceive him. In the same way we can touch a mountain with our hands but we cannot put our arms around it as we could put them around a tree or something else not too large for them. To grasp something is to embrace it in one's thought; to know something it is sufficient to touch it with one's thought." Descartes to Mersenne, May 27, 1630, AT I 151 and CSMK 25.

38. Third Meditation, final paragraph.

39. Nor should anything I say here be taken to imply that this elaboration is not worth detailed analytic scrutiny—something I have offered elsewhere. See ch. 3 of John Cottingham, *Descartes* (Oxford: Blackwell, 1986), 48–57.

40. René Descartes, *Rules for the Direction of Our Native Intelligence (Regulae ad directionem ingenii,* ca. 1628], AT X 421 and CSM I 46.

41. Third Meditation, AT VII 46 and CSM II 31.

42. Bonaventure, *Itinerarium* 3.3, my translation.

43. The wording here is not that of Levinas himself but comes from the admirable discussion by Hilary Putnam in his "Levinas and Judaism," in *The Cambridge Companion to Levinas,* ed. Simon Critchley and Robert Bernasconi (Cambridge: Cambridge University Press, 1986), 42. The relevant Levinas text is *Ethique et infini* (1982), trans. as *Ethics and Infinity* (Pittsburgh: Duquesne University Press, 1985), 91 ff.

44. "The entire luminous power of the argument depends on the fact that this ability to have within us the idea of God could not belong to our intellect if the intellect were simply a finite entity (as indeed it is) and did not have God as its cause." *Meditations,* First Replies, AT VII 105 and CSM II 77.

45. Anselm of Canterbury, *Proslogion,* ch. 1. Just to avoid any possible confusion: I am not, of course, suggesting for one moment that Descartes's Third Meditation reasoning is a kind of ontological argument. The quite separate Cartesian version of the ontological argument, found in the Fifth Meditation, raises very different issues, which there is no space to explore in the present paper.

46. Indeed, Descartes himself even went so far as to attempt a formalized treatment of it, yielding to the demands of the authors of the Second Objection for something more "geometrical" (AT VII 160 and CSM II 113). The result seems to me a classic case of more turning out to be less. The lesson bears out Galen Strawson's general and, to my mind, very persuasive claim about philosophy that "tight argument can be very fine, but it constantly degrades the quality of philosophical debate, scholasticizing it and pushing it into unimportant minutiae and fantasy. It obstructs vision if overdone, and it invites overdoing." Galen Strawson, *Real Materialism* (Oxford: Oxford University Press, 2008), 3.

47. *Discourse on the Method,* pt. 1 (AT VI 1 ff. and CSM I 111 ff.).

48. Nietzsche envisages a "new philosopher with a spirit 'strong enough to revalue and invent new values.'" Friedrich Nietzsche, *Beyond Good and Evil* [1886], trans. Walter Kaufmann (New York: Random House, 1966), sec. 203. Some of the relevant considerations against the Nietzschean position are raised in John Cottingham, *The Spiritual Dimension* (Cambridge: Cambridge University Press, 2005), ch. 3, esp. sec. 2. See also sec. 2 of John Cottingham, "Impartiality and Ethical Formation," in *Partiality and Impartiality: Morality, Special Relationships, and the Wider World,* ed. Brian Feltham and John Cottingham (Oxford: Oxford University Press, 2011).

49. Immanuel Kant, *Grundlegung zur Metaphysik der Sitten* [1785], ch. 2, Akademie ed. (Berlin: Reimer/De Gruyter, 1900–), 4:436, 431; for English translation, *Groundwork for the Metaphysics of Morals,* ed. Thomas E. Hill Jr. and Arnulf Zweig, trans. Arnulf Zweig (Oxford: Oxford University Press, 2003), 236, 232.

50. Thus, for Kant, moral imperatives cannot be construed as conditional on whatever contingent desires one happens to have, for "in these cases the will never determines itself directly by the thought of an action, but only by the motivations which the anticipated effect of the action exercises on the will— *I ought to do something because I want something else.*" (*Grundlegung,* 4:444; *Groundwork,* 244.) Because of its dependency on the contingencies of inclination, action of this kind is always for Kant heteronomous.

51. Fourth Meditation, AT VII 57 and CSM II 40. For a detailed account of the implications of Descartes's position here, see John Cottingham, "Descartes and the Voluntariness of Belief," and "The Intellect, the Will and the Passions," chs. 11 and 10, respectively, in *Cartesian Reflections.* The phrase "because of divinely produced disposition of my inmost thought" refers to the "supernatural light" of faith, that other source of truth which Descartes acknowledges alongside the "natural light of reason." See further *Meditations,* Second Replies

(AT VII 148, line 27, and CSM II 106). But aside from a few excursions (e.g., into the Transubstantiation, AT VII 248 ff. and CSM II 172 ff.), Descartes's writings resolutely avoid discussion of the revealed truths of faith (see especially AT V 176 and CSMK 350, where he draws firm boundaries between the provinces of philosophy and theology). Restoring Descartes to his rightful place in the long line of Christian philosophers does not, of course, in any way imply erosion in his thought of the standard distinction between reason and revelation. To desecularize Descartes is not to "appropriate" him for Christianity; his reasoning in the *Meditations* was designed to be accessible, as he put it, "even among the Turks" (*Conversation with Burman* [1648], AT V 159 and CSMK 342). Coming to awareness of God by reflecting on the weakness of the human mind in confronting the infinite is, of course, an approach that is equally at home in Judaic or Islamic thought.

52. For the former, see *Discourse* pt. 5 (AT VI 41 and CSM I 131); for the latter, *Discourse* pt. 6 (AT VI 64 ff. and CSM I 144 ff.).

53. See *Discourse,* pt. 1, AT VI 2 and CSM I 111; *The Search for Truth by Means of the Natural Light* [*La recherche de la vérité par la lumière naturelle,* ca. 1641 or 1649], AT X 496 and CSM II 400.

Chapter 2

Law and Self-Preservation in *Leviathan*

On Misunderstanding Hobbes's Philosophy, 1650–1700

A. P. MARTINICH

Let him go with this Elogy, That he was a Man much blam'd,
but little understood.

—Mercurius Anglicus

Thomas Hobbes's philosophy was by and large misunderstood by his critics in the second half of the seventeenth century.[1] In this chapter I explain some of the principal sources for this misunderstanding and then give three substantive examples of it. Of these three examples, the third, Hobbes's grounding of obligation in the irresistible power of God, is both the most important one for philosophy and the one that most affected later thought about revealed religion. Hobbes, I shall argue, attempted to preserve a religion and politics of the early seventeenth century with methods that would become characteristic of the Enlightenment.

Hobbes's Jacobeanism

Hobbes was once described as a "radical in the service of reaction."[2] The accuracy of that description has not been sufficiently appreciated.

He was a reactionary in the sense that he defended a form of Jacobean-ism in the third quarter of the seventeenth century when already that view had largely disappeared by the beginning of the English Civil War. Thus we need to understand what Jacobeanism consists of in order to understand Hobbes's philosophy. It has two parts, subscription to absolute sovereignty and English Calvinism.

Absolute sovereignty is the view that the sovereign (1) has all political power in the state; and (2) has authority over (virtually) every aspect of life. For Hobbes, the "virtually" condition is needed in order to exempt the sovereign from authority over the steps a subject may take to avoid imminent death. As regards English Calvinism, it consists roughly of being (1) orthodox in doctrine,[3] (2) Calvinist in theology, (3) preferring an episcopal and Erastian church government, (4) non-Puritan in liturgy, and (5) professing the Bible to be the "true religion of Protestants," to use William Chillingworth's phrase.[4] Each of these latter elements deserves some explanation.

Regarding *orthodoxy,* one criterion was acceptance of the decrees of the first four ecumenical councils; and Hobbes did accept them. Another criterion during most of the seventeenth century in England was profession of the Thirty-Nine Articles. One might argue that Hobbes could not have professed all of them because some of his teachings are inconsistent with some of them. For example, according to Hobbes, the monarch had priestly powers, and the Thirty-Nine Articles denies this. But that Hobbes had a different understanding of Christianity than some of the doctrines in the Thirty-Nine Articles is irrelevant. What was required was profession of them, and that could be done in good conscience even if one disagreed with or did not understand part of their content. The phrase "implicit faith" was used to describe the faith of people who had an imperfect or incomplete understanding of Christian doctrine, and an implicit faith was sufficient. Also, all of Hobbes's Arminian opponents, notably Bishop John Bramhall, also did not accept some of the articles, specifically, the ones on predestination.

Regarding *Calvinist theology,* it is important to distinguish between beliefs in propositions and the theories that are used to explain, account for, or fill out that belief. Augustinianism and Thomism in the fourteenth century and Arminianism and Calvinism in the seventeenth

century were competing Christian theologies. People could be orthodox in the sense described above and yet hold different theologies.
In the late sixteenth and early seventeenth centuries, the dominant
theology was Calvinism, in contrast with Lutheranism and Thomism.
Hobbes, whose formative years were precisely in this period, was a
Calvinist, and not just any kind of Calvinist, such as a Dutch or Swiss
Calvinist, but an English Calvinist, like his monarch, James I. To point
out that some Calvinists outside England held theological views opposed to those of Hobbes is as irrelevant as pointing out that during
the middle of the twentieth century a communist in the Soviet Union
had different beliefs from one in the People's Republic of China. Even
to point out that some Calvinists in England held views different from
Hobbes's would not in itself prove that Hobbes was not an English
Calvinist. Characteristic elements of English Calvinism were that God
is incomprehensible and the cause of all things, that God predestined
the elect to heaven and the damned to hell, that Jesus died only for
the elect and not for all human beings, and that the work of redemption was wholly a work of mercy and contained no element of justice
(*Leviathan* 41.2).[5]

The first element I mentioned, that God is incomprehensible,
calls for a special comment. God is radically unlike human beings or
anything else of which they can have sense experience. God's nature
is "capable properly of no definition. . . . God is an incomprehensible,
first, and absolute Being."[6] Not only was it impious to try to speculate
about God's nature, it could not yield anything that could be known.
Perry Miller summarized the belief in this way: "God is not to be understood, but to be adored. This supreme and awful essence can never
be delineated in such a way that He seems even momentarily to take
on any shape, contour, or feature recognizable in the terms of human
discourse, nor may His activities be subjected to the laws of human
reason or natural plausibility."[7] Substantive beliefs about God beyond,
say, that he exists and is omnipotent, the two things Hobbes said could
be known about God, could be had only from revelation—thus the
importance of biblical interpretation. This explains why Hobbes in
fact does not speculate about the nature of God. His view of God fits
the character of modern thought if we accept, as I think we should,
Alexander's Pope's attitude:

Say first, of God above, or man below
What can we reason, but from what we know?
Of man, what see we but his station here[?]
. . . .
Know, then, thyself, presume not God to scan;
The proper study of mankind is man.
Essay on Man 1.17–19, 2.1–2

Hobbes's modesty about the scope of human knowledge included the sensory world: "The principles of natural reason . . . are so far from teaching us anything of God's nature, as they cannot teach us our own nature, not the nature of the smallest creature living" (*Leviathan* 31.33). In contrast, Arminian theologians thought that natural theology could discover a great deal about God. And although they may have said that God was incomprehensible, since this was a standard view, their philosophical starting point was that God was good. From this premise, they argued that since a good person would not condemn people to hell unless they were responsible for their actions, and since responsibility required free will, people had free will. The attitude of many Calvinists was that an Arminian understanding of free will presupposed that God was not the cause of everything and was not the ultimate cause of reality, two propositions at variance with the long tradition of Christianity. As for the relationship between free will and responsibility, Calvinists thought either that it was a mystery or, like Hobbes, that human responsibility was consistent with God's causality.

Hobbes showed a *preference for an episcopal and Erastian church government* over other forms. He thought that Independency, essentially Congregationalism, was acceptable, especially in the confused circumstances shortly after the Civil Wars (*Leviathan* 47.20). So he was not as adamant about the issue as James I, who said "No bishop, no king." What he detested was Presbyterianism, according to which the church had authority over everyone, including the monarch.

Concerning *liturgy,* Hobbes thought that it should consist of "words and phrases not sudden, nor light, nor plebian, but beautiful and well composed; for else we do not give God as much honour as we can" (*Leviathan* 31.34). For him, this described the liturgy of the Church of England before the Independents and Presbyterians took control of the church. It largely explains why he attended worship services conducted according to the rights of the Church of England during the Commonwealth, even though they were officially banned.[8]

The last element, *professing the Bible to be the "true religion of Protestants,"* is consonant with Calvinist modesty about the limits of human reason. Because God is incomprehensible, he had to reveal to human beings the things that they needed to know for salvation. If human reason were sufficient for knowledge of God, the Bible would be otiose. It is no good to object that only the weak of mind need the Bible to achieve heaven, because that position denies the inherent need for revelation.[9]

The reason for introducing the issue of Hobbes's Jacobeanism is twofold. First, typically when people add new beliefs to their system of beliefs, they are unlikely to change basic beliefs of that system; and religious propositions—for Hobbes, Jacobeanism—are usually part of the basic ones. Second, because Jacobeanism was passé in the second half of the seventeenth century, many of Hobbes's critics were unable to understand what he believed and why because they were ignorant of his religious and political foundations. It should be remembered that Hobbes was about two decades older than some of his critics, such as John Wallis, Seth Ward, Ralph Cudworth, and Thomas Pierce, and more than three decades older than many others, such as John Tillotson, Thomas Tenison, and Samuel Parker. All of these critics achieved their success either as part of the anti-Calvinist, Laudian clergy; as part of the subsequent Laudian generation of Restoration clergy; or as opponents of absolute sovereignty. Robert Filmer, who shared Hobbes's commitment to absolutism, and John Bramhall, a Laudian and Arminian, were two of the few critics who were also roughly his age.

At least three other elements contributed to Hobbes's alienation from the prevailing views of the latter half of the seventeenth century. One is that he was committed to the new science, which seemed to be inconsistent with traditional doctrine. Another is that his particular version of that new science was unique.[10] Still another is that Hobbes was familiar with and accepted much of the latest biblical scholarship of the time, and his critics were not or did not. (Most of these views are accepted by theistic biblical scholars today.) In short, rather than rejecting the basic beliefs he held as a young adult during the reign of James I, Hobbes tried to reconcile Jacobeanism with the new science. This reconciliation consisted in large part of working in the spirit of Enlightenment thinking. The new science could be put to work to solve long-standing religious and political issues.

My interpretation of Hobbes, as a philosopher trying to reconcile traditional religious content with the new science, is consonant with interpretations that have been given of his friends and colleagues Marin Mersenne, Pierre Gassendi, Thomas White, Kenelm Digby, and, more generally, a large part of the early modern period.[11] Scholars who do not attend to these aspects of religion are prone to be mistaken about the nature of his project, his beliefs, and the significance of the opposition of his contemporaries. The attacks by Presbyterians, Independents, and certain members of the Church of England may lead one to think that no space remains on the spectrum of Christian beliefs for Hobbes to stand on. I contend that such space exists, but, unfortunately for him, this space was sparsely populated during the second half of the seventeenth century.

Eleven Charges against Hobbes and Their Relation to Hobbism

Because Hobbes's actual views are so different from the views attributed to him, we need to distinguish between Hobbes's actual views and Hobbism, the distorted set of doctrines that were attributed to him from at least the Restoration onwards. Hobbism consists in large part of eleven propositions, which are tantamount to charges against him. His critics claim that Hobbes held the following:

1. There was a time when the state of nature was universal.
2. Self-preservation is a law of nature.
3. The most important obligation human beings have is the obligation to preserve themselves.
4. An entity that has power over a group of people is a legitimate government (de facto-ism).
5. Sovereigns have absolute authority.

6. Subjects are permitted to rebel against their sovereign.[12]
7. The foundation of all political authority is a contract.
8. Property rights do not exist prior to the establishment of a civil state; they are granted by the sovereign.
9. The laws of nature are not commanded by God.
10. God does not exist because only bodies exist.
11. No religion is true.

Of these charges Hobbes holds only 5 and 8, neither of which is antireligious.[13] Many of Hobbes's critics themselves assert 5. To us, it may look as if the large majority, 1 through 8, are about politics alone, 10 and 11 are about religion, and 9 is about both. However, for Hobbes's contemporaries, all except perhaps 8 are about religion; and for John Locke even 8 is squarely about religion. God commands humans to preserve themselves, and they cannot do this very well without property.[14]

The apparent discrepancy between the way we see these eleven propositions and the way seventeenth-century intellectuals did may be explained by their belief that politics and religion were inextricably connected. This point can be illustrated by considering propositions 1 through 3. Both 1 and 2 were thought to be inconsistent with the goodness of God, who commanded that people love one another. According to Jesus, the fundamental law of human relations is "Love your neighbor as yourself" (Mark 12:28–30). Concerning 3, some of Hobbes's critics objected that his political theory makes sovereigns as powerful as God and that his statement that Leviathan is a mortal God is blasphemous. But it is not, judged by the standards of Jacobeanism. Referring to Psalm 82, James I, in his *Speech to the Lords and Commons of the Parliament at White-Hall,* says,

> The state of monarchy is the supremest thing on earth, for kings are not only God's lieutenants upon earth, and sit upon God's throne, and even by God are called Gods. Kings are justly called gods for that they exercise a manner or resemblance of divine power upon earth. For if you will consider the attributes to God, you shall see how they agree in the person of a king. God has

power to create, or destroy, to make, or unmake at his pleasure, to give life, or send death, to judge all, and to be judged nor accountable to none; to raise low things, and to make high things low at his pleasure, and to God are both soul and body due. And the like power have kings: they make and unmake their subjects; they have power of raising and casting down, of life and of death; judges over all their subjects, and in all cases, and yet accountable to none but God only.[15]

In the rest of this chapter, propositions 1 through 3 will be considered in some detail and shown to be false generalizations of Hobbes's actual position.

Charge 1: There was a time when the state of nature was universal

Most of those who criticized Hobbes's conception of the state of nature thought he was making a historical claim about primeval times. Robert Filmer begins with God and the first humans: "If God created only Adam and . . . the woman . . . ; if also God gave to Adam not only the dominion over the woman and the children that should issue from them, but also over the whole earth to subdue it, . . . I wonder how the *right of nature* can be imagined by Mr Hobbes, [to be] 'a condition of war of everyone against everyone.'"[16] Filmer realizes that Hobbes acknowledges that the state of nature "never generally" existed over the entire world but does not stop to consider that such an acknowledgment might indicate a misinterpretation of Hobbes's position. Nor does Filmer consider that Hobbes's supposition of people "sprung out of the earth like mushrooms without any obligation one to another" might mean that Hobbes was not talking primarily about history.[17] I'll return to this point in a moment. Bramhall, Seth Ward, William Lucy, and Edward Hyde, Earl of Clarendon, are other good examples of famous critics who criticized Hobbes's use of the state of nature on the grounds that it was not a historical condition.[18]

When Hobbes's concept of the state of nature was accepted, it was interpreted as the condition of people after the fall of Adam and Eve. In *Killing is Murder, and No Murder,* Michael Hawke writes, "For after the fall of our first Parents the natural State of men, before they were setled in a Society, as Master *Hobbs* truely sayeth, was a meer Warre."[19]

The principal reason that Hobbes's critics did not understand the character of the state of nature was that for them the origin of things had to be explained in terms of the history that they believed was reported in the book of Genesis.[20] But Hobbes's approach to origins is completely different. His political philosophy is not historical but scientific. In *De corpore,* Hobbes brags that political science is no older than he.[21] For him, science consists of definitions and the consequences of these definitions. As such, all the propositions of science are necessary and a priori. This is how Hobbes thinks that he avoids skepticism (not "I think; therefore, I am," but "I define x as y; therefore, x is y"). Scientific propositions are universal but also necessarily true; and as a priori, they are nonempirical. In contrast, experience is always of the particular and always empirical. Some propositions that express experience may be universal in form, but they are not scientific because they are not necessarily true. Hobbes says that the proposition "Every crow is black" is universal and true but contingent because while true today it may happen to be false at another time ["Hodie quidem contingere potest ut sit vera, alio tempore ut sit falsa"] (*OL* 1:33–34). According to Hobbes's understanding of philosophy, "It is evident that we are not to account as any part thereof that original knowledge called experience, in which consisteth prudence, because it is not attained by reasoning, but found as well in brute beasts as in man" (*Leviathan* 46.2).

Understanding Hobbes's approach is made more difficult by the fact that his idea of science is unusual. His paradigm is geometry, and his understanding of it nonstandard. Points have length and width, and lines have width in addition to length.[22] Also, Hobbes conceives geometry as generative or constructive. In *Leviathan,* he says, "By PHILOSO-PHY is understood *the knowledge acquired by reasoning, from the manner of the generation of anything, to the properties; or from the properties, to some possible way of generation of the same*" (*Leviathan* 46.1; see also *OL* 1:2).

When it is systematized, a science like geometry begins with the simplest elements and builds on them: "So the geometrician, from construction of figures, findeth out many properties thereof, and from the properties, new ways of their construction by reasoning" (*Leviathan* 46.1). In geometry, one begins with a definition of a point and then a straight line; ideally these definitions are formulated in terms of how to construct them. One then proceeds to deduce whatever follows from these definitions. One goes on to define a plane figure and do the same for it, then to define various kinds of plane figures, and so on. The analogous operation in political philosophy is to begin with the simplest case, that is, the condition of human beings in which no laws exist. For expository purposes, I call this the "primary state of nature."

After drawing the appropriate conclusions, such as that war is generated by competition, diffidence (that is, distrust of others), and the desire for glory, one adds the definition of a law of nature. The deductions resume. The specific laws of nature are deduced from the definition of a law of nature, plus other definitions that Hobbes has supplied, notably, the definitions of a human being and the right of nature. This yields what I call the "secondary state of nature." It is a state of nature because the civil state has not yet appeared, but it is not the primary state of nature because it contains the laws of nature.[23] In *On the Citizen (De cive)*, Hobbes described his general procedure by saying that he began "with the matter of which a commonwealth is made," that is, people in the state of nature, and then went on to describe how the civil state "comes into being and the form it takes, and to the first origin of justice" (Preface, 9).

I have already mentioned that Hobbes's contemporary critics did not appreciate the geometric and generative character of Hobbes's scientific method. Hyde cannot understand how Hobbes could hold that it is "unavoidably necessary for every man to cut his neighbour's throat."[24] He cannot see how people could fall "into that condition of war" if "Nature hath thus providently provided for the Peace and Tranquility of her Children, by Laws immutable & eternal, that are written in their hearts."[25] What Hyde does not understand is that the laws of nature cannot be appealed to in the primary state of nature. (I will return to this theme of science as deduction from definitions in the next section, in which the second charge against Hobbes is at issue.)

Strategically and perhaps rhetorically, Hobbes wants to begin only with the state of nature because he wants to show how horrible the condition of human beings is without government. Having discussed the concept of the state of nature in science, I can now describe its empirical application. Hobbes thinks that it exists in three kinds of situations: during civil war, in highly primitive conditions, and in international relations. But these empirical applications do not change the character that the concept of the state of nature has in Hobbes's science of politics.

In short, the state of nature, for Hobbes, is primarily a concept in a thought experiment. For my purposes, what is important about the groundlessness of charge 1 is that it illustrates how feeble the understanding of Hobbes's philosophy by some of his critics was. They did not appreciate his aspirations to develop a science of politics as rigorous as Galileo's physics and Euclid's geometry, even though *On the Citizen* had been published five years before *Leviathan.*

Charge 2: Self-preservation is the fundamental law of nature

Like the first, this proposition, the second charge made against Hobbes, is false. In *Leviathan,* the first law of nature is "to seek peace" (*Leviathan* 14.4), and the law is similar in *On the Citizen* (*OC* 2.3).[26] Rather than being a law, self-preservation is the object of the dominant desire of human beings and a concept in the definition of a law of nature. As Hobbes states, "A Law of Nature (lex naturalis) is a precept or general rule, found out by reason, by which a man is forbidden to do that which is destructive of his life, or taketh away the means of preserving the same, and to omit that by which he thinketh it may be best preserved" (*Leviathan* 14.3). But the definition of a law of nature is not a law any more than the definition of a horse is a horse. Nonetheless, the reason his critics made the mistake they did is understandable. In *Leviathan,* Hobbes says that the general rule of reason is *"that every man ought to endeavor peace, as far as he has hope of obtaining it; and when he cannot obtain it, that he may seek and use all helps and advantages of war"* (14.4). If the reader is not attentive to the slight changes of wording, she might identify the general rule of reason with the first law of nature; and since the general rule of reason contains what Hobbes describes as "the sum of the right of nature" (that is, "the liberty each man hath . . . for the preservation of his own nature" [14.4, 14.1]), she might conclude that self-preservation is a law of nature.[27] However, both this identification and the slide from the sum of the right of nature to a law of nature are illegitimate. The first law of nature is only the "first branch" of the general rule of reason, not the whole of it. And while the rule of reason contains the right of nature, containing something is not identical with being it. The right to self-preservation is the "second" branch of the general rule of reason and is no part of the first law of nature (14.4).

As with the first charge, many critics leveled the second charge against Hobbes.[28] In *A Discourse of Ecclesiastical Politie,* Samuel Parker writes that for Hobbes "self-preservation [is] the first and fundamental law of nature" and self-interest and self-preservation is an obligation; thus when the "Tye [of self-interest] happens to cease, their Obligation becomes Null and Void."[29] Writing about the same time as Parker, Thomas Tenison implies that for Hobbes self-preservation is the most "ancient" law.[30]

One of the most interesting critics who charged that, for Hobbes, self-preservation is a law is the anonymous author, supposedly one J. Shafte, of *The Great Law of Nature, or Self-Preservation Examined, Asserted and Vindicated from Mr. Hobbes his Abuses* (1673).[31] The title tells the story, but the point is reinforced in the text where Shafte wrote that, for Hobbes, "that Great Law of Nature [is] Self-preservation."[32] He assumes that "the Law of Nature" is operating as soon as Hobbes introduces the state of nature. He says that if the right of nature permitted a person to do things that actually led to his destruction, then "the Law of Nature will *re vera,* really and truly be broken, contrary to design and apparence."[33] As this quotation indicates, Shafte repeats the mistake that critics made with respect to charge 1. He illicitly uses propositions that are not yet in play. Writing about the state of nature, which occurs in chapter 13 of *Leviathan,* Shafte tries to use propositions that are introduced only in chapter 14, "Of the Laws of Nature." Given the logical resources in chapter 13, nothing yet can be just or unjust, as Hobbes says (*Leviathan* 13.13). Another problem with Shafte's interpretation is that he seems to think of the right of nature as a claim right, "granted [to a human being] . . . by God." This is the reason he thinks that the right of nature and the equality of men entail that each person has a right to "a just and equal portion" of all things: "Seeing men are equal by Nature, one man ought not to take to himself a greater liberty in his actions, which respect or concern another man."[34] But obviously, for Hobbes, the right of nature does not give people the right to an equal share of things, only an equal right to compete for whatever they desire.[35]

The misunderstanding that self-preservation is a law of nature for Hobbes was still alive in 1683 when Oxford University, which wanted to support the claim of James, Duke of York, to succeed Charles II, condemned various propositions by such diverse thinkers as the Presbyterian Richard Baxter, the republican John Milton, and the Independent John Owens. Proposition 7 is directed against Hobbes: "Self-preservation is the fundamental law of nature, and supersedes the obligation of all others, whenever they stand in competition with it. *Hobbes de Cive, Leviathan.*"[36] Motivated by the Oxford Judgment, several sermons further spread the idea that self-preservation was a law of nature according to Hobbes, such as one given by James Brome, a royal chaplain, who condemns "our Republican *Leviathans.*"[37] Brome's misunderstanding is about as perfect as one might hope to imagine.[38] Roman republicanism is the view that a healthy state is one in which the citizens participate in governance, while Hobbes's view is that the sovereign decides who participates and to what extent. Chapter 21 of *Leviathan* is a relatively explicit attack on Roman republicanism.[39]

During the Exclusion Crisis (1678–81), some intellectuals began to accept a role for Hobbes's concept of self-preservation in political philosophy. For Locke, people have an obligation to defend themselves because God commanded human beings to multiply and fill the earth: "Everyone is . . . *bound to preserve himself,* and not to quit his Station willfully."[40] Although Locke prefers to talk about the law of the preservation of society, that obligation, it seems, gives way to the obligation of self-preservation if one's own life is endangered.

Like the de facto controversy, the Allegiance Controversy of 1689–90 concerned the problem faced by people of conscience who had sworn allegiance to one monarch and were then pressured to swear allegiance to the person or persons who displaced that monarch. In 1688, James II had left England for the safety of France because William of Orange had come from the Netherlands, ostensibly to observe the election of a new parliament. But in the absence of James, William was made monarch, even though he was not the next person in the line of legal succession. Those who refused to swear allegiance of William were called nonjurors.

William Sherlock began as a nonjuror and defended Charles and his brother James after the Rye House Plot in his pamphlet *The Case of Resistance of the Supreme Powers Stated and Resolved,* in which he presented "ways of proving and confirming *the Doctrine of Non-resistance,* or *Subjection to the Sovereign Princes.*"[41] When he decided to swear allegiance to William, he felt the need to explain his reasons. In *The Case of Allegiance Due to Sovereign Powers,* Sherlock argues that an obligation to obey de facto powers is created by the fact that they are ordained by God. So it seems possible to have obligations to two sovereigns, to the de facto sovereign and to the deposed sovereign, who retains his political legitimacy. He supports his view by citing Canon 28 of the Church of England, as set down in Bishop John Overall's *Convocation Book* for the year 1606. That canon declared that it was a mistake to think that the authority in "new Forms of Government, begun by Rebellion, and after thoroughly settled, . . . [are] not of God."[42] Sherlock takes this to be an endorsement of de facto-ism.[43]

Sometimes acceptance of one of Hobbes's central concepts was combined with an important misunderstanding of his theory. For example, Sherlock appeals to the "inward principle of Self-Preservation."[44] It is not clear what status this "principle" is supposed to have, whether a psychological law, a normative law, or something else. Whether he would want to maintain this at all costs or not, at one point Sherlock does say, "Self-Preservation is as much a Law to Subjects, as to the Prince."[45] And one of Sherlock's critics, Thomas Browne, understands Sherlock to be asserting that "*Hobbs's Self-preservation* [is] . . . the *primary Law of* Nature."[46] In any case, Sherlock appeals to self-preservation to justify the view that whatever "settled" entity is in control of a person's life is a legitimate government in the sense that it has "God's Authority, and must be obeyed."[47] This is a version of the de facto theory of legitimacy espoused by some thinkers during the Engagement Controversy. (It is connected with charge 4 above.) For Sherlock, a usurper on the throne is owed as much obedience as a rightful ruler is, even if consent is not given. So, while he helps himself to Hobbes's concept, he does not end up with Hobbes's view.

It might seem that, for Sherlock, a subject could have a double allegiance, one to the de jure sovereign, who is legitimate, and one to the de facto one, who is illegitimate. But he denies this. A person owes allegiance only to the person who has power over his life; and this is often the de facto sovereign, who has authority from God. The de jure sovereign might have the right to the government but not the authority of the government. That is, right and authority and hence right and allegiance are pulled apart. Since authority is given by God alone, not by the consent of the subjects or any other fact or property, God sometimes ignores what is right; but Sherlock does not consider this consequence. At the end of 1688, James II had possession of "Legal Right" but not the authority of government. At the same time, William III had the authority of government but not the legal right. According to Sherlock, both nonjurors and most jurors made the same mistake, namely, in thinking that legal right was the only ground for allegiance. Sherlock's identification of a supposed error common to both jurors and nonjurors is clever, if not convincing, so it is not surprising that he shores up his position by appealing to principles of the Church of England and the Bible. One of the biblical texts is Daniel 4:21, "*He [God] taketh away Kings, and setteth up Kings.*" Sherlock understands this passage to have the consequence that God removed James II via William's invasion. However, another possible interpretation is exploited by one of Sherlock's critics. Browne uses the same quotation plus a similar one, "*He* removeth *Kings, and* setteth up *Kings*" (Dan. 2:21), on the title page of his *An Answer to Dr. Sherlock's Case of Allegiance to Sovereign Powers.*[48] The implication that Browne intends the reader to draw is that only God removes kings, not human beings. Since James II was not removed by God, he remains king.

A non-biblically based objection to Sherlock's views is that, for him, "Strength always has Right," and the source of that strength is of no importance. For him, "Strength, or Power, still carrys right from God inseparably along with it. . . . And *Right* always carried by *Power* is not a Right to settle Peace but to make *War.* . . . So his *Power carrying Right,* throws all into a state of War, as much, I conceive as Mr. *Hobbs's*

Power giving it."[49] Sherlock replies by denying that his views are the same as Hobbes's. The key difference between them, Sherlock claims, is that he holds that "no Man is a Subject, without his own Consent, or Submission. . . . The greatest Conqueror cannot Compel us to be his Subjects without our own submission."[50] And he says: "We do not Assert, with Mr. *Hobbs,* That as soon as any Prince or Rebel has got Possession of the Throne, we immediately thereby become his Subjects."[51] Sherlock's defense against the charge is ironic, since at this point it looks exactly the same as Hobbes's view, and it is not de facto-ism. Sherlock's use of the claim that "no Man is a Subject, without his own Consent," echoes Hobbes's claim that there is "no obligation on any man which ariseth not from some act of his own" (*Leviathan* 21.10).[52] As for the claim of Sherlock's opponent that for Hobbes "Strength always has Right," it is simply false. Only irresistible power, which belongs only to God, always has right (*Leviathan* 31.5).[53] For human beings, "right" in the sense of authority requires the consent of the subjects.

Charge 3: The most important obligation human beings have is the obligation to preserve themselves

One reason that Hobbes's critics recoiled from the idea that self-preservation could be a law of nature or in some way be obligatory was that such a connection undermined the traditional view that obligation was opposed to self-interest. They feared something like this Hobbist line of reasoning:

1. All acts of self-preservation are acts of self-interest. (Analytic)
2. If self-preservation is a law of nature, then all people have an obligation to preserve themselves. (Analytic)
3. Self-preservation is a law of nature. (Hobbism)
4. Therefore, all people have an obligation to preserve themselves (perform acts of self-preservation). (2 and 3)
5. Therefore, all people have an obligation to perform acts of self-interest. (4 and 1)

According to ordinary morality, obligation and self-interest were largely incompatible. So, if the above argument stood, the ordinary sense of obligation seemed to be destroyed. And since this ordinary sense was thought to prevent society from falling into chaos, the Hobbist argument seemed to be "destructive to all Society."[54] Hobbes's critics were especially worried about the obligation to keep oaths and covenants. (This is related to charge 6 above.)

If Hobbes's critics had not thought that he had made it the first law of nature, they probably would have accepted self-preservation as an obligation.[55] After all, as Locke argues, people are created by God, and hence are God's property; and each person has an obligation to protect God's property from destruction.[56] If some other law had been first, say, "Love your neighbor as yourself," then the obligation of self-preservation would not have trumped all other obligations. However, if self-preservation is the first law of nature, then it seems to be logically prior to all other obligations, and hence the highest obligation. As mentioned above, the Oxford Condemnation expresses its opposition to this.

Although they were mistaken to think that self-preservation was an obligation according to Hobbes, they were right in sensing that his project threatened one of their central beliefs, namely, that reality contains goodness and value as an essential part. The striking refrain of the first creation story in Genesis is that what God created was "good" and that the entire creation was "very good." Even more important than the belief that creation was good was their belief that God was inherently good. The premise that creation is good, combined with the principle that nothing can give what it does not have, entails that God the Creator is inherently good. Hobbes thinks that to attribute properties like mercy and goodness to God is to engage in anthropomorphism. Only beings that have feelings can be merciful, and God does not have them. Most philosophers in the Judeo-Christian tradition would agree with Hobbes that God does not have feelings. However, they would contest the claim that no account of mercy and goodness can be given independent of feelings. No such option is available to Hobbes, for whom to be good is to be desired (*Leviathan* 6.7). It is appropriate for humans to say that God is good and merciful, as well as that he sees and understands, because such statements are "signs of honor" and show honor to God that is owed to him, not because he is the Creator, but because he is sovereign over humans by nature by virtue of his irresistible power (*Leviathan* 31.5–6). Because Hobbes eliminates inherent goodness from both the world and God, the traditional foundation of morality is undermined. His own account of the source of morality is supposed to show how moral obligation is generated from or grounded in something that is not obligation and does not have inherent normative value. To do this, he of course cannot include or presuppose the existence of obligation in the state of nature. (To understand the force of this condition, consider the treatment of the state of nature by Locke, who assumes that it contains laws, obligations, and values.)[57] Thus Hobbes begins his account of obligation with a condition that contains no obligations, that is, a condition in which there are no laws at all. One sees this clearly at the end of chapter 13 of *Leviathan*, "Of the Natural Condition of Mankind," where he says that in the condition of "mere," that is, pure, nature, "The notions of Right and Wrong, Justice and Injustice have there no place" (*Leviathan* 13.13).

Now Hobbes gives the impression that obligation arises in the state of nature only when the laws of nature have been added to it, the secondary state of nature, because he first explains the origin of obligation in chapter 14, "Of the Laws of Nature," after the first law of nature has already been proved. He says, "And when a man hath . . . abandoned or granted away his right, then is he said to be OBLIGED or BOUND, . . . and that he ought, and it is DUTY, not to make void that voluntary act of his own" (*Leviathan* 14.7). What Hobbes means is that obligation is nothing more than "a declaration or signification by some voluntary and sufficient sign or signs" that he no longer has his right (*Leviathan* 14.7). The consequences of giving up a right are solely behavioral. People will say that the person *P*, who gave up the right to do *A*, is obliged or has an obligation not to do *A*. If someone asks *P* to do *A, P* may say that he cannot because he is obliged or has an obligation not to do *A*. If *P* subsequently acts as if he still has the right to do *A*, other people will object or may interfere with his attempt to do *A*.

It is difficult to explain what Hobbes means because he is saying something so new that it is difficult to express using our ordinary words. No matter how his point is stated, it is subject to being misunderstood as meaning something relatively conventional. This problem notwithstanding, it is necessary to try to convey his point as precisely as possible. He means that an obligation is not a new entity in the world. The world continues to consist of nothing more than bodies in motion. What is different is that the speaker, in uttering some words, has indicated his intention to other people that he will not exercise his right to O. The obligation of the speaker consists of nothing extra. To use some contemporary terminology, it is not correct to quantify over obligations. It is not the case that once one has laid down a right, there now exists an X such that X is an obligation. There are no non-natural properties in the sense that G. E. Moore believed there were. Hobbes's view about obligations may be helpfully contrasted with his view about the civil state. Although Hobbes generally does not want to be committed to any entities other than bodies in motion, he seems to commit himself to the existence of artificial persons such as the civil state when he says that it is a "real unity" (*Leviathan* 17.13).

I said above that Hobbes gives the "impression" that obligation arises only when the laws of nature have been added to the state of nature because he introduces the concept of obligation along with the laws of nature. However, it might seem that, given his principles, obligations should be able to arise in the pure or primary state of nature because "a declaration or signification by some voluntary and sufficient sign or signs" that a person no longer has a right does not depend on the existence of any law of nature. One way to remove this appearance of obligation in the state of nature is to appeal to a principle used above. One cannot infer propositions from definitions that have not yet been introduced. Since Hobbes does not define "laying down of right" when he discusses the mere state of nature, one cannot infer that one can lay down a right in the mere state of nature.

If certain empirical changes in behavior are the only consequences of acquiring an obligation, then obligations seem to be rather weak. This is exactly Hobbes's view of them: the words and actions that signify the laying down of a right are "the BONDS, by which men are bound and obliged, bonds that have their strength not from their own nature (for nothing is more easily broken than a man's word), but from fear of some evil consequence upon the rupture" (*Leviathan* 14.7). Obligations without fears of not fulfilling them are empty. This is a wholly naturalistic account of human obligation. But it is not a complete account of human obligation or of obligation in general.

In addition to saying that obligation arises from laying down a right, Hobbes speaks of the laws of nature as obliging: "From that law of nature by which we are obliged to transfer to another such rights as, being retained, hinder the peace of mankind, there follows a third, . . . *that men perform their covenants made*" (*Leviathan* 15.1); "The laws of nature oblige *in foro interno*" (15.36); and "The same laws . . . oblige only to a desire and endeavor" (15.39). That he is speaking of moral obligation is indicated by his table of sciences, where the laws of nature are named moral laws; and he says that "the true doctrine of the laws of nature is the true moral philosophy" (15.40).

These quotations raise the question of whether Hobbes thinks that the obligation that attaches to the laws of nature is grounded in something more basic. Most Hobbes scholars think that Hobbes's laws are merely prudential and not moral, that they are not genuine laws. For them, the laws of nature are dictates of reason—full stop. If this interpretation of the laws of nature is correct, then Hobbes has completely separated the foundations of obligation and morality from God. That's what many of Hobbes's contemporaries thought. I hold a contrary view, that for Hobbes the laws of nature are genuine laws,[58] because he says that in doing science one must speak literally, because he holds that all laws are the commands of someone, and because he often asserts that the laws of nature are God's commands. The law of nature, which "dictateth to men that have no civil government what they ought to do, . . . dictateth the same . . . to the consciences of sovereign princes . . . where not man, but God reigneth, whose laws, such of them as oblige all mankind in respect of God, as he is King of kings" (*Leviathan* 30.30; see also 40.1 and 42.37). This quotation from chapter 30 occurs in part 2 of *Leviathan,* which applies to commonwealths in general. The special treatment of Christian commonwealths has not yet begun. A sticking point for philosophers who believe that the laws of nature are commands of God is how to explain how one knows that God does command them. Hobbes says that one way that God speaks to people is through reason, that the laws of nature are discovered by reason, and that "our natural reason" is "the undoubted word of God" (*Leviathan* 32.2). Hobbes, like almost all intellectuals in the seventeenth century, thought this last point was obvious.

Granted that the obligation attached to the laws of nature is grounded in their being commands of God, we can ask, "In virtue of what are God's imperatives commands?" This is to ask, "In virtue of what does God have authority to command anything?" Most seventeenth-century English intellectuals gave one or both of two standard answers. One is that God has authority over humans in virtue of being their creator; the other is that God has authority over humans in virtue of being good. Sherlock opted for creation grounding authority in order to avoid being convicted of Hobbism.[59]

Hobbes rejects both. He is right to say that creating something does not give one authority over that thing. A workman who makes something, say, a bowl, does not have "authority" over that bowl if he is employed by someone else. The employer has the authority or control over it. Since it is odd to say that anyone has authority over a bowl, let's change the example. A slave who creates a child does not have authority over that child. The owner of the slave has authority over the child. The owner may authorize the slave parent to care for the slave child, but the authority remains in the owner. The reason is that the owner has power over the slave. (Shortly, we shall see what lies at the foundation of this.) It is also incorrect to say that God has authority over humans in virtue of his goodness. The best person in the world does not have authority over anyone in virtue of her goodness. Goodness is logically irrelevant to authority.

Therefore, Hobbes's answer to the question, "In virtue of what does God have authority to command anything?" is different. He says, "The right by nature whereby God reigneth over men and punisheth those that break his laws is to be derived, not from his creating them, as if he required obedience as of gratitude for his benefits, but from his *irresistible power*" (*Leviathan* 31.5). Many of Hobbes's critics thought that locating the source of authority in God's irresistible power was religiously suspect.[60] However, it was an idea that many intellectuals were themselves committed to because it is the straightforward interpretation of a famous text in the epistle to the Romans: "Let every soul be subject unto the higher powers: for there is no power but of God" (Rom. 13:1, Authorized Version).[61] "Power" (ἐξουσία) here has the additional sense of authority. It is a concept that others made use of at the same time. In *Killing is Murder, and No Murder,* Michael Hawke writes, "The Power of all Kings, Princes, and Rulers, immediately proceeds from God. . . . There is no power but from God."[62] In his pamphlet *Transcendent and Multiplied Rebellion and Treason Discovered,* Hyde writes, "*Political Authority, is the power which the Supreame Magistrate hath over men's Persons and Estates. . . . The original thereof is from God; who is the only Potentate,* The King of Kings, and Lord of Lords, 1. Tim. 6, 15, *and from none other, Men or Angells.*"[63]

In short, Hobbes first says that human obligation arises from the laying down of rights. He then connects the laying down of rights to the second law of nature and maintains that all the laws of nature oblige. Ultimately, they are obligatory because of the irresistible power of God. Although obligation is grounded in a kind of power, that power can only be divine.

.   .   .

Hobbes's views look particularly odd for several reasons. He was defending a religious and political view that had gone out of style at least two decades before *Leviathan* appeared. He tried to reconcile traditional Christian doctrine with the new science, which would dominate Enlightenment ideology before the seventeenth century ended. His own version of the new science was eccentric. His biblical understanding was more sophisticated than that of almost all of his critics. Given these elements, it is not surprising that his contemporaries largely misunderstood him on a number of basic issues. I illustrated this point by considering and disarming three of the most common and volatile charges made against him. We thus have good reason to look with suspicion at the caricature of Hobbes in Hobbism and to take seriously the uniquely theological and indeed Christian character of Hobbes's thought, even if his particular brand of theology is thought, even by those in his own time, to be somewhat passé.

Notes

The epigraph from *Mercurius Anglicus,* a short-lived seventeenth-century newspaper, is taken from Jon Parkin, *Taming the Leviathan* (Cambridge: Cambridge University Press, 2007), 346.

1. Showing that several of Hobbes's contemporaries misunderstood his philosophy is not the same as showing that most did, but producing all the evidence for my view is not possible within the limits of this chapter. I am illustrating my point by producing representative examples of the misunderstanding. Also, I am indebted to Parkin's *Taming the Leviathan,* an impressive work of scholarship, for leading me to many of the works cited here. His interpretation of the evidence greatly differs from mine.

2. John Tulloch, *Rational Theology and Christian Philosophy in England in the Seventeenth Century,* 2nd ed. (Edinburgh: William Blackwood and Sons, 1874), 26.

3. Hobbes's orthodoxy is the most controversial of the elements listed. If private individuals make judgments about orthodoxy, then very often one person's orthodoxy is another person's heresy. If someone with authority to make judgments about orthodoxy judges someone's doctrine to be heterodox, then that person's doctrine is heterodox, relative to the community that accepts that judge's judgment. But no such authoritative person made such a judgment about Hobbes's doctrine; and it is unlikely that he could since Hobbes satisfied the criterion for orthodoxy in seventeenth-century England. I distinguish between orthodox and standard views. Of course, many of Hobbes's religious views were nonstandard, as were many of his political and mathematical ones; and he prided himself on holding paradoxical views.

4. Although James I was more interested in dogmatic theology than the Bible, his commitment to the Bible is indicated by his support for a new translation of the Bible into English, the Authorized Version of the Bible, more commonly known as the King James Bible. His Bible-oriented Protestantism is also indicated by his preference for sermons in church services, since sermons were always based on biblical texts.

5. All citations to this work are by chapter and paragraph number and are taken from Thomas Hobbes, *Leviathan,* rev. ed., ed. A. P. Martinich and Brian Battiste (Peterborough, ON: Broadview Press, 2011).

6. John Preston, *Life Eternall, or, A Treatise of the Knowledge of the Divine Essence and Attributes* (1631), 94. See also William Ames: "What God is, none can perfectly define, but that hath the Logicke of God himselfe"; *Marrow of Sacred Divinity* (1643), 11. Cf. *Leviathan* 34.4.

7. Perry Miller, *Errand into the Wilderness* (Cambridge, MA: Harvard University Press, 1984), 51.

8. A. P. Martinich, "Thomas Hobbes's Interregnum Place of Worship," *Notes and Queries* 252 (2007): 433–36.

9. For more about Hobbes's Calvinism and the proper way to interpret him, see A. P. Martinich, *The Two Gods of Leviathan: Thomas Hobbes on Religion and Politics* (Cambridge: Cambridge University Press, 1992), "On the Proper Interpretation of Hobbes's Philosophy," *Journal of the History of Philosophy* 34 (1996): 273–83, and "Interpretation and Hobbes's Political Philosophy," *Pacific Philosophical Quarterly* 82 (2001): 309–31, which also contain references to the works of my critics.

10. See, e.g., Steven Shapin and Simon Schaffer, *Leviathan and the Air-Pump* (Princeton: Princeton University Press, 1985).

11. Margaret Osler, *Divine Will and Mechanical Philosophy: Gassendi and Descartes on Contingency and Necessity in the Created World* (Cambridge: Cambridge University Press, 1994); Beverley Southgate, *"Covetous of Truth": The Life and Work of Thomas White, 1593–1676* (Dordrecht: Kluwer Academic Publishers, 1993); Peter Dear, *Mersenne and the Learning of the Schools* (Ithaca: Cornell University Press, 1988); and Steven Gaukroger, *The Emergence of a Scientific Culture* (Oxford: Oxford University Press, 2006).

12. One might notice that charges 5 and 6 are either contradictory or almost so. This does not indicate a mistake on his critics' part. If Hobbes's theory is contradictory, then both complaints would be correct.

13. As regards charge 10, many scholars think that Hobbes was an atheist.

14. John Locke, *Two Treatises of Government,* ed. Peter Laslett (Cambridge: Cambridge University Press, 1967), 286–88.

15. James I, *The Political Works of James I,* ed. Charles Howard McIlwain (Cambridge, MA: Harvard University Press, 1918), 307. James had said "kings are in the word of GOD it selfe called Gods, . . . and so adorned and furnished with some sparkles of the Diuinitie" (281). Even at midcentury, some of Hobbes's critics believed that sovereigns had something akin to divinity. Eutactus Philodemius, the pseudonym of a defender of the Commonwealth, acknowledged that the "best of Magistrates . . . are called Gods." Eutactus Philodemius, *An Answer to the Vindication of Doctor Hammond, Against the Exceptions of Eutactus Philodemius. Wherein is Endeavored to be Cleared What Power Man Hath* (1650), 18. See Stephen Baskerville, *Not Peace but a Sword* (London: Routledge, 1993), 5, 103, and 118, for other examples.

16. Robert Filmer, *Patriarcha* (1652), in *Patriarcha and Other Writings* (Cambridge: Cambridge University Press, 1991), 187.

17. Thomas Hobbes, *On the Citizen* 8.1; translation from *On the Citizen,* ed. and trans. Richard Tuck and Michael Silverthorne (Cambridge: Cambridge University Press, 1998). Subsequent citations to this work, abbreviated *OC,* are given in the text by chapter and section number.

18. John Bramhall, *The Catching of Leviathan, of the Great Whale* (1658), 567–68; Seth Ward, *In Thomae Hobbii philosophiam* (Oxford, 1656), 287; William Lucy, *Observations, Censures and Confutations of Notorious Errours in Mr Hobbes his Leviathan* (1663), 147–48; and Edward Hyde, *A Brief View and Survey of the Dangerous and Pernicious Errors of Mr. Hobbes His Leviathan* (1676), 28.

19. Michael Hawke, *Killing is Murder, and No Murder* (1657), 7.

20. An intellectual who did understand Hobbes on the state of nature was Matthew Wren, who in *Monarchy Asserted* wrote: "Originally every man had Right to every thing. . . . There was no settled Propriety before the Establishment of Propriety; . . . I must alwayes assert, That though Originally in the state of nature . . . every particular Man had Right to prosecute his own Advantage, though to the Ruine of other Men." Matthew Wren, *Monarchy Asserted* (1660), 18–19, 48–49.

21. *De corpore,* in Thomas Hobbes, *Opera Latina,* ed. William Molesworth (London: John Bohn, 1839–45), 1: [cv]. Subsequent citations to this work, abbreviated as *OL,* are given in the text with volume and page number.

22. Thomas Hobbes, *English Works,* ed. William Molesworth (London: John Bohn, 1839–45), 7:211.

23. Martinich, *Two Gods of Leviathan,* 76–86.

24. Hyde, *Brief View and Survey,* 37.

25. Hyde, *Brief View and Survey,* 38.

26. Somewhat confusingly, Hobbes says, "The first *of the Natural Laws* derived from this fundamental natural law [the first one]" is "*that the right of all men to all things must not be held onto; certain rights must be transferred or abandoned*" (*OC* 2.3). So the first *law of nature* (the foundation) is "to seek peace when it can be had; when it cannot, to look for aid in war" (*OC* 2.2).

27. The mistake of identifying self-preservation with the first law of nature is abetted by the text of *Of the Citizen,* which includes the right of war in the first law of nature: "*to seek peace when it can be had; when it cannot, to look for aid in war*" (2.3).

28. To broaden the historical scene, my examples will focus on authors writing after 1669.

29. Samuel Parker, *A Discourse of Ecclesiastical Politie* (1670), 120–21, 116.

30. Thomas Tenison, *The Creed of Mr. Hobbes Examined* (1670), 147. John Cosin was unhappy with Hobbes for holding that "God's dominion is founded in his power" (Parkin, *Taming the Leviathan,* 63). Also, Skinner quotes a seventeenth-century commonplace book that says that for Hobbes "The prime law of nature in the soul of man is that of temporal self-love." Quentin Skinner, *Visions of Politics: Hobbes and Civil Science* (Cambridge: Cambridge University Press, 2002), 283.

31. Shafte is identified as the author in Early English Books Online. His book is interesting because, though he is virtually unknown, his description of Hobbes's views is more accurate than that of most of Hobbes's critics.

32. J. Shafte, *The Great Law of Nature, or, Self-Preservation Examined, Asserted and Vindicated from Mr. Hobbes his Abuses* (1673), A2r–A2v; see also 19.

33. Shafte, *Great Law of Nature*, 5. There is one place where Shafte's language accurately captures Hobbes's view: "The rules of reason, [are] grounded upon Equality and Self-preservation" (15). It is possible of course that Shafte's wording is correct because he is using a shorthand expression for "law of Self-preservation."

34. Shafte, *Great Law of Nature*, 13.

35. There are other problems with Hobbes's account of rights. In the primary state of nature, a person is supposed to have a right to everything, that is, an absence of external impediments to do whatever he or she likes. However, other people in the state of nature often are external impediments to a person—I owe this point to Kevin Smith—and so, as a matter of logic, there is no right to everything in the state of nature, given that there is some density of population that forces people to interact with others. Also, even if one person were in the state of nature, she would not have a right to everything according to Hobbes's definition if something were inaccessible because of external impediments to objects such as mountains, valleys, or quicksand. One reason it is important to realize that the rights in the state of nature are liberty rights is that Hobbes claims that a certain principle applies to them, when in fact that principle is not true of liberty rights. The principle, which I call "The Principle of the Right to the Means Necessary to an End," is "Whoever has a right to an end has a right to the means necessary to achieving that end." Hobbes clearly holds the principle (*Leviathan* 18.8). He thinks it allows him to argue that sovereigns are absolute: that is, since a sovereign has the right to govern his subjects and one of these rights is to judge what means are necessary to achieve that end, the sovereign can judge that he needs all the rights of his subjects (except for the right of self-preservation and related ones). In short, he is an absolute sovereign.

36. *The Judgment and Decree of the University of Oxford Past [sic] in their Convocation July 21, 1683, against Certain Pernicious Books and Damnable Doctrines Destructive to the Sacred Persons of Princes, their State and Government, and of all Humane Society* (Oxford, 1683), 3.

37. See Parkin, *Taming the Leviathan*, 374–75. Skinner has incisively discussed Hobbes's philosophy within the context of republicanism, or, more precisely, the differences between Hobbes's philosophy and republicanism. See, e.g., Quentin Skinner, *Hobbes and Republican Liberty* (Cambridge: Cambridge University Press, 2008).

38. Parkin may be subject to this judgment when he says, "In some ways Hobbes's own project might be regarded as a highly original variant of conservative republican themes" (*Taming the Leviathan*, 179; cf. 178).

39. See Skinner's *Hobbes and Republican Liberty* and the literature referred to there, as well as A. P. Martinich, "Hobbes's Reply to Republicanism," in *New Critical Perspectives on Hobbes's Leviathan,* ed. Luc Foisneau and George Wright (Milan: FrancoAngeli, 2004).

40. Locke, *Two Treatises,* 2:6; see also Jeremy Waldron, *God, Locke, and Equality* (Cambridge: Cambridge University Press, 2002), 157.

41. William Sherlock, *The Case of Resistance of the Supreme Powers Stated and Resolved* (1684), 2.

42. John Overall, *Bishop Overall's Convocation-Book* (1690), 59.

43. Parkin, *Taming the Leviathan,* 382–84.

44. William Sherlock, *The Case of Allegiance Due to Sovereign Powers* (1691), 3.

45. Sherlock, *Case of Allegiance,* 42.

46. Thomas Browne, *An Answer to Dr. Sherlock's Case of Allegiance to Sovereign Powers* (1691), 17.

47. Sherlock, *Case of Allegiance,* 5.

48. Browne, *Answer to Dr. Sherlock's Case.*

49. John Kettlewell, *The Duty of Allegiance Settled upon its True Ground* (1691), 53.

50. William Sherlock, *Their Present Majesties Government Proved to by Thoroughly Settled* (1691), 14, 16.

51. Sherlock, *Their Present Majesties Government,* 19.

52. One difference between the two philosophers is that Hobbes thinks that human authority arises when subjects consent to be governed by a sovereign and Sherlock holds that human authority is given by God. The submission of the subjects is "the Visible Evidence, that such a Prince has receiv'd his Authority from God" (Sherlock, *Their Present Majesties Government,* 7; see also 14).

53. When Sherlock supported Charles II and his brother after the Rye House Plot, he wrote, "*God* himself set up a Soveraign and Irresistible Power in the *Jewish Nation*" (Sherlock, *Case of Resistance,* 3). This suggests that he had read Hobbes by this time.

54. Daniel Scargill, *The Recantation of Daniel Scargill* (Cambridge, 1669), 6.

55. See, e.g., Parker, *Discourse of Ecclesiastical Politie,* 122; and William Barclay in Locke, *Two Treatises,* 420.

56. Locke, *Two Treatises,* 271.

57. In general, Locke helps himself to too many concepts. For example, he assumes that the world is common property and then explains how private property comes about. It would have been more interesting if he had begun from a state in which there was no property and explained the origin of property.

58. For a full defense of my view, see Martinich, *Two Gods of Leviathan* and "On the Proper Interpretation."

59. Sherlock, *Case of Allegiance,* 15.

60. Parkin, *Taming the Leviathan,* 57.

61. Hobbes uses this text in his argument against Robert Bellarmine's case for the indirect temporal authority of the pope (*Leviathan* 42.10). He also uses other biblical texts with the same force (e.g., Col. 3:30, 3:22; 1 Pet. 2:13–15, and Titus 3:1).

62. Hawke, *Killing is Murder,* 10, 11.

63. Edward Hyde, *Transcendent and Multiplied Rebellion and Treason Discovered* (1645), 1.

Chapter 3

The Religious Spinoza

PHILIP CLAYTON

Perhaps no figure in the two-century history from Descartes through Hegel has been more thoroughly identified with secularization and atheism than Baruch de Spinoza. In Christian Europe, for almost a century after Spinoza's death, the mere hint that a philosopher was sympathetic to Spinozism was enough to bring scandal and sometimes professional ruin. One thinks of the controversy that surrounded the writings of Lessing, Jacobi, and Mendelssohn, and even the 1799 essay by Fichte that launched the Atheism Dispute *(Atheismusstreit)* and eventually cost him his professorship at Jena.[1] Nowhere is the antireligious Spinoza more clearly evident than in the monumental Enlightenment work by Pierre Bayle, the *Dictionnaire historique et critique*: "[Spinozism] is the most absurd and monstrous hypothesis that can be imagined, and the most contrary to the most evident notions of our mind."[2]

Indeed, one proof that the Enlightenment was not a thoroughly antireligious epoch is the vehemence with which Spinoza was attacked because of the threat that he allegedly posed to all things religious. Louis Dupré—to mention just the best in a series of important recent works—has shown how deep and ubiquitous were the religious underpinnings for most of the great Enlightenment thinkers.[3] Indeed, religiously motivated dismissals of Spinoza, based on his criticisms of personal theism, teleology, and divine action, continue in an unbroken line to the present day.

But the initial equation of Spinozism with atheism, fatalism, and irreligion was only the first of four major schools in Spinoza interpretation. The second, which I skip over here, was dominated by empiricist and positivist assumptions and tended also to deride Spinoza, this time *because of* his metaphysical interests. In the third school, to which we turn in a moment, Spinoza is most significant as the philosopher who opened the door to the scientific study of the world without religious interference. Whatever religious interests he may have had—and it is hard to spend time with Spinoza's texts without being struck by the depth of his religious interest—Spinoza is here given credit for construing religion in such a way that it does not interfere with rational inquiry into the natural world.

The fourth school gained influence in the second half of the twentieth century, although it has antecedents in Lessing and all the great German idealists (Kant, Fichte, Schelling, and Hegel). To these interpreters Spinoza becomes the author of a new form of religious metaphysics and religious ethics, one that is deeply tied to the mystical strands of Judaism and Christianity and yet fully compatible with the pursuit of science and the commitment to democracy and the "open society."[4] It is this school about which philosophers in the twentieth century have been strangely silent; we will speculate on the reasons for that silence in due course.

In general, however, Spinoza is the early modern philosopher who is most often tied to the absence of God. Most modern thinkers associate theism with transcendence, for example. So if Spinoza emphasizes immanence, he must be the opponent of transcendence. Worse, he takes a "naturalized" approach to ethics, human nature, and the world as a whole. Combining these factors leads to the popular equation: naturalism + immanence = the absence of God.

In this essay, I resist the simple identifications of immanence with presence and transcendence with absence. More positively, I hope to show how wrestling with Spinoza's reflections on the nature of God and seeking to grasp the role of theistic metaphysics in his system help in understanding his philosophy and its subsequent influence. We will find that the debate between the metaphysics of immanence and the metaphysics of transcendence is far more complex than the standard, simple oppositions suggest. Spinoza's work helps to problematize both terms—that is, render them problematic or, better, uncover the complex and dialectical nature of the distinction itself. Since in theistic metaphysics the primary meanings of the term *God* are strongly determined by the semantic field of immanence and transcendence, the rethinking to which Spinoza's work led subsequent philosophers inevitably began to "relocate" God-language in ways that became highly significant for subsequent European debates about metaphysics and the nature of the divine.[5]

Complexifying "Naturalism" and "Immanence"

We begin with the standard reading of Spinoza. Is it not clear that he has denied all transcendence? The Jewish philosopher Yirmiyahu Yovel defends this conclusion in *The Adventures of Immanence*. He writes, "[Spinoza] rejected both the dualistic transcendence of the Christians and the denaturized, transcendence-ridden this-worldliness of his fellow Jews. A 'Marrano of reason,' he shed all historical religions (though not all religious concerns), and offered salvation neither in Christ nor in the Law of Moses, but in his own kind of religion of reason—naturalistic, monistic, and strictly immanent."[6] As one of the great outsiders of the tradition, and as a clear opponent to any God who is separate from and transcendent of the world, Spinoza appears (to Yovel and to others) to represent the perfect starting point, the opening chapter in a new narrative of the birth and blossoming of the postmodern philosophy of pure immanence, which runs from Spinoza to Richard Rorty, Jean François Lyotard, and their followers. This fact explains Yovel's choice of thinkers for his two-volume work *Spinoza and Other Heretics*, namely Kant, Hegel, Heine, Hess, Feuerbach, Marx, Nietzsche, and Freud, most of whom are only tangentially connected to Spinoza—or connected to him more by opposition than by agreement.

Yovel and other commentators are right: Spinoza remains one of the great representatives, if not *the* greatest representative, of the philosophy of immanence *within modern metaphysics*. Note the last phrase carefully: there are *post*-metaphysical thinkers who match or exceed Spinoza in their emphasis on immanence. But Spinoza is a metaphysician, a rationalist, a direct successor to Descartes. Even today, when naturalism dominates virtually every major philosophy department in Europe and America, few philosophers offer a metaphysical defense of naturalism that can rival Spinoza's. (The truth is that few philosophers feel much need to provide a metaphysical defense of naturalism—when they defend it at all. One finds some good epistemic defenses of naturalism, but that is something different.)

So let us begin by granting Spinoza the role of premier spokesperson for the metaphysics of immanence. After all, he did develop a naturalist metaphysics that is congenial to many of our contemporaries. On his view, if the term *God* is to play any role in philosophy at all, it must say something about the natural world rather than designate a supernatural, transcendent being. For Spinoza, God exists if and only if the equation *deus siva natura* ("God, that is, nature") holds. By implication, then, all those who advocate a purely immanent account of divinity—the viewpoint that has traditionally been called *pantheism*—will check in as "Spinozists," at least at the outset of our discussion.[7]

Immanence and naturalism, it is assumed, stand in tension with transcendence. Consider again Yovel's quick reference (cited above) to "the *dualistic transcendence* of the Christians." Note what this move assumes: all transcendence language is dualistic. Presumably, Yovel has in mind the dualism between naturalism and supernaturalism. In his text, it certainly appears that he is equating transcendence language with supernaturalism and immanence language with naturalism.

But what *is* this naturalism that has realigned all talk of God? A recent collection entitled *Naturalism in Question* highlights the problem.[8] The authors are unanimous in rejecting what they call "supernaturalism," that is, appeals to deities, the "occult," or "magic." As Barry Stroud so profoundly puts it, "Naturalism on any reading is opposed to supernaturalism."[9] But it is not very helpful, is it, to find that naturalism is nothing more than the negation of supernaturalism—especially when one recognizes that supernaturalism, for *its* part, only began to be used in the early modern period as a negative term to describe religious positions that were not *naturalistic* enough!

In fact, the problem is even deeper. Note how David Papineau opens his 2007 encyclopedia article on naturalism: "The term 'naturalism' has no very precise meaning in contemporary philosophy. Its current usage derives from debates in America in the first half of the last century. The self-proclaimed 'naturalists' from that period included John Dewey, Ernest Nagel, Sidney Hook and Roy Wood Sellars. These philosophers aimed to ally philosophy more closely with science. They urged that reality is exhausted by nature, containing nothing 'supernatural,' and that the scientific method should be used to investigate all areas of reality, including the 'human spirit.'"[10] So understood, *naturalism* is not a particularly informative term as applied to contemporary philosophy. The great majority of contemporary philosophers would happily accept naturalism as just characterized—that is, they would both reject "supernatural" entities and allow that science is a possible route (if not necessarily the only one) to important truths about the "human spirit."[11]

One begins to see the problem. Naturalism must be *positively* defined, not just used as a privative, that is, to designate that which is *not* supernatural. But the task seems impossible. For example, philosophers sometimes equate "being naturalistic" with "being scientific," that is, being committed to the "empirical" study of phenomena in the natural world. Yet it turns out to be rather difficult to show that *any* commitment to empirical study requires one to deny all transcendence. Of course, commitment to science may well require that one not treat God as present in the same way that natural objects are present, or as a cause alongside other natural causes. But that is hardly news; for centuries theologians have provided strong theological reasons not to treat God as analogous to a natural object or finite being.[12]

I suggest that some interesting new readings of Spinoza open up once one takes into account these complexities in the notions of immanence and naturalism. Let us see how they affect our understanding of the absence and presence of God in Spinoza.

An Atheist for Whom God Was Indispensable

For centuries, Spinoza has been viewed as the most dangerous atheist in early modern thought. This might seem like a strange judgment on the author of *Ethics,* a book that opens and closes with a lengthy defense of God-language. What justifies Spinoza's reputation as the *advocatus diaboli*, the great advocate of the absence of God? And what significant role, if any, does God still play in Spinoza's thought?

First, a scientific worldview, it is often said, does not allow for teleology. Recall Jacques Monod's confident assertion that "pure, blind chance" alone is the basis of evolution. Richard Dawkins famously makes a similar argument in *The Blind Watchmaker:* "All appearances to the contrary, the only watchmaker in nature is the blind forces of physics, albeit deployed in a very special way. A true watchmaker has foresight. . . . Natural selection . . . has no purpose in mind. . . . If it can be said to play the role of watchmaker in nature, it is the blind watchmaker."[13] Spinoza is equally skeptical of teleological accounts of nature, that is, accounts given in terms of final causes: "Nature has no fixed goal and . . . all final causes are but figments of the human imagination."[14]

Second, Spinoza insists as a result that there can be no action of God as an intentional being acting in the world, hence no personal divine action. All anthropomorphic attributes are inappropriate to God. For example, Spinoza writes in letter 56 to Hugh Boxel:

> When you say that you do not see what sort of God I have if I deny in him the actions of seeing, hearing, attending, willing, etc., and that he possesses these faculties in an eminent degree, I suspect that you believe that there is no greater perfection than can be explicated by the aforementioned attributes. I am not surprised, for I believe that a triangle, if it could speak, would likely say that God is eminently triangular, and a circle that God's nature is eminently circular. In this way each would ascribe to God its own attributes, assuming itself to be like God, and regarding all else as ill-formed.[15]

Third, Spinoza argues that it is impossible that multiple substances should exist. Thus God cannot be present as one substance among other substances, and definitely not as a personal presence, as one person is present to another. Here Spinoza's inspiration comes from Descartes. In the *Principles of Philosophy,* Descartes had written, "By substance, we can understand nothing else than a thing which so exists that it needs no other thing in order to exist. And in fact only one single substance can be understood which clearly needs nothing else, namely, God."[16]

One can clearly see the inspiration of this observation in the opening definitions of book 1 of Spinoza's *Ethics*:

III. By *substance,* I mean that which is in itself, and is conceived through itself; in other words, that of which a conception can be formed independently of any other conception.

IV. By *attribute,* I mean that which the intellect perceives as constituting the essence of substance.

V. By *mode,* I mean the modifications *[Affectiones]* of substance, or that which exists in, and is conceived through, something other than itself.

VI. By *God,* I mean a being absolutely infinite—that is, a substance consisting in infinite attributes, of which each expresses eternal and infinite essentiality.

From these definitions and the opening axioms, Spinoza derived his famous conclusions about the nature of the one substance. There exists only the one infinite substance; hence what we call things and persons in the world are merely modes or modifications of that one substance. The one infinite substance has a fully independent existence; it requires nothing else in order to be thought—which is, after all, what Spinoza meant by writing of "that of which a conception can be formed independently of any other conception" in definition III above. This is not true of us: we are clearly contingent; we require other things in order to be understood. So we must in some way be expressions of the one infinite substance, which is God: "Particular things are nothing but affections of the attributes of God; that is, modes wherein the attributes of God find expression in a definite and determinate way" (*Ethics* I, P25, cor.). We are distinct "not really but only modally" (*Ethics* I, P15).[17] H. F. Hallett thus speaks of each mode as a "microcosm," a locus of relations that reflects the relations below it and is reflected in those above.[18] Under this conception, Nature is "an infinite 'web' or 'lattice,'" and finite agents are "the 'modes' operating so as to form the indivisible integrity of the 'whole.'"[19]

Yet Spinoza retains the God-word, *deus*. What can it mean? Certainly, as we have seen, it cannot mean personal presence, or the presence of one substance to others. For Spinoza, then, God is the framework, the one absolute substance or context, within which all else exists.[20] The existence and functioning of human reason are possible only because of this framework. God is that within which we exist, that without which no finite being would be possible.

In fact, Spinoza argues, reason requires the encompassing frame of God in multiple areas and with regard to multiple attributes of the world. Consider another example from Spinoza. Reflection on the nature of bodies, he argues, inevitably moves human reflection up through a hierarchy of frames to the one substance:

> If, however, we now conceive another individual composed of several individuals of diverse natures, we shall find that the number of ways in which it can be affected, without losing its nature, will be greatly multiplied. Each of its parts would consist of several bodies, and therefore (by Lemma vi.) each part would admit, without change to its nature, of quicker or slower motion, and would consequently be able to transmit its motions more quickly or more slowly to the remaining parts. If we further conceive a third kind of individual composed of individuals of this second kind, we shall find that they may be affected in a still greater number of ways without changing their actuality. If we thus continue to infinity, we shall readily conceive the whole of Nature as one individual whose parts—that is, all the constituent bodies *(omnia corpora)*—vary in infinite ways without any change in the individual as a whole. (*Ethics* II, P13, lemma vii, scholium)

Recall, however, that in Spinoza's system the mind is the idea of that body: "The object of the idea constituting the human mind is the body . . . and nothing else" (*Ethics* II, P13). And for *each* body there is a corresponding idea. Thus the order of ideas likewise includes ideas within ideas within ideas. The structure of the order of ideas precisely mirrors that of bodies; like two congruent triangles, they exist in perfect symmetry. Hence it is not surprising that there is one idea, which Spinoza calls the idea of all ideas, which encompasses all others. The ultimate context for bodies is *natura,* and the ultimate context for ideas— the only context in which we can make sense of the ever-expanding scope of mind or thought—is *deus.* The two terms describe the same totality of reality, though from the standpoint of two different attributes (hence, "dual-aspect theory"). Hence, Spinoza argues, they must be identical: *deus siva natura,* God, that is, nature.

Some contemporary naturalists have argued that this is the ideal way to speak of God (if one must), because God does not do anything and does not get in the way. Thus Jonathan Bennett in his *Study of Spinoza's Ethics* praises Spinoza for leaving the field of empirical phenomena open to scientific study.[21] The God-term, having been moved to the margins, as it were, can no longer impede the pursuit of knowledge. The frame no longer gets in the way. If one's sole interest is empirical explanation and control, the frame becomes irrelevant. On this reading, Spinoza becomes the great modern metaphysician of the absence of God. Is this reading accurate?

"Der Gott betrunkene Mensch"

Things have been brought into being by God with supreme perfection.
—Spinoza, *Ethics* I, P33, scholium 2

I have now explained the nature and properties of God: that he necessarily exists, that he is one alone, that he is and acts solely from the necessity of his own nature, that he is the free cause of all things and how so, that all things are in God and are so dependent on him that they can neither be nor be conceived without him.
—Spinoza, *Ethics,* I, Appendix, opening

As I hope now to show in the remainder of this essay, the judgment just expressed is only half the truth. There is another side to Spinoza that pushes in a completely different direction. It is the side that led Novalis to label Spinoza "der Gott betrunkene Mensch"—"that God-intoxicated man"—who "rightly saw the divine presence in all things."[22] The following paragraphs bring out the dimensions of Spinoza's thought that bring him close to theism or, more precisely, panentheism. Let it be said in advance, however: Spinoza is in fact an advocate of neither view. If one *had* to place the *Ethics* into a metaphysical camp, one would call it pantheism—perhaps more fully pantheistic than the work of any other major philosopher in the West. These seven points may bring the *Ethics* close to the complex boundary between pantheism and panentheism. They represent a direction that Spinoza could have gone and perhaps—depending on one's sense of the arguments and the directions in which they point—a direction he ought to have gone. But let it be said clearly: Spinoza himself never actually took this step.

(1) Book 5 of the *Ethics* uses language that is difficult to dismiss as "merely" naturalistic. For example, "Our mind, insofar as it knows both itself and the body under a form of eternity, necessarily has a knowledge of God, and knows that it is in God and is conceived through God" (*Ethics* V, P30); "God loves himself with an infinite intellectual love" (V, P35); and again, "Blessedness is not the reward of virtue, but virtue itself" (V, P42). Such assertions are hard to mesh with contemporary naturalism. One encounters here a deeply religious construal of human existence, wedded to a metaphysical framework that is very foreign to the spirit of naturalism. And God is somehow crucial to this mode of existing and thinking.

(2) The last book of the *Ethics* also increasingly emphasizes "the intellectual love of God" and the primary reality of essences, which is known only from the perspective of eternity, *sub specie æternitatis*. Thus Spinoza writes toward the end: "It is impossible that we should remember that we existed before the body, since neither can there be any traces of this in the body nor can eternity be defined by time, or be in any way related to time. Nevertheless, we feel and experience that we are eternal" (V, P23, scholium). The focus here is on "the third kind of knowledge" as the most fundamental and as "the highest virtue of the mind" (V, P25). This unique kind of knowledge "proceeds from the adequate idea of certain of God's attributes" (V, P25). It is

definitely not purely immanent, as Bennett's commentary would have us believe. For "the more we understand things in this way, the more we understand God" (V, P25).

(3) Book 5 employs a form of values language that is difficult, if not impossible, to naturalize. It certainly cannot be naturalized in anything like the way that contemporary philosophers are pursuing the "naturalization of ethics" or "naturalized epistemology." Spinoza writes, "The mind's intellectual love towards God *[Mentis amor intellectualis erga Deum]* is the love of God wherewith God loves himself not in so far as he is infinite, but in so far as he can be explicated through the essence of the human mind considered under a form of eternity. That is, the mind's intellectual love towards God is part of the infinite love wherewith God loves himself" (V, P36). Not only is the theological dimension irreducible here, but Spinoza appears to ascribe a kind of agency to God as well. We will return to the question of divine agency in a moment.

(4) We have seen that a number of traditional predicates of God also apply in Spinoza's system, some of them robustly. Does the predicate of transcendence apply? Clearly Spinoza would say no; the intent of the *Ethics* is to obviate the need for a transcendent God. The most one can show here is that Spinoza's metaphysics includes an element of transcendence, that it is not a *pure* philosophy of immanence in the way that, say, Daniel Dennett's philosophy is. There is transcendence only in the sense that Spinoza's absolute substance *(deus siva natura)* is the defining metaphysical unit for all that takes place within it. If *deus* is the whole, then all actions are (in this specific sense) divine actions. As we have seen, this ultimate dimension is indispensable to knowledge; it is the third kind, the highest kind of knowledge. Far from being irrelevant, this One Whole is the defining feature of all else that exists.

(5) In a forthcoming essay, Anselm Min argues effectively that God cannot be an efficient cause in the sense of efficient cause that came to dominate in modern (Newtonian) science and the scientific disciplines derived from it.[23] He claims, rightly I think, that most of the Thomistic tradition would likewise resist ascribing efficient causality, in this sense, to God (though I will not pause here to make that case). The comments Spinoza has to make about divine causality offer a re-

markable echo of the same argument. God is not a transient but the immanent cause of all things (*Ethics* I, P18). God's causes do not pass over to the modes like the motion of billiard balls; rather, God as indwelling cause is *in* his effects. In this sense, Spinoza's attribution of efficient causation to God would appear to be even stronger than the claims St. Thomas makes. After all, Spinoza is willing to assert that "God is the efficient cause not only of the existence of things but also of their essence" (*Ethics* I, P25).

(6) When it comes to the specific respects in which Spinoza resists ascribing activity to *deus siva natura,* we can see why he has done so. Critics (especially theistic critics) have argued that his reasons are inadequate and that the more consistent position would have been to attribute activity to God, which would have pushed Spinoza in the direction of a metaphysics of transcendence. The critique begins with Spinoza's philosophy of mind. At times, he recognizes mind as activity. Human mind is *res cogitans* (note the active participle); it includes an active principle of thought, and this active thinking is constitutive of who we are. Elsewhere, Spinoza famously construes mind only as "the idea of the body," which is a fundamentally passive definition. As Hegel complains, Spinoza's definition of mind does not do justice to *thinking*—to mind as activity.[24]

Spinoza's actual treatment of persons, especially in books 3 and 4 of *Ethics,* generally acknowledges the importance of activity: for example, good as defined in his ethics involves remaining active rather than passive. But when it comes to mind, he falls back on his strict definition: "the idea of the mind, that is, the idea of an idea *[idea Mentis, hoc est, idea ideae]*" (*Ethics* II, P21, scholium).[25] Now recall that God is defined in terms of the two divine attributes that humans can grasp: thought and extension. When Spinoza defines thought only as the idea of ideas, God becomes the idea of *all* ideas. Activity is strikingly absent from this definition.

Yet note the tension here. *Nature,* Spinoza insists elsewhere, has an active element; it is not only *natura naturata* but *natura naturans,* nature "naturing" (*Ethics* I, P29, scholium). Critics allege that this is an inconsistency. Nature's activity takes place, in part, through humans and other living things. That activity manifests not only through the attribute of extension but also through the activity of thought. We are mentally active; we evidence mental creativity; and we consciously synthesize. Spinoza's view becomes more consistent if we explicitly include mental as well as physical activity in the description of persons.

But now recall that all finite individuals are modes of the One. How can the modes be active unless the one Whole of which they are modes *also* includes activity? Can Spinoza say that mental activity is crucial for us, while the One who has the idea of us has no mental activity? According to Spinoza, "[God] constitutes the essence of our mind" (*Ethics* II, P34, proof); the two are understood as fully parallel. If there is any active conscious activity in humans, if there is anything more to thinking than a one-to-one mirroring of the body in the language of ideas, and if there is any activity in God that is not just the idea of physical processes, then (critics argue) there has to be a part of God-as-mental that is more than just a mirroring of the physical universe. *Something about God would have to be more than the physical universe.* As long as God possesses the attribute of thought, then this "more than" seems unavoidable. For it is basic to the phenomenon of reflection, the later idealists would argue, to be aware of the contents of one's thought (an awareness that is more than those contents), to synthesize them, to judge them. In creative reflection, as Whitehead realized, "the many become one, and are increased by one."[26] The moment one acknowledges mental activity and the creative drive of thinking, the German idealists maintained, Spinoza's pantheism is tugged toward panentheism. A thinking God, a God with the attribute of thinking, is a God who encompasses the world but at the same time also transcends it. And this difference, they argued, is enough to transform God from a basic framework—the One within which all else exists—to the God who is also in some sense an active agent.

(7) The argument to this point has attempted to bring out a dilemma that is latent in Spinoza's thought and that became a guiding theme in the later reception of his work, especially in German philosophy. Subsequent readers have cited multiple considerations that likewise count against his attempt to retain a pure, monistic pantheism, thereby pushing in the same direction. One classic problem in Spinoza interpretation that has this effect concerns the problem of the origin of the modes. Why do the modes exist? Why is the one Whole differ-

entiated into a vast number of what appear to be finite objects? As a rationalist, Spinoza cannot simply say, "Well, isn't it empirically obvious that there are many things (modes) within the world?" Since he famously treats reasons and causes as identical, he needs to be able to explain the existence of modes.

Two paths were open to Spinoza, had he discerned this dilemma and wished to move beyond it. He could have derived the modes from the One, or he could have shown how the existence of finite things entails the existence of the one divine substance. In fact, Spinoza did not provide, and probably could not have provided, an account of how and why (note that the two questions are identical in his system) the one absolute substance should be differentiated in the way it is. Conversely, even if the move from individual modes (taken as extended spatiotemporal moments) to the whole of the physical universe were unproblematic, it is not clear that one can move in a precisely symmetrical way from modes as thinking individuals to the one substance understood as the activity of thought (as opposed to "the idea of all ideas").

In fact, the only way Spinoza could make the latter argument would be to ascribe some form of consciousness to God. But that move would again push him over the line from pantheism to panentheism. (It is interesting to see "the Spinoza of the East," the great monist philosopher of classical Hindu thought, Shankara, struggling with the same precariousness in his attempt to defend *nirguna Brahman,* the Absolute without attributes. At times he conceives *Brahman* as beyond all attributes, at other times as necessarily having the attribute of consciousness.)[27]

Spinoza's work thus poses a crucial dilemma to subsequent philosophers. On the one hand, one can preserve the monism of the *Ethics,* in which case the source of finite modes and their individuality remains unexplained. On the other hand, one can grant some element of de facto autonomy for the modes (that is, for physical and mental entities in the world), in which case monism is abandoned in all but name. As other Spinoza scholars have recognized, the problem of explaining the individuation of the modes is probably insoluble as long as one works within the precise parameters within which Spinoza worked.[28]

No other philosophical system in the modern period brings home the force of this dilemma as clearly as Spinoza's *Ethics*—which helps to explain the continuing value of his work for constructive meta-physicians. To recognize the incompatibility of the relations between monism and autonomy is to recognize fundamental constraints on how the relationship between God and world, or God and human freedom, can be conceived. The fact that both philosophers and theologians (for different reasons) tend to draw back from exploring these relations may express prejudice, fear, or ignorance, but it does not in any way detract from the force of conceptual dilemma that Spinoza's work helps to demonstrate. If the subsequent tradition, particularly in German philosophy, was correct in its exposition of the dilemma, one has to make a choice. One can affirm absolute monism, monism without differentiation. But in that case, the appearance of distinctions within the world becomes, ultimately, illusory. Alternatively, one can affirm the metaphysical view that came to be known as panentheism: the modes are contained within the Divine, but God is also more than the world; *deus* is more than *natura*.

The *Ethics* claims to offer the reader a single system that perfectly blends the infinite and the finite. Critics have argued that the system is not fully coherent; despite Spinoza's intentions we are left, they claim, with two realms—the one infinite substance, and the interconnected field of modes—which are linked in name alone. Spinoza could resolve this dualism (if such it is) into ultimate and complete monism; certain tendencies in this direction are already present in the *Ethics*. Thus, as the mind begins to see clearly, it intuits a final unity. It sees *sub specie aeternitatis,* perceiving the connection of all together. At the ultimate limit, William Sacksteder argues, in Spinoza's system "the distinction between part and whole absconds entirely."[29] By contrast, if the critics are right and Spinoza wants to retain the real activity of the modes *qua* mental agents, he must apply that activity to *deus* as well.

Further Confirmations: Influences on and the Influence of Spinoza

In the past, analytic philosophers enjoyed reconstructing textual arguments but spent somewhat less time working on historical sources and historical influence. This tendency, while it led to some great textual analysis, tended to foster an ahistorical, even atomistic treatment of certain modern philosophers. In the case of Spinoza, I suggest, that approach has been particularly damaging. (Spinoza's claim to write *more geometrico*—after the fashion of geometry, with what are supposed to be purely formal arguments—when combined with his habit of not citing his sources by name, also bears its responsibility for the ahistorical treatment of his work.) It is worth taking a moment to dispel the resulting misimpressions.

We know that Spinoza was well read in medieval Jewish philosophy. In addition to his extensive study of Maimonides, he was familiar, it seems, with Abraham ibn Ezra, Gersonides, and Leone Ebreo.[30] Many of the ideas about God that readers take to be distinctive of Spinoza's thought turn out not to be original to him—including his ultimate philosophical monism. The philosophers who represented for him the deepest Jewish reflection on the nature of God had come to similar conclusions. As Leon Roth concludes in his classic study, "The monism of Spinoza is a direct derivative of the characteristic form which the monotheistic idea . . . had assumed in the mind of Maimonides."[31] And Shlomo Pines even claims at one point that Maimonides' God is "something coming perilously close to Spinoza's attribute of thought (or to his 'Intellect of God')."[32] Carlos Fraenkel, at the end of his masterful study of Spinoza and Maimonides, is equally unambiguous: "It is clear that in my view the distance separating Maimonides' God from Spinoza's is rather small. If we imagine a discussion between the two philosophers I would not expect metaphysics to be a very controversial issue."[33]

That Spinoza is not a "traditional theist" should be obvious. But the *distance* between Spinoza and traditional theism has frequently been overstated. Such judgments often use creedal statements (in the case of Christianity) and the standards of Orthodoxy (in the case of Judaism) as their point of comparison. But each of the Abrahamic traditions has also included sophisticated philosophical reflection on the nature of God. When one uses the Jewish, Christian, and Islamic *philosophers* as the standard—those influenced by Aristotle, by Neoplatonism, and by the Kabbalistic tradition, just to name a few examples—the lines of continuity and influence emerge rather more vividly.

What of Spinoza's influence on subsequent reflection in theistic metaphysics? One finds him cited as a defender of personal immortality, as an authority on the nature of faith, and as a model for eco-spirituality.[34] Far from being an advocate of modern materialism, Amihud Gilead argues, he "would reject physicalism of any sort, and most, if not all, of today's [physicalist] views."[35] Yovel's famous attempt to link Spinoza to the antitheism and atheism of subsequent Continental thought, discussed earlier, has prompted a wave of scholarship in response, which works to show Spinoza's theological roots and his importance for contemporary philosophical reflection on the nature of God.[36] Martin Yaffe goes so far as to claim that "modern Judaism seems scarcely understandable apart from Benedict Spinoza."[37]

I have no doubt that these connections exist. But Spinoza has had an even deeper impact on subsequent theistic metaphysics than these various specific claims reveal. That he played a crucial role in these subsequent developments is not lessened by the fact that they grew out of the unsolved paradox in his philosophy that we explored in the previous section. The view that emerged in the work of Spinoza's closest readers in the period from Lessing to Hegel—partly through appropriation and partly through criticism—is not difficult to state. Thought is not just the sum of ideas but also *activity:* in finite thinkers, in nature's activity, and in God. Thus there is causality at the level of God, the ultimate principle. This causality is not transcendent, as in classical theological dualism, but immanent. Yet if there is activity and causality within the Absolute, then God is also *more than* the whole of nature. What applies to the creative synthesis of every actual occasion also applies to God, as we saw above: "The many become one, and are increased by one."[38]

In short, Spinoza's pantheism spawned a new form of philosophical panentheism. Whatever else one wants to say about this history in general, and its German idealist form in particular, it is clearly a story of agency, subjectivity, and activity being ascribed more explicitly and more robustly to the Ultimate. It is precisely this gradual transformation that one can observe in the history of Continental philosophy over the following two centuries. The movement extends from Lessing through Jacobi, Mendelssohn, Kant, Fichte, Schleiermacher, Schelling, and Hegel . . . and on to Whitehead and others in the twentieth century.[39] It helps explain why Michael Brierley can speak of "the panentheistic turn in modern theology" in his carefully documented essay on the history of panentheism in the twentieth century.[40]

In short, the well-known links between Spinoza and the secular Enlightenment need not be denied. But to interpret Spinoza's impact and significance only in this sense is to foster a truncated view of his work and its subsequent influence. Spinoza's continuation of the tradition of radical philosophical reflection on the nature of God as the highest (and for him the only) substance is hardly orthodox. But nor was the work of many of the Jewish and Christian philosophers who engaged in this same project before him. To recognize Spinoza's location within this tradition is to recognize how misleading is the mantle of atheism and irreligion that is often used to define his life's project.

Notes

1. I have told these stories in *The Problem of God in Modern Thought* (Grand Rapids, MI: Eerdmans, 2000).

2. Pierre Bayle, "Spinoza," in *Mr. Bayle's Historical and Critical Dictionary*, 2nd ed. (London, 1738), vol. 5; for the original French, see *Dictionnaire historique et critique de Pierre Bayle*, new ed. (Paris: Desoer Libraire, 1820), 13:416–68. The Spinoza article is the longest in the entire *Dictionnaire*. Typically, Bayle notes, "Few people are suspected of adhering to his doctrine; and among those who are suspected of it, few have studied it; and among the latter, few have understood it, and most of them are discouraged by the difficulties and impenetrable abstractions that attend it" (*Mr. Bayle's*, 217; *Dictionnaire historique*, 418).

3. Louis Dupré, *The Enlightenment and the Intellectual Foundations of Modern Culture* (New Haven: Yale University Press, 2004).

4. See Karl Popper's classic, *The Open Society and Its Enemies* (New York: Harper, 1962).

5. An earlier version of some of the following material was read at the annual Danforth conference on the philosophy of religion at the Claremont Graduate University in February 2008. It appears under the title "The Hiddenness of God in Spinoza: A Case Study in Transcendence and Immanence, Absence and Presence," in the volume of conference proceedings *The Presence and Absence of God*, ed. Ingolf Dalferth (Tubingen: Mohr, 2009).

6. Yirmiyahu Yovel, *The Adventures of Immanence*, vol. 2 of *Spinoza and Other Heretics* (Princeton: Princeton University Press, 1989), 169.

7. See Michael Levine, *Pantheism: A Non-Theistic Concept of Deity* (New York: Routledge, 2003).

8. Mario DeCaro and David Macarthur, eds., *Naturalism in Question* (Cambridge, MA: Harvard University Press, 2004).

9. Barry Stroud, "The Charm of Naturalism," in DeCaro and Macarthur, *Naturalism in Question*, 23.

10. David Papineau, "Naturalism," in *The Stanford Encyclopedia of Philosophy*, Spring 2007 ed., ed. Edward N. Zalta, http://plato.stanford.edu/archives/spr2007/entries/naturalism/. At the end of this passage Papineau parenthetically cites Yervant Hovhannes Krikorian, ed., *Naturalism and the Human Spirit* (New York: Columbia University Press, 1944), and Jaegwon Kim, "The American Origins of Philosophical Naturalism," *Journal of Philosophical Research* 28 (2003): 83–98.

11. Papineau, "Naturalism."

12. See, e.g., Ingolf Dalferth, "God, Time, and Orientation: 'Presence' and 'Absence' in Religious and Everyday Discourse," and Anselm Min, "The Dialectic of God's Presence and Absence in the World," both in Dalferth, *Presence and Absence*.

13. Richard Dawkins, *The Blind Watchmaker* (New York: Norton, 1986), 5.

14. See Baruch Spinoza, Appendix to *Ethics* [part] I, which follows P [= proposition] 36. Here and subsequently, I am citing the Samuel Shirley translation, *Ethics and Selected Letters* (Indianapolis, IN: Hackett, 1982), abbreviated as *Ethics*, parenthetically in the text with part and proposition numbers.

15. Spinoza to Hugh Boxel, letter 56, in Shirley, *Ethics*, 247.

16. René Descartes, *Principia philosophiae* 1.51; I have modified the English translation in *The Philosophical Writings of Descartes*, trans. John Cottingham, Robert Stoothoff, and Dugald Murdoch (Cambridge: Cambridge University Press, 1985), 1:210.

17. "Modaliter tantum distinguuntur, non autem realiter."

18. H. F. Hallett, *Benedict de Spinoza* (London: Athlone, 1957), quoted from the reprint in *Spinoza*, ed. Marjorie Grene (Garden City, NY: Doubleday Anchor, 1973), 154–60.

19. Hallett, *Benedict de Spinoza*, 158.

20. Spinoza claims to have shown "the nature and properties of God: that he necessarily exists, that he is one alone, that he is and acts solely from the necessity of his own nature. . . , that all things have been predetermined . . . from the absolute nature of God, his infinite power" (*Ethics* I, P36, start of Appendix).

21. Jonathan Bennett, *A Study of Spinoza's Ethics* (Indianapolis, IN: Hackett, 1984).

22. Novalis, *Novalis' Werke in vier Teilen,* ed. Hermann Friedemann (Berlin: Bong, 1908), no. 562, 3:651; Frederick C. Beiser, *German Idealism: The Struggle against Subjectivism, 1781–1801* (Cambridge, MA: Harvard University Press, 2002), 419, citing the influence of Jacobi's *Briefe* on Novalis and many in his generation, including Schelling, Hölderlin, and Hegel.

23. Min, "Dialectic of God's Presence."

24. The criticism goes back to Hegel and his followers—and even earlier, as we will see below. See, e.g., Wolfgang Cramer, *Spinozas Philosophie des Absoluten* (Frankfurt: Vittorio Klostermann, 1966), 96–108.

25. Joseph Moreau actually argues that Spinoza has already moved in this direction. He argues that the metaphor of the body is the key for combining substantial monism and modal pluralism: "The diversity of singular things . . . is a collection of single modes that are unified as the organs of one body. The universe must be considered as an individual Soul, of which the parts change without its ceasing still to persist in its form as a total Individual." Joseph Moreau, "Spinoza est-il monist?" *Revue de Théologie et de Philosophie* 115 (1983): 26.

26. A. N. Whitehead, *Process and Reality,* corrected ed. (New York: Free Press, 1978), 21.

27. See Natalia Isayeva, *Shankara and Indian Philosophy* (Albany: SUNY Press, 1993); Michel Hulin, *Sankara et la non-dualité* (Paris: Bayard, 2001); and, classically, J. H. Woods and C. B. Runkle, trans., *Outline of the Vedanta System of Philosophy according to Shankara* (1906; repr., Cambridge, MA: Harvard University Press, 1927).

28. See Amihud Gilead, "Spinoza's *Principium individuationis* and Personal Identity," *International Studies in Philosophy* 15 (1983): 41–57; Richard V. Mason, "Spinoza on the Causality of Individuals," *Journal of the History of Philosophy* 24 (1986): 197–210; Marx W. Wartofsky, "Nature, Number and Individuals: Motive and Method in Spinoza's Philosophy," *Inquiry* 20 (1977): 457–79; Amélie Oksenberg Rorty, "The Two Faces of Spinoza," *Review of Metaphysics* 41 (1987): 299–316; and Hermann de Dijn, "The Articulation of Nature, or the Relation God-Modes in Spinoza," *Giornale Critico della Filosofia Italiana* 8 (1977): 337–44.

29. William Sacksteder, "Simple Wholes and Complex Parts: Limiting Principles in Spinoza," *Philosophy and Phenomenological Research* 45 (1985): 403.

30. See Manuel Joel, *Spinozas theologisch-politischer Traktat auf seine Quellen geprüft* (Breslau: Schletter'sche Buchhandlung, 1870). Carlos Fraenkel draws extensively from Joel's book but also adds to the evidence, in his recent article, "Maimonides' God and Spinoza's *Deus sive Natura,*" *Journal of the History of Philosophy* 44, no. 2 (2006): 169–215.

31. Leon Roth, *Spinoza, Descartes, and Maimonides* (Oxford: Clarendon Press, 1924), 145.

32. Shlomo Pines, *Studies in the History of Arabic Philosophy,* ed. Sarah Stroumsa (Jerusalem: Hebrew University Press, 1996), quoted in Fraenkel, "Maimonides' God," 211.

33. Fraenkel, "Maimonides' God," 207. This conclusion is based on the more specific thesis that "there is no fundamental break between the medieval doctrine of the Aristotelian God and Spinoza's *Deus sive Natura*" (203). Although the evidence for Fraenkel's claims is strong, it should be acknowledged that the conclusions of Harry Austryn Wolfson, Leon Roth, Carlos Fraenkel, and others are resisted by a significant number of Spinoza scholars.

34. On Spinoza as a defender of personal immortality, see Alan Donagan, "Spinoza's Proof of Immortality," in *Spinoza: A Collection of Critical Essays,* ed. Marjorie Grene (Garden City, NY: Anchor Books, 1973); Tamar Rudavsky, *Time Matters: Time, Creation and Cosmology in Medieval Jewish Philosophy* (Albany: SUNY Press, 2000), 18–86. Wolfson even argues that Spinoza affirms the traditional belief that "the bliss and happiness of the immortal souls consist in the delight they take in the knowledge of the essence of God." Harry Austryn Wolfson, *The Philosophy of Spinoza* (Cambridge, MA: Harvard University Press, 1934), 2:310–11. On Spinoza as an authority on the nature of faith, see David Cockburn, "Self, World and God in Spinoza and Weil," *Studies in World Christianity* 4 (2001): 173–86. Cockburn argues that Spinoza's thought shows what it means "to take [all that] happens as the work of God" (183). And on Spinoza as a model for ecospirituality, see Arne Naess, *Spinoza and the Deep Ecology Movement* (Delft: Eburon, 1993); Eccy de Jonge, *Spinoza and Deep Ecology: Challenging Traditional Approaches to Environmentalism* (Aldershot: Ashgate, 2004).

35. Amihud Gilead, "Substance, Attributes, and Spinoza's Monistic Pluralism," *European Legacy* 3 (1998): 1–14.

36. Thus, for example, Dov Schwartz argues that "one may establish that Spinoza, in many respects, is none other than a disciple of Maimonides and his followers." Dov Schwartz, review of *Spinoza and Other Heretics,* by Yirmiyahu Yovel, *Jewish Quarterly Review* 83 (1993): 452–57.

37. Martin D. Yaffe, "Two Recent Treatments of Spinoza's 'Theologico-Political Treatise' (1670): A Review Essay," *Modern Judaism* 13 (1993): 309. It should be added that Yaffe's concern for orthodoxy leads him (apparently) to wish that modern Judaism had never happened.

38. Whitehead, *Process and Reality,* 21.

39. I have pursued this line of thought is some detail in Clayton, *Problem of God.*

40. Michael Brierley, "Naming a Quiet Revolution: The Panentheistic Turn in Modern Theology," in *In Whom We Live and Move and Have Our Being,* ed. Philip Clayton and Arthur Peacocke (Grand Rapids, MI: Eerdmans, 2004), 1–15.

Chapter 4

God and Design in the Thought
of Robert Boyle

RICHARD A. MULLER

In the last half century, historians of early modern science have recognized the importance of the religious, indeed, the theological dimension to the thought of the natural philosophers or scientists of the late seventeenth and early eighteenth centuries, reversing the older claims of a "warfare" between science and religion.[1] Historians in other fields, namely philosophy and theology, have been slow to integrate these results into their understandings of the era. Historians of theology, certainly, have argued the case for more positive relations between theology and science, but there has been little examination of the theological and philosophical implications of the works of natural philosophers and scientists,[2] nor has there been any convincing analysis of the implications of the gathering revolt against a more or less traditional "substance metaphysics" for theological formulation in the early modern era. Historians of philosophy have studied the impact of religion on the philosophies in the early modern era but have not typically endeavored to close the circle of research by examining the theological works of the era and their relationships to philosophical developments.[3]

These connections between philosophy, natural science, and theology and the implications of the various natural philosophies old and new for theology were, however, seldom ignored by the writers of the early modern era, whose works consistently disoblige the more recent disciplinary boundaries of theology, philosophy, and science. In the case of the members of the Royal Society, the so-called virtuosi of the latter decades of the seventeenth century, scientific advance was often connected with renewed interest in divine providence and concerted attempts to write theology in and for their own era. A significant example of this approach is the thought of Robert Boyle, whose approach to theology and science rejected both the explicit notion of double truth (namely, that something can be true in philosophy but false in theology or true in theology and false in philosophy) proposed by some theologians of the era and the implicit acceptance of double truth embedded in the Baconian approach to learning.[4] Although one would be hard put to identify any developed form of a confessional orthodoxy in his thought, he nonetheless evidences a concerted interest in maintaining an alliance between science and religion and in stressing the underlying theological or religious implications of science itself—while at the same time indicating a clear differentiation of methodologies.[5] A significant illustration of this assumption is his emphasis on the importance of final causality for understanding both the world order and the divine involvement in it, an emphasis that not only distinguishes his thought from the deductive rationalisms of the era but also represents a conscious effort on his part to show the defect of a science or philosophy not directed toward issues of penultimate and ultimate purpose in the universe.

Previous analyses of Boyle's approach to causality have mainly presented his relationship to early modern science and to the mechanical philosophies of the era, claiming either that his approach to final causality was intended primarily as an argument for the legitimacy of teleological conclusions in experimental science or that it serves primarily as the basis for a form of natural philosophical theology intended specifically to argue for the existence of God.[6] The present essay will take up the question of Boyle's intention in pressing the issue of final causality by identifying relationships or parallels between his understanding and lines of argument found in the theologies and philosophies of Reformed and Puritan writers in his time. Whereas the Mechanical phi-

losophy, in which Boyle's role was pivotal, is typically known for its attack on the Aristotelian substance metaphysic (which was engrained
in the orthodox theologies of the day), we will see that Boyle himself
held significant reservations over the dissolution of final causality in
the sciences and in related philosophies and ultimately argued that a
strong view of providence, and thus of providentially ordered teleology, is essential not only to religion but to science as well.[7]

Boyle on Providence and Final Causality

The impact of the atomist or mechanistic critique of older Aristotelian
models is evident in Boyle's philosophical and theological argumentation.[8] Boyle's approach to theology and science assumed not only their
cooperation but also their conjunction. He declared that rightly understood "nothing is false in philosophy . . . that is true in Divinity."[9]
His use of the rather Baconian view of the distinction of theology and
natural philosophy in matters of research also insisted—contrary
to Bacon—on the importance of understanding "the first *original of
things*" and the constructive relationship of philosophical examination
of "the subsequent *course of Nature*" to religion and theology.[10] He did
not, in other words, understand the distinction of the realms of investigation as removing the necessity for discourse between the two fields
of inquiry. As Harold Fisch pointed out, like the Hermetic (and, we
add the Scriptural and Mosaic) philosophers of his time, Boyle viewed
nature and divinity as interconnected, with natural philosophy serving
divinity.[11] It is, for example, necessary for the naturalist to recognize
that "God is not onely the Author, but the Creator of the World";
since the philosophers differed on the point and since even those who
thought the world had a beginning assumed that matter as such had no
beginning and that creation out of nothing was impossible, theology
rightly informs natural philosophy.[12] Theology also informs philosophy concerning the time, order, circumstances, and manner of the creation and completion of "the Fabrick of the World."[13]
   It is therefore quite significant and a sign of his relationship to a
more traditional understanding of the relationship of God and world

that Boyle spoke not only of the original divine framing of the world
order but also of an ongoing providential concurrence:

> the *first original of things,* and the subsequent *course of Nature*
> teaches . . . not onely that God gave Motion to Matter, but that in
> the beginning He so guided the various Motions of the parts of
> it, as to contrive them into the World he design'd they should com-
> pose (furnish'd with the *Seminal* Principles and Structures of Mod-
> els of Living Creatures,) and establish'd those *Rules of Motion,* and
> that order amongst things Corporeal, which we are wont to call the
> *Laws of Nature.* And having told this as to the *former,* it may be al-
> lowed as to the *latter* to teach, That the Universe being once fram'd
> by God, and the *Laws of Motion* being setled and all upheld by his
> incessant concourse and general Providence; the Phaenomena
> of the World thus constituted, are physically produc'd by the Me-
> chanical affections of the parts of Matter, and that they operate
> upon one another according to Mechanical Laws.[14]

The providential concourse is evident primarily in constancy of the
mechanical laws,[15] but Boyle's argument for an "incessant concurrence" nonetheless also reflects an understanding of creation ex nihilo
and the traditional assumption, held by his Reformed and Puritan contemporaries, that the material order is radically contingent.[16]

Boyle was sensible of the danger to traditional religion posed by the
scientific critique of traditional notions of causality and substance —
but he was also intent on identifying a similar danger to natural philosophy if the connection between scientific and religious thought was
severed. He did, of course, identify his task as that of the "Christian
virtuoso," recognizing that the work of the scientific adept was not to
be separated form religion.[17] From one perspective, Boyle's *Disquisition about the final causes of natural things,* published two years before his
Christian virtuoso, can be understood as an apologetic essay, reminding
his colleagues, the virtuosi, of the theological and metaphysical underpinnings of scientific endeavor and defending that endeavor from
the charge that science was detrimental to religion.[18] The apologetic
mode had been evident in his *Usefulnesse of experimental philosophy,*[19] and

the positive relation between science and theology had been a theme of Boyle's earlier works *The Excellence of theology* and *Of the high veneration man's intellect owes to God.*[20]

What is remarkable about Boyle's definitions is that they consistently return to the idea of providence and to the importance of an understanding of providence to the scientific endeavor itself, an emphasis that he knew ran counter to the tendencies of Cartesian and Epicurean science in his time.[21] What is more, Boyle's definitions had significant affinities with the Reformed and Puritan theologies of the era as well as with more traditional natural philosophies.

Manifesting an affinity with the Scriptural and Mosaic philosophies and with the eclectic natural philosophy of Daniel Sennert, favored by many of the Reformed, Boyle points out that the "vulgar notion of nature" can undermine religion if it tends to explain all the operations of the world order without reference to providence, thus removing "the necessity of acknowledging a deity." This problem is particularly acute among the Epicurean philosophers. Those who exhibit this excessive admiration for the world order "fear to affirm, that God and nature are the same thing, and will confess that she is but his viceregent; yet, in practice, their admiration, and their praises, are frequently given to nature, not to God."[22] A right understanding of "nature" forestalls "an excessive veneration" for it, such as was evident in "many of the old heathen philosophers." In addition, right understanding of nature conduces to a sound doctrine of providence—which, among other things, recognizes (with the theological orthodoxy of the era) that God "is a most free agent" who "created the world, not out of necessity, but voluntarily; having framed it as he pleased, and thought fit, at the beginning of things; when there was no substance but himself, and, consequently, no creature, to which he could be obliged, or by which he could be limited."[23]

This double concern for the mutual relationship of science and religion and for the integrity of both is highly evident in Boyle's approach to final causality—perhaps because Boyle's voluntaristic understanding of God as an utterly free creator would require a notion of final causality. He begins his *Disquisition about the final causes of natural things* with the comment that no single subject belonging to natural philosophy is more worthy of discussion among "Christian Philoso-phizers" than the subject of the knowability of final causes—all the more so in his own time given that the two major schools or "sects," the Epicureans and the Cartesians, "though upon differing Grounds, deny that the Naturalist ought at all to trouble or busie himself about *Final Causes*" (A2r–A3r).[24] On the one hand, the Epicureans (with the exception of Gassendi) deny any consideration of final causes or "the Ends of Things" because the world, in their view, arose "by Chance" without any ends or goals in view—specifically through the interaction of atoms, without any divine activity. On the other hand, Descartes and his followers identify the divinely intended ends of corporeal things as "so Sublime" that they are far beyond the ability of reason to discern (A3v–A4r).[25] Boyle notes the irony of his inquiry: he finds himself an adversary of two groups that might have been thought to be his "Assistants" in scientific investigation and hardly an ally of the older Aristotelianism, which, though in agreement on the existence and importance of final causes, had argued the case on grounds to which he could not assent or had used examples that he deemed less than "Comprehensive," such as "how Bodies, that were devoid of Knowledg, could Act for Ends" (A6r). The Cartesian critique, at least, demanded a new way of handling the question (A8r). Accordingly, Boyle frames his argument in terms of four questions:

I.   Whether, generally or indefinitely speaking, there be any Final Causes of things Corporeal, knowable by Naturalists?

II. Whether, if the first Question be resolv'd in the Affirmative, we may consider Final causes in all sorts of Bodies, or only in some peculiarly qualified ones?

III. Whether, or in what sense, the Acting for Ends may be ascribed to an Unintelligent, and even Inanimate Body?

IV. And lastly, How far, and with what Cautions, Arguments may be fram'd upon the supposition of Final Causes? (2)

Boyle sets aside the Epicurean objection as so universally disavowed and ably confuted by nearly all other schools of thought that he need not argue against it separately. The Cartesian objection, however, demands close examination. "Perhaps," Boyle opines, "one thing that alienated that excellent Philosopher [Descartes], from allowing the Consideration of *Final* Causes in Physicks" was the incautious way that "School-Philosophers" and theologians had appealed to the concept. Boyle adduces the example of a "famous Writer" who had argued the eschatological annihilation of the world order on the ground that the human race, having moved past its *viator* state to the state of final rest, would no longer need a world. Such presumptuous and indiscrete argumentation ought not, however, "to prejudice Truth, which must not be cast away, with the unwarrantable Conceits that some men have pinn'd upon it" (4–6).[26]

To respond to his first question, "whether . . . there be any Final Causes of things Corporeal, knowable by Naturalists," Boyle proposes a fourfold distinction of ends or final causes that has notable parallels in the more orthodox theological and philosophical literature of his time (sec. 1, 3–39). He clearly echoes the traditional theological assumption that the creation has several ends, "some *generall,* some *speciall and subordinate.*"[27] Thus, first, when the issue of final causality is raised, there are "the *Universal Ends* of God or Nature," such as the manifestation of divine glory or the display of divine power and wisdom (7).[28] Second, at a somewhat more limited level, there are the ends intended in or accomplished by the world process—as in the movement of the tides in relation to the disposition of earth and sea. These ends "may, for distinctions sake, be called *Cosmical* or *Systematical* of the great System of the world" (7–8).[29] Third, Boyle pointed toward a finality not typically noted by the theologians but identified by the Scriptural or Mosaic philosophers of the seventeenth century: there are "*Animal* Ends" that can be identified in the functions of animal life. According to these "*Animal* Ends," the "Parts of Animals" together conduce to the welfare of the individual animal "as he is an entire and distinct System of organiz'd parts, destinated to preserve himself, and propagate his *Species*" (8).[30] Fourth are those ends that relate specifically to human beings—"*Human* Ends," both mental and corporeal. These are distinct from animal ends inasmuch as human beings can be said to be "framed" or designed not merely for their own preservation and the preservation of the species but also to have dominion over animals and nature to use them "to His service and benefit" (9–10).[31] As to this fourth distinction, Boyle adds that he would never claim that all things in the visible world were made for human use, only that "any thing was made for ends Investigable by Man" (10).

What is significant here is that Boyle's primary interest in his *Disquisition* is the ends engineered or conceived by rational or intelligent agents, although his arguments do not exclude the ends that belong to nonrational animal life or to the natural order generally. He thus retains a view of finality indebted to Aristotle and the older tradition of Christian philosophy[32]—specifically one that is intimately related to the understanding of providence and, moreover, to his voluntaristic understanding of God's free agency. His argument relates directly to the traditional theologies and philosophies of his time that had argued the very nature of free choice as resting on the assignment of final causes by rational agents in their engagement with concatenations of efficient and material causality in the natural order—what could be identified as necessities of the consequence (i.e., contingencies), specifically as "complex hypothetical necessities."[33] Final causality, in this view, was intrinsic to the freedom of rational agents—without it, free agency, even in the case of God, might be excluded.

As a first point against the Cartesian position, Boyle notes that the Cartesians argue a constant "quantity of Motion" in the world at all times on the ground of the divine immutability: an immutable God, in making the world, would convey to it precisely the amount of motion that was needed and in such a manner that it would not need to be augmented or decreased. The argument, from Boyle's perspective, is little more than a judgment or claim made concerning God's design, indeed, a speculation about final causality that the Cartesian philosophy itself has ruled out. Moreover, there is no reason why an immutable God could not at times vary "the Quantity of Motion he has put into the world" (*Disquisition,* 14). Such a question may well be incapable of resolution—but a more restricted examination of ends is another matter.

Whereas all of God's ends cannot be known, some of them may be, and these may in fact be known from examination of the world order itself. Thus, against the Cartesians, there is no reason to conclude that since the higher end of something in the world order cannot be known a lesser end or use is to be ruled out. Examination of the eye surely leads to the conclusion that "the Author of Nature intended It should serve the Animal, to which it belongs, to See with" (*Disquisition,* 16). Against the Epicureans who argue that all things arise by the chance interaction of atoms, the point can be made that if one claims that human eyes arose by chance, one might just as well claim that the human use of eyes is also fortuitous. Clearly, however, the use of the eye is based on knowledge and not merely an accident of nature—and, even so, when the eye is dissected, it is easily seen to be an organ perfectly fitted to a task, implying an artificer. Nor does it matter, Boyle notes, if there are (as the Cartesians might object) ends intended by God that are beyond human comprehension: the fact that some ends can be definitively identified establishes the importance of discussing ends or final causes in the examination of the natural order (17–18).[34]

The Cartesians are also demonstrably mistaken when they assert that all of the ends intended by God in and for his "Corporeal Works . . . lie equally hidden in the abyss of Divine Wisdom," given the large number of uses of various things in the world order that are evident to human beings generally (*Disquisition,* 21).[35] Nor, conversely, is it correct to claim that all of the grounds or reasons identified in Physics need be physical grounds or reasons: "If we be treating, not *of* any particular *Phaenomenon,* that is produc'd according to the course of Nature establish'd in the *World,* already constituted as *this* of ours is: but *of* the first and general Causes of the World it self; from which Causes, I see not why the Final Causes, or Uses, that appear manifestly enough to have been design'd, should be excluded" (23). This point ought even to be obvious to Cartesians, given that "the Fundamental Tenets of Mr. *Des-Cartes's* own Philosophy, are not by himself prov'd by Arguments strictly Physical; but either by Metaphysical ones, or the more Catholick Dictates of Reason, or the particular testimonies of Experience" (24). Specifically, says Boyle, Descartes holds that all of the motion in the material world derives from God—an argument that cannot be physical given that God is presumed to be an "Immaterial Agent." Descartes also argues a constancy of motion in the universe on the ground of divine immutability—an argument not at all physical but properly metaphysical (24–25).

Having dismissed the Epicureans and shown Descartes to have been inconsistent in his own premise, Boyle takes as a particular example of the problem of excluding ends or goals from causality the Cartesian denial that God created the sun to shed light on human beings, given the vast bulk of the sun and the small part of its light that actually shines on humans. This Cartesian claim is "somewhat invidiously propos'd," Boyle comments, given that those who identify this end in the divine creation of the sun do not claim that it is the sole end of God's creative act—or that God's unknowable ultimate ends rule out the possibility of identifying penultimate ends (28–29). "I see not why the Belief," Boyle continues, "that a Man may know God's Ends in things Corporeal, should more derogate from our Veneration of Wisdom, than to think we know some of his Ends in other Matters, of which the Scripture furnishes us with a multitude of Instances . . . since God may, if He pleases, declare Truths to Men, and instruct them by his Creatures and his Actions, as well as by his Words" (30). How incongruous it would be, Boyle avers, for God to require that human beings praise him and his works and at the same time deny them the knowledge that would lead to a "reasonable service" (31).

Boyle makes clear that he does not accept the arguments of those who accuse Descartes of favoring atheism.[36] Nonetheless, following Descartes's "rejection of Final Causes from the consideration of Naturalists" would undermine "one of the best and most successful Arguments" for the existence of God (*Disquisition,* 32–33). It is true that Descartes and his followers do establish the existence of God, specifically, on the basis of "the Innate Idea" or an "Inbred Notion of God" and also hold that God created matter out of nothing, but such argumentation ought not to militate against discussion of God's existence and work "as well *without,* upon the *World,* as *within,* upon the *Mind*" (35–36). "Bare Speculation of the Fabrick of the World" unaccompanied by consideration of the God who created it and the uses or ends to which he "destinated" it was, after all, a characteristic of philosophies that erroneously drew the conclusion of the eternity of the world and either identified "Nature" as the ultimate Being or set nature as coequal or "co-ordinate" with God—a point shared by Boyle with the more traditionalistic theologies and philosophies of the era (36–37).[37]

Assuming that he has carried the day on his first question, Boyle passes on to the second, whether "we may consider Final causes in all sorts of Bodies, or only in some peculiarly qualified ones" (*Disquisition,* sec. 2, 39–86). The second argument proceeds by a primary division of the corporeal order into inanimate and animate bodies, the latter category including vegetative as well as animal life. The "Noblest" bodies in the inanimate order, "the Sun, Planets, and other Coelestial Bodies," move with such regularity, giving light and heat, and producing the seasons, that the conclusion that they were framed by "some Divine Being" and work to the benefit of human beings has been universally drawn and may be held, if not as a precise demonstration, certainly as a high probability. Still, these motions are so remote and human knowledge of the vast world system so incomplete that they do not offer arguments for design as clear and cogent as those drawn from the "bodies of Animals and Plants" or from the human frame or, indeed, from the eye of a fly, which, Boyle declares, appears to be "a more curious piece of Workmanship, than the Body of the Sun" (42–44).

The objection that the growth and development of plants and animals could be a result of "Chance" or be similar to the natural polishing of a stone or the growth of crystalline structures cannot be accepted:

> There are some effects, that are so easy, and so ready, to be produc'd, that they do not infer any knowledge or intention in their Causes; but there are others, that require such a number and concourse of conspiring Causes, and such a continued *series* of motions or operations, that 'tis utterly improbable, they should be produced without the superintendency of a Rational Agent, Wise and Powerfull enough to range and dispose the several intervening Agents and Instruments, after the manner requisite to the production of such a remote effect. And therefore it will not follow, that if Chance could produce a slight contexture in a few parts of matter; we may safely conclude it may produce so exquisit and admirable a Contrivance, as that of the Body of an Animal. (45–46)

It is quite acceptable to argue that the patterns observed in cut marble to appear like towns or woods are fortuitous—but to infer from this that the complex images of "a real Town or wood" should arise by chance would be absurd. Equally absurd is the inference from chance patterns in nature that "the great multitude of Nerves, Veins, Arteries, Ligaments, Tendons, Membranes, Bones, Glandules, &c. that are required to the compleating of a human Body," each of which "must have it's determinate size, figure, consistence, situation, connexion, &c.," is merely fortuitous and not the product of design: "There is incomparably more Art express'd in the structure of a Doggs foot, than in that of the famous clock of *Strasburg*" (46–47).

Having made these preliminary observations concerning design, Boyle discourses at length on the ability of the eye to focus and to adjust to different lights. He notes also the membrane that can cover the eye of a frog, protecting it from water and other dangers, but nonetheless transparent and not interfering with sight. The eyes of humans are designed for a particular kind of use — and the eyes of frogs designed differently to suit different circumstances of life (48–54). Even so moles, whose eyes are unsuited to existence on the surface of the ground, are designed for life under the ground (60–61). Thus "The differing structures and Situations of the Eyes in several Animals, are very fit to shew the fecundity of the Divine Authors Skill . . . in being able to frame so great a Variety of exquisite Instruments of Vision" (65).

Against those who argue chance in the natural order, Boyle argues "that Chance is really no natural Cause or Agent, but a Creature of Man's Intellect" used to characterize effects that are brought about in ways that we do not fully understand. Chance is, therefore, an "Extrinsical Denomination" signifying only "that *in our apprehensions,* the Physical Causes of an Effect, did not Intend the Production of what they nevertheless produc'd" (71–72). It is no wonder that Aristotle did not raise the issue of chance in his examination of natural causes. Boyle's point is significantly reflective of the Reformed and Puritan theology of the era, specifically its rebuttal of Epicurean and early deist argumentation: as Turretin indicated, the attribution of "all things to fortune and chance" would either "remove God himself away from the world or make him listless."[38]

In general, Boyle concludes, the "Naturalist" will "discourse merely upon Physical Grounds," as he has in fact done in the examination of uses and ends in the natural order. Such discussion rightly belongs to "bare Philosophy"—but there is no reason not to augment philosophy with considerations of ultimate divine intentions grounded in the revelation found in Scripture. Scripture itself declares clearly that the sun, moon, and stars are placed in the heavens to give light, to distinguish day and night, and to measure the seasons and years. Those Cartesians who are also theologians ought to admit such final causality! (*Disquisition,* 78–80).

The third question—Whether, or in what sense, the Acting for Ends may be ascribed to an Unintelligent, and even Inanimate Body?—does represent a more difficult issue, one that "ever since *Aristotles* time, and even before that, Perplex'd those that allow in Natural Philosophy, the Consideration of *Final Causes*" (sec. 3, 87). Bodies that are devoid of knowledge or, indeed, devoid both of knowledge and of life, would not appear to be able to act toward ends or for purposes—they cannot "predesign" a course of action or use "Means that they have no Knowledge wherewith to make choice of" (87–88). Without explicitly raising the issue, Boyle here points to the assumption that final causality is intrinsic to free choice; Aristotle rightly taught "that Nature does nothing in vain, and rightly judg'd, that the Actions of Natural Agents tended to certain Ends" but failed to give a satisfactory answer to the question of how this might be so (88).

Boyle's resolution of the issue is to distinguish between two different understandings of the ways in which actions tend toward ends—"*One,* when the Agent has a Knowledge of that End, and acts with an Intention to obtain it; as, when a man shoots and Arrow to hit a mark: The *Other* is, when the Action of the Proximate Agent, is indeed so directed as it ought to be to obtain an End, and yet that End is neither Known nor Intended by the Proximate Agent, but by a Remoter Agent that is Intelligent" (89). In the former sense, it would be difficult if not impossible to imagine that inanimate objects in the world order act toward ends, given that they are incapable of knowledge. In the latter sense, however, natural objects can be understood as acting toward ends—specifically when they are identified as instruments used by a "remoter" agent (90).

Still, Boyle adds, this understanding of ends in the natural order is also subject to objection and must be explained with care. Given that vastness of the divine intellect, God was able at the very "Beginning of Things" not only to see the condition of the universal order he had made and put in place universal laws but also to "to Foresee all the Effects, that particular Bodies so and so qualify'd, and acting according to the Laws of Motion by him establish'd, could have in such and such circumstances, have on one another," without any such foreknowledge or understanding of finality on the part of the created objects—just as a wise clockmaker determines the future functions of a clock by designing its mechanisms (91–92). This is indeed difficult to understand on the analogy of a comparatively "simple Instrument" and its "Local motion" given the vast multitude and diversity of agents and motions in the world order—but a vast system such as the world is in fact "manifestly fitted for the attainment of Ends" intended by an "Omniscient and Almighty Agent" such as God is (93).[39] The clock metaphor not only is explicitly theistic but also has resonances in the older Reformed tradition.[40]

When he comes to his fourth question, Boyle rewords it: what had read, "How far, and with what Cautions, Arguments may be fram'd upon the supposition of Final Causes?" (*Disquisition,* 2), now reads, "With what Cautions final Causes are to be considered by the Naturalist?" (103). Arguably, Boyle has not changed his meaning—but he has definitely narrowed possible interpretations of the scope of his question, having moved from a general question about the relation of final causality to argumentation to a specific question about the consideration of final causes by the "Naturalist" operating in his own field. The narrowing of scope is clear from his further, explicitly Baconian, distinction between the ends intended by God for "things Corporeal" and "the End designed by Nature" for a particular corporeal thing: the latter he identifies as "purely and simply *Physical* Ones," the former as "*Physico-Theological* Ones," or, he adds, "if we will with *Verulamius* refer Final Causes to the Metaphysicks, . . . *Metaphysical* Ones" (105). This question also addresses the issue least addressed by the theology of the era, the argument that most clearly identifies the kind of final causality suitable to experimental natural philosophy taken as distinct from theology, and the most detailed portion of Boyle's treatise: the argument remains positive toward theology and toward a doctrine of providence, but it is here that Boyle specifically argues the case for a finality that is distinctly scientific, intrinsic to science, and to be respected as distinct by theologians.

Boyle does not rule out the consideration of physico-theological or metaphysical ends in scientific investigation but notes that it is unsound to propound arguments about the specifically human ends of celestial bodies intended by God in the framing of the universe. He views unacceptable the claim made by some—specifically some theologians of his time—that the entire creation exists for the use of human beings and that the nature of "celestial bodies" can be properly discussed from the perspective of human ends (107).[41] Some of the theological works of the era did comment on the divine purpose in creation to provide "all things necessarie both for the use and command of man,"[42] but they were seldom oblivious either to purposes in creation beyond the needs of human beings or to the ultimate purposes of God that cannot be fully known by finite creatures.[43] Boyle's understanding of divine ends is quite conformable to assumptions of Reformed and Puritan theology that the divine decrees to create and order the universe are in no way grounded on any conditions in the creature but are determined solely by God's own ends—and that use by human beings is only a penultimate end of the creation.[44]

Boyle does not dispute the assumption that contemplation of the heavens is of great use in drawing human beings "to Admire and Praise, the Greatness and Power of the Divine Maker," but he identifies such argumentation as belonging to the "*Physico-Theological*" rather than to the "purely *Physical*" category. This premise of Boyle's argument not only identifies the place where science has a unique claim to speaking of final causality but also establishes much of the argumentative foundation for later natural theology in the form of the physico-theologies of the eighteenth century.[45] Such arguments refer to "*Cosmical Ends*" and do not "Prove any thing about the determinate Nature of particular Bodys." Certainly the "Good of Man" is an intended end of God belonging to the design of the universe, but this cannot be argued restrictively as the only end intended by God for remote stars that cannot be discerned "without good Telescopes" (*Disquisition,* 111–[113]).[46] A similar caution and logic applies in the consideration "of particular Bodies that are Inanimate in the Sublunary World," such as "Clays, Chalks, and Stones," the motions or movements of which are not regularized like those of heavenly bodies; and since so much of these inanimate materials lies far beneath the surface of the earth and inaccessible to human beings, identification of their purpose or end in relation to human beings is not possible (135–37). Indeed, Boyle speculates, given that God can "justly be suppos'd to have made nothing in Vain," it may very well be that such things as cannot be of any "service" to human beings may have been created "not out of a Primary Intention, but as Productions that will naturally follow upon the Establishment and Preservation of those Grand Laws and Rules of Motion, that were most fit to be setled among Things Corporeal" (137–38). The ultimate ends of such things may well be unknowable (139–40).

Having stated his reservations, Boyle passes on to identify precisely where and how a "Naturalist" can identify final causes, what Osler has called "immanent finality"[47]—with no subject being more conducive to such argumentation than "the Structure of the Bodies of Animals." Such structures cannot result from mere chance. Boyle notes a dialogue of Cicero in which a Stoic philosopher asks an Epicurean why, if mere chance has produced the human body, mere chance has not also produced "Palaces and other Buildings." The houses in which the bodies of human beings dwell "are far less curious structures than the Mansions their Souls reside in" (*Disquisition,* 143–44). The Epicurean objection that the various anatomical parts of animals existed before human beings conceived of their uses is "sophistical" and not to the point, inasmuch as the "inner parts" of animals such as the heart and liver all perform their functions apart from anyone's knowledge of the fact: they are not "applyed to such Uses by Our Sagacity" (150–51).[48]

Examination of the functioning parts of bodies in the light of the "known Ends of Nature" can yield knowledge of the purpose of individual parts, particularly when observation can discern that a particular organ is more suited to a particular use than any other organ (*Disquisition,* 155–56). Acknowledgment of the truth of this assumption, moreover, leads Boyle to his next proposition: "It is Rational, from the Manifest Fitness of some things to Cosmical or Animal Ends or Uses, to Infer that they were Fram'd or Ordain'd in reference there-unto, by an Intelligent and Designing Agent" (160). This proposition stands quite specifically against "that part of the *Epicurean Hypothesis,* which Ascribes the Origine of Things to *Chance,* and Rejects the Inter-est of a *Deity,* and the Designing of Ends, in the Production and Man-agement of Natural Things" (160). Boyle notes the problem, quite ap-parent in some of the writings of his time, of adopting, together with the more "innocent" views of Epicureanism, the "irreligious" aspect of the philosophy, specifically the assumption that "the Deity and Providence" can be "quite Excluded from having any Influence upon the Motions of Matter, all whose Productions are refer'd to the Ca-sual Concourse of Atoms" (161). To reinforce his point, Boyle notes that nature does not merely furnish the bodies of animals with organs suited to simple or ordinary needs but offers "Superabundant Provi-sion for Casualties"—such as two eyes and two ears, when one would have been sufficient (162–63). What is more, the natural instincts of animals intended for self-preservation and propagation of the species also argue design: whether the "Untaught Skill of Spiders in Weaving their Curious Webs," or the structure of wasps' nests, or the hanging nests of birds so suitable to protect their eggs from apes (171, 176, 179). Boyle also urges that, given the complexity of nature, "we be not Over hasty in Concluding, nor too Positive in Asserting, that This or That must be, or is, the particular Destinated Use of such a Thing, or the Motive that induc'd the Author of Nature to Frame it thus" (214).

Finally, Boyle warns that even the suitably defined consideration of final causes ought not to be taken to such excess that the natural-ist "undervalue or Neglect the studious Indagation of . . . Efficient Causes" (229). The proper task of the naturalist is to examine not why a thing is the way it is but "how Particular Effects are Produc'd." By way of example, he adduces a watch—knowing its final cause, namely, that it is intended to mark the hours of the day, does not go very far toward an understanding of the nature of the watch and certainly offers no information about how to construct a watch if one is needed. To make such an instrument one must understand the materials, the num-ber and interrelationship of the wheels, the function of the spring, and the means by which the measured movement of the whole is produced

(230–31). On the other hand, the careful investigation of efficient causes ought not to "Prejudice the Contemplation of *Final Causes*": recognizing the "Sufficiency of the Intermediate Causes" does not render unnecessary the recognition of "a First and Supreme Cause" (232–33). The implication of Boyle's point parallels the orthodox Reformed understanding of levels of causality, in which the primary causality of God so concurs with the secondary causality of the crea-ture as neither to remove its freedom or contingency nor to impede it in any way, but rather to ensure its free or natural operation.[49] In short, Boyle concludes that neither should the consideration of final causality be excluded from natural philosophy nor should the examination of efficient causality be removed from its central place in that particular discipline (*Disquisition*, 235, 237).

Some Conclusions

Robert Boyle's critique of traditional understandings of substance and causality, intrinsic to his experimental science, was balanced with con-cern for a broader philosophical and theological understanding of the universe in which the direct results of the observation and analysis of nature conjoined with a strongly defined doctrine of providence. Not only did Boyle argue the necessity of such a doctrine at the heart of re-ligion, but he insisted on its centrality to scientific endeavor as well. In connection with this broader understanding, he was pressed to retain one major element of the older Aristotelianism, the language of final causality. Where the tendency of the Cartesian and Epicurean philoso-phies had been to reduce all causality to the motions of corpuscles or atoms, namely to efficiency and materiality, Boyle insisted that efficient and material causation itself could not be properly understood with-out the identification of ends, of final causality—just as he retained much of the traditional understanding of providence characteristic of his Reformed and Puritan contemporaries. These commonalities with the orthodox tradition of Reformed theology in no way detract, cer-tainly not in Boyle's own self-understanding, from the scientific inves-tigation at the heart of Boyle's work.

Is Boyle's treatise on final causes primarily a contribution to the science of his time or primarily a work of natural theology? The answer to the question must be mixed. Boyle's *Disquisition* contains more in the way of theological concerns than might be expected in a treatise devoted simply to the referencing of teleological issues in experimental science. As Shanahan has argued, it is far too immersed in the religious and theological issues of its time to be understood solely as an argument advocating consideration of final causality in experimental science. But it also contains far more reference to experimental science than was typical of the theological treatises of the era. Given that it was published in 1688, several years in advance of the theological naturalism of John Ray and several decades in advance of the *Physico-theology* and *Astro-theology* of William Derham and the *Philosophical principles of religion* of George Cheyne, it should perhaps be viewed more as a prelude to the future of natural theology, perhaps even the prototype, than as a work on natural theology as such.[50] Derham's *Physico-theology,* in fact, began as the Boyle lectures of 1711–12. The significance of works like Derham's and Cheyne's arises from their assumption, grounded in the line of argumentation found in Boyle's treatises, that the teleological implications of science as such had positive application in theology—indicating at very least an equal partnership of disciplines.

Arguably, Boyle intended to demonstrate the common interest of science and theology and to identify the danger to both fields of study in the total rejection of traditional patterns of thought. His treatise accordingly drew detail upon detail from experimental philosophy/science and argued the scientific necessity of considering final causality in several senses, the "Cosmical," the "Animal," and the "corporeal" human. At the same time, Boyle also insisted on the positive relationship of these experimental interests to religion and theology, which considered "Universal" and human ends, the latter relating chiefly to human use of the created order. And in the common ground between science and theology, Boyle saw a religious use of scientific knowledge in the confirmation of divine providence and the existence of God. Without final causality, there would be no purpose in the universe— a barrier both to religion and to science. Thus, at the same time that he rejected aspects of the older Aristotelianism like the theory of substantial forms, Boyle retained and emphasized, for both positive and apologetic purposes, elements of this tradition not as extraneous aspects of an otherwise scientific method but as fundamental premises without which he believed that the very progress of his science would be undermined as well as the foundation of religion. His model was not, in other words, a clumsy amalgam of old theology and new science, or indeed a clear prelude to deism, but a conscious fusion of the new scientific or mechanical philosophy with some elements of the theological and philosophical tradition intended for the benefit of both.

Notes

1. See, e.g., Edwin A. Burtt, *The Metaphysical Foundations of Modern Science,* rev. ed. (New York: Humanities Press, 1951); Marie Boas, "The Establishment of the Mechanical Philosophy," *Osiris* 10 (1952): 412–541; Richard S. Westfall, *Science and Religion in Seventeenth-Century England* (New Haven: Yale University Press, 1958); Margaret J. Osler, "Providence and Divine Will in Gassendi's Views on Scientific Knowledge," *Journal of the History of Ideas* 44, no. 4 (1983): 549–60; Amos Funkenstein, *Theology and the Scientific Imagination from the Middle Ages to the Seventeenth Century* (Princeton: Princeton University Press, 1986); Hans Blumenberg, *The Genesis of the Copernican World,* trans. Robert M. Wallace (Cambridge, MA: MIT Press, 1987).

2. A partial exception is John Dillenberger, *Protestant Thought and Natural Science: A Historical Interpretation* (Nashville, TN: Abingdon, 1960).

3. E.g., James E. Force and Richard H. Popkin, eds., *Essays on the Context, Nature, and Influence of Isaac Newton's Theology* (Dordrecht: Kluwer, 1990); Richard Popkin, "The Religious Background of Seventeenth-Century Philosophy," in *The Cambridge History of Seventeenth-Century Philosophy,* 2 vols., ed. Daniel Garber and Michael Ayers (Cambridge: Cambridge University Press, 1998).

4. Cf. Jan W. Wojcik, "The Theological Context of Boyle's *Things above Reason,"* in *Robert Boyle Reconsidered,* ed. Michael Hunter (Cambridge: Cambridge University Press, 1994), 139–55; Harold Fisch, "The Scientist as Priest: A Note on Robert Boyle's Natural Theology," *Isis* 44, no. 3 (1953): 252–65; and Dillenberger, *Protestant Thought,* 113; and on the problem of double truth, see Richard A. Muller, *After Calvin: Studies in the Development of a Theological Tradition* (New York: Oxford University Press, 2003), 122–36.

5. See Thomas F. Gieryn, "Distancing Science from Religion in Seventeenth-Century England," *Isis* 79, no. 4 (1988): 582–93.

6. For an example of the former position, see James Lennox, "Robert Boyle's Defense of Teleological Inference in Experimental Science," *Isis* 74 (1983): 38–58. For the latter position, see Timothy Shanahan, "Teleological Reasoning in Boyle's *Disquisition about Final Causes*," in Hunter, *Robert Boyle Reconsidered,* 177–92. On the issue of final causality, also see Margaret J. Osler, "Whose Ends? Teleology in Early Modern Natural Philosophy," *Osiris,* 2nd ser., 16 (2001): 161–67, and "From Immanent Natures to Nature as Artifice: The Reinterpretation of Final Causes in Seventeenth-Century Natural Philosophy," *Monist* 79 (1996): 388–407, as well as Burtt, *Metaphysical Foundations,* 177–80.

7. On reaction to the mechanical philosophy, see Keith Hutchison, "Supernaturalism and the Mechanical Philosophy," *History of Science* 21 (1983): 297–333; and Richard A. Muller, "Thomas Barlow on the Liabilities of 'New Philosophy,'" in *Scholasticism Reformed: Festschrift Willem van Asselt,* ed. Maarten Wisse, Marcel Sarot, and Willemien Otten, Studies in Theology and Religion 13 (Assen: Van Gorcum, 2008), 180–96.

8. Note the topical division of Boyle's efforts in the early eighteenth-century collections: *The Philosophical Works of the Honourable Robert Boyle Esq.; abridged, methodized, and disposed under the general heads of physics, statics, pneumatics . . . , by Peter Shaw, M.D.,* 3 vols. (London: for W. Innys, R. Manby, and T. Longman, 1725) (2nd ed., corrected, 1738); and *The Theological Works of the Honourable Robert Boyle, Esq.; epitomiz'd . . . by Richard Boulton,* 3 vols. (London: for W. Taylor, 1715). See J. F. Fulton, "Robert Boyle and His Influence on Thought in the Seventeenth Century," *Isis* 18, no. 1 (1932): 77–102, and "The Honourable Robert Boyle, F. R. S. (1627–1692)," *Notes and Records of the Royal Society of London* 15 (1960): 119–35; also Dillenberger, *Protestant Thought,* 112–17.

9. Robert Boyle, *Some Considerations about the Reconcileableness of Reason and Religion,* in *Theological Works,* 1:395. Cf. Robert Boyle, *A Disquisition about the final causes of natural things: wherein it is inquir'd whether, and (if at all) with what cautions, a naturalist should admit them? . . . To which are subjoyn'd, by way of appendix Some uncommon observations about vitiated sight* (London: H. C. for John Taylor, 1688), 105, 229–37, subsequently abbreviated as *Disquisition* and cited parenthetically in the text, first by folio numbers (beginning with A) for the unpaginated preface and then by page number for the main text. Also see Francis Bacon, *Instauratio Magna. Of the Advancement and Proficiencie of Learning of the Partitions of Sciences in IX Bookes,* interpreted by Gilbert Wats (Oxford: Leonard Lichfield, 1640), I.i and III.iv.6 (pp. 9 and 161); Dillenberger, *Protestant Thought,* 113; Fisch, "Scientist as Priest"; and, on the problem of double truth, Muller, *After Calvin,* 122–36.

10. Robert Boyle, *About the excellency and grounds of the mechanical hypothesis,* in *The excellency of theology compar'd with philosophy (as both are objects of men's study). Discours'd of in a letter to a friend by T. H. R. B. E. . . . ; to which are annex'd some occasional thoughts about the excellency and grounds of the mechanical hypothesis* (London: T. N.

for Henry Herringman, 1674), 4 (the two works in this volume have separate pagination). Note Gieryn, "Distancing Science from Religion."

11. Fisch, "Scientist as Priest," 253, 255; on the Scriptural and Mosaic philosophies, see Ann Blair, "Mosaic Physics and the Search for a Pious Natural Philosophy in the Late Renaissance," *Isis* 91, no. 1 (2000): 32–58.

12. Boyle, *The excellency of theology compar'd with philosophy (as both are objects of men's study). Discours'd of in a letter to a friend by T. H. R. B. E. . . . ,* in *Excellency of theology,* 19–20; cf. Zacharias Ursinus, *The Summe of Christian Religion, delivered by Zacharias Ursinus, first, by way of Catechism, and the afterwards more enlarged by a sound and judicious Exposition, and Application of the same* (London: James Young, 1645), 181–85.

13. Boyle, *Excellency of theology,* 25; cf. Robert Boyle, *A Discourse of Things Above Reason, Inquiring whether a Philosopher should admit that there are any such* (London: F. T. and R. H., 1681); and Wojcik, "Theological Context," 140.

14. Boyle, *About the excellency,* 4. On the theological side of Boyle's work, see Fisch, "Scientist as Priest," and Margaret G. Cook, "Divine Artifice and Natural Mechanism: Robert Boyle's Mechanical Philosophy of Nature," *Osiris,* 2nd ser., 16 (2001): 133–50.

15. Boyle, *Origin of Forms* 1.3, in *The Works of the Honourable Robert Boyle, Esq. Epitomized by Richard Boulton,* 4 vols. (London: J. Phillips and J. Taylor, 1699–1700), 1:36. On Boyle's understanding of concurrence, note Burtt, *Metaphysical Foundations,* 198–200; Burtt does not, however, recognize how much Boyle's argument accorded with the theological orthodoxy.

16. Richard Baxter, *The Reasons of the Christian Religion* (London: R. White, 1667), 518–20; cf. Francis Turretin, *Institutio theologicae elencticae,* 3 vols. (Geneva, 1679–85), VI.iv.6–13, translated as *Institutes of Elenctic Theology,* 3 vols., ed. James T. Dennison, trans. George Musgrave Giger (Phillipsburg: Presbyterian and Reformed Publishing, 1992–97).

17. Robert Boyle, *The Christian virtuoso: shewing, that by being addicted to experimental philosophy, a man is rather assisted, than indisposed, to be a good Christian. The first part. To which are subjoyn'd, I. A discourse about the distinction, that represents some things as above reason, but not contrary to reason. II. The first chapters of a discourse, entituled, Greatness of mind promoted by Christianity* (London: Edw. Jones, for John Taylor, 1690); and cf. Westfall, *Science and Religion,* 43–44.

18. Note, e.g., the polemic in Richard Baxter, *The Arrogancy of reason against divine revelations, repressed. Or, proud ignorance the cause of infidelity, and of mens quarrelling with the Word of God* (London, 1655), 16–21, and *Reasons,* 495–534, where Gassendi's understanding of matter is identified as particularly problematic; cf. the discussion in Westfall, *Science and Religion,* 13–25.

19. Robert Boyle, *Some considerations touching the usefulnesse of experimental naturall philosophy, propos'd in a familiar discourse to a friend by way of invitation to the study of it* (Oxford: Henry Hall, 1671).

20. Robert Boyle, *Of the high veneration man's intellect owes to God; peculiarly for His wisedom and power* (London: M. F., 1685).

21. Cf. Lennox, "Robert Boyle's Defense," 39.

22. Robert Boyle, *Free Inquiry into the Vulgar Notion of Nature,* in *Philosophical Works* [1725], 2:118–19; cf. Lambert Daneau, *The wonderfull woorkmanship of the world wherin is conteined an excellent discourse of Christian naturall philosophie, concernyng the fourme, knowledge, and vse of all thinges created: specially gathered out of the fountaines of holy Scripture,* trans. T. T. (London: John Kingston for Andrew Maunsell, 1578), 1r; Johann Amos Comenius, *Naturall philosophie reformed by divine light, or, A synopsis of physicks* (London: Robert and William Leybourn, 1651), preface and 6; Gulielmus Scribonius, *Naturall Philosophy: or, a Description of the World, and of the severall Creatures therein contained,* 2nd ed., corrected and enlarged (London: Tho. Cotes, 1631), 1; Johann Wecker, *Eighteen Books of the Secrets of Art & Nature, being the summe and substance of naturall philosophy, methodically digested, augmented and inlarged by Dr. R. Read* (London: for Simon Miller, 1660), I.i–ii (pp. 1–2); and Daniel Sennert, *Thirteen Books of Natural Philosophy* (London: Peter Cole, 1660), appended discourses, 416–19. On Boyle's treatise, see Michael Hunter and Edward B. Davis, "The Making of Robert Boyle's 'Free Enquiry into the Vulgarly Receiv'd Notion of Nature," *Early Science and Medicine* 1 (1996): 204–71.

23. Boyle, *Free Inquiry,* 148; cf. John Downame, *The Summe of Sacred Divinitie briefly and methodically propounded: and then more largely and cleerly handled and explaned* (London: W. Stansby, 1625), I.ii (pp. 63–64); William Twisse, *A Discovery of D. Jacksons Vanitie. Or, a Perspective glasse, whereby admirers of D. Jacksons profound discourses, may see the vanitie and weaknesse of them* (London, 1631), 289; Turretin, *Institutio theologicae elencticae* III.xiv.6; cf. Richard A. Muller, *Post-Reformation Reformed Dogmatics: The Rise and Development of Reformed Orthodoxy, ca. 1520 to ca. 1725,* 4 vols. (Grand Rapids, MI: Baker, 2003), 3:446–50.

24. Note the analysis of the treatise as an argument for teleology in science in Lennox, "Robert Boyle's Defense," 38–58; cf. Shanahan, "Teleological Reasoning," where the treatise is discussed as a contribution to natural theology; and Osler, "Whose Ends," 161–67.

25. On Gassendi's approach to finality, see Osler, "Whose Ends," 158–61.

26. Note that the argument to which Boyle objects can be found in Johannes Wollebius, *The Abridgement of Christian Divinitie,* ed. and trans. Alexander Ross (London: T. Mab and A. Coles, 1650), I.36 (pp. 237–38).

27. Ursinus, *Summe of Christian Religion,* 187.

28. Cf. Ursinus, *Summe of Christian Religion,* 187; Daneau, *Wonderfull woorkmanship* xix, fols. 44r–45r; Edward Leigh, *A Systeme or Body of Divinity: consisting in ten books wherein the fundamentals of religion are opened* (London: A. M. For William Lee, 1662), III.ii (p. 285).

29. Cf. Downame, *Summe of Sacred Divinitie* I.iii (p. 67); George Walker, *The History of the Creation, as it is written by Moses in the first and second chapters of Genesis . . .*

Whereunto is added a short Treatise of Gods actuall Providence (London: for John Bar-
let, 1641), 138–44.

30. Comenius, *Naturall philosophie reformed,* 162–66.

31. Cf. Ursinus, *Summe of Christian Religion,* 187; Downame, *Summe of Sacred
Divinitie* I.iii (pp. 66–67); Leigh, *Systeme* III.ii (p. 285).

32. Cf. Osler, "Whose Ends," 164.

33. Note, e.g., Johannes Combachius, *Joh. Combachii Metaphysicorum: libri
duo vniversam primæ philosophiæ doctrinam theorematibus brevissimis comprehendentes, &
commentariis necessariis illustrantes: studiosis ejus disciplinæ perquam utiles &fructuosi*
(Oxford: W. Hall, 1662), I.xiii, commentarius (pp. 183–84).

34. Cf. Lennox, "Robert Boyle's Defense," 41.

35. Citing René Descartes, *Objections and Replies, Fifth Set* [contra Gassendi]
iv.1, in Boyle, *Philosophical Writings,* 2:258; cf. Burtt, *Metaphysical Foundations,* 169.

36. Boyle, unfortunately, does not identify these critics of Descartes.
Among the British writers of the era, Henry More and Edward Stillingfleet argued that Cartesian assumptions conduced to atheism; various Continental
theologians, such as Gisbertus Voetius, Leonardus Rijssenius, and Petrus van
Mastricht, drew similar conclusions. See Theo Verbeek, "Descartes and the
Problem of Atheism: The Utrecht Crisis," *Nederlands Archief voor Kerkgeschiedenis*
71, no. 2 (1991): 211–23.

37. Cf. Daneau, *Wonderfull woorkmanship* ix, xv, xvi (fols. 26r, 31v, 34v);
Gulielmus Bucanus, *Institutions of the Christian Religion, framed out of God's Word,*
trans. R. Hill (London, 1659), v (pp. 56–57); Leigh, *System or Body of Divinity*
III.ii (pp. 282–83); Turretin, *Institutio theologicae elencticae* V.iii.10.

38. Turretin, *Institutio theologicae elencticae* VI.i.3; cf. Bucanus, *Institutions* xiv
(pp. 169–70, 175); Stephen Charnock, *Discourses upon the Existence and Attributes
of God,* II, "On Practical Atheism," in *The works of the late learned divine Stephen
Charnock, B. D.,* 2 vols. (London: for Tho. Cockerill, 1699), 1:29–67.

39. Cf. Westfall, *Science and Religion,* 75.

40. E.g., Theodore Beza, *A Booke of Christian Questions and Answers. Wherein
are set forth the chief points of the Christian religion in manner of an abridgement* (London: William How, 1572), 1:60r–61r.

41. Cf. Shanahan, "Teleological Reasoning," 181.

42. Downame, *Summe of Sacred Divinitie* I.iii (pp. 66–67); cf. Edward
Leigh, *A Systeme or Body of Divinity: consisting in ten books wherein the fundamentals of
religion are opened* (London: A. M. For William Lee, 1662), III.ii (p. 285).

43. Downame, *Summe of Sacred Divinitie* I.iii (p. 67); Leigh, *System* III.ii
(p. 285).

44. Cf. Daneau, *Wonderfull woorkmanship* xxxi (fol. 65v); Bucanus, *Institutions* v (pp. 54–55, 63, 69–70); Turretin, *Institutio theologiae elencticae* IV.iii.3–4.

45. E.g., William Derham, *Physico-theology: or, A demonstration of the being and attributes of God, from his works of creation. Being the substance of sixteen sermons preached*

in St. Mary-le-Bow-Church, London; at the Honorable Mr. Boyle's lectures, in the years 1711, and 1712 (London: for W. And J. Innys, 1713), and *Astro-theology: or, A demonstration of the being and attributes of God, from a survey of the heavens* (London: for W. Innys, 1715); George Cheyne, *Philosophical principles of religion: natural and revealed* (London: for George Strahan, 1715).

46. Note that the text reads continuously but the pagination shifts at this point, with 112 being followed by 129; cf. the epitome of the *Disquisition* in *Theological Works,* 2:245.

47. Cf. Osler, "Whose Ends," 166–67, and "From Immanent Natures," 388–407.

48. Cf. Lennox, "Robert Boyle's Defense," 42.

49. Cf., e.g., Bucanus, *Institutions* xiv (p. 172); Turretin, *Institutio theologiae elencticae* VI.vi.6.

50. John Ray, *The Wisdom of God manifested in the Works of the creation. Being the substance of some common places delivered in the chappel of Trinity-College, in Cambridge* (London: for Samuel Smith, 1691); John Ray, *Three physico-theological discourses . . . wherein are largely discussed the production and use of mountains, the original of fountains, of formed stones, and sea-fishes bones and shells found in the earth, the effects of particular floods and inundations of the sea, the eruptions of vulcano's, the nature and causes of earthquakes: with an historical account of those two late remarkable ones in Jamaica and England* (London: for Sam. Smith, 1693); Derham, *Physico-theology* and *Astro-theology*; Cheyne, *Philosophical principles.*

Chapter 5

God in Locke's Philosophy

NICHOLAS WOLTERSTORFF

To write about the role of God in Locke's philosophy is to confront a daunting hermeneutical challenge. In what Locke says about God and God's role in human existence, there are contradictions, ambiguities, obscurities, and gaps. The question the interpreter has to face is what accounts for these flaws in Locke's mode of presentation and how to deal with them in one's interpretation. No one holds that they are due to incompetence on Locke's part, though of course Locke was no more immune to error than other writers are. (As for the *Essay concerning Human Understanding,* Locke says, in the "Epistle to the Reader," that it was written in "disconnected" snatches over a long period of time and never thoroughly revised—a method of composition that, as we all know, is guaranteed to create problems of consistency and continuity.)

There is a school of thought, of which Leo Strauss was the twentieth-century *pater familias,* which holds that the flaws in Locke's mode of presentation are due to the fact that he was an esoteric writer who played it safe by concealing his true thoughts on religious, moral, and political matters from all but the most discerning (though why Locke would assume that only the sympathetic would be discerning is not explained). My own view is that it is not Locke's way of writing that accounts for the flaws but his peculiar way of articulating his philosophical thought, and that this way of articulating his thought is manifested not just in his writings on religious, moral, and political matters but in all his writings, including those where there was no need to play it safe. In fact, Locke was astonishingly daring in his writing. He rubbed lots of people the wrong way and when challenged seldom backed down.

In none of my previous writings on Locke did I engage the esotericist alternative to my own line of interpretation. I explained my own way of accounting for, and dealing with, the flaws in Locke's mode of presentation and proceeded in my own interpretations to employ that way of dealing with the flaws. In ignoring the esotericist line of interpretation, I was doing what most of my fellow philosophers have done. The esotericist line of interpretation has its home not in philosophy departments but in political theory departments.

On this occasion, I propose taking the esotericist line seriously. There have been esoteric writers; and if there is persuasive evidence that Locke was one of those, it behooves those of us who write about Locke to take that evidence seriously. It is especially important that we do so when considering the role of God in Locke's philosophy, for it is at this point that the two lines of interpretation clash most sharply.

I propose the following sequence. First, I will sketch out the principles and motivations of the esotericist line of interpretation. Then, after indicating my own line of interpretation, I will employ that line of interpretation in describing Locke's project of a rational theology and the role of God in his thought. Last, I will engage the arguments of the esotericists for the conclusion that my own, more or less traditional, understanding of the role of God in Locke's philosophy is radically mistaken, and I will look at what they propose instead.

I

Rather than making a survey of the esotericist writers, I propose working with the latest and most thorough esotericist interpretation, one that, by its frequent citation of other writers, presents itself as incorporating the best of preceding esotericist interpretations. I have in mind part 3 of Thomas L. Pangle's *The Spirit of Modern Republicanism: The Moral Vision of the American Founders and the Philosophy of Locke.*[1]

In the conclusion of his discussion, Pangle summarizes his strategy for interpreting Locke in the following words:

> As nearly as possible, [I] have tried to read [Locke's texts] as Locke himself indicates he intends them to be read by his most careful and sympathetic or philosophic readers. This has required in the first place a constant and careful attention to the many strange things Locke says about the proper way in which a politic writer expresses himself in order to avoid persecution, achieve the greatest influence, and educate the few truly openminded and reflective readers. Only when one's reading is guided by these explicit clues does Locke's radical and shocking intrepidity begin to appear through his well-wrought veil of conventional sobriety and caution. . . . My efforts have been directed to uncovering and then critically assessing the trail of induction and deduction that Locke has left in his system of writings for the faithful reader to rethink and retrace for himself. (*SMR,* 276–77)

What is not clear from this passage, or explicitly stated in any other, is that Pangle assumes that there are two levels and degrees of concealment in Locke. The first level pertains to Locke's overt teaching, the line of thought that, with due allowance for disagreements, has traditionally been ascribed to him. This was already a radical line of thought, as witnessed by the controversies in which Locke found himself embroiled. Thus Locke casts a pious haze over this teaching by enlisting such traditional writers as Hooker in his support, by quoting snippets from Scripture, by using traditional language, and the like. Pangle says, in one passage, that "Locke confines himself mainly to endless repetitions of pious affirmations. He deliberately cultivates the image of an earnest but somewhat forgetful or woolly-headed believer, revealing only in flashes the application, to religious questions, of his amazingly ruthless reasoning capacity" (*SMR,* 215). The second level of concealment pertains to Locke's true position, in contrast to his overt teaching.

Pangle alludes to the two levels of concealment in the following passage:

> Locke may also have reflected that the pious and moral censure of the learned authorities and literate leisured class was potentially much more dangerous to him and his project than the restlessness of the illiterate working class—and that he therefore needed above all to conciliate or drug, or at least try to toss some red herrings before, the former. The learned class has, of course, one enormous redeeming merit: among its children or students there may be a few who, as they study the respectable if bumbling and somewhat unorthodox theology of the *Essay Concerning Human Understanding* (and the *Reasonableness of Christianity* as well), begin to notice and follow a path of subversive, critical thought. The path leads—with appropriate, weeding-out, mazes or tests—from a surface of earnest but totally inadequate support for a liberal Christianity or at least deist theology to a new and *very* liberal, un-Christian and even un-deist outlook. (*SMR,* 205; see also 133)

Let me summarize Pangle's hermeneutic strategy: Locke overtly espoused what we now know as liberal Christianity. That was a radical position in Locke's day; accordingly, to minimize controversy and increase his readership, he cast a haze of traditional piety over his position in order to evoke in his readers the feeling that it was not all that far out of the tradition. The liberal Christianity that Locke overtly espoused was not, however, what he actually believed. His actual position was "a new and *very* liberal, un-Christian and even un-deist outlook." Locke expected that only a few "faithful" readers, "less easily satisfied" students (*SMR,* 133) and children of "the learned class," would follow the clues that he scattered about and arrive at his true view, a view probably best described as atheistic libertarianism. What initially seem to be flaws in Locke's mode of presentation prove instead to be hints that his overt teaching is not his true view and clues to his covert, esoteric, teaching.

Why adopt this strategy for interpreting Locke? I assume that Pangle does not want readers of his own book to treat flaws in his mode of presentation as clues to the fact that he is an esoteric writer; certainly I do not want readers of what I have written to treat flaws in my mode of presentation that way. So why treat Locke this way?

For one thing, Locke was living in a much less open society than Pangle and I are; a large range of opinions that would cause Pangle and me no trouble, were we to espouse them, would have gotten Locke into a lot of trouble had people thought he held them. And Locke was like most people in having a preference for avoiding ecclesiastical and political persecution. Furthermore, Locke seems to have been a rather secretive fellow. So we should not be surprised if it turns out that Locke was an esoteric writer.

These considerations do no more, however, than make it not unlikely that Locke was an esoteric writer. Pangle bases his positive case for Locke's being an esoteric writer on some things that Locke says about writing. Pangle remarks, "In the truly fundamental *First Treatise*, Locke discloses the principles which he believes ought to govern the writing, and perforce the reading, of political theory—and which must be followed if his own political-theoretical writings are to be read and understood as he intended. In his detailed analysis of Robert Filmer's works Locke does more than offer a model of how he believes a text in political theory should be approached; he makes explicit reference to some of the general canons of interpretation he applies" (*SMR*, 137).

So what are these principles, formulated in his discussion of Filmer, that Locke suggests "must be followed if his own political-theoretical writings are to be read and understood as he intended"? One passage from the *First Treatise* that Pangle cites in support of his position is section 7 of the *Treatise* (*SMR*, 137). Pangle quotes and rearranges fragments from the passage; I think it is important to have the passage before us almost in its entirety:

> I do not think our author so little skilled in the way of writing discourses of this nature, nor so careless of the point in hand, that he by oversight commits the fault that he himself . . . objects to [in] Mr. Hunton in these words: "Where first I charge the A. that he hath not given us any definition or description of monarchy in

general; but by the rules of method he should have first defined."
And by the like rule of method, sir Robert should have told us
what his fatherhood, or fatherly authority is, before he had told
us in whom it was to be found, and talked so much of it. But, perhaps, sir Robert found, that this fatherly authority . . . would make
a very odd and frightful figure, and very disagreeing with what either children imagine of their parents, or subjects of their kings,
if he should have given us the whole draught together, in that gigantic form he had painted it in his own fancy; and therefore, like
a wary physician, when he would have his patient swallow some
harsh or corrosive liquor, he mingles it with a large quantity of that
which may dilute it, that the scattered parts may go down with
less feeling, and cause less aversion.

Another passage that Pangle refers to is section 110 of the *First Treatise* (*SMR,* 137). Whereas Pangle again quotes only fragments, in this
case too I think we should have almost the entire passage before us:

The obscurity cannot be imputed to want of language in so great
a master of style as sir Robert is, when he is resolved with himself
what he would say; and therefore, I fear, finding how hard it would
be to settle rules of descent by divine institution, and how little it
would be to his purpose . . . if such rules of descent were settled, he
chose rather to content himself with doubtful and general terms,
which might make no ill sound in men's ears who were willing to
be pleased with them; rather than offer any clear rules of descent
by the fatherhood of Adam, by which men's consciences might be
satisfied to whom it descended, and know the persons who had
a right to regal power, and with it to their obedience.

A third passage that Pangle refers to is the last sentence of section 23:
"But he [Filmer] begs your pardon in that point; clear distinct speaking not serving every where to his purpose, you must not expect it in
him, as in Mr. Selden, or other such writers." A fourth passage comes
from section 109: "Though the chief matter of his writing be to teach
obedience to those who have a right to it, which he tells us is conveyed

by descent; yet who those are, to whom this right by descent belongs, he leaves like the philosopher's stone in politics, out of the reach of any one to discover from his writings." And a fifth is the last sentence of section 141: "This is but a flourish of our author's to mislead his reader, that in itself signifies nothing."[2]

Pangle then says that "these remarkably frank hints [in the *First Treatise*] accord perfectly with what Locke says elsewhere about the esoteric mode of communication that must be understood to have been adopted by theological and philosophical innovators who sought to express in a constructive manner their disagreements with reigning moral dogmas. Taken all together, these Lockean pronouncements about speech and writing give us our only nonarbitrary starting point for an adequate interpretation of Locke according to his own principles of interpretation" (*SMR,* 137–38). The reference is to remarks that Locke makes in *The Reasonableness of Christianity* about Jesus sometimes concealing his full meaning, and about the ancient philosophers often participating in public religious ceremonies while disagreeing in their writings with the theology of those ceremonies.

I find it astonishing that these passages from the *First Treatise* would be cited as evidence for Locke's being an esoteric writer — or, indeed, as evidence for any principle whatsoever that Locke followed in composing his writings. Locke does not treat Filmer as an esoteric writer; he treats him as a *cunning* writer who resorts to playing rhetorical tricks on his readers. And nowhere does Locke suggest that, when writing on political matters, it is acceptable to play such tricks. Locke regards them as reprehensible; he abuses Filmer for his cunning. Though he does indeed recognize the presence of esoteric speaking and writing in Jesus and in the ancient philosophers, in what he says about such esoteric speaking and writing there is no hint whatsoever that he too is an esoteric writer. In short, there is no basis whatsoever for holding that, in these passages, Locke is giving us the hermeneutic key to how he himself is to be interpreted, namely, as an esoteric writer who has constructed a two-stage concealment of his thought.

But though Locke nowhere so much as hints that he is to be interpreted as an esoteric writer, it may nonetheless be the case that that is the best way to account for, and to deal with, the apparent or real flaws in his mode of presentation. To arrive at the point where we can consider this suggestion, we must have before us Locke's overt teaching concerning God's role in human affairs and his project of a rational theology. Before we turn to that, however, let me present my own view as to what accounts for the perceived flaws in Locke's mode of presentation.

II

Some of the flaws in Locke's mode of presentation seem to me quite clearly to be due to carelessness on Locke's part; others seem to me due to the fact that, on some important issues, he found it difficult to make up his mind. And with respect to the *Essay*, I think there is no reason to doubt him when he says that it was written in snatches over a considerable length of time and that he never subjected the whole of it to a thorough revision. But I hold that a good many of the perceived flaws are not due to these factors but are instead manifestations of two pervasive features of Locke's way of thinking and presenting his thought.

First, while it is true that Locke is sometimes tediously prolix—witness the *First Treatise*—he also has a fondness for arresting declarations. "Reason must be our last judge and guide in everything" is just one of many examples of the point (*Essay* 4.19.14).[3] But invariably when one reads with care the full context in which one of these sloganeering declarations occurs, one notices that Locke qualifies the ringing declaration, usually without bothering to complete the circle by restating the declaration in its fully qualified form. In my book on Locke, *John Locke and the Ethics of Belief,* I spoke of the *visionary* side of Locke and the *craftsmanly* side and observed that it was typical of him to let these two sit side by side, unintegrated.[4]

A second feature of Locke's way of thinking, to which I perhaps gave insufficient emphasis in my Locke book, is the following. Locke had a grand philosophical program in mind, namely, the construction of a rational religion and a rational morality. It is a program that has gripped the imagination of a great many thinkers since Locke. Locke was not very industrious in carrying out the program, however, and not very good at carrying it out when he tried; others have done it far better than he did. With respect to the construction of a rational morality, he got stuck; late in his life he conceded as much, without, however, concluding that the project was misguided. And with respect to the construction of a rational religion, he treated important parts of the program in what strikes me, at least, as an offhand, bored sort of way. He spent the bulk of his time and energy in articulating the epistemological foundations for his program of a rational ethic and a rational religion rather than in carrying it out.

Let me move on, now, to Locke's program of a rational religion and the place of God in his thinking. On this occasion, I shall have to confine myself to a mere sketch of Locke's views; a full treatment would require a book.[5]

Locke's thought as a whole and, in particular, his thought about religion were profoundly shaped by his reflections on the phenomenon of human disagreement and the woes it so often brings. It motivated his discussion of the limits of human knowledge, and it motivated his proposals concerning the proper role of reason in human existence. I will interweave my treatment of these two topics.

In 1671, Locke had a discussion with some five or six friends in his apartment at Exeter House in London on matters of morality and revealed religion.[6] The discussants, says Locke, "found themselves quickly at a stand by the difficulties that arose on every side. After we had awhile puzzled ourselves, without coming any nearer a resolution of those doubts which perplexed us, it came into my thoughts that we took a wrong course, and that before we set ourselves upon enquiries of that nature it was necessary to examine our own abilities, and see what objects our understandings were or were not fitted to deal with" (*Essay*, Epistle to the Reader). This thought, says Locke, "was that which gave the first rise to this Essay concerning the Understanding" (*Essay* 1.1.7).

Over and over in the *Essay*, when Locke wants to draw our attention to the main features of his picture of our place as knowers and believers in the world, he uses three terms as a metaphor cluster: *daylight, darkness,* and *twilight.* The sort of "half-light" he has in mind when he speaks of twilight is not only the half-light produced by the sun just below the horizon but also the half-light produced by the glow of a candle.

If I feel dizzy on a certain occasion, then, to use Kantian conceptuality, my dizziness belongs to the intuitional content of my mind. It is present to me; conversely, I am acquainted with it. The term Locke himself favored was *perceive*. To keep before us the fact that Locke is using it metaphorically, I shall, when presenting his thought, speak of *mentally perceiving*. We mentally perceive certain entities, including certain facts, or, to use Locke's parlance for what I call facts, certain *agreements* and *disagreements* among ideas. For Locke, the only live question was the scope of mental perception (acquaintance, presence, intuition). His answer, famously, was that it is only with one's own ideas, and their agreements and disagreements, that one can have acquaintance. On this occasion, I shall resist the temptation to say exactly what Locke meant by *ideas*—if, indeed, he did mean anything precise by the term.

Locke's official account of knowledge was that knowledge is mental perception of one's ideas and the agreements and disagreements among them. I call this his "official account" because, in the fine mesh of his discussion, he knowingly backs away from the identification of knowledge with mental perception. This is perhaps most clear in his discussion of memory. He observes that we remember many things that we do not actively have in mind—things that are not present to us; and he concedes that some such rememberings are knowings. In his unsteady attempts to sort out the relation between knowledge and mental perception, one sees conflicting impulses at work. On the one hand, one knows that which one mentally perceives; on the other hand, one knows that which is certain for one. Locke found the latter understanding to be broader in scope than the former, and that is what gave him trouble: some of our memories are certain for us even when the relevant ideas are not present to the mind.

And now for the first use of the metaphor cluster: "Light, true light in the mind is, or can be nothing else but the evidence of the truth of any proposition" (4.19.13). The light that evidence throws on the truth of some proposition has its source in the facts, present to the mind, that constitute the evidence. These facts cast light on those other facts for which they are evidence; they illuminate those others. They are the light sources. They are to the mind what the light of the sun is to the physical eye. Such a fact "is irresistible, and like the bright sunshine, forces itself immediately to be perceived, as soon as ever the mind turns its view that way; and leaves no room for hesitation, doubt, or examination, but the mind is presently filled with the clear light of it" (4.11.1).

Everything not illuminated by those light sources is in darkness. And when we duly note that the facts susceptible of being mentally perceived are "very short and scanty" (4.14.1) compared to the totality of things, we realize that these light sources are tiny dots of light in what, apart from the illumination they cast on a few other facts, is an "abyss of darkness" (4.111.22). Our "knowledge [is] limited to our ideas, and cannot exceed them either in extent, or perfection." These are "very narrow bounds, in respect of the extent of all being, and far short of what we may justly imagine to be in some even created understandings, not tied down to the dull and narrow information, is to be received from some few, and not very acute ways of perception, such as are our senses" (4.3.6).

Items of intuitive knowledge, when present to the mind, force themselves to be mentally perceived "as soon as ever the mind turns its view that way," says Locke. The will thus has an important but secondary role to play in what we come to know. The analogy to vision is again instructive. Though "a man with his eyes open in the light, cannot but see; yet there be certain objects, which he may choose whether he will turn his eyes to" (4.12.1). So too, "the employing, or withholding any of our faculties from this or that sort of objects" is a matter of volition on our part, as is our "more, or less accurate survey of them" (4.8.2). Apart from that, however, "our will hath no power to determine the knowledge of the mind one way or other, that is done only by the objects themselves, as far as they are clearly discovered" (4.8.2).

Choosing to attend to certain mental facts is not, however, the whole of the will's role in the formation of knowledge. We have it in our power to construct arguments in which, as Locke sees the matter, we come to mentally perceive agreements and disagreements among ideas that we would have missed but for the fact that, in the argument, we interpose between those "extremes" a greater or less number of "middle terms" whose interrelations we mentally perceive as we move along the argument. By and large, we have to *construct* such arguments; we do not just passively receive them. "We have, here and there, a little of this clear light, some sparks of bright knowledge: yet the greatest part of our ideas are such, that we cannot discern their agreement, or disagreement, by an immediate comparing them. And in all these, we have need of reasoning, and must, by discourse and inference, make our discoveries" (4.17.15). There is thus considerable scope for what Locke calls "the improvement of our knowledge." "I do not question, but that human knowledge, under the present circumstances of our beings and constitutions may be carried much farther, than it hitherto has been, if men would sincerely, and with freedom of mind, employ all that industry and labour of thought, in improving the means of discovering truth, which they do for the colouring or support of falsehood, to maintain a system, interest, or party, they are once engaged in" (4.3.6). Though nature is hardly at all susceptible to being known by us, the situation for religion and morality—along with mathematics—is quite different. In principle, it is possible to go a long way in the construction of a demonstrative theology and a demonstrative morality. One might even say that "morality [that is, the acquisition of moral knowledge] is the proper science, and business of mankind in general (who are both concerned, and fitted to search out their *summum bonum*)" (4.12.11).

Demonstrative arguments are like the objects of intuitive knowledge in that they are sources of light. At bottom, it is the same kind of light, namely, "the evidence of the truth of [a] proposition." The light cast by demonstrative arguments is less intense, however, its brilliance dimmed by the presence of those middle terms and the need for memory.

Even when demonstrative arguments are added to intuitive knowledge, however, it remains the case that "our understandings [come] exceedingly short of the vast extent of things" (1.1.5); genuine knowledge is "short and scanty." Locke devotes page after page to this theme of "how disproportionate our knowledge is to the whole extent even of material beings," not to mention spirits, "which are yet more remote from our knowledge, whereof we have no cognizance," so that "almost the whole intellectual world" is concealed from us "in an impenetrable obscurity" (4.3.27).

One might expect the rhetoric of a writer so profoundly impressed with the extent of our ignorance to be intense and anguished. There is intensity in some of Locke's rhetoric, but no anguish; all is serene. Instead of anguish, Locke urges contented acceptance of our limits.

> Our knowledge being so narrow, as I have shewed it, it will, perhaps, give us some light into the present state of our minds, if we look a little into the dark side, and take a view of our ignorance: which being infinitely larger than our knowledge, may serve much to the quieting of disputes, and improvement of useful knowledge; if discovering how far we have clear and distinct ideas, we confine our thoughts within the contemplation of those things, that are within the reach of our understandings, and launch not out into that abyss of darkness (where we have not eyes to see, nor faculties to perceive anything) out of a presumption that nothing is beyond our comprehension. (4.3.22)

Instead of railing against the gods for giving us a nature incapable of knowing very much, Locke urges us to note what we are capable of knowing, to acknowledge that our capacities for knowledge have been bestowed on us by God, and to thank God accordingly. Though "the comprehension of our understandings, come exceedingly short of the vast extent of things; yet, we . . . have cause enough to magnify the bountiful author of our being, for that portion and degree of knowledge, he has bestowed on us, so far above all the rest of the inhabitants of this our mansion" (1.1.5).

What is it about our capacities for knowledge for which we should be thankful? We should be thankful that God has given us "whatsoever is necessary for the conveniences of life, and information of virtue; and has put within the reach of their discovery the comfortable provision for this life and the way that leads to a better. How short soever their knowledge may come of an universal, or perfect comprehension of whatsoever is, it yet secures their great concernments, that they have light enough to lead them to the knowledge of their maker, and the sight of their duties" (1.1.5).

> We shall not have much reason to complain of the narrowness of our minds, if we will but employ them about what may be of use to us; for of that they are very capable: And it will be an unpardonable, as well as childish peevishness, if we undervalue the advantages of our knowledge, and neglect to improve it to the ends for which it was given us, because there are some things that are set out of the reach of it. It will be no excuse to an idle and untoward servant, who would not attend his business by candlelight, to plead that he had not broad sunshine. The candle, that is set up in us, shines bright enough for all our purposes. (1.1.5)

We have heard Locke speaking of sunlight, of varying degrees of brightness, and of darkness; now, suddenly, he is talking about candles and candlelight. How so? He has abruptly changed the subject.

Let me begin laying out what he has to say on the new subject by quoting from the next sentence: "We shall then use our understandings right, when we entertain all objects in that way and proportion, that they are suited to our faculties; and upon those grounds, they are capable of being proposed to us; and not peremptorily, or intemperately require demonstration, and demand certainty, where probability only is to be had." Just as we had not previously heard of candles and candlelight, so too we had not previously heard of probability.

Locke spends the first thirteen chapters of book 4 of the *Essay* discussing one and another aspect of knowledge. At the beginning of chapter 14 he turns to a new topic, on which he then spends the remainder of the *Essay*. That new topic is *belief* and *judgment*. He introduces the topic like this: "The understanding faculties being given to man, not barely for speculation, but also for the conduct of his life, man would be at a great loss, if he had nothing to direct him, but what has the certainty of true knowledge. For that being very short and scanty, as we have seen, he would be often utterly in the dark, and in most of the actions of his life, perfectly at a stand, had he nothing to guide him in the absence of clear and certain knowledge" (4.14.1).

But we do have something more than knowledge to direct and guide us, something that is also part of our creaturely endowment. It has two aspects. One is the twilight of probability. "As God has set some things in broad daylight, as he has given us some certain knowledge, though limited to a few things in comparison, probably, as a taste of what intellectual creatures are capable of, to excite in us a desire and endeavour after a better state: So in the greatest part of our concernment, he has afforded us only the twilight, as I may so say, of probability, suitable, I presume, to that state of mediocrity and probationership, he has been pleased to place us in here" (4.14.2). The other aspect is our faculties for judgment and belief. "The faculty which God has given man to supply the want of clear and certain knowledge in cases where that cannot be had, is judgment: whereby the mind takes its ideas to agree, or disagree; or which is the same, any proposition to be true or false, without perceiving a demonstrative evidence in the proofs" (4.14.3).

Knowledge is acquaintance with a fact—or, to use Lockean terminology, the perception of some agreement or disagreement among ideas. Judgment and belief, by contrast, consist of *taking* certain ideas to agree or disagree. Obviously, there is no hope whatsoever of understanding Locke if we read him through the lens of the contemporary epistemological consensus, which holds that knowledge is a species of belief.

We saw that corresponding to God's gift to us of the capacity for knowledge is the divine command to expand our knowledge while yet remaining content with its limits. A divine command also comes along with our capacity for judgment and belief. We are to *regulate* the operation of our belief-forming faculties. Assent of the mind, that is, belief,

> if it be regulated, as is our duty, cannot be afforded to anything, but upon good reason. . . . He that believes, without having any reason for believing, may be in love with his own fancies; but neither seeks truth as he ought, nor pays the obedience due to his maker, who would have him use those discerning faculties he has given him, to keep him out of mistake and errour. He that does

not this to the best of his power, however he sometimes lights on truth, is in the right but by chance; and I know not whether the luckiness of the accident will excuse the irregularity of his proceeding. This at least is certain, that he must be accountable for whatever mistakes he runs into: whereas he that makes use of the light and faculties God has given him, and seeks sincerely to discover truth, by those helps and abilities he has, may have this satisfaction in doing his duty as a rational creature, that though he should miss truth, he will not miss the reward of it. For he governs his assent right, and places it as he should, who in any case or matter whatsoever, believes or disbelieves, according as reason directs him. He that does otherwise, transgresses against his own light, and misuses those faculties, which were given him to no other end, but to search and follow out the clear evidence, and greater probability. (4.17.24)

Light and *faculties, clear evidence, greater probability:* we must try to understand what Locke has in mind in speaking of these. First, though, a comment about the scope of doxastic obligation is in order. The passage just quoted is ringingly universalistic in tone: *everyone ought always.* But in the course of his discussion it becomes clear that Locke does not really mean this. The method he recommends takes time to employ; no one has time to employ it for all her beliefs, and some have time to employ it for only a few. Locke's thought is that all of us are obligated, regarding certain issues, to try to do our best to bring it about that we believe what is true and do not believe what is false. Let us say that some proposition is of *maximal concernment*—*concernment* is Locke's term—to a person just in case that person is obligated to try to do the best to bring it about that she believes it if and only if it is true. The method Locke outlines is the method that, in his judgment, one must use when some proposition is of maximal concernment to one. Only in the light of a person's total obligations can one determine which issues are of maximal concernment for her. And the results of that determination will differ from person to person—with this extremely important qualification: fundamental matters of morality and religion are of maximal concernment for everyone.

Now we turn to the method. Suppose that the proposition *P* is a matter of maximal concernment for me. I am under obligation to try to do the best to bring it about that I believe *P* if and only if *P* is true. What do I do? What method do I employ? I begin by gathering a satisfactory body of evidence concerning the truth or falsehood of *P.* That body of evidence must consist of things that I know—*know* in Locke's stringent sense of the term; otherwise I am not doing the best. And it must be a satisfactory collection of items of knowledge. Locke does not say much about what that comes to. But clearly the body of evidence must be of sufficient amplitude, and it must not be skewed. In its totality it must be a reliable indicator of whether *P* is true or false.

Once I have gathered a satisfactory body of evidence, I then determine the probability of *P* on that evidence. That done, I then believe or disbelieve *P* with a firmness that fits its probability on that evidence.

Where is reason in all this? Reason has not been mentioned. Locke wavers in what he calls reason. Sometimes the set of mental activities that he calls reason is wide in its scope, sometimes narrow. Probably the widest is that indicated in this passage: "We may in Reason consider these four degrees; the first and highest, is the discovering, and finding out of proofs; the second, the regular and methodical disposition of them, and laying them in a clear and fit order, to make their connection and force be plainly and easily perceived; the third is the perceiving their connection; and the fourth, the making a right conclusion" (4.17.3). Locke's subsequent discussion leaves no doubt that he regards the third in this list as central.

It is easy now to see why Locke spoke of the *twilight of probability*— that is, the half-light of probability. The only sources of light are facts that the mind mentally perceives. When mentally perceived facts are assembled into some demonstrative proof, the light cast by all of those together on the agreement or disagreement of the ideas in the conclusion is dimmed somewhat by the presence of the middle terms in the proof and by the need for memory. When mentally perceived facts are assembled into evidence for some probabilistic inference, the light they cast on the conclusion is dimmed yet further—so much so that, unless the probability is very high, the conclusion lies in a sort of half-light.

The picture would be woefully incomplete if we did not intro-
duce yet one more use of the metaphor of light in Locke. In *The Reasonableness of Christianity,* Locke says this:

> Though the works of nature, in every part of them, sufficiently evi-
> dence a Deity, yet the world made so little use of their reason that
> they saw him not where, even by the impressions of himself, he
> was easy to be found. Sense and lust blinded their minds in some,
> and a careless inadvertency in others, and fearful apprehensions in
> most . . . gave them up into the hands of their priests, to fill their
> heads with false notions of the Deity. . . . The belief and worship
> of one God was the national religion of the Israelites alone; and if
> we will consider it, it was introduced and supported amongst the
> people by revelation. They were in Goshen and had light, while
> the rest of the world were in almost Egyptian darkness. (§ 238)

The Israelites "were in Goshen and had light." Once again, we find
Locke employing the light metaphor. But the light that the Israelites
uniquely enjoyed was not the light thrown off by facts that they mentally perceived. It was the light of revelation. On a few occasions, Locke
speaks of reason as a mode of revelation (e.g., 4.7.11). But when he
does so, he distinguishes reason as revelation from revelation proper, in
which "God himself affords [a truth] immediately to us, and we see the
truth of what he says in his unerring veracity" (4.7.11). It is this that
Locke sometimes describes as "the light of revelation." In revelation,
God "illuminates the mind with supernatural light" (4.19.14). God
"enlighten[s] the understanding by a ray darted into the mind immediately from the fountain of light" (4.19.5); "God, in giving us the light
of Reason, has not thereby tied up his own hands from affording us,
when he thinks fit, the light of revelation" (4.18.8).

Must we then qualify the claim that the only "true light in the
mind" is that which emanates from facts that we mentally perceive?
Locke thinks not. He reasons as follows. Revelation is at bottom testimony, *divine* testimony; and testimony in general, if it be veridical, is
a form of evidence—hence, a form of light. Indeed, testimony is "all
the light we have in many cases; and we receive from it a great part of
the useful truths we have, with a convincing evidence" (4.16.11).

But history is filled with people thinking that divine revelation occurred on some occasion when it did not. Accordingly, anyone who is not willing to "give himself up to all the extravagencies of delusion and error" concerning the occurrence of revelation "must bring this guide of his light within to the trial"—that is, must allow reason to render judgment as to whether some purported episode of revelation was really an episode. To act otherwise would be irresponsible, a violation of the commands of God (4.19.14).

III

The outlines of Locke's program of a rationally grounded natural religion, a rationally grounded revealed religion, and a rational morality are now before us, as are the outlines of the epistemological basis of his program. What we do not yet have is any indication of how Locke carried out the program—any indication of what Locke's rational religion and morality actually looked like. The truth, as I mentioned earlier, is that Locke does not do much by way of carrying out the program. He spent far more time and energy working out its epistemological foundations than in carrying it out; clearly it was those foundations that gripped his attention.

The most extensive implementation of the program is Locke's *Reasonableness of Christianity*. Looking back on *Reasonableness* from our place in history, it is clear that this is one of the founding documents in the history of liberal Christianity. What we get in *Reasonableness* is a very low Christology coupled with a take on Christianity that treats it as being focused far more on human well-being and morality than on the glory and majesty of God. The Bible is "the good book." Of course, if we recall Locke's ruminations on the scope of human knowledge at the beginning of the *Essay,* there is nothing surprising in this; it is exactly what we should have expected. Our capacities are fitted not for speculation about the transcendent but for guiding us in the living of our lives. If one is looking for articulate theology, one does not go to Locke. And just as *Reasonableness* is one of the founding documents in the history of liberal Christianity, so too Locke's *Paraphrase and Notes on the Epistles of Paul* is one of the founding documents in the tradition of modern biblical interpretation.

Although there are important parts of Locke's program of a rationally grounded religion that he never worked out, he helps himself to theological principles at various points in his moral and political theory, as indeed we have seen him doing in his epistemology. For example, as Jeremy Waldon argues in his *God, Locke, and Equality*, Locke's argument for human equality in the *Second Treatise* is an argument whose theological premises are intrinsic to the argument.[7]

A full treatment of God in Locke's philosophy would note all these many ways in which Locke employs theological principles. Such a full treatment is impossible here and, for our purposes, unnecessary. What will be necessary, when we return to the issue of whether Locke was an esoteric writer, is a grasp of what is arguably the most important point at which Locke appeals to theological principles in his moral and political theory.

Locke was a eudaemonist in his understanding of the human good. "All men seek happiness," he says (2.21.54). And as to what constitutes happiness, his view was that things "are good or evil, only in reference to pleasure or pain. That we call good, which is apt to cause or increase pleasure, or diminish pain in us; or else to procure, or preserve us the possession of any other good, or absence of any evil. And on the contrary, we name that evil, which is apt to produce or increase any pain or diminish any pleasure in us; or else to procure us any evil, or deprive us of any good" (2.20.2).

This explanation of what constitutes happiness has led some commentators to call Locke a hedonist. That seems to me an extremely wooden interpretation of his thought. Apart from the fact that many of his examples are not examples of pleasure or pain in the usual sense, Locke himself says that "by *pleasure* and *pain* . . . I must all along be understood . . . to mean, not only bodily pain and pleasure, but whatsoever delight or uneasiness is felt by us, whether arising from any grateful, or unacceptable sensation or reflection" (2.20.15). I submit that what Locke means is that the good life, the happy life, is the *experientially satisfying* life. This is the concept of the good life that the modern utilitarian tradition works with. What separates Locke from the utilitarians is that the rule of application he employs is not the classical utilitarian principle of the greatest good of the greatest number but rather the eudaemonist principle that we are each to seek our own greatest good.

What is experientially satisfying for one person is, to a considerable extent, different from what is experientially satisfying for another. Hence, Locke makes a point of saying, "the same thing is not good to every man alike" (2.21.54). "The mind has a different relish, as well as the palate; and you will as fruitlessly endeavour to delight all men with riches or glory, (which yet some men place their happiness in,) as you would to satisfy all men's hunger with cheese or lobsters; which, though very agreeable and delicious fare to some, are to others extremely nauseous and offensive" (2.21.55).

If we are to understand Locke's moral theory, it is important that we note that Locke distinguishes between *the good* and *the obligatory.* Everything said so far is only about the good. As to the nature of the obligatory, Locke holds what Robert Adams, in his *Finite and Infinite Goods,* has called a "social requirement" theory of obligation.[8] Locke's theory is that an act is morally obligatory if it is required of us by God.

In general, a law is a rule of a certain sort for voluntary action (2.28.4–5). Specifically, a rule for voluntary action is a *law* if someone who wills that the rule be followed and has the right to do so attaches sanctions to its observance and breach (2.28.6). Three sorts of laws may be distinguished, says Locke: "1. The *divine* law. 2. The *civil* law. 3. The law of *opinion* or *reputation,* if I may so call it. By the relation they bear to the first of these, men judge whether their actions are sins, or duties; by the second, whether they be criminal, or innocent; and by the third, whether they be virtues or vices" (2.28.7).

What duty is can thus not "be understood without a law; nor a law be known, or supposed without a lawmaker, or without reward and punishment" (1.3.12). Specifically, moral duty is what is required by divine law. "That God has given a rule whereby men should govern themselves, I think there is nobody so brutish as to deny," says Locke. "He has a right to do it, we are his creatures: He has goodness and wisdom to direct our actions to that which is best; and he has power to enforce it by rewards and punishments, of infinite weight and duration, in another life: for nobody can take us out of his hands. This is the only true touchstone of moral rectitude" (2.28.8). The sanctions attached to divine law, as indeed to any law, are, of course, goods and evils—satisfying experiences and dissatisfying experiences.

It is important to realize that the very same rule for action that occurs in divine law might also occur in civil and social law; when that is the case, and the question is raised why the rule should be followed, one can reply by appealing to any one of the statuses it has—or to all of them. Furthermore, people may agree that something is a law while disagreeing about its status—if indeed they think of its status at all. One person may think it belongs to divine law, another only to civil or social law. Thus a law that is *in fact* a divine law may be acknowledged as a law without being acknowledged as a divine law.

> That men should keep their compacts, is certainly a great and undeniable rule in morality. But yet, if a Christian, who has the view of happiness and misery in another life, be asked why a man must keep his word, he will give this as a reason: Because God, who has the power of eternal life and death, requires it of us. But if an Hobbist be asked why; he will answer: Because the public requires it, and the Leviathan will punish you, if you do not. And if one of the old heathen philosophers had been asked, he would have answered: Because it was dishonest, below the dignity of a man, and opposite to virtue, the highest perfection of human nature, to do otherwise. (1.3.5–6)

And how do we come to believe that some specific rule for action is a law of moral obligation? Locke's answer is that we come to believe that something is obligatory in many different ways: by believing what our teachers tell us, by reason, by accepting revelation, and so forth (see 1.2.8).

Locke regularly used the term *law of nature* to refer to a law of moral obligation that can *in principle* be known by reason without the assistance of revelation. The qualification "in principle" is important. To call something a law of nature is not to imply that everybody is acquainted with it, that everybody mentally perceives it. Locke's repeated references to laws of nature in the *Second Treatise* do not carry the implication that the laws of nature belong to a *consensus gentium*. It is true that God's laws for our lives, to be genuine laws for us, must be *promulgated*—made available to us by reason or revelation. But to say that a law of moral obligation is available to unaided reason is not to imply that any of us, let alone all of us, have capitalized on that availability. And it is not to imply that any of us, let alone all of us, accept Locke's "divine social requirement" *theory* of obligation. The existence of God, says Locke, "is so many ways manifest, and the obedience we owe him, so congruous to the light of Reason, that a great part of mankind give testimony to the law of nature: But yet I think it must be allowed, that several moral rules, may receive, from mankind, a very general approbation, without either knowing, or admitting the true ground of morality; which can only be the will and law of a God, who sees men in the dark, has in his hand rewards and punishments, and power enough to call to account the proudest offender" (2.3.6).

IV

We now have enough of Locke's views in hand to deal with the question of whether he was an esoteric writer. Recall that Pangle thinks he sees two levels of concealment in Locke. Since Locke's overt teaching is already radical, Locke casts a haze of "conventional sobriety and caution" over it so as to make his readers feel good about what he says; and for those few readers who are truly discerning, he plants clues that will lead them away from his already-radical overt teaching to the truly "radical and shocking intrepidity" of his covert teachings, these being his true views. Let me discuss, in the order of mention, these two levels of concealment that Pangle professes to find in Locke.

I mentioned Locke's abusive treatment of Filmer. Locke's abuse of Filmer pales in comparison to Pangle's abuse of Locke. As one would expect, much of the abuse that Pangle heaps on Locke is focused on Locke's supposed deceptiveness. But a good deal of it is focused on Locke's overt teaching, or what Pangle takes to be his overt teaching. Pangle does not like Locke's rationalism, does not like his liberal Christianity, does not like his protomodernist way of treating Scripture, does not like his version of eudaemonism, and so forth.

Pangle is especially hostile to Locke's biblical interpretation. Locke's basic offense was to espouse and follow the hermeneutical principle that "we must approach Paul's letters ('as well as other parts of sacred Scripture') as we would approach any other letters written by and to someone living long ago. To understand any such letter we must try to reconstruct the exact historical and personal occasion for the epistle" (*SMR,* 152). Locke, along with Spinoza, must be held accountable for "the eclipse, at least among the sophisticated, of the humanly gripping questions ('What could God be?' 'What ought I to be, as a consequence?'). In their stead arose the academic or historical questions which have become so familiar in every divinity school curriculum and are so much less troubling to the spirit: 'How did the texts, with their simple and uncontroversial message, get written'" (*SMR,* 153).

Pangle's hostility to Locke's biblical interpretation goes well beyond his hostility to the general principles that Locke follows, however; it goes to the details of Locke's interpretation. He speaks of "the amazing feats of Lockean casuistry contained in the paraphrases" of the Pauline epistles (*SMR,* 156); he describes the paraphrases as "a commentary suffused with a pedestrian reasonableness so sober as to be soporific, peppered here and there with some of the most delicious pieces of benevolent blasphemy and playful sophistry ever written" (156); he speaks of Locke's "subversion of the received Scriptures" (153) and of his "attempt to undermine the Bible's supreme and suprarational authority" (147); he describes Jesus, on Locke's interpretation, as "that master of benevolent duplicity" (152); and so forth, on and on. On Locke's view, says Pangle, "the Bible contradicts itself, and not in secondary ways, but on the fundamental issue: the Bible's depiction of God is morally incoherent." He adds that he takes this "to be the nerve of Locke's theologico-political argument; this, the attempted refutation of biblical faith on its own terms, would appear to be the bedrock of all his philosophizing" (145).

This summary judgment on Locke's biblical interpretation comes as the conclusion to Pangle's discussion of a particular point of Locke's biblical interpretation. It will be instructive to look at what that is. The issue is the curse pronounced on Adam and Eve in Genesis 3:16–19. Locke, says Pangle, "anticipates some reader objecting 'that these words are not spoken personally to Adam, but in him, as their representative, to all mankind, this being a curse upon mankind because of the fall'—this interpretation," says Pangle, being "the orthodox Christian interpretation" (*SMR,* 144). But Locke rejects this interpretation, his reason for doing so being that he assumes "that God is *just.* Adam and Eve were the only humans who sinned in Paradise; they alone deserve condign punishment" for that sin (*SMR,* 144).

But if these "curses" are not deserved punishment upon all humankind, what then is their status? Locke's view, as Pangle correctly states, is that "God does not in this place of Scripture lawfully punish the innocent unborn women of the future; 'the weaker sex' is not 'by a law so subjected to the curse'; no, God 'only foretells what should be the woman's lot, how by his providence he would order it so'" (*SMR,* 145). Accordingly, says Locke, "there is here no more law to oblige a woman to such a subjection, if the circumstances either of her condition or contract with her husband should exempt her from it, than there is, that she should bring forth her children in sorrow and pain, if there could be found a remedy for it, which is also a part of the same curse upon her" (145).

The implication of this line of interpretation, says Pangle, is that "one may indeed save the omnipotent and all-seeing God from the appearance of being an outrageously vindictive and unjust judge, but in order to do so one is compelled to conceive of his providence as capriciously cruel to all the innocent generations of the future" (*SMR,* 145). In short, "Locke has forced us to confront" the thought that there is "no other alternative: the God of whom and for whom the Bible speaks is either grotesquely unjust in his punishments or tyrannically cruel in his providential care (or both)" (145). What Locke is up to is nothing less than "the attempted refutation of biblical faith on its own terms," says Pangle.

What are we to say about this charge by Pangle, that Locke's aim in his interpretation of Genesis was to show that the biblical depiction of God is "morally incoherent"? The charge is preposterous.

Consider Locke's position: the pain and subjection that we experience are to be understood as somehow falling within God's providential care for humankind; they are not to be understood as God's punishment of all of us for the sin of Adam and Eve. Is a person who holds this position—as many do—thereby committed to holding that God is tyrannically cruel? Is the problem of the relation among God's goodness, God's providence, and human misery really as simple as that? If human misery somehow falls within God's providence, then God is tyrannically cruel? Suppose one holds this position, as Locke did, because one doesn't see how God's justice is compatible with the alternative view. Does that amount to implicitly trying to show that the biblical picture of God is morally incoherent? Though Pangle is not forthcoming on the matter, he apparently embraces the traditional interpretation of the curse.[9] He gives no clue, however, as to how that is compatible with the justice of God. Are we to take Pangle's interpretation of Locke as a model for our interpretation of Pangle and give a malign interpretation to his silence on how God's punishment of all of us for the sin of Adam and Eve fits with the justice of God?

V

I have allowed myself to be diverted from our topic. I have noted some—only some—of Pangle's hostility to what he understands to be Locke's overt teaching. Our topic, however, is Pangle's charge that Locke casts a haze of traditional piety over his overt teaching, so that his ordinary readers will not recognize, or will not be alarmed by, its radical character. Locke employs "biblical language and references . . . to elude persecution, and avoid offending pious potential adherents" (*SMR,* 150). Locke's "subtle deployment of pious and conservative rhetoric testifies to his acute awareness of a continuing need for a degree of traditional piety and moralism in large portions of the populace" (*SMR,* 271).

I have no wish to deny that Locke sometimes gave the impression of being more traditional, less radical than in fact he is—so what's new?

I judge, however, that Locke does this far less often than Pangle suggests. And before we make a big thing of the instances in which he does do this, we had better, in our overall interpretations, take full cognizance of the fact that, just as often, he comes across as more radical than in fact he is. Locke's opposition to innate ideas, and thus to innate knowledge, is a good example of the point. From the time of the publication of the *Essay* until today, this has been taken by many of Locke's readers to be a truly radical feature of his thought. But anyone who reads the *Essay* with even a modicum of care will notice that, though Locke denies innate ideas and innate knowledge, he postulates all sorts of innate faculties. And on his view, the activation of those innate faculties yields knowledge of pretty much the same body of principles that earlier thinkers had held to be innate. Another example of the point is one that we discussed earlier. Locke gives the impression of holding that everybody is always to employ the method he proposes for the governance of belief; reason is to be our judge and guide in everything. But then, as we read along, we discover that he is far from affirming any such grand universalistic principle.

Why Locke was willing, rather often, to give his readers the impression that he was more radical than he actually was is an interesting question that I do not propose trying to answer; my point is only that, before we draw conclusions and make accusations about Locke's deceptiveness, we had better take into account not only those passages in which he comes across as less radical than he is but also those in which he comes across as more radical than he is.

There is no point in looking at all the instances in which Pangle charges Locke with casting a deceptively pious haze over his radical teaching; and in any case, it would take much too long. Let me confine myself to looking at just one instance. It is a case of supposed deceptiveness to which Pangle himself assigns central importance, and is found in section 15 of Locke's *Second Treatise of Government*.

Locke has been talking, in the preceding sections, about the state of nature; his discussion presupposes the existence of laws of nature.[10] At the beginning of section 14 of the *Second Treatise,* Locke says, "It is often asked as a mighty objection, *where are,* or ever were there any *men in such a state of nature?*" His answer is that "all princes and rulers of *independent* governments all through the world, are in a state of nature."

It is a very acute reply, given what Locke means by a state of nature. Two or more people are in a state of nature with respect to each other if there is no executive authority over them. Now suppose that there is no system for the enforcement of international law and of inter-governmental compacts. And then consider the rulers of two independent governments. Those rulers, and the states of which they are the heads, exist in a state of nature with respect to each other. That is to say, there is no executive authority over the two of them.

After further illustrating the point, Locke says, in the next section, section 15, that in response to those who say that there were never any men in the state of nature he will enlist in support "the authority of the judicious Hooker."[11] Pangle says that in this reference to Hooker, Locke is appealing to "the greatest political theorist of the established church and the direct Anglican heir to Thomas Aquinas's synthesis of Aristotle and the Bible. Locke claims to demonstrate that the doctrine of the state of nature derives from the most authoritative and patriotic interpreter of both Christianity and classical political philosophy. In other words, immediately after drawing attention to the alien character of his teaching, Locke loudly asserts its familiar and traditional origin" (*SMR,* 132). Pangle then goes on to say:

> This invocation of Hooker has always proved enormously successful in establishing Locke's credentials with most readers as a pious and relatively conservative English gentleman. Yet attentive or questioning readers, once they recover from the barrage of authority and poke their heads up out of the trenches, must ask just where it is in Hooker's text that one discovers an endorsement of anything like the state of nature Locke has been describing. For surely there is nothing of the kind in the passage Locke here adduces, nor in the lengthy passage he quoted a few sections previously. And when one refers to the whole of the *Laws of Ecclesiastical Polity* one finds that Hooker never so much as mentions, let along embraces, the concept of the state of nature. (132)

So what, then, are we to make of Locke's quotation of this passage from Hooker? "The amazing incongruity of Locke's appeal to Hooker does not usually make itself felt on first reading," says Pangle, but if we read a few more times it becomes clear that Locke is providing "a modest and respectable cloak for what is in truth an intransigently iconoclastic stance toward received moral teaching. By clothing himself in the garb of a disciple of Hooker, he makes it easier for Christian and gentlemanly readers to entertain his new principles and categories without feeling their moral foundations shaking; at the same time he pricks the curiosity and guides the questioning of a few less easily satisfied readers" (133).

To decide whether this charge of craven cunning is on target, we should have before us the passage from Hooker that Locke quotes:

> The laws which have been hitherto mentioned, i.e., the laws of nature, do bind men absolutely, even as they are men, although they have never any settled fellowship, never any solemn agreement amongst themselves what to do, or not to do, but forasmuch as we are not by ourselves sufficient to furnish ourselves with competent store of things, needful for such a life as our nature doth desire, a life fit for the dignity of man; therefore to supply those defects and imperfections which are in us, as living single and solely by ourselves, we are naturally induced to seek communion and fellowship with others; this was the cause of men's uniting themselves at first in politic societies. (*Second Treatise,* § 15)

Was it really deceptive of Locke to cite this passage from Hooker in support of his position?

First, let us remind ourselves that in antiquity, and on through the Middle Ages and into the Renaissance, quotation functioned very differently from how it functions among us. Suppose one took Pangle's tacit principle of responsible quotation and applied it to St. Paul's quotations from the Old Testament, or to Aquinas's quotations from numerous of his predecessors. One would have to conclude that St. Paul and Aquinas were grossly irresponsible, if not cunning deceivers. Locke, along with the other writers of his day, was living in the transition from the old way of quoting to our new way. (Perhaps, under the pressure of deconstruction, we are again in a period of transition, this time back to something close to the old way.)

Be that as it may, the (ahistorical) question that you and I want to ask concerning the Hooker quotation is whether Locke was justified, *by our lights,* in his claim that in this passage one finds the idea of certain human beings living without there being an executive authority over them. If Locke is not justified by our lights in that claim, then it is relevant to ask why he quoted the passage. And wanting to deceive his readers is one, but only one, of several options to consider; St. Paul was not trying to deceive his readers with those quotations and allusions to the Old Testament that we find so strange.

I judge that Locke was indeed justified in believing that he found his idea of the state of nature in the Hooker passage. The laws of nature bind men, says Hooker, even though they never had any solemn agreement among themselves as to what to do and what not to do. Living without any solemn agreement among themselves—and thus perforce living without any executive to enforce that solemn agreement—is exactly what Locke means by living in a state of nature. Nowhere in all his writings, says Pangle, does Hooker use the term *state of nature.* I take his word for that. The idea can be present without the term being used.

But suppose Locke disagreed with Hooker's statement at the end of the passage that "we are naturally induced to seek communion and fellowship with others." Would it then be deceptive on his part to quote Hooker as he does? Locke's claim that some people live in the state of nature with respect to each other carries no implications, one way or the other, as to what it is that induces human beings to seek communion and fellowship with each other. To say it yet again: on Locke's concept of state of nature, for two or more people to live in a state of nature with respect to each other is just for there to be no executive authority over them to enforce laws or compacts.

VI

We have been considering Pangle's first level of purported concealment in Locke. Only when we consider the second level is the topic, strictly speaking, Locke as an esoteric writer. So let's move on to that.

What reason is there to suppose that Locke's overt teaching was not what he himself believed?

Not everything that Locke believed entered into his overt teaching. In his *Paraphrase and Notes on the Epistles of St. Paul,* Locke makes clear that he does not like conciliar Christianity; he wants to leap over the councils and read the New Testament "neat." Thereby Locke helped to give birth to a wide swath of Protestant Christianity in the modern world: "no creed but Christ." Where Locke differed from many of those who followed him in this regard was that, as already mentioned, his reading of the New Testament was a rational liberal reading rather than a conservative evangelical reading. It is pretty clear from the *Reasonableness* that Locke did not think that the Gospels taught the two natures of Christ; and it seems a fair inference from letters written by him and to him that he was a Socinian—that is, a Unitarian. The question before us, however, is not whether there were things Locke refrained from saying in his writings because he thought they might get him into trouble, but whether there are fundamental components of his overt teaching that he himself did not believe, and whether he planted clues in his overt teaching to his real thoughts.

The textual evidence for Locke's supposed esotericism consists of what I called, at the beginning of our discussion, "flaws in Locke's mode of presentation"—contradictions, ambiguities, obscurities, gaps, and the like. "The apparent arbitrariness, the puzzling ambiguity or seeming contradictoriness, of Locke's point of departure in the *Second Treatise*" can be accounted for, Pangle argues, only by the conclusion that Locke was an esoteric writer. It was just too dangerous for him to express his true views openly.

Now there is an a priori reason for finding this explanation dubious. The flaws in question are everywhere in Locke. Locke's account of knowledge is at least as messy as his account of the state of nature. And his ringing declarations about the role of reason in human life are seriously misleading as to what he really has in mind. But nobody was poised to persecute Locke for his account of knowledge—or, indeed, for his views about the role of reason, though many readers disliked what he said on the matter. Thus it cannot, in general, be the case that Locke's mode of presentation is flawed because he was an esoteric writer trying to play it safe. Of course, if the flaws were different in those passages where playing it safe was an issue from those in which playing it safe was not an issue, then the esotericist interpretation could appeal to that difference. But the esotericists do not point to any such difference; and I submit that there is none.

Who is the esoteric Locke? What did Locke really believe, on Pangle's interpretation? Pangle is remarkably elusive on this point. I would have thought that if Locke really were an esoteric writer and Pangle had discerned his covert teaching, it would prove to be a rich, interesting, and arresting body of thought. If those who succeed in following the clues to the covert Locke find that there is nothing much there, it is they who have been duped.

Though Locke's supposed covert teaching proves not to come to much, I think I do see, in a general sort of way, what Pangle thinks the real Locke believed (see *SMR* 206–9). Locke, if I understand Pangle, was a rationalist who was an atheist in religion, a hedonist in ethics, and a libertarian in politics and who believed there were no objective moral laws. Anybody in Locke's day who held such views would, if he wrote at all, either write on topics that didn't touch on his true views, or express his true views in such a way that only the initiates would discern them, or openly express his true views but conceal his authorship. Anything else would spell trouble. And Locke, strange to say, did not like trouble.

So once again, what is the evidence for Locke's being an esoteric writer? So far as I have been able to determine, all those who espouse the esoteric interpretation hold that the only way to account for the messiness of what Locke says about the state of nature is to conclude that he was secretly a Hobbesian.[12] The best way to undercut this argument would, of course, be to offer an interpretation of Locke's teaching on the state of nature that shows it to be coherent and non-Hobbesian. Though I judge that such an interpretation is possible, here is not the place to present it. And in any case, though the esotericists do cite the messiness of what Locke says about the state of nature as a consideration in favor of their interpretation, it appears to me that they do not regard this as the decisive consideration. So let me move on to what Pangle quite clearly regards as decisive. Locke does not really believe, so Pangle argues, that there are any laws of nature or any principles of moral obligation.

As a preliminary point, it is worth noting that Pangle either does not notice Locke's distinction between a theory of the good and a theory of the obligatory or does notice it but declines to acknowledge its validity. It is a distinction that is commonplace in contemporary ethics, however;[13] the fact that something would be a good thing for me to do does not imply that it is morally required of me, obligatory. Against Locke's account of moral obligation, says Pangle, "a deep current in the classical tradition . . . would strongly protest. The true ground of morality, these adherents of the older view would contend, is the beauty of nobility *(to kalon)*" (*SMR*, 191). But this just misses Locke's point, that an account of the good is not an account of obligation. Pangle goes on to say that "all the precepts of traditional natural law, Stoic or Christian, are understood to be categorical imperatives. They may also be backed up by providential sanctions" (192). But this again misses Locke's point. On Locke's view, divine sanctions are not tacked on to moral imperatives; the sanctions *make* them moral imperatives. Or better put: God requiring something of us is what makes it morally obligatory; the sanctions are a component of the requiring.

Let us move on to the main point. Recall that a law of nature, for Locke, is a principle of moral obligation of a certain sort, namely, one that is knowable in principle by "the use and due application of our natural faculties, . . . without the help of positive revelation" (1.3.13). Recall also that, on Locke's view, a principle of moral obligation is a rule for voluntary action that God requires us to follow, a central component of the requiring being that God attaches sanctions to our following the rule, in this life but especially in the life to come. And recall, lastly, Locke's program of a rational natural theology, a rational revealed theology, and a rational morality.

So what would Locke have to do, Pangle asks, to assure us that he really believes there is moral obligation and isn't just fobbing off the unenlightened herd with the impression that he believes this when he does not? He would have to give us "a rational proof of the immortality of the soul" and "a demonstration of the existence of an 'Omnipotency' which can make matter as well as spirit think, and which can bring either type of thinking thing or self back to lasting life in such a way as to enable the thinking thing to suffer painful retribution or blissful reward" (*SMR*, 198).

Now Locke did in fact offer a demonstration of the existence of a "most powerful," "most knowing," and benevolent God (4.10). Though I think there is rather more to be said for Locke's argument than is customarily thought, it is certainly not what I would cite if someone asked me for the most subtle and weighty argument for God's existence. As for immortality, Locke says that this doctrine is *above Reason*—not contrary to reason but above reason (4.17.23). It is one of those doctrines that, "when revealed, [is] the proper matter of faith" (4.18.7). It is clear that Locke believed the doctrine had in fact been revealed by God, though he nowhere assembles the evidence for this belief, evidence that the implementation of his program of a rational revealed religion requires of him.

So what are we to make of this lack of arguments? Pangle leaves no doubt as to what he makes of it.

> Locke's failure to prove the existence (or even to give a quasi-rational argument, however exiguous, for the bare possibility of the existence) of future reward and punishment, happiness and misery, is so naked and clear, and the task at which he fails has been so built up by him in importance, that we are compelled to reconsider that importance. Locke in effect shocks his demanding readers into rethinking the fundamental and popular or conventional assumption upon which he at first appears to build: the assumption that belief in divine judgment in the afterlife is "the only true" ground of morality, or of the principles required to guide human life. (*SMR*, 201)

In short, Locke is "not ultimately serious about the afterlife" (204); he is not "serious about the necessity for divine sanctions in the afterlife" (209). Hence, he is not serious when he says that there are moral obligations and that there is a law of nature.

This charge—that Locke is helping himself to a theological principle, without having satisfied the conditions of his own program of a rational theology for being entitled to do so, indicates that he does not really believe that principle—would perhaps have some weight if this were the only occasion on which Locke did this sort of thing; but, as I indicated earlier, he does it frequently. Or should we go in the opposite direction and conclude that, since Locke does this all the time, there is not much of anything in his overt teaching that he actually believed?

It is scarcely unusual for philosophers to help themselves to principles that some program they espouse implies they are not entitled to. What do we make of that? That they do not believe those principles? Almost always the thing to make of it is that, though they have not actually carried out their program, they believe it can be carried out; so, in the meanwhile, they help themselves to what they believe would be the results of carrying it out. Why treat Locke differently?

Or is the problem that, whereas those other philosophers usually treat the implementation as an ideal to be aimed at, Locke holds that he is not *entitled* to hold theological principles unless he has rationally grounded them? But if this is the problem, then, once again, it is a problem that pervades Locke's thought. Hume showed that, given Locke's program, he is not entitled to inductively formed beliefs about the future; Reid showed that he is not entitled to perceptual beliefs. Locke's classical foundationalist criterion is fundamentally flawed as a criterion for belief entitlement; that is the problem. Locke's failure to satisfy the requirements of his own theory of entitlement in his account of obligation no more shows that he does not believe in obligation than his failure to do so in his account of perception indicates that he does not believe that there is an objective world to be perceived.

One final point. The laws of nature are, for Locke, a species of moral obligations, namely, those that can in principle be known by the employment of our innate faculties of belief formation without the assistance of revelation. Now as we saw, Locke holds that one can recognize that something is morally obligatory without embracing what he (Locke) regards as the correct account of moral obligation—indeed, without embracing any account. And should an estericist interpreter pounce on this as a deceptive evasion on Locke's part, let me observe that Robert Adams espouses the very same view in his *Finite and In-*

finite Goods. And surely it is the correct view. Now, Locke holds that, though some principles of moral obligation are self-evident, most of them, if they are to be known, need to be demonstrated. Thus Locke holds out the ideal of a demonstrative system of moral principles not unlike what is to be found in mathematics. He seems to have labored for quite some time at developing such a system; he conceded, late in life, that he had been unsuccessful.[14] An implication, given Locke's concept of laws of nature, is that neither he nor anyone else has much more than a faint adumbration of which principles of obligation are in fact included in the law of nature.

Locke's mode of presentation was filled with what we—rightly, I think—regard as flaws. Are those flaws not really flaws but cunningly placed indicators of the fact that Locke's overt teaching was not what he really believed and consisted instead of clues for the initiates to follow to his truly radical and subversive covert teaching? We have found no reason to think so.

Notes

1. Thomas L. Pangle, *The Spirit of Modern Republicanism: The Moral Vision of the American Founders and the Philosophy of Locke* (Chicago: University of Chicago Press, 1988), hereafter cited parenthetically in the text as *SMR.*

2. Pangle also refers to §§ 111, 119, and 151. Locke's charges against Filmer are more indirect in these passages than in the ones quoted in the above text.

3. All subsequent citations to Locke are to the *Essay* unless otherwise indicated and are given parenthetically in the text by book, chapter, and paragraph number.

4. Nicholas Wolterstorff, *John Locke and the Ethics of Belief* (Cambridge: Cambridge University Press, 1996).

5. I have treated the topic more fully than I can here in three of my writings: *John Locke,* "Locke's Philosophy of Religion," in *The Cambridge Companion to Locke,* ed. Vere Chappell (Cambridge: Cambridge University Press, 1994), 172–98, and "John Locke's Epistemological Piety: Reason Is the Candle of the Lord," *Faith and Philosophy* 11, no. 4 (October 1994): 572–91. In my discussion in this section, some material has been drawn from these writings.

6. See Maurice Cranston, *John Locke: A Biography* (London: Longmans, 1957), 140–41.

7. Jeremy Waldon, *God, Locke, and Equality: Christian Foundations in Locke's Political Thought* (Cambridge: Cambridge University Press, 2002).

8. Robert Adams, *Finite and Infinite Goods* (Oxford: Oxford University Press, 1999).

9. A bit later in his discussion, Pangle speaks of "the clarity with which the Bible speaks" on the issue of the "morally obliging" subjection of women to men (*SMR,* 173).

10. Even the most charitable interpreter of Locke has to concede that what he says about the state of nature is scarcely a model of consistency—though in the course of my discussion I have pointed out that the same problem erupts at a good many other points in Locke. I myself think that a careful and sympathetic reading of what Locke says on the state of nature does yield a coherent interpretation and that Locke's thought about the state of nature is not crypto-Hobbeanism; but for our present purposes that is neither here nor there.

11. What he says, to speak more precisely, is that he "not only" will cite the authority of Hooker but will "moreover" affirm a more expansive point in his own voice.

12. Cf. *SMR,* 246: "Locke exaggerates . . . the peaceful and reasonable possibilities of the precivil condition in order to mask the extent of his agreement with the unpalatable Hobbesian conception of human nature; he thus seduces most of his readers into accepting or entertaining the essentials of that account without being shocked into quite realizing what they are doing, and at the same time compels a few to puzzle out and thus to comprehend the full picture."

13. See, e.g., Adams, *Finite and Infinite Goods.*

14. See my discussion in *John Locke.*

Chapter 6

The Myth of the Clockwork Universe

Newton, Newtonianism, and the Enlightenment

STEPHEN D. SNOBELEN

[The Lord God] is eternal and infinite, omnipotent and omniscient,
that is, he endures from eternity to eternity, and he is present from
infinity to infinity; he rules all things, and he knows all things that
happen or can happen.

—Isaac Newton, General Scholium
to the *Principia* (1726)

The myth of Newton's clockwork universe is one of the most persistent and pervasive myths in the history of science, perhaps almost as widespread as the mistaken and essentialistic belief that the Galileo Affair involved some sort of clash between "science" and religion (even though one of the main dynamics was a clash between two forms of science). Like the popular conception of Galileo's troubles with the hierarchy of the Catholic Church, the myth of Newton's clockwork universe is recognized as a myth by most informed historians of science but not by the wider public. The myth of the clockwork universe as applied to Newton has several components, not all of which are always present in any given articulation of it. These include the idea that the universe is like a machine or clockwork mechanism; that God created the cosmos and set it in motion but now no longer intervenes in it or governs it; that the cosmos follows deterministic laws; that Newton was a deist or protodeist; and that Newton through his physics either unwillingly or even willingly excluded God from the universe.

Examples of the myth abound. In an agenda-driven article commemorating the 150th anniversary of Darwin's theory, Johnjoe McFadden blithely states that two hundred years before Darwin "Newton had banished God from the clockwork heavens."[1] On this sort of reading, Newton is part of a metanarrative about the secularizing influence of science through the ages.[2] In an extra feature of "Beyond the Big Bang," the final episode for the 2007 season of the History Channel series *The Universe,* respected physicist Michio Kaku says: "Newton believed that the universe was a clock. A gigantic clock—a machine—that God wound up at the beginning of time, and it's been ticking ever since due to his laws of motion."[3] Science writer Edward Dolnick's 2011 book *The Clockwork Universe: Isaac Newton, the Royal Society and the Birth of the Modern World* will help keep the myth alive.[4] This is no straw man. The myth of the clockwork universe is both common and for many seemingly assumed. Regrettably, while the scholarly community has begun to outgrow this myth, it had a hand in perpetuating it, especially during the first half of the twentieth century.[5]

The situation changed dramatically in the second half of the twentieth century, although not all at once. The single most important development was the sale of Newton's nonscientific papers at Sotheby's in London in 1936. A large number of the theological and alchemical papers were purchased by the economist John Maynard Keynes, who left them to King's College, Cambridge, at his death in 1946; selections from the theological portion were published in 1950 by Herbert McLachlan. A second large collection of Newton's theological and alchemical papers, assembled by the Jewish Orientalist A. S. Yahuda, arrived at the Jewish National and University Library in Jerusalem in the late 1960s and subsequently became accessible to researchers. Even wider access began in 1991 with the release of the majority of Newton's manuscripts. The next stage came with the founding of the Newton Project in 1998, which soon after began to mount professional transcriptions of the papers on the Internet. Partway through this decades-long process of manuscript revelations came a new historiographical mood among Newton scholars, who now had increasing access to Newton's massive manuscript corpus. One outcome was a greater tendency among scholars, secular or otherwise, to argue for the importance of Newton's religion to his science.[6]

The purpose of this essay is to demonstrate the conceptual distance between Newton's actual worldview and the metaphor of the secularizing clockwork universe by drawing on the wealth of resources in Newton's published works and his manuscript corpus. This essay consists of two parts. In the first part I show that a deistic clockwork view of the world contrasts with an authentic and accurate presentation of Newton's theology and providentialist physics. The second part looks at the interpretations of Newton's theology and physics offered by Newton's early disciples. I show that Newton's closest followers reassert the central features of his theological conception of the world, including the role of supramechanical forces, the reality of processes of degeneration in the cosmos, the true rather than nominal omnipresence of God, and the rejection of mere mechanism and the God-banishing clockwork universe. I conclude with a brief postscript on Newton and his secularization in the European Enlightenment.

Providential Themes in Newton's Cosmology

The first step in undoing the clockwork myth is to correct the notion that a clockwork view of the cosmos is necessarily secular or ultimately born out of deism. It was not during the Renaissance or Scientific Revolution that the clockwork metaphor was born,[7] but centuries before among pious medieval monks. The clockwork analogy of the universe — popular conceptions of its association with deism and materialism notwithstanding — is tied to the medieval conception of the cosmos as an assembly of nested and regularly moving crystalline spheres. The expression *machina mundi* ("world machine" or "machine of the universe") was employed in works on astronomy in the late medieval period by Robert Grosseteste (ca. 1175–1253),

Johannes de Sacrobosco (fl. 1230), and Nicholas of Cusa (1401–64).[8] It appears in Nicholas Copernicus's *De revolutionibus* (1543) as well.[9] Nicole Oresme (ca. 1325–82) took the step from the term *machina mundi* to a universe-clockwork comparison.[10] Comparisons of God with a clockmaker are used by the archbishop of Canterbury, Thomas Bradwardine (ca. 1290–1349), as well as Henry of Langestein (d. 1397).[11] The clockwork analogy is also used in medieval literary contexts by the French poets Jean Froissart (1333?–1400/1) and Christine de Pisan (1364–ca. 1430) and the great Florentine poet Dante Alighieri (ca. 1265–1321).[12] In these early theological contexts, the clockwork analogy has two essential features: God as creator of the clockwork and God as sustainer of the clockwork. Thus it differs from eighteenth-century, nonprovidentialist deism that is committed only to the first element.[13]

While the accompanying philosophy and theology change in the seventeenth century, the theologically positive use of the clockwork analogy does not. This can be seen among three leading advocates of the mechanical philosophy, all French Catholics: the friar Marin Mersenne, the priest Pierre Gassendi, and the Jesuit-educated René Descartes. Mersenne contends for a clockwork analogy of the universe, convinced that the mechanical philosophy can serve as a defense of theistic belief.[14] Gassendi, famous for reviving and Christianizing Epicurean atomism, compares the wisdom evident in creation with the intentionally designed clock.[15] As for Descartes, while not advocating a cogged machine per se, he does describe the world as a machine and is fond of describing animals as clocks and humans as clocks with souls.[16] The Protestant advocates of the mechanical philosophy Johannes Kepler and Robert Boyle also employ the clockwork analogy.[17] Kepler speaks of his efforts to understand the physical causes of the planetary system in clockwork terms;[18] Boyle uses the clockwork metaphor to argue for both divine transcendence and the radical contingency of creation.[19] Whatever the uses of the clockwork metaphor in later Enlightenment and post-Enlightenment thought, the clockwork view of the universe was seen by these Christian thinkers as a friend of Christianity and a powerful defense against atheism.[20]

In this light, advocacy of the clockwork metaphor prior to the publication of Newton's *Principia* need not imply some kind of protodeistic conception of the world. The early advocates of the clockwork universe were pious, believing Christians. Had Newton advocated the clockwork metaphor, he would have joined the ranks of those Christian natural philosophers who went before him. Did Newton adopt this metaphor? Although examples abound of people declaring, after Newton's time, that Newton espoused a clockwork universe, quotations from his writings that specifically support this assertion are never proffered. There is a good reason for this. To date, not a single example of Newton unambiguously referring to the universe as a clockwork system has surfaced. Given that others in his own day and before did use this analogy (including Boyle, with whom Newton was personally acquainted), and given the voluminous nature of his published and unpublished writings, his omission of it is all the more striking.

In this section, I will show that, contrary to common conceptions that he held to a semideistic, clockwork model of the universe, Newton had a providentialist view of the cosmos that was informed by a belief in an omnipresent and omniscient God continuously in control of his creation. The evidence brought forward to demonstrate these elements of Newton's thought will also show that this pioneer of modern physics cannot be classified with strict accuracy as a mechanist. Newton's status as an active lay theologian is now well established in Newton scholarship, so there is no need to go over this now well-trodden ground here. The question that concerns us here is the degree to which Newton's theological beliefs informed or infused his cosmology.[21]

A useful place to start is Newton's most well-known book, the *Principia mathematica*. Although there is a misconception that the first edition of 1687—unlike the second and third editions of 1713 and 1726—was published bereft of theological language, this is in fact not the case.[22] It is true, however, that the first edition is *almost* bereft of theological language. When the *Principia* was first published, it contained only one reference to the Bible and one to God. The reference to the Scriptures occurs near the beginning of the book in the Scholium on the Definitions. Here Newton says that it is just as important to distinguish between absolute and relative language in the Bible as it is to distinguish between absolute and relative senses of time, space, place, and motion in physics.[23] The reference to God occurs in book 3, proposition 8, corollary 5, where Newton discusses the felicitous arrangement of the planets around the sun—including the earth's location in a position that allows the existence of liquid water. He concludes this discussion by stating: "Therefore God placed the planets at different distances from the sun so that each one might, according to the degree of its density, enjoy a greater or smaller amount of heat from the sun."[24] In 1713, Newton removed the word *God* from this passage and replaced it with a passive verbal construction in a reworked section of what would become corollary 4. Nevertheless, the revised material is a palimpsest that not only continues to articulate an argument from design based on the arrangement of the solar system but in its reworked form arguably presents a *more* powerful case for design by virtue of being more intuitive and less weighed down with mathematical detail.[25]

But even in the first edition, there is more material of theological significance than meets the eye. Thus Newton's discussion of the absolute and the relative in the Scriptures as part of an argument about the absolute and the relative in physics suggests a structural relationship between Newton's biblical hermeneutics and his study of the cosmos. The drafts of this material show that Newton had more theological ideas when writing this portion of the *Principia* than he allowed to appear in print.[26] Also, we now know that Newton's discussion of absolute time and space in the Scholium on the Definitions emanates in part from his theological notions of God's eternal duration and omnipresence. Newton's comment about God's placement of the stars is additionally connected with his providentialist understanding of the creation of the cosmos. All of this takes on added significance in light of Newton's manuscript "De gravitatione"—likely composed shortly before he began work on the *Principia*—which not only attacks the deficiencies of the Cartesian cosmology but also speaks about God's omnipresence and action in the world and argues that the notion of matter existing independently of God offers a path to atheism.[27]

The first edition of the *Principia* also needs to be seen in the light of two sets of documents Newton produced shortly after its publication: his correspondence with Richard Bentley in 1692–93 and his Classical Scholia, drafted around the same time. Bentley sought Newton's aid in late 1692 when writing up his Boyle Lectures for publication.[28] He intended to enlist the new physics of the *Principia* in support of the design argument and hence the existence of God. The words with which Newton began the first of his four letters to Bentley are now famous: "When I wrote my treatise about our system, I had an eye upon such principles as might work with considering men, for the belief of a deity, and nothing can rejoice me more than to find it useful for that purpose."[29] The arguments for design that Newton presents in his letters to Bentley focus on the providential arrangement of the structure of the solar system and God's continuous upholding of this system in some way through gravitation. With respect to the first dynamic, Newton stresses in his first letter that the complex arrangement of the planetary system points to a cause that is "not blind and fortuitous, but very well skilled in mechanics and geometry."[30] In his second letter, he contends that the force of gravity on its own would not have been sufficient to create the motions of the planets: "So then gravity may put the planets into motion, but without the divine power it could never put them into such a circulating motion as they have about the sun; and therefore, for this, as well as other reasons, I am compelled to ascribe the frame of this system to an intelligent agent."[31] In his fourth letter Newton strongly rejects as an "absurdity" the idea that gravity is innate in matter and that it can operate across distances without the mediation of something else. He writes: "Gravity must be caused by an agent acting constantly according to certain laws; but whether this agent be material or immaterial, I have left to the consideration of my readers."[32] Bentley proved to be a quick study, and in the published version of his Boyle Lectures he expands on Newton's hints, declaring gravitation to be a supramechanical force that "proceeds from a higher principle, a Divine energy and impression."[33]

Newton himself crafted even bolder statements in his Classical Scholia, a set of scholia written in the early 1690s for a second edition of the *Principia* that he was planning. These additions were meant to show the continuity between the wisdom of the ancients and Newton's physics, including his understanding of gravitation and the inverse-square law. But the Classical Scholia also include discussions of God's omnipresence and activity in the world. The following passage from this collection is an example:

> That God is an entity in the highest degree perfect, all agree. But the highest idea of the perfection of an entity is that it should be one substance, simple, indivisible, living and life-giving, always everywhere of necessity existing, in the highest degree understanding all things, freely willing good things; by his will effecting things possible; communicating as far as is possible his own similitude to the more noble effects; containing all things in himself as their principle and location; decreeing and ruling all things by means of his substantial presence . . . ; and constantly co-operating with all things according to accurate laws, as being the foundation and cause of the whole of nature, except where it is good to act otherwise.[34]

Along similar lines, a new corollary to proposition 9 in book 3 of the *Principia* reads: "There exists an infinite and omnipresent spirit in which matter is moved according to mathematical laws."[35] And in another place, Newton records, in similar terms, what he believes the ancients thought about gravity: "Quite apparently [they thought] the heavens are nearly free of bodies, but nevertheless filled everywhere with a certain infinite *spiritus,* which they called God."[36] It seems likely that some of Newton's thinking about the universal spirit in the cosmos (which is ultimately linked to God's omnipresence) was shaped by his study of and practice of alchemy, which also posits a nonmechanical, active spirit in the world.[37]

Newton's own mature views were published in the two versions of the General Scholium to the *Principia.*[38] The General Scholium, a sort of general-purpose appendix, first appeared with the second edition of the *Principia* in 1713. An amended and elaborated version appeared in the third edition of 1726. The beginning of the General Scholium is devoted to comments on the complex motions of the planets and

comets in the solar system. This discussion leads naturally for Newton to a consideration of the designer of this system—a system whose
operations it was Newton's honor to explain through a detailed mathematical description for the first time in his *Principia.* Newton expostu-
lates: "This most elegant system of the sun, planets, and comets could
not have arisen without the design and dominion of an intelligent and
powerful being."[39] Here, in a memorable line, are identified Newton's
two essential theological roles of God in the cosmos: God as creator
and sustainer of the heavens and earth. Newton's God has complete
dominion not merely in word but in actuality: "He rules all things, not
as the world soul but as the lord of all. And because of his dominion
he is called Lord God *Pantokrator.*"[40] God's sovereignty is truly universal, and his rule is that of a personal God, not the vague, impersonal
anima mundi of Greek philosophical schools, such as the Stoics. Instead, Newton's view of God's sovereignty can be compared with that
of John Calvin, who declared: "We mean by providence not an idle
observation by God in heaven of what goes on in earth, but His rule
of the world which He made; for He is not the creator of a moment,
but the perpetual governor."[41] Newton also distances his thought
from pantheism, by explicitly denying that God's dominion involves
dominion over the world as over his body, such as is the case with the
world soul.[42] By speaking of classic Jewish and Christian notions of
God's sovereignty and deploying biblical names and titles of the deity,
Newton was making his theological affiliations clear.

Newton offers further detail on God's omnipresence and universal dominion later in the General Scholium. In elaborating on God's
omnipresence, he writes: "He is eternal and infinite, omnipotent and
omniscient, that is, he endures from eternity to eternity, and he is present from infinity to infinity; he rules all things, and he knows all things
that happen or can happen. He is not eternity and infinity, but eternal
and infinite; he is not duration and space, but he endures always and
is present everywhere, and by existing always and everywhere he constitutes duration and space."[43]

For Newton, the nature of God's omnipresence involves his literal presence everywhere at all times: "He is omnipresent not only *virtually* but also *substantially;* for action requires substance. . . . In him all

things are contained and move, but he does not act on them nor they on him. God experiences nothing from the motions of bodies; the bodies feel no resistance from God's omnipresence."[44] To the quotation from Acts 17:28 ("In him all things are contained and move"), Newton adds his footnote on space. This note contains a series of references to classical authors who offer analogies to the notion of a ubiquitous spirit, along with Philo Judaeus and a *florilegium* of quotations about God's omnipresence from the Bible.[45] After further discussions of God and his attributes, Newton moves on to consider gravity, for which he refuses to assign a cause: "I do not feign hypotheses" *(Hypotheses non fingo),* he says.[46] The placement of a consideration of universal gravitation immediately after a discussion of God that includes statements about his omnipresence, however, may have been intended to suggest that it was God who was behind this power. After all, for Newton, only two things are truly universal in the spatial sense: gravity and God's omnipresence.

The General Scholium offers another important insight into Newton's understanding of God's activity in the world. In a comment on the distribution of the fixed stars, which was added to the third edition shortly after his bold declaration of the "most elegant system of sun, planets, and comets," Newton states: "And so that the systems of the fixed stars will not fall upon one another as a result of their gravity, he has placed them at immense distances from one another."[47] Here Newton speaks of an element of his system that is rarely discussed: gravity can be a *destabilizing* force just as it can be a *stabilizing* force. When we recognize that gravity can be both for Newton, we see the significance of his careful comments about God placing the stars at appropriate distances from each other. But Newton contemplated an even stronger statement for this place in the third edition. In an annotation to his copy of the second edition, Newton wrote: "et fixarum systemata per gravitatem suam in se mutuo paulatim caderent nisi omni consilio Entis summi regerentur," that is, "and the fixed stars would, through their gravity, gradually fall on each other, were they not carried back by the counsel of the supreme Being."[48] Once more, God is essential to the ongoing stability of the system.

Newton's *Opticks* (first published in English in 1704) provides further examples of Newton's dynamic cosmos.[49] When Newton had the *Opticks* translated into Latin in 1706 by his supporter Samuel Clarke, he used the opportunity to add seven new and elaborative queries to the original sixteen concise queries. These appeared with some amendments in the second English edition of 1717. The two queries that interest us are those eventually numbered 28 and 31. In a place in query 28, where he rejects an ether-filled plenum and notes the ancient belief in a vacuum, Newton writes that "the main Business of Natural Philosophy is to argue from Phænomena without feigning Hypotheses, and to deduce Causes from Effects, till we come to the very first Cause, which certainly is not mechanical."[50] This cause, for Newton, is God—not the closed, self-contained, and thoroughly mechanical system of some later French thinkers.

Further on, in query 31, Newton considers both the power of gravity in the heavens and the active powers that operate between the smallest particles. He writes:

> And thus Nature will be very conformable to her self and very simple, performing all the great Motions of the heavenly Bodies by the Attraction of Gravity which intercedes those Bodies, and almost all the small ones of their Particles by some other attractive and repelling Powers which intercede the Particles. The *Vis inertiæ* is a passive Principle by which Bodies persist in their Motion or Rest, receive Motion in proportion to the Force impressing it, and resist as much as they are resisted. By this Principle alone there never could have been any Motion in the World. Some other Principles was necessary for putting Bodies into Motion; and now they are in Motion, some other Principle is necessary for conserving the Motion.[51]

Once again we see (indirectly, in this case) Newton's two roles for God in the universe at work: creating and sustaining. Newton adds to this a remark about the tendency for motion to decrease over time: "By reason of the Tenacity of Fluids, and Attrition of their Parts, and the Weakness and Elasticity in Solids, Motion is much more apt to be lost than got, and is always upon the Decay."

Query 31 also provides an elaborate and colorful description of active principles at work in the world:

Seeing therefore the variety of Motion which we find in the World
is always decreasing, there is a necessity of conserving and recruit-
ing it by active Principles, such as are the cause of Gravity, by
which Planets and Comets keep their Motions in their Orbs, and
Bodies acquire great Motion in falling; and the cause of Fermen-
tation, by which the Heart and Blood of Animals are kept in perpetual Motion and Heat; the inward Parts of the Earth are constantly warm'd, and in some places grow very hot; Bodies burn and
shine, Mountains take Fire, the Caverns of the Earth are blown
up, and the Sun continues violently hot and lucid, and warms all
things by his Light. For we meet with very little Motion in the
World, besides what is owing to these active Principles. And if
it were not for these Principles the Bodies of the Earth, Planets,
Comets, Sun, and all things in them would grow cold and freeze,
and become inactive Masses; and all Putrefaction, Generation,
Vegetation and Life would cease, and the Planets and Comets
would not remain in their Orbs.[52]

This is not a world whose motion is merely dependant on an initial divine push. It is a dynamic world in which decline is mixed with renewal.

Three pages later Newton explicitly mentions the gradual buildup
of irregularities in the solar system that bring about the need for a correction: "For while Comets move in very excentrick Orbs in all manner of Positions, blind Fate could never make all the Planets move one
and the same way in Orbs concentrick, some inconsiderable Irregularities excepted which may have risen from the mutual Actions of Comets and Planets upon one another, and which will be apt to increase,
till this System wants a Reformation. Such a wonderful Uniformity in
the Planetary System must be allowed the Effect of Choice."[53] This,
evidently, is the statement that provoked Leibniz to claim that Newton's God was a clockmaker without sufficient foresight to make the
world a perpetual-motion machine (see below). Thus Newton's providentialist cosmology was not merely a part of his private faith: it appears in both the *Principia* (including the first edition) and the *Opticks*.

Newton's use of such a religiously charged term as *reformation* and
the implication that this "reformation" would be effected by God leads

us to Newton's unpublished theological manuscripts. Anyone who is familiar with the hundreds of thousands of words Newton wrote on Daniel and the Apocalypse, along with other biblical prophecies, will know that he spent a good part of his life living in the world of prophecy, both fulfilled and unfulfilled. Newton also held to a premillennial eschatology, believing that Christ would one day return to set up the Kingdom of God on earth. One of the central themes of Newton's prophetic writings is the cycle of apostasy and reformation in salvation history. Newton believed that the Jews had corrupted their religion by the time of Christ and that the Christians had corrupted theirs in the centuries following the first advent of Christ. The chief problem was lapsing into idolatry. It happened to ancient Israel and it happened to Christianity (especially the Roman Church), although God always preserved a faithful remnant. But, in biblical times at least, God had sent reformers to lead his people back to the true faith.

Newton outlines this pattern in his "Irenicum," a theological manuscript that dates to the early eighteenth century. In speaking about the Two Greatest Commandments (loving God and loving neighbor), he asserts:

> These two commandments always have and always will be the duty of all nations and The coming of Jesus Christ has made no alteration in them. For as often as mankind has swerved from them God has made a reformation. When the sons of Adam erred and the thoughts of their heart became evil continually God selected Noah to people a new world and when the posterity of Noah transgressed and began to invoke dead men God selected Abraham and his posterity and when they transgressed in Egypt God reformed them by Moses and when they relapsed to idolatry and immorality God sent Prophets to reform them and punished them by the Babylonian captivity.[54]

But it did not end with the Babylonian Captivity. When the exiles returned, the Jews once again became corrupted by mixing "human inventions with the law of Moses under the name of traditions" and thus "God sent Christ to reform them." When they rejected Christ,

"God called the Gentiles." But the Christians were no better than the Jews: "Now the Gentiles have corrupted themselves we may expect that God in due time will make a new reformation."[55]

Thus, like the system of the world, the human sphere has destabilizing tendencies, and for Newton religion in particular tended to degenerate over time. In both his views of prophecy and his physics, time is a great corrupter: physical beings and physical entities tend to wind down, thus showing their dependence on the timeless and immutable deity. And in both his views of prophecy and his physics, the Lord God of Israel is the Great Restorer. It is perhaps noteworthy that on the same page that Newton outlined the patterns of apostasy and reformation in salvation history he also spoke about God's omnipresence in the universe: "We are to conceive him void of external shape or bounds, a being intangible and invisible whom no eye hath seen or can see, and therefore also incorporeal. A being immoveable and the first cause of motion in all other things. For he is necessarily in all places alike so that no place can subsist without him or be emptier or fuller of him then it is by the necessity of nature."[56]

Newton's biblical view of providence does not make a neat separation between providence in the natural world and intervention in human affairs. This may explain why the themes of degeneration and renewal, along with God's role in these cycles, occur in Newton's understanding of both prophetic history and cosmic history. But an awareness of Newton's powerfully prophetic worldview also puts to rest another common myth about Newton, namely, that he was a deist or protodeist. Despite increasing evidence to the contrary, Richard Westfall maintained that Newton was a protodeist or religious rationalist who was racked by anxieties about the supposed erosion of the Christian faith in the face of the new authority of science.[57] Even without knowledge of his vast prophetic manuscripts it is should be apparent that Newton's conception of the universe is not that of a deist— not even a providentialist deist. But his prophetic manuscripts make this absolutely clear. No deist would accept biblical prophecy (of all genres in the Scriptures) as a revelation from God that has been fulfilled and will be fulfilled in history. No deist would hold to the millenarian views Newton embraced.[58] Newton's views of providence in the natural and human worlds accord with the classical theism of the Judeo-Christian tradition, not deism.

Perhaps the closest Newton came to applying the clockwork analogy to the universe is in the draft of a letter written around May 1712 and intended to respond to Leibniz in the pages of *Memoirs of Literature*. The letter remained unpublished, but near the end Newton argues for understanding that gravity can keep the planets in their courses without a miracle: "To understand the motions of the planets under the influence of gravity, without knowing the cause of gravity, is as good a progress in philosophy as to understand the frame of a clock, and the dependence of the wheels upon one another, without knowing the cause of the gravity of the weight which moves the machine, is in the philosophy of clockwork."[59] Close though it may be, this argument has specific ends and falls short of an explicit description of the world as a clockwork mechanism. Newton did not have a view of the cosmos as a mechanical clock in the rational sense. He may not have even held a view of the cosmos as a clockwork in the pious sense of Kepler or Boyle.

Having worked hard to try to dispel one myth about Newton, I want to be exceptionally careful that I do not provide the seeds for an opposite myth, namely, that Newton's system of the world was *primarily* dependent on ideas of God's providence derived from Scripture. A reckless statement made by Christopher Hitchens helps demonstrate the propensity for such a reverse myth to develop. In a two-page advertisement sponsored by the John Templeton Foundation and containing statements on the relationship of science and religion from a range of notable figures, Hitchens offers the following declaration about Newton: "For Sir Isaac Newton—an enthusiastic alchemist, a despiser of the doctrine of the Trinity and a fanatical anti-Papist—the main clues to the cosmos were to be found in Scripture."[60] Everything between the two em-dashes is true, although one may want to quibble about the use of the qualifier *fanatical*. What comes at the end of Hitchens' declaration, however, is a gross distortion. No one who knows anything about the massive amounts of observational data and theoretical work Newton put into the development of his laws of motion and his theory of gravitation could make such a statement—at least not in good faith. Yes, the evidence suggests that the *structure* of Newton's cosmology was in certain respects informed by his prophetic conception of God's providence. But let there be no mistake: while his commitments to a providentialist view of the universe cannot now be doubted, Newton's theology was not the primary source for his physics. Newton was an empiricist in his understanding of the cosmos. Although he believed that his physics was compatible with the Scriptures and that the *Principia* provided evidence for God's creative and sustaining hand at work, he nevertheless found the main clues to the cosmos in the cosmos.

Newton's Early Followers

How, then, did those who knew Newton best interpret his view of the universe? An authoritative witness can be found in the writings of the early Newtonians William Whiston, Samuel Clarke, Roger Cotes, and Colin Maclaurin. Whiston, who succeed Newton as Lucasian Professor of Mathematics at Cambridge, enjoyed intimate contact with Newton until the latter broke with him around 1714. Clarke was a close confidant of Newton who was also a near neighbor in London for most of the last two decades of Newton's life (as well as being Newton's parish priest). As already mentioned, he was the translator of the Latin edition of Newton's *Opticks*. Roger Cotes, a young Fellow of Trinity College who was also the Plumian Professor of Astronomy and Experimental Philosophy at Cambridge, was the editor of the second (1713) edition of Newton's *Principia*. As for Maclaurin, a Scottish mathematician who became an ardent supporter of Newton, although he did not enjoy the sustained contact with Newton that Whiston and Clarke did, he nevertheless knew Newton personally and had a detailed understanding of his physics, as evinced by the introduction to Newtonian physics he published in 1748.

Rather than turning immediately to these friends and acquaintances of Newton, we will start with the famous Leibniz-Clarke correspondence of 1715–16. Among other criticisms of Newton's thought, Gottfried Leibniz claimed the following in the fourth paragraph of his first paper:

Sir *Isaac Newton,* and his Followers, have also a very odd Opinion concerning the Work of God. According to their Doctrine, God Almighty wants to *wind up* his Watch from Time to Time: Otherwise it would cease to move. He had not, it seems, sufficient Foresight to make it a perpetual Motion. Nay, the Machine of God's making, is so imperfect, according to these Gentlemen; that he is obliged to *clean* it now and then by an extraordinary Concourse, and even to *mend* it, as a Clockmaker mends his Work; Who must consequently be so much the more unskilful a Workman, as he is oftner obliged to mend his Work and to set it right.[61]

Leibniz's notion of a perpetual motion machine implies an idealized clock of Platonic perfection; what he attributes to Newton is an unreliable clock that requires frequent rewinding—the kind of clock that would have been familiar to the original readers of this debate. In his note to the first published edition of the correspondence, Clarke surmises that Leibniz is here responding to the statement in the final query of the *Opticks,* where Newton contends that the irregularities of the comets and planets "will be apt to increase, till this System wants a Reformation."[62] And it does seem likely that Leibniz had this text in mind. Leibniz next contrasts Newton's putative view of things with his own understanding of the cosmos, the preestablished divine order, and the nature of miracles: "According to *My* Opinion, the *same* Force and Vigour remains always in the World, and only passes from one part of Matter to another, agreeably to the Laws of Nature, and the beautiful *pre-established* Order. And I hold, that when God works Miracles, he does not do it in order to supply the Wants of Nature, but those of *Grace.* Whoever thinks otherwise, must needs have a very mean Notion of the Wisdom and Power of God."[63] Thus Leibniz lays down the gauntlet.

In the section of his first reply that corresponds to Leibniz's fourth paragraph, Clarke is careful to answer Leibniz's attribution to Newton of a divine Clockmaker without perfect foresight. First, Clarke argues against the analogy between God and the human clockmaker, noting that the latter is responsible for making the clock and its component parts but not the forces that drive it. These are "only *adjusted,* by the Workman."[64] "But with regard to *God,* the Case is quite different;

because *He* not only composes or puts Things together, but is himself the Author and continual Preserver of their *Original Forces* or *moving Powers*: And consequently tis not a *diminution,* but the true *Glory* of
his Workmanship, that *nothing* is done without his *continual Government*
and *Inspection.*"[65]

Thus, in contradistinction to Leibniz's proposal, the Newtonian conception emphasizes God's role as both creator and sustainer
through continuous Providence. Far from cowering before Leibniz's
accusation of theological infelicity, Clarke takes the high road and
declares God's continuous care of the cosmos a thing worthy of
great glory.

Second, Clarke offers a direct, forceful, and unambiguous repudiation of the clockwork analogy: "The Notion of the World's being a
great *Machine,* going on *without the Interposition of God,* as a Clock continues to go without the Assistance of a Clockmaker; is the Notion of
Materialism and *Fate,* and tends, (under pretense of making God a *Supra-
Mundane Intelligence,*) to exclude *Providence* and *God's Government* in reality out of the World."[66] Thus Clarke does not merely reject the clockwork analogy but, without hesitation, associates it with materialism
and fate and, what is more, is at pains to emphasize the deleterious
theological consequences of such a view of the cosmos for the sovereignty of God.

The remainder of Clarke's reply to Leibniz's use of the clockwork
model involves the explication of two theological problems that could
arise from viewing the cosmos as a clock. First, he presents a slippery-
slope argument about Leibniz's "pre-established order": "And by the
same Reason that a *Philosopher* can represent all Things going on from
the beginning of the Creation, *without* any Government or Interposition of Providence; a *Sceptick* will easily argue still farther backwards,
and suppose that Things have from Eternity gone on (as they now do)
without any true Creation or Original Author at all, but only what such
Arguers call *All-Wise and Eternal Nature.*"[67] Clarke here is prophetic.
This is essentially what some thinkers in the eighteenth century began
to argue.[68] His second concern is met with a royal analogy. Just as a
king whose kingdom continued "*without* his Government or Interposition, or *without* his Attending to and Ordering what is done therein"

would in effect be merely a king of "a *Nominal* Kingdom" and not merit the titles "King or Governor," so it would be with God if He did not exercise continuous dominion over the world—an argument that echoes the treatment of the God of continuous dominion in Newton's General Scholium. Clarke also extends this analogy in an interesting way by arguing that just as treasonous men who in "Earthly Government" believe things can go on without the oversight of the king "may reasonably be suspected that they would like very well to set the King aside," "whosoever contends, that the Course of the World can go on *without* the Continual direction of *God,* the Supreme Governor; his Doctrine does in Effect tend to Exclude God out of the World."[69] Is Clarke suggesting that his opponent is guilty of some kind of theological sedition?

Although he does not explicitly say so, Clarke may also have been implying that Leibniz's view of God's action (or nonaction) in the world was tantamount to deism.[70] Clarke's familiarity with Newton's natural philosophy and theology endows his rejection of the clockwork analogy with a great deal of authority. The evidence of Newton's behind-the-scenes involvement in Clarke's responses to Leibniz also strongly suggests that Clarke's statement either met with Newton's approval or originated with Newton.[71]

Clarke added detail to his conception of Newton's theologically informed cosmology in subsequent replies to Leibniz. In his second reply, Clarke further elaborates on his conception of God's continuous providence. Agreeing with Leibniz that God's workmanship should show both his power and his wisdom, Clarke argues: "This *Wisdom of God* appears, not in making Nature (as an Artificer makes a Clock) capable of going on *without him:* (For that's *impossible;* there being *no Powers* of Nature *independent* upon *God,* as the *Powers* of *Weights* and *Springs* are *independent* upon *Men:*) But the *Wisdom of God* consists, in framing *originally* the *perfect* and *compleat Idea* of a Work, which *begun and continues,* according to that Original perfect Idea, by the *continual uninterrupted Exercise* of his *Power* and *Government.*"[72] Leibniz's clockwork analogy, based as it is on the notion of the independent power of weights and springs, is theologically problematic precisely because it does not do justice to the continuous sovereignty of the Almighty.

Another notable statement comes in the tenth paragraph of his second reply, in which he declares that God is both transcendent over the world and immanent in the world: "God is neither a *Mundane* Intelligence, nor a *Supra-Mundane* Intelligence; but an *Omnipresent* Intelligence, both *In* and *Without* the World. He is *In* all, and *Through* all, as well as *Above* all."[73] Clarke also denies that the only kind of "natural forces" are mechanical, contending that this would make animals and men "as *mere Machines* as a *Clock*." "Natural forces" for Clarke are not to be exclusively equated with mechanical forces. If they are not (as Clarke argues), "then *Gravitation* may be effected by *regular* and *natural* Powers, though they be *not Mechanical*."[74] Clarke rejects both the clockwork analogy and a universe that can be reduced to mere mechanism. Although Clarke provides a robust repudiation of Leibniz's implied clockwork analogy, it seems likely that Leibniz's criticism of Newton on this point ultimately fed into the common myth that Newton problematically introduced a clockwork universe.

Although Whiston does feel able to use the clockwork analogy for the purposes of the design argument, he too accepts only a strongly providentialist view of the universe.[75] Whiston does, however, employ the clockwork analogy in a way very similar to the way Leibniz does in this First Paper of 1715—albeit to very different ends. In his 1696 *New theory of the earth,* Whiston argues that God would have created the cosmos in such a way that "external Nature was even, uniform, and regular" but that the various eccentricities and anomalies now observed were the result of secondary causes.[76] "'Tis most Philosophical, as well as most Pious, to ascribe only what appears wise, regular, uniform, and harmonious, to the First Cause; (as the main *Phænomena* of the Heavenly Bodies, their Places, and Motions, do, to the degree of wonder and surprize) but as to such things as may seem of another nature, to attribute them intirely to subsequent changes, which the mutual actions of Bodies one upon another, fore-ordain'd and adjusted by the Divine Providence, in various Periods, agreeably to the various exigencies of Creatures, might bring to pass."[77]

This much is more or less consistent with the views of Newton and Clarke. But shortly after this, Whiston introduces the analogy of the clock to explain his distinction between the original perfection and uniformity of the creation and its subsequent decline: "If any one of us should observe that a curious Clock, made and kept in order by an excellent Artist, was very notably different from the true time of the day, and took notice withal of a certain rub or stoppage, which was very capable of causing that Error in its Motion; he would easily and undoubtedly conclude that such an Error was truly occasion'd by that visible Impediment; and never design'd at first, or procur'd by the Artist."[78] Two decades later, in his *Astronomical principles of religion* (1717), when speaking of those predisposed to accept the doctrine of the eternity of the world, Whiston compares the universe to a clock losing its motion over time. Whiston argues that such a person cannot suppose there to be an "Equality of Motion . . . in every Part of the Universe" and "that a certain Clock or Watch will of itself go for ever" while also observing "such wearing of the Wheels and Pivots, such decay of the Spring, and such Rust and Foulness over the whole, (besides the Necessity of its being wound up every Revolution) as must, by Calculation, put a Stop to its Motion in 20 Years time."[79] Whiston completed his *Astronomical principles* on September 1, 1716, and the book appeared for sale in early April 1717,[80] so he likely composed this argument before becoming aware of Leibniz's challenge to Newton using the example of the clockwork universe that requires constant rewinding.

But this language is consistent with Whiston's advocacy of Newton's argument against the eternity of the world based on the degeneration of the cosmos elsewhere in the same book, where he asserts that the stars and their systems "are not of Permanent and Eternal Constitutions; but that, unless a miraculous Power interposes, they must all, in length of Time, decay and perish, and be rendred utterly incapable of those noble Uses for which at present they are so wonderfully adapted."[81] Further clarification of Whiston's views comes in his corollaries at the beginning of the *New theory*. In the first two corollaries Whiston contends that the power of gravity "*is not a result from the Nature of Matter,*" but rather that "*this universal force of Gravitation being so plainly above, besides, and contrary to the Nature of Matter . . . must be the Effect of a Divine Power and Efficacy which governs the whole World, and which is absolutely necessary to its Preservation.*"[82] Additional detail comes in the fifth corollary: "*The Providence of God in the Natural World is not merely a Conservation of its being, or a Non-annihilation thereof; but a constant, uniform, active Influence or Energy in all the Operations done in it.*"[83] If God were to withdraw this sustaining power, even if he preserved the being of the bodies of the world, "*the whole would immediately be dissolv'd, and each of the Heavenly Bodies be crumbled into Dust.*"[84] This is not deism or merely preordained design; this is the continuous providence of a truly omnipresent and everlasting God.

When Roger Cotes crafted his preface to the second edition of the *Principia,* he devoted some space to theological apologetics, including articulations of natural theology and the claim that Newton's magnum opus acted as an incentive to piety as well as a buttress against atheism. His articulations of natural theology include echoes of the General Scholium's design argument and God of dominion. Cotes writes: "Surely, this world—so beautifully diversified in its forms and motions—could not have arisen except from the perfectly free will of God, who provides and governs all things."[85] Newton through his great work the *Principia* has "unlocked the gates" and "opened our way to the most beautiful mysteries of nature." The *Principia* has now made it "possible to have a closer view of the majesty of nature, to enjoy the sweetest contemplation, and to worship and venerate more zealously the maker and lord of all."[86] Once again, the emphasis is on the continuous sovereignty of God.

Finally, these themes reverberate in Colin Maclaurin's 1748 *Account of Sir Isaac Newton's philosophical discoveries.* Early in this book, Maclaurin rejects Epicureanism and all systems that view the universe in purely mechanical ways.[87] Toward the end of the book Maclaurin takes up themes relevant to the relationship between Newtonian physics and theology. Like Newton, he uses the example of the decay of the sun to argue against the eternity of the world. The argument against the eternity of the world is further bolstered by the new theory of comets, "since the supply which they afford must have been long ago exhausted, if the world had existed from eternity."[88] Maclaurin also summarizes the arguments made in the General Scholium about God's dominion, namely that "the structure of the visible world" demonstrates that it "is governed by *One Almighty,* and *All-Wise Being,* who rules the world, not as its *Soul* but as its *Lord,* exercising an absolute sovereignty over the universe."[89] Alluding to Leibniz's views, Maclaurin states "that as the Deity is the first and supreme cause of all things, so it is most unaccountable to exclude him out of nature, and represent him as an *intelligentia extramundana.*"[90] He elaborates on this as follows:

> On the contrary, it is most natural to suppose him to be the chief mover throughout the whole universe, and that all other causes are dependent upon him; and conformable to this is the result of all our enquiries into nature; where we are always meeting with powers that surpass mere mechanism, or the effects of matter and motion. The laws of nature are constant and regular, and, for ought we know, all of them may be resolved into one general and extensive power; but this power itself derives its properties and efficacy, not from mechanism, but, in a great measure, from the immediate influences of the first mover. It appears, however, not to have been his intention, that the present state of things should continue for ever without alteration; not only from what passes in the moral world, but from phænomena of the material world likewise; as it is evident that it could not have continued in its present state from eternity.[91]

Two elements of this passage are worthy of comment. First, we see Maclaurin explicitly deny mere mechanism and emphasize the necessary role of *supramechanical* powers. Second, Maclaurin strikingly asserts not only that the current state will not "continue for ever without alteration" but also that we know this in part from the analogy of the moral world. Here Maclaurin speaks with the same voice as Newton.

In sum, Newton's closest followers reassert the central features of his theological conception of the world, including the role of supramechanical forces, the reality of processes of degeneration in the cosmos, the true rather than nominal omnipresence of God, and the rejection of mere mechanism and a God-banishing clockwork universe. When a clockwork analogy is raised (as it is by Whiston), it is used to describe a universe in perpetual decline rather than a static cosmos that has no need of the deity beyond the initial creative act. Newton's followers also echo the two most basic elements of Newton's theological conception of the world, that God is creator *and* sustainer; while Newton and the Newtonians embrace both elements, the deistic conception of the world accepts only the first element. Finally, it is noteworthy that these close followers of Newton were without exception antideistic in theological orientation.

Postscript on Newton and the Enlightenment

Newton was committed to a powerful biblical faith and saw his physics in providentialist terms. We have seen this in both Newton's own writings and his reception among his closest followers, who reassert the central features of his theological conception of the world. Yet in the decades after his death these important elements of his thought, already little known and not very well understood while he was alive, were distanced even further from Newton in the writings of both supporters and opponents. As Newton biographer Gale E. Christianson concludes: "Few things would have angered or dismayed him more than the Enlightenment belief that the *Principia* contained the framework of a universe in which God was no longer a vital, or even necessary, part."[92] But this is precisely what occurred. Both popular and scholarly (mis)conceptions of Newton today are due in no small part to readings and misreadings of his thought during the European Enlightenment of the eighteenth century—readings and misreadings that led to a diversity of portrayals of Newton, some of them mutually contradictory. While space does not allow detailed elaboration, I think it is worth outlining six likely factors that can be identified as contributory to the distortion of Newton's thought during this time.[93]

First, Newton engaged in self-censorship—no doubt motivated in part by his desire to conceal his antitrinitarian theological heresy. Second, Newton's own followers in Britain, some of them chosen by him, tended to emphasize the success of Newton's physics, champion his philosophical method, celebrate his genius, and explicate the natural theological relations of his work, while avoiding the wider theological dynamics of his thought.[94] Third, a number of less friendly voices in Britain began to provide readings of Newton different from those being disseminated by the British Newtonians. On the one hand, a small number of deists and freethinkers began to radicalize his thought;[95] on the other hand, some vocal religious opponents of Newton's system in Britain began to contend that Newtonianism was bad for religion.[96] Fourth, the leading thinkers of the French Enlightenment, headed by Voltaire, produced deistic, secularizing, and even occasionally materialistic interpretations of Newton's physics. Voltaire himself was happy to point to elements of Newton's religion—such as his natural theology and antitrinitarianism—that he found compatible with his rationalism, but in his three major works popularizing Newton's physics he maintained a studied silence on Newton's prophetic beliefs—although elsewhere he derogates Newton's prophetic beliefs.[97] And nothing signals Newton's distance from the *philosophes* like his deep commitment to biblical prophecy and millenarianism. Fifth, the British Romantics—partly responding to distortions of Newton's thought already current—constructed an image of Newton as a cold, malevolent rationalist who helped bring about the God-banishing, soul-destroying, imagination-sapping, and materialistic forms of science that they decried in their poetry and prose.[98] William Blake epitomizes the Romantic reaction. It was he who wrote, "May God us keep / From Single vision & Newtons sleep."[99] If only Blake had known Newton the alchemist and providentialist! Sixth, and finally, Newton's cosmology is read through the lens of Pierre-Simon de la Place, the "Newton of France" who transformed Newtonianism into the deterministic, clockwork universe that so many now anachronistically associate with Newton himself.

Such factors as these go a long way to explaining how Newton came to be known as the father of the deistic clockwork universe. Yet, thanks in large part to our access to the material hidden away by Newton's self-censorship, we are able to see how far removed such a portrait of Newton is from his actual visage. A careful reading of Newton's massive corpus, both published and unpublished, reveals that he was, without question, committed to biblical Christianity—even if not always orthodox—and understood his own work, particularly his physics, in providentialist terms, reflective of his theistic and prophetic understanding of the cosmos. In a certain sense, Blake was right. Newton had a single vision rather than a double vision. But it was a single vision of the cosmos as a whole that contained both matter and spirit and that involved both nature and the superintendence of the God of Israel.

Notes

For helpful discussions about the themes of this essay, I would like to thank Edward Davis, Mordechai Feingold, Andrew Janiak, and Jeffrey Wigelsworth. I am also grateful to the two editors of this volume for their help and advice.

1. Johnjoe McFadden, "'Survival of the Wisest': It Is 150 Years since Darwin Expounded the Theory That Illuminates Our World to This Day," *Guardian*, June 30, 2008. For similar caricatures, see also Christopher Hitchens, *God Is Not Great: How Religion Poisons Everything* (Toronto: McClelland and Stewart, 2007), 80; Carl Sagan, *The Varieties of Scientific Experience: A Personal View of the Search for God*, ed. Ann Druyan (New York: Penguin Press, 2006), 63–64; Robert M. Hazen and James Trefil, *Science Matters: Achieving Scientific Literacy* (1991; repr., New York: Anchor Books, 1992), 5, 14; Roger S. Jones, *Physics for the Rest of Us: Ten Basic Ideas of Twentieth-Century Physics That Everyone Should Know . . . and How They Have Shaped Our Culture and Consciousness* (Chicago: Contemporary Books, 1992), 101–2; Paul Davies and John Gribbin, *The Matter Myth: Dramatic Discoveries That Challenge Our Understanding of Physical Reality* (New York: Touchstone, 1992), 12, 13, 15, 17, 42, 62, 221, 260; Peter Aughton, *The Story of Astronomy: From Babylonian Stargazers to the Search for the Big Bang* (London: Quercus, 2008), 80–91; Ivars Peterson, *Newton's Clock: Chaos in the Solar System* (New York: W. H. Freeman, 1993); Richard Baum and William Sheehan, *In Search of Planet Vulcan: The Ghost in Newton's Clockwork Universe* (New York: Plenum, 1997); John David Ebert, *Twilight of the Clockwork God: Conversations on Science and Spirituality at the End of an Age* (San Francisco: Council Oak Books, 1999); Fritjof Capra, *The Web of Life: A New Scientific Understanding of Living Systems* (New York: Anchor Books, 1996), 5, 19, 20, 107, 120, 188, and *The Turning Point: Science, Society, and the Rising Culture* (1982; repr., Toronto: Bantam Books, 1983), 53–74, 99 (heading of Part III) and 164–87 (chapter entitled "Newtonian Psychology"); Franz J. Broswimmer, *Ecocide: A Short History of the Mass Extinction of Species* (London: Pluto Press, 2002), 57; Jane Jakeman, *Newton: A Beginner's Guide* (Abingdon: Hodder and Stoughton, 2001), 63. An increasingly popular source of knowledge is the online encyclopedia Wikipedia. For several years up to early 2011, its entry "Clockwork Universe Theory" asserted that the clockwork universe was "established by Isaac New-

ton." Happily, Ted Davis's enterprising students corrected the entry, which now stresses that Newton *opposed* the clockwork universe theory (Ted Davis, pers. comm., August 8, 2011).

2. Often presented in tandem with the clockwork myth is the claim that Newton himself did not realize that his physics spelled the end of faith. See, e.g., Steven Weinberg, letter to the editor, *Times Literary Supplement,* February 16, 2007, http://entertainment.timesonline.co.uk/tol/arts_and_entertainment /the_tls/article2341817.ece. However, there have also been attempts to correct mythologies about Newton in the public sphere. See, e.g., Jean F. Drew, "Newton vs. the Clockwork Universe," July 19, 2004, www.freerepublic.com/focus /f-news/1174268/posts.

3 "Beyond the Big Bang," *The Universe,* History Channel, 2007, video clip of extra feature available at www.history.com/shows/the-universe/videos /playlists/beyond-the-big-bang#beyond-the-big-bang-sir-isaac-newtons-law -of-gravity (current as of August 12, 2011). One assumes that if Professor Kaku had committed a scientific solecism in his interview, it would have been caught and thus not included in the documentary. However, in science documentaries errors about the history of science or theology do not seem to receive this kind of scrutiny.

4. Edward Dolnick, *The Clockwork Universe: Isaac Newton, the Royal Society and the Birth of the Modern World* (New York: Harper, 2011).

5. To be sure, the Newtonian clockwork myth has not completely disappeared among scholars today. See, e.g., William A. Stahl et al., *Webs of Reality: Social Perspectives on Science and Religion* (New Brunswick: Rutgers University Press, 2002), 81. On the role of the scholarly community in perpetuating the myth, see, e.g., George S. Brett, "Newton's Place in the History of Religious Thought," in *Sir Isaac Newton, 1727–1927: A Bicentenary Evaluation of His Work,* ed. F. E. Brasch (Baltimore: Williams and Williams, 1928), 263; and Samuel Leslie Bethell, *The Cultural Revolution of the Seventeenth Century* (London: D. Dobson, 1951), 63. To be fair to scholars of this earlier era, assessments of Newton's thought were of necessity limited mostly to his published works.

6. See, e.g., J. E. McGuire and P. M. Ratansi, "Newton and the 'Pipes of Pan,'" *Notes and Records of the Royal Society of London* 21 (1966): 108–42; David Kubrin, "Newton and the Cyclical Cosmos: Providence and the Mechanical Philosophy," *Journal of the History of Ideas* 28 (1967): 325–45, and "Providence and the Mechanical Philosophy: The Creation and the Dissolution of the World in Newtonian Thought" (PhD diss., Cornell University, 1968); J. E. McGuire, "Force, Active Principles, and Newton's Invisible Realm," *Ambix* 15 (1968): 154–208, and *Tradition and Innovation: Newton's Metaphysics of Nature* (Dordrecht: Kluwer, 1995); Frank E. Manuel, *The Religion of Isaac Newton* (Oxford: Clarendon Press, 1974); Betty Jo Teeter Dobbs, *The Foundations of Newton's Alchemy: The Hunting of the Greene Lyon* (Cambridge: Cambridge University Press, 1975) and

The Janus Faces of Genius: The Role of Alchemy in Newton's Thought (Cambridge: Cambridge University Press, 1991); Richard S. Westfall, *Never at Rest: A Biography of Isaac Newton* (Cambridge: Cambridge University Press, 1980); Gale E. Christianson, *In the Presence of the Creator: Isaac Newton and His Times* (New York: Free Press, 1984); James E. Force and Richard H. Popkin, *Essays on the Context, Nature, and Influence of Isaac Newton's Theology* (Dordrecht: Kluwer, 1990); James E. Force and Richard H. Popkin, eds., *Newton and Religion: Context, Nature and Influence* (Dordrecht: Kluwer, 1999); James E. Force, "Newton and Deism," in *Science and Religion / Wissenschaft und Religion,* ed. Änne Bäumer and Manfred Büttner (Büchum: Brockmeyer, 1989), 120–32, and "Newton's God of Dominion: The Unity of Newton's Theological, Scientific and Political Thought," in Force and Popkin, *Essays on the Context,* 75–102; Edward B. Davis, "Newton's Rejection of the 'Newtonian World View': The Role of Divine Will in Newton's Natural Philosophy," *Fides et Historia* 22 (1990): 6–20, republished in *Science and Christian Belief* 3 (1991): 103–17 and, with additions, in *Facets of Faith and Science,* vol. 3, *The Role of Beliefs in the Natural Sciences,* ed. Jitse M. van der Meer (Lanham: University Press of America, 1996), 75–96, and "Myth 13: That Isaac Newton's Mechanistic Cosmology Eliminated the Need for God," in *Galileo Goes to Jail and Other Myths about Science and Religion,* ed. Ronald L. Numbers (Cambridge, MA: Harvard University Press, 2009), 115–22; Edward B. Davis and Robin Collins, "Scientific Naturalism," in *The History of Science and Religion in the Western Tradition: An Encyclopedia,* ed. Gary B. Ferngren (New York: Garland, 2000), 203; Edward B. Davis and Michael P. Winship, "Early-Modern Protestantism," in Ferngren, *History of Science,* 283–84; Otto Mayr, "Clockwork Universe," in *Encyclopedia of the Scientific Revolution: From Copernicus to Newton,* ed. Wilbur Applebaum (New York: Garland, 2000), 145; William E. Burns, *The Scientific Revolution: An Encyclopedia* (Santa Barbara, CA: ABC-CLIO, 2001), 240; Dan Falk, *In Search of Time: Journeys along a Curious Dimension* (Toronto: McClelland and Stewart, 2008), 134; Keith Ward, *Pascal's Fire: Scientific Faith and Religious Understanding* (Oxford: Oneworld Publications, 2006), 24–33, 40–48, 108; Alvin Plantinga, "What Is 'Intervention'?" *Theology and Science* 6 (2008): 369–401.

7. Cf. Christopher B. Kaiser, *Creational Theology and the History of Physical Science: The Creationist Tradition from Basil to Bohr* (Leiden: Brill, 1997), 108.

8. See John North, *God's Clockwork: Richard of Wallingford and the Invention of Time* (London: Continuum, 2005), 201. Otto Mayr sees the notion of the *machina mundi* as a stepping stone to the clockwork metaphor. See Mayr, "Clockwork Universe," 146.

9. Copernicus, *On the Revolutions,* vol. 2, ed. Jerzy Dobrzycki, trans. Edward Rosen (London: Macmillan, 1978), 4.

10. Nicole Oresme, *Le livre du ciel et du monde* 2.2, cited in Edward Grant, *A History of Natural Philosophy: From the Ancient World to the Nineteenth Century* (Cambridge: Cambridge University Press, 2007), 284. See also Kaiser, *Creational The-*

ology, 106–7. Mayr dates Oresme's first conception of the world as a clockwork to ca. 1350. See Mayr, "Clockwork Universe," 146.

11. See North, *God's Clockwork,* 202; and Kaiser, *Creational Theology,* 107–8.

12. Mayr, "Clockwork Universe," 145–46.

13. Stanley L. Jaki, "God, Nature, and Science," in Ferngren, *History of Science,* 48.

14. William B. Ashworth Jr., "Catholicism and Early Modern Science," in *God and Nature: Historical Essays on the Encounter between Christianity and Science,* ed. David C. Lindberg and Ronald L. Numbers (Berkeley: University of California Press, 1986), 138.

15. William B. Ashworth Jr., "Christianity and the Mechanistic Universe," in *When Science and Christianity Meet,* ed. David C. Lindberg and Ronald L. Numbers (Chicago: University of Chicago Press, 2003), 72–74; Pierre Gassendi, *Syntagma philosophicum,* cited in Margaret J. Osler, "Whose Ends? Teleology in Early Modern Natural Philosophy," *Osiris* 16 (2001): 159.

16. René Descartes, *Philosophical Essays and Correspondence,* ed. Roger Ariew (Indianapolis: Hackett, 2000), 42–43, 69, 73, 138, 270–71, 276. See also Ashworth, "Christianity," 70, 74. For an argument that God plays a continuing role in Descartes's universe, see Gary Hatfield, "Force (God) in Descartes' Physics," *Studies in History and Philosophy of Science* 10 (1979): 113–40.

17. On Boyle's version of the mechanical philosophy, see Margaret G. Cook, "Divine Artifice and Natural Mechanism: Robert Boyle's Mechanical Philosophy of Nature," *Osiris* 16 (2001): 133–50; and Eugene Klaaren, *Religious Origins of Modern Science* (Grand Rapids, MI: Eerdmans, 1977), 149–59.

18. See Kepler to Herwart von Hohenburg, February 10, 1605, quoted in the original Latin in Alexandre Koyré, *The Astronomical Revolution: Copernicus—Kepler—Borelli,* trans. R. E. W. Maddison (1973; repr., New York: Dover Publications, 1992), 378: "My aim is this, to show that the celestial machine is not like a divine creature, but like a clock (he who believes the clock to be animate assigns the glory of the artificer to the work), insofar as nearly all the diversity of motions are caused by a simple, magnetic and corporeal force, just as all the motions of a clock are caused by a most simple weight. I will also show how this physical account is to be brought under mathematics and geometry" (my translation).

19. Klaaren, *Religious Origins,* 149.

20. See Ashworth, "Christianity."

21. For recent studies on the relationship between Newton's science and his religion, see Stephen D. Snobelen, "To Discourse of God: Isaac Newton's Heterodox Theology and His Natural Philosophy," in *Science and Dissent in England, 1688–1945,* ed. Paul B. Wood (Aldershot: Ashgate, 2004), 39–65, and James E. Force, "The Nature of Newton's 'Holy Alliance' between Science and Religion: From the Scientific Revolution to Newton (and Back Again)," in

no178 • *Stephen D. Snobelen*

Rethinking the Scientific Revolution, ed. Margaret J. Osler (Cambridge: Cambridge University Press, 2000), 247–70.

22. Some use this misconception—and others the *relative* lack of theological language in the first edition—to argue that the addition of the General Scholium in 1713 represents a turn to theology and a turn away from theological neutrality in the *Principia.* The accessibility of Newton's theological manuscripts, many of which predate the *Principia,* along with a better understanding of the theological contexts of the work, has rendered this position untenable. On the continuing presence of theology in all three editions of the *Principia,* see I. Bernard Cohen, "Isaac Newton's *Principia,* the Scriptures, and the Divine Providence," in *Philosophy, Science, and Method: Essays in Honor of Ernest Nagel,* ed. Sidney Morgenbesser, Patrick Suppes, and Morton White (New York: St. Martin's Press, 1969), 523–48. See also Stephen D. Snobelen, "The Theology of Isaac Newton's *Principia mathematica:* A Preliminary Survey," *Neue Zeitschrift für Systematische Theologie und Religionsphilosophie* 52 (2010): 377–412.

23. Isaac Newton, *The Principia: Mathematical Principles of Natural Philosophy,* trans. I. Bernard Cohen and Anne Whitman with Julia Budnez (Berkeley: University of California Press, 1999), 413–14. The Cohen-Whitman translation of the *Principia* is based on the third (1726) edition.

24. Newton, *Principia,* 814 n. cc.

25. Newton, *Principia,* 814–15.

26. See Cohen, "Isaac Newton's *Principia,*" and Snobelen, "Theology of Newton's *Principia.*"

27. For a recent edition of "De gravitatione," see Isaac Newton, *Philosophical Writings,* ed. Andrew Janiak (Cambridge: Cambridge University Press, 2004), 12–39.

28. For background, see Henry Guerlac and Margaret Candee Jacob, "Bentley, Newton and Providence (the Boyle Lectures Once More)," *Journal of the History of Ideas* 30 (1969): 307–18.

29. Newton to Bentley, December 10, 1692, in Newton, *Philosophical Writings,* 94.

30. Newton to Bentley, December 10, 1692, in Newton, *Philosophical Writings,* 96.

31. Newton to Bentley, January 17, 1693, in Newton, *Philosophical Writings,* 98.

32. Newton to Bentley, February 25, 1693, in Newton, *Philosophical Writings,* 103. A 1698 memorandum by the Scottish mathematician David Gregory is also suggestive: "Mr C. Wren says that he is in possession of a method of explaining gravity mechanically. He smiles at Mr Newton's belief that it does not occur by mechanical means, but was introduced originally by the Creator." *The Correspondence of Sir Isaac Newton,* ed. J. F. Scott (Cambridge: Cambridge University Press, 1967), 4:267.

33. Richard Bentley, *A confutation of atheism from the origin and frame of the world. The third and last part* (London, 1693), 32.

34. Isaac Newton, Classical Scholia, in David Gregory MS. 245, fol. 14a, Library of the Royal Society, quoted in English in McGuire, "Force, Active Principles," 216.

35. Newton, Cambridge University Library, Add. MS. 3965.6, fol. 266v.

36. Newton, Classical Scholia, in Volkmar Schüller, "Newton's *Scholia* from David Gregory's Estate on the Propositions IV through IX Book III of His *Principia*," in *Between Leibniz, Newton, and Kant: Philosophy and Science in the Eighteenth Century*, ed. Wolfgang Lefèvre (Dordrecht: Kluwer, 2001), 241. See also Newton, Cambridge University Library Add. MS. 3965.12, fol. 269, cited in McGuire and Rattansi, "Newton," 120.

37. Betty Jo Teeter Dobbs, "Newton's Alchemy and His Theory of Matter," *Isis* 73 (1982): 511–28.

38. On the theology of the General Scholium, see Stephen D. Snobelen, "'God of Gods, and Lord of Lords': The Theology of Isaac Newton's General Scholium to the *Principia*," *Osiris* 16 (2001): 169–208; Larry Stewart, "Seeing through the Scholium: Religion and Reading Newton in the Eighteenth Century," *History of Science* 34 (1996): 123–64.

39. Newton, *Principia*, 940.

40. Newton, *Principia*, 940.

41. John Calvin, *Concerning the Eternal Predestination of God*, trans. J. K. S. Reid (London: James Clarke, 1961), 162.

42. Newton, *Principia*, 940. Newton later makes it clear that God is "not at all corporeal" (942).

43. Newton, *Principia*, 941.

44. Newton, *Principia*, 941–42.

45. Newton, *Principia*, 941–42 n. j. The note on space was enlarged for the 1726 edition.

46. Newton, *Principia*, 943.

47. Newton, *Principia*, 940.

48. Isaac Newton, *Isaac Newton's Philosophiae naturalis principia mathematica: The Third Edition (1726) with Variant Readings*, ed. I. Bernard Cohen and Alexandre Koyré (Cambridge, MA: Harvard University Press, 1972), 2:760. Michael A. Hoskin points to the significance of this variant reading when discussing the difference between the cosmologies of Leibniz and Newton in "Newton and the Beginnings of Stellar Astronomy," in *Newton and the New Direction in Science*, ed. G. V. Coyne, M. Heller, and J. Życiński (Vatican City: Specola Vaticana, 1988), 60. I have adapted Hoskins's translation to bring out with greater clarity Newton's description of God and his will (Hoskins has simply "the divine plan").

49. A survey of theological themes in the various editions of the *Opticks* can be found in Stephen D. Snobelen, "'La lumière de la nature': Dieu et la philosophie naturelle dans l'*Optique* de Newton," *Lumières* 4 (2004): 65–104.

50. Isaac Newton, *Opticks: or, a treatise of the reflexions, refractions, inflexions and colours of light* (London, 1717), 344.

51. Newton, *Opticks* [1717], 372–73.

52. Newton, *Opticks* [1717], 375.

53. Newton, *Opticks* [1717], 378.

54. Isaac Newton, "Irenicum," Keynes MS. 3, 35 (normalized text).

55. Newton, "Irenicum," 35.

56. Newton, "Irenicum," 35.

57. Various iterations of Westfall's protodeist and incipient rationalist theses can be found in Richard S. Westfall, "Newton and Christianity," in *Religion, Science and Public Policy,* ed. Frank T. Birtel (New York: Crossroad, 1987); "The Rise of Science and the Decline of Orthodox Christianity: A Study of Kepler, Descartes, and Newton," in Lindberg and Numbers, *God and Nature,* 218–37; "Isaac Newton's *Theologiae gentilis origines philosophicae*," in *The Secular Mind: Transformations of Faith in Modern Europe,* ed. W. Warren Wagar (New York: Holmes and Meier, 1982), 15–34; *Science and Religion in Seventeenth-Century England* (New Haven: Yale University Press, 1958), 193–220; and "Isaac Newton: Religious Rationalist or Mystic?," *Review of Religion* 22 (1957–58): 155–70. Westfall was still insisting on this view of Newton's secularizing role in culture and the history of ideas in one of his last papers, published after his death. See Richard S. Westfall, "The Scientific Revolution Reasserted," in Osler, *Rethinking the Scientific Revolution,* 54. It is possible that Westfall's position was shaped by the mistaken belief that Newton's biblicist antitrinitarian theology was either incipient deism or tantamount to deism.

58. James Force has provided the most robust criticisms of Westfall's protodeism thesis. See James E. Force, "Samuel Clarke's Four Categories of Deism, Isaac Newton, and the Bible," in *Scepticism in the History of Philosophy,* ed. Richard H. Popkin (Dordrecht: Kluwer, 1996), 53–74, "Newton and Deism," 120–32, and "The Newtonians and Deism," in Force and Popkin, *Essays on the Context,* 43–73.

59. Newton to the editor of *Memoirs of Literature,* ca. May 1712, in *Philosophical Writings,* 117.

60. "Does Science Make Belief in God Obsolete?," advertisement, *Atlantic,* May 2008, 44–45.

61. Gottfried Leibniz, "First Paper," in *A collection of papers, which passed between the late learned Mr. Leibnitz, and Dr. Clarke, in the years 1715 and 1716* (London, 1717), 3, 5. The correspondence between Leibniz and Clarke was conducted in French but was published in 1717 with an English translation by Clarke

facing the original French. The English text of the 1717 edition is available at www.newtonproject.sussex.ac.uk.

62. Samuel Clarke, *Collection of papers,* 5 n *. Leibniz would have been referring to Clarke's 1706 Latin translation of the *Opticks* (Newton, *Optice,* 345–46). In this edition the final query is numbered 23.

63. Leibniz, "First Paper," 5.

64. Samuel Clarke, "First Reply," in *Collection of papers,* 13 and 15 (quotation on 15).

65. Clarke, "First Reply," 15.

66. Clarke, "First Reply," 15.

67. Clarke, "First Reply," 15 and 17.

68. It also roughly corresponds to the position of modern pantheists and materialists. One is reminded of Carl Sagan's opening statement in his 1980 documentary *Cosmos*: "The cosmos is all that is or ever was or ever will be," a secular inversion of Rev. 1:8.

69. Clarke, "First Reply," 17.

70. See Clarke's arguments against deism and his quadripartite taxonomy of deism in his 1705 Boyle Lectures: Samuel Clarke, *A discourse concerning the unchangeable obligations of natural religion, and the truth and certainty of the Christian revelation* (London, 1706), 19–45.

71. I. Bernard Cohen and Alexandre Koyré, "Newton and the Leibniz-Clarke Correspondence," *Archives Internationales d'Histoire des Sciences* 15 (1962): 63–126; A. Rupert Hall and Marie Boas Hall, "Clarke and Newton," *Isis* 52 (1961): 583–85. This is not to say that Clarke was merely Newton's mouthpiece or that he showed no originality in the debate.

72. Clarke, "Second Reply," in *Collection of papers,* 45.

73. Clarke, "Second Reply," 47.

74. Clarke, "Fourth Reply," in *Collection of papers,* 151.

75. For Whiston's use of the clockwork analogy, see William Whiston, *Astronomical principles of religion, natural and reveal'd* (London, 1717), 106, 255.

76. William Whiston, *New theory of the earth* (1696), 114–15 (quotation on 115).

77. Whiston, *New theory,* 116.

78. Whiston, *New theory,* 116–17.

79. Whiston, *Astronomical principles,* 109–10.

80. Whiston, *Astronomical principles,* 301; *Daily Courant,* advertisement, April 4, 1717.

81. Whiston, *Astronomical principles,* 89–90.

82. Whiston, *New theory,* 5–6.

83. Whiston, *New theory,* 6.

84. Whiston, *New theory,* 6–7.

85. Roger Cotes, preface to Newton, *Principia,* 397.

86. Cotes, preface to Newton, *Principia,* 398.

87. Colin Maclaurin, *An account of Sir Isaac Newton's philosophical discoveries, in four books* (London, 1748), 4–5.

88. Maclaurin, *Account,* 375–76.

89. Maclaurin, *Account,* 377.

90. Maclaurin, *Account,* 387.

91. Maclaurin, *Account,* 387.

92. Christianson, *In the Presence,* 60.

93. On Newton in the Enlightenment, see Stephen D. Snobelen, ed., "Isaac Newton in the Eighteenth Century," special issue, *Enlightenment and Dissent* 25 (2009); J. B. Shank, *The Newton Wars and the Beginning of the French Enlightenment* (Chicago: University of Chicago Press, 2008); Jonathan I. Israel, *Enlightenment Contested: Philosophy, Modernity, and the Emancipation of Man, 1670–1752* (Oxford: Oxford University Press, 2006), 201–22, 751–80; Brian Young, "Newtonianism and the Enthusiasm of Enlightenment," *Studies in the History and Philosophy of Science* 35 (2004): 645–63; Stephen D. Snobelen, "Isaac Newton," in *Encyclopedia of the Enlightenment,* ed. Alan Charles Kors (Oxford: Oxford University Press, 2003), 3:172–77; Jonathan I. Israel, *Radical Enlightenment: Philosophy and the Making of Modernity, 1650–1750* (Oxford: Oxford University Press, 2001), 515–27; Paolo Casini, "Newton's *Principia* and the Philosophers of the Enlightenment," *Notes and Records of the Royal Society of London* 42 (1988): 35–52; P. M. Rattansi, "Voltaire and the Enlightenment Image of Newton," in *History and Imagination: Essays in Honour of H. R. Trevor-Roper,* ed. Hugh Lloyd-Jones, Valerie Pearl, and Blair Worden (London: Duckworth, 1981), 218–31; Robert E. Schofield, "An Evolutionary Taxonomy of Eighteenth-Century Newtonianisms," *Studies in Eighteenth-Century Culture* 7 (1978): 175–92; Margaret C. Jacob, "Newtonianism and the Origins of the Enlightenment: A Reassessment," *Eighteenth-Century Studies* 11 (1977–78): 1–25; Peter Gay, *The Enlightenment: The Science of Freedom* (New York: W. W. Norton, 1969), 2:128–50 (the sections "The Enlightenment's Newton" and "Newton's Physics without Newton's God"); Henry Guerlac, "Newton's Changing Reputation in the Eighteenth Century" [1965], "Where the Statue Stood: Divergent Loyalties to Newton in the Eighteenth Century" [1965], and "Three Eighteenth-Century Social Philosophers: Scientific Influences on Their Thought" [1958], all in *Essays and Papers in the History of Modern Science* (Baltimore: John Hopkins University Press, 1977), 69–81, 131–45, and 451–64, respectively.

94. See Patricia Fara, *Newton: The Making of Genius* (London: Macmillan, 2002); Maureen McNeil, "Newton as National Hero," in *Let Newton Be! A New Perspective on His Life and Works,* ed. John Fauvel et al. (Oxford: Oxford University Press, 1988), 223–39. The notable exception is William Whiston, who published extensively on prophecy (although Newton is only one of the sources of

his prophetic and strongly millennial ideas). On Whiston's prophetic views, see Stephen D. Snobelen, "William Whiston: Natural Philosopher, Prophet, Primitive Christian" (PhD diss., University of Chicago, 2000), ch. 4; James E. Force, *William Whiston: Honest Newtonian* (Cambridge: Cambridge University Press, 1985); and Maureen Farrell, *William Whiston* (New York: Arno Press, 1981).

95. See, e.g., John Toland, *Letters to Serena* (London, 1706), 183. Two valuable studies of Toland's appropriation of Newton are Jeffrey R. Wigelsworth, "Lockean Essences, Political Posturing, and John Toland's Reading of Isaac Newton's *Principia*," *Canadian Journal of History* 38 (2003): 521–35; and Margaret C. Jacob, "John Toland and the Newtonian Ideology," *Journal of the Warburg and Courtauld Institutes* 32 (1969): 307–31. See also Wigelsworth's more recent study "A Sheep in the Midst of Wolves: Reassessing Newton and English Deists," *Enlightenment and Dissent* 25 (2009): 260–86. Wigelsworth sees Toland as a kind of deist, while Jacob portrays him as a kind of pantheist, and thus more radical. On Toland and Newton, see also Shank, *Newton Wars*, 126–29, and Jacob, *The Newtonians and the English Revolution, 1689–1720* (Hassocks, Sussex: Harvester Press, 1976), 201–50.

96. Orthodox concerns over Newton's heterodoxy are explored in Scott Mandelbrote, "Eighteenth-Century Reactions to Newton's Anti-Trinitarianism," in *Newton and Newtonianism: New Studies,* ed. James E. Force and Sarah Hutton (Dordrecht: Kluwer, 2004), 93–111; Stephen D. Snobelen, "Isaac Newton, Heretic: The Strategies of a Nicodemite," *British Journal for the History of Science* 32 (December 1999): 381–419. See also George Hickes to Roger North, May 23, 1713, British Library Add. MS. 32551, fol. 34; Joseph Spence, *Observations, Anecdotes, and Characters of Books and Men Collected from Conversation,* ed. James M. Osborn (Oxford: Clarendon Press, 1966), 1:387; George Berkeley, *A treatise concerning the principles of human knowledge* (London, 1710), 156–68 (secs. 110–17). For more on Berkeley's anti-Newtonianism, see Fara, *Making of Genius,* 103–5; M. Hughes, "Newton, Hermes and Berkeley," *British Journal for the Philosophy of Science* 43 (1992): 1–19; Geoffrey N. Cantor, "Anti-Newton," in Fauvel et al., *Let Newton Be!,* 212–15; D. J. Greene, "Smart, Berkeley, the Scientists and the Poets: A Note on Eighteenth-Century Anti-Newtonianism," *Journal of the History of Ideas* 14 (1953): 327–52.

97. Voltaire, *Letters concerning the English nation* (London, 1733), *The Elements of Sir Isaac Newton's Philosophy,* trans. John Hanna (London, 1738), and *The Metaphysics of Sir Isaac Newton,* trans. David Erskine Baker (London, 1747). For Voltaire's discomfort with Newton's prophetic studies, see, for example, the reference to Newton in the entry "Esprit faux" ("False minds") in his *Dictionnaire philosophique, II,* vol. 36 of *The Complete Works of Voltaire* (Oxford: Voltaire Foundation, 1994), 63. On the reception of Newton in France, see Shank, *Newton Wars*; Derek Gjertsen, "Newton in France," in *The Newton Handbook* (London: Routledge and Kegan Paul, 1986), 382–84; A. Rupert Hall, "Newton in France: A

New View," *History of Science* 13 (1975): 233–50; I. Bernard Cohen, "Isaac Newton, Hans Sloane, and the Académie Royale des Sciences," in *Mélanges Alexandre Koyré,* ed. I. Bernard Cohen and René Taton (Paris: Hermann, 1964), 1:61–116; Charles Coulston Gillispie, "Fontenelle and Newton," in *Isaac Newton's Papers and Letters on Natural Philosophy,* ed. I. Bernard Cohen (Cambridge, MA: Harvard University Press, 1958), 427–43. The classic study is Pierre Brunet, *L'introduction des théories de Newton en France au XVIII siècle, I: Avant 1738* (Paris: Libraire Scientifique Albert Blanchard, 1931). No further volumes were published.

    98. For an overview, see Cantor, "Anti-Newton," 203–21.

    99. William Blake to Thomas Butts, November 22, 1802, in *The Complete Poetry and Prose of William Blake,* ed. David V. Erdman (New York: Anchor Books, 1982), 722.

· *Chapter 7* ·

Pierre Bayle

A "Complicated Protestant"

HUBERT BOST

The expression "complicated Protestant" needs some explaining. It comes from Antony McKenna's response to the invitation from a certain university to speak on Pierre Bayle. McKenna had to decline but instead proposed the names of two colleagues: Gianluca Mori and myself. Mori, he wrote, "interprets Bayle as a crypto-materialist," while Bost views him "as a complicated Protestant." I found this characterization as to how I interpret Bayle to be right on the mark, since my reading of him aims to do away with all simplistic ones. To take just one example, in the *crux interpretum* of the relationship between faith and reason, my view fully admits Bayle's complexity and allows one to place a reading that would favor fideism side by side with one that tends more toward atheism.

But why is Bayle a "complicated Protestant"? It is because, in his life and in his thought, the question of Protestantism took different forms at different stages and in different contexts. I will list a number of these factors before grouping them under three broader rubrics:

- Confessional adherence. Bayle's adherence to Protestantism comes both from his education (as son of a pastor) and from a personal

185

choice (he returned to it after, at one time, renouncing his child-
hood religion).

- Position in a social group. Wherever he goes (with the exception
of his stay at Toulouse), Bayle never ceases to frequent Protestant
networks, but this does not prevent him from connecting with
Catholics wherever he goes as well.
- The strong solidarity he shows with the Protestants when they
suffer persecution and exile, as expressed in his correspondence
and other writings from the time immediately preceding and following the Revocation of the Edict of Nantes.
- The critical—at times even conflict-laden—relationship Bayle
has with certain representatives of his church on a philosophico-
political or theologico-political level over such events as the Revocation or the Glorious Revolution—as illustrated especially in the
affair of the "cabale de Rotterdam" that broke out with his *Avis
aux réfugiés*.
- The thankless battle against any and every form of religious hi-
jacking of politics. This criticism evolved throughout the course
of Bayle's life. At the beginning of his literary career, it comes to
expression in his condemnation of superstition and the constraints
of the conscience, but later it grows in intensity and is instead directed against the inspirations of the Enthusiasts and all other fa-
naticist manifestations. The initial anti-Catholicism gives way, at
least in terms of intensity, to a criticism that is *internal,* directed
against deviations within the Protestant camp.
- The demand of epistemological coherence with respect to doctrine and the theologians who are supposed to defend it. This
demand results in a clear and oft-repeated distinction between
the method, objectives, and regulating authority of theology on the
one hand and his own work as historian and philosopher on the
other.
- The question as to whether on the literary level there is such a
thing as a "Protestant writing" or perhaps a "Reformed style,"
which I will not treat here, but which is all the same most perti-
nent, as Roger Zuber and Ruth Whelan have recently shown at a
conference in Paris.[1]

The above complexity of Bayle's relationship to Protestantism becomes even greater when one considers the impact of certain personal circumstances. Bayle is also a "complicated Protestant" in that his status as Protestant, his adherence to Protestant doctrine, is never unaccompanied by torments and upheavals. When it comes to *torments,* we must think of the hundreds of pages Bayle devoted to the persistent problem of evil, an issue that surfaces particularly in Reformed theology because of its insistence on the sovereignty of God.[2] With *upheaval,* we have in mind Bayle's polemics and conflicts with a number of theological leaders (e.g., Jurieu or the "rationalists"), or even those affairs that on two occasions earned him an appearance before the consistory of the Walloon Church in Rotterdam.

I will attempt to account for all the issues above by uniting them under three broader rubrics:

- *Biographical:* This part considers the existential choices Bayle makes in his journey to belong to a particular social group and the conflicts that these choices cause.
- *Historical and political:* Here we find the ideas Bayle forms concerning the evolution of Protestantism since the Reformation, what characterizes it, and any deviations there might be.
- *Theological and moral:* In this context I will deal with Bayle's doctrinal discussions, especially on the relationship between faith and reason as focused on the Bible, the idea of God, and providence.

Of course, these issues cannot be treated exhaustively, and I will instead just mention them so as to highlight the complexity of the subject.

It may seem somewhat redundant to dwell on the *biographical* aspect, since the main details of Bayle's Protestantism are well known. However, we absolutely need to remind ourselves of them because they have been worked into a reading of his Protestantism that admits its reality only to empty it: *Yes, Bayle was indeed born a Protestant, but he stayed Protestant only formally and externally; for him, the truth lay elsewhere.* However, few historians would do well to ignore a particular thinker's education or what that thinker writes about it himself. In fact, these two aspects form the basis for evaluating various interpretations of any thinker's work. And Bayle's Protestantism was not just imposed on him because of his family background, for later in his life it took the shape of a personal choice.

That Bayle belonged in the Protestant camp by choice, and not just by birth, should at the very least nuance or counterbalance an exclusively rationalist reading of his thought. Of course, one could emphasize that there were sociological or psychological factors to this decision—such as Bayle's conformism—but these factors in no way render his Protestantism empty. One cannot deny that group mechanics played a role in Bayle's decisions and actions, but this does not imply that his claim to Protestantism was empty.

For, to quote Elisabeth Labrousse, Bayle is a "Protestant by choice" insofar as he chose to return to the Reformed confession.[3] This is not the place to repeat the reading I suggested of Bayle's reconversion to Protestantism in 1670, where I emphasized its existential dimension, in contrast to the more intellectual dimension that had led him to embrace Catholicism a year and a half earlier.[4] I consider it equally pointless here to dwell on the consequences that followed and led him to relapse, to enter a period of exile, and then to live in hiding in Rouen, Paris, and Sedan. But even if we do not return in depth to all these details in Bayle's life, let us remind ourselves how costly this confessional choice was. Bayle never wanted to return, in spite of the opportunities presented to him when he left Sedan, and the many offers made to him by correspondence in the Paris milieu when he worked to have his brother freed.[5] Then, when his brother died, Bayle lost his last remaining family member. Therefore, if before his brother's death the only thing that had kept Bayle from leaving the Protestant confession was his family, he could afterwards have left his church quietly without any direct consequences for his family relations.

After establishing himself in Rotterdam, Bayle on various occasions showed his solidarity toward his fellow Protestants. One could point to the sarcasm launched against Catholic superstitions in the *Pensées diverses sur la comète,* the polemically charged questions of the *Critique générale de l'Histoire du calvinisme de M. Maimbourg,* and the remarks directed toward the moderate Catholics in the *Nouvelles de la République des Lettres.* In 1685, Bayle launches sharp attacks in the *Nouvelles lettres critiques* against Louis XIV's politics aimed at the eradication of the "Religion prétendue réformée." In 1686, he shows his indignation in the pamphlet *Ce que c'est que la France toute catholique,* which can hardly contain the rage and the pain he felt at the ravages caused by the Revocation.[6] Finally, the *Commentaire philosophique* shows a rationalist tendency, though it is also based on values that Bayle considers to be clearly evangelical. As such, his plea for the rights of the erring conscience can be taken as a desperate attempt to try and undo that fatal knot that invariably ties intolerance and defense of religious truth in each and every religious group.

Jacob Bayle, pastor and Pierre's oldest brother, died in the persecutions under Louis XIV. Bayle never forgets that. Even in the heat of the "cabale de Rotterdam," he brings up the painful memory again and connects it to his own confessional identity. Though one should be careful in interpreting the following passage because of its rhetoric of persuasion and its polemical context, and though we very rarely find such a direct outpouring of feelings in Bayle's writings, it is telling of the state of mind in which he lays claim to, and appropriates for himself, his confessional identity:

> If there was anything else but my attachment to the religion that I took in with the milk, as the son of and brother to ministers, both the most zealous ministers one could find in France, and of whom the latter died in the Château-Trompette where he had been shut up for his Religion, crowning the piety which he had shown throughout his entire life with a most noble death that was admired even by those who had done everything in their power to make him die a papist, and by the attacks over which he triumphed gloriously; if, I say, there was anything else that keeps me here, according to the new hypothesis of M. J. it would be the desire to serve my first divinity, Louis XIV.[7]

That Bayle speaks of his Protestantism as if by procuration should not be misinterpreted. As soon as the sincerity of his confessional adherence is questioned, it seems normal to him to seek some form of legitimacy in his family background. He probably brandishes the

Huguenot banner in this manner because his efforts to liberate his brother Jacob galled Jurieu, who in his *Examen d'un libelle* accused Bayle of being a loyal servant of the Sun King. Bayle sums up the theologian's allegations as follows: "In order to procure the freedom of a brother who was very dear to me, I would have sacrificed my religion, had it not been more dear to me than anything else."[8]

That there is an aspect of social conformism in Bayle's adherence to Protestantism cannot be questioned. This is indeed true for the education he received, and the way he speaks of the religion that he "took in with the milk" shows that he does not consider himself exempt from parental influence under the pretext of being a philosopher. He allows that the "préjugés de l'enfance" apply to him as much as anyone else. This sociological dimension is also clear when we consider Bayle's social leaning and inclinations after becoming Protestant once again. The Huguenot Refuge and, more precisely, the Walloon Church in Rotterdam, formed all at once a national (French), linguistic (francophone), and confessional (Huguenot) context.[9] Bayle's social habits in this period are also fully in line with those of other times. They correspond to his homebound psychology, in that where he lived he was closely surrounded by friends (of the same confession), printer/bookstore, church, and school.[10] For this reason, it is also hardly surprising that Bayle turned down the offer to teach at the Academy of Franeker in 1684. The position would certainly have been more prestigious than the one at the school in Rotterdam, but going to Friesland also meant losing all the benefits of the homogenous culture in Rotterdam. The small French, francophone, and Huguenot colony made exile somewhat easier to bear. To distinguish these three elements as such would be anachronistic. Or, more precisely, it would prevent one from seeing the rift that tore through the heart of this colony after the Revocation and the Glorious Revolution, exactly because with them patriotism and confessional adherence came into conflict. This aspect of Bayle's social context in Rotterdam also largely explains why Bayle battled and fought so fiercely during the affair of the *Avis des réfugiés,* as well as later during the months that led up to his destitution in 1693. It was not only his honor that would suffer in being driven from Rotterdam; Bayle would also lose his friends. We here also find a key to explain the violent attacks he launched in the second part of his life. Earlier Bayle had denounced the deviations of Catholicism in France, but gradually he turned his attention to the deviations found in his own confessional "camp" and attacked them with renewed ardor. But to take these attacks as an expression of hostility toward Protestantism, and perhaps even of an anti-Protestantism, would be to forget one of Bayle's most common moral imperatives, namely, to sweep one's own front porch first.[11]

One cannot but notice the respect Bayle shows—even if it may have been with a certain secret irony—toward the consistory before which he was summoned to appear in connection with two "affairs" in which he was implicated,[12] not allowing himself to utter any provocation and rather showing all cooperation. Yet at the same time, we see that he never backs down from what seems important to him. Far from being constrained to resort to trickery to elude censure or threats, Bayle in both "affairs" comes across very strong, and it can hardly be doubted that he knew he had the support of a part of the *compagnie* against Jurieu.

But what about Protestantism as a *historical* reality and a *political* factor? Here we again cannot let ourselves get caught up in all the necessary nuances on the way Bayle views it. I will limit myself to noting that this issue has already been the subject of a number of studies.[13] However, we do need to remind ourselves that the term *Protestantism,* though convenient, must be used carefully.[14] After all, to what does it refer? To the Reformation of the sixteenth century? Adherence to the Canons of Dordt and the more narrow Consensus Helveticus? A polemical mind-set (antipapist),[15] or the attachment to rediscovered values (especially the Bible)? A developing synthesis between orthodoxy and rationalist tendencies, which at that time took shape in a "rational orthodoxy" in Switzerland,[16] and which throughout the course of the eighteenth century developed into a number of attempts at reconciliation that were more or less deist? There is thus a great chasm between the intuitions of the Reformers and the institutional forms they took on during the period of "confessionalization" that no historian can cross without sizing up the leap he is about to make. As we will see, Bayle designates the doctrinal heritage to which he holds as

"Calvinism of the old rock," but we cannot overlook the mutations
that had taken place, or the rhetorical value of the broad term he uses
there. Above all, it is not only this difficult doctrinal and institutional
aspect that holds Bayle's attention. His approach as historian, and
his reflection as philosopher, superimpose themselves on it and even
build on it. He thus applies his formidable knowledge of history, and
his cutting analysis of the politico-religious phenomena, to the confessional party to which he himself belongs. He knows that whatever
side of the religious divide they may be on, the clergy will not speak
or act the same way when they are in power as when they are in the
minority. Bayle had argued this a long time ago already in connection
with the birth and early expansion of Christianity, and afterward repeated it several times, especially in his *Commentaire philosophique*. The
truth of this observation was confirmed to Bayle throughout his life,
and he personally suffered its consequences. For within his own camp
he saw how those who had been Protestantism's prudent and cautious
defenders and spokesmen in France showed a remarkable tendency
to become inquisitors and downright terrors once they came to the
United Provinces of Holland. Bayle clearly wrote his *Réponse d'un con-
verti à la lettre d'un réfugié,* and most likely the *Avis aus réfugiés* as well,
from a minority position.[17] But to make sense of the sharp criticism he
directs in these works against his fellow Protestant compatriots there
is no need to interpret it as "anti-Protestant" on the doctrinal level. It
is instead brotherly admonition with a political aim, where the phrase
Qui bene amat bene castigat applies. One need only mention the firmly loy-
alist opinions Paets expressed in his *De nuperis angliae motibus epistola,* to
which Bayle fully adhered,[18] his review of Elie Merlat's *Traité du pouvoir
absolu des souverains* in the *Nouvelles de la République des Lettres*[19]—two texts
that were published in the year of the Revocation—to note that he saw
the temptations offered by the House of Orange and millenarianism as
posing a mortal threat to the French Protestants.[20] It is impossible to
overestimate the impact of the image Catholic propaganda had drawn
of the French Protestants in linking their heresy (religion) with the
threat of rebellion (politics). Bayle's efforts in the *Critique générale* show
that he was afraid of this link and sought to undo it at all costs. His loy-
alty to Louis XIV and his calls to obedience—seeing resistance possible only in a nonviolent form—agree with his Christian ideals, in-

spired by the ideal of an evangelical compassion, and with his Protestant convictions on the need to differentiate carefully between political and ecclesiastical power. The combination of moral, political, *and religious* factors explains his desperate efforts to remind his people of one constant (at least, theoretically) of his confessional heritage — and, at the same time, his efforts to discredit the apocalyptic speculations. Developments on the international scene, and the deterioration of his relationship with Jurieu, led Bayle to become more and more vehement on this issue, but one should not forget that the attack on millenarianism was explicit already in the *Pensées diverses*. Noting the prophecies of the Protestant pastor Drabicius, Bayle took care to distance his confessional camp from them:

> The Protestants themselves are not all that persuaded that Drabicius was a prophet. Many are convinced that he was a fanatic whose imagination simply ran wild on reading commentaries on the Old Testament prophecies, as well as those of the Apocalypse; that, filled with such ideas, he saw the emperors of Germany as Pharaos, Sennacheribs, Nebuchadnezzars and emissaries of the Great Whore, *drunk on the wine of the wrath of her adultery;* and that he finally persuaded himself that God destined him to command a number of princes to kill these persecutors. The people who had suffered under these persecutions, and who were convinced that divine providence would sooner or later punish those who had inflicted such monstrosities, apparently had to give themselves over to Drabicius' visions. Yet the greatest part of the Protestants have largely ignored him, especially after it became clear that he was deluded and that he plainly contradicted himself so often that it would be impossible to excuse him except by resorting to innumerable glosses, which would be even more laughable than the simple admission of his errors; for if these kinds of glosses are going to be multiplied as needed, there would never be any false prophet one could not defend.[21]

As philosopher and as historian, Bayle thinks he needs to denounce such wild ideas. What he writes here about Drabicius with a touch of humor he will repeat later with a much greater polemical thrust when Jurieu blows his prophetic trumpet. And Bayle cares little what confessional party those who proclaim such foolishness belong to: "I claim to have a legitimate call to oppose the progress of superstitions, visions and popular gullibility. Who better than one of my own confession to claim this right to guard the breach against such waves of disorder?"[22]

After having treated Bayle as "complicated Protestant" from a biographical angle, and then from the perspective of history and politics, we need to turn to *theology* and *morality*. A summary of what is at stake in the debate, and later the conflict, is certainly not out of place. Calvinist orthodoxy claimed to explain providence and grace in a way that agreed most closely with the idea of a sovereignly perfect Being—that is, without the smallest concession to human freedom. A passage from the *Nouvelles de la République des Lettres* gives a good summary of all that is involved in this complicated issue. In the article devoted to the *Jugement sur les méthodes rigides et relâchées d'expliquer la providence et la grâce,* where Pierre Jurieu examines and compares various competing theological systems, Bayle writes the following:

> Having established this condition [i.e., conformity to the idea of the sovereignly perfect Being], Mr. Jurieu looks for it in vain in all other systems. For he finds that neither the approach of the Socinians, nor the indifferent *concursus* of the Scotists, nor the middle knowledge of the Molinists, nor the general laws of Father Malebranche, nor the hypothesis of the Remonstrants, nor that of Mr. Pajon, nor the grace of the universalists, satisfy the two criteria he was seeking: first, that the idea of the sovereignly perfect Being pass unscathed; second, that these systems resolve all the difficulties that trouble that idea in the doctrine of St. Augustine. And since he finds no one who satisfies his condition, he stays where he is. For it is a principle of both good sense and natural light that, *unless you gain something by changing, you should stay right where you are.* In the physical domain, it is an inviolable law of nature that bodies never change in state unless the reasons for changing are greater than those for not changing. The same should be true in the spiritual domain, so that if it is not by mere chance or coincidence that

we belong to a particular sect, we should live and die in that same place if the others are no better.[23]

Bayle's comment, which dates from the time when the dispute between Jurieu and him had not yet broken out, is doubly significant, for as journalist, Bayle here provides a key to understanding the Calvinist doctrine, its "particularism" rooted in double predestination. It certainly does not resolve all the problems or smooth out all the difficulties, but Bayle thinks that there are just as many objections to the other systems. We can therefore speak of a kind of *reasonable* (i.e., more moderate than *rational*) adherence to this doctrine. It is no worse than the others, and on the point of the "idea of the sovereignly perfect Being," the Calvinist doctrine even has some advantages over the others. One could object that this reasonable adherence applies only to Jurieu and not to Bayle himself. This would seem to be all the more true considering that this article on the *Jugement* dates from only several months after the decision of the Walloon synod to tighten the bounds of orthodoxy for the pastors of the Refuge[24] and that Bayle shortly thereafter strongly expressed his disapproval of that decision in the short preface he wrote to a work by Isaac Papin.[25] However, in the passage that follows the citation above, Bayle himself appeals to a sort of status quo ethic that flows into the doctrinal domain when he argues that one should not change unless there are valid motives for change. The phrase "if it is not by mere chance or coincidence that we belong to a particular sect" should make us immediately think of Bayle's bold proposal in the *Supplément du Commentaire philosophique,* when he amuses himself in considering the uncertain fate of the children of Jewish, Muslim, or Christian parents, and, within this last group, of the orthodox and heterodox.[26] But this phrase especially clarifies the later passages where Bayle identifies himself as a "Calvinist of the old rock." It is not that he believes the doctrinal position of his confessional group to be absolutely superior or that he adheres to it unconditionally. He only thinks that the others are hardly better, and he decides to assume what he considers to be part of his confessional identity.

The same can be found in Bayle's *Dictionnaire,* where he also emphasizes that none of the doctrinal systems solve all the problems. By this time the conflict with Jurieu had broken out, so Bayle exposes all the difficulties: "So that this professor, finding nothing better elsewhere, stays with St. Augustine's hypothesis which is the same as that of Luther and Calvin, and that of the Thomists and Jansenists; he stays there, I say, *troubled by* the astonishing *difficulties* which he has revealed, and *buckled over under these weights*."[27] The citations Bayle takes directly from his opponent are therefore also intended to show that it is not he himself who, as if just to kill some time, invented or even merely collected these difficulties. As a philosopher, it is his duty to show the rational dead ends in which theologians find themselves. And he does this with a clear conscience, convinced that he is not raising any new objections but simply listing those that have been raised before by the theologians themselves.

Throughout his life, Bayle reminded his readers that doctrinal orthodoxy does not guarantee good morals, although morals do in a way still validate the authenticity of one's faith. The primacy of this ethical principle reinforced his view on confessional status quo that he had advanced already at the beginning of his career in the Netherlands. In the end, he argued, one should not decide the value or credibility of a religious idea on the level of doctrine. The issue deserves attention because precisely it is what triggered Bayle to reflect on the virtuous atheists. For does it mean that, since Bayle conceived of his own relationship to Protestantism above all in moral terms, he had to lay out the entire question again and abandon the purely metaphysical questions in favor of the moral one? I do not think so, since as a philosopher and metaphysician—and even as moralist—he still tended to engage the doctrinally dense theology of Protestantism (or more generally, Christianity).

I pass over the *Dictionnaire,* since it has already been given much attention in the Paris conference.[28] Instead, I would like to consider more closely such later expressions as "Calvinist of the old rock," or "theologians of the trunk of the tree," which Bayle uses to identify his confessional partisans.[29] In a Straussian reading, they are like sleeping pills intended to put orthodoxy's censors to sleep. But this is a poor solution and does nothing but exasperate his interlocutors. According to the fideist interpretation, it is a reference to such slogans as *o altitudo*

divitiarum sapientiae et scientiae Dei! quam incomprehensibilia sunt (Rom.
11:33) and becomes part of a rhetoric that aims at "humbling reason"
when confronted with the impenetrable mysteries of the faith.[30] However, there is still that question: Why allow reason to have its say if it
is only to make it keep quiet?[31]

That there is an irreducible tension between faith and reason is
undeniable; Bayle does not cease to oppose those "rationalist" authors who claim that the two can be reconciled. But since, for Bayle,
faith and reason do not operate on the same level, we cannot speak of
contradictions in him when he favors first one, then the other. This
observation also illustrates that the hermeneutical dead end in which
Bayle studies find themselves in fact results from an unsatisfactory
way of posing the question. The exclusively rationalist and fideist readings must be placed back to back as soon as they claim to hold the
one key to unraveling Bayle's thought. For a reading of Bayle to be satisfactory, it should be able to account for a cognitive framework that
maintains at one and the same time (1) that reason can show this or
that article of faith to be invalid and (2) that reason will never be able
to take account of certain affirmations to whose logic it has no access.
It is precisely here that the *complexity* of Bayle's relationship to Protestantism must prevail. When it comes to theology, Bayle time and again
notes the relative and ever-unsatisfactory character of doctrinal formulations when they are tested according to reason; yet one maintains
this or that position for lack of a better one. When it comes to the believers, Bayle insists that the doctrine they hold (only rarely after an actual examination, and most often simply by having received it through
their education) imposes itself on them and then becomes part of their
confessional identity. Even if they do not want to, they can believe
only from within the conceptual context they were taught. Bayle, having himself gone through changes in confession and so having reflected on the mechanics of faith, is too sharp to suppose that he
himself is not subject to this human law. Rather, he assumes what his
education and personal choices have made of him and knows he cannot change that.

Bayle approaches these topics also as metaphysician: the debates
with theologians are in the form of an interdisciplinary dialogue. He

does not pretend to impose a particular philosophical perspective on them, but he does challenge them insofar as they tend toward a form of dogmatic rationalism. At the beginning of his *Commentaire philosophique,* Bayle had identified the hegemony of reason in theology—and ridiculed it. The later emergence of a rationalist current did nothing but confirm this intuition. The theologians who attack him cannot admit that Bayle may doubt that faith and reason can be combined, because their whole apologetic edifice is based on that foundation. In contrast, "Calvinism of the old rock," at the risk of appearing out of date, calmly affirms the impossibility of combining faith and reason. Against Jacques Bernard, Bayle mentions a number of Calvinist theologians before he points him to the Confession of Faith of the French churches: "However great man's ability to distinguish good and evil may be, we nevertheless say that whatever light there is in him turns to darkness when it comes to the search for God, *such is his absolute inability to approach him by his intelligence and reason.*"[32]

Bayle thinks and works within the context of a Calvinist paradigm—as noted above, one that insists more than any other on the absolute sovereignty of God. However, we could point out that a number of the objections he raises would not have the same weight in a Lutheran paradigm. We can go further: Bayle is one of the first to be acutely aware of the metaphysical impasse into which Calvinism gradually enclosed itself between the end of the sixteenth century and the beginning of the seventeenth (with the Synod of Dordt) and to realize that this impasse is in fact the impasse of Christianity as a whole. Even if he can hardly break with the paradigm in which he is confronted with problems, he sees clearly that it is the paradigm itself that is problematic: a good and omnipotent God (the a priori necessity) and the existence of evil and misery (the a posteriori reality) are irreconcilable in reason, but in faith they coexist. When the rationalists, who have no room for anything that might even have the semblance of being contradictory, claim to have found the solution, they are ridiculed by Bayle, who can, with full integrity, hold to a traditional, but solid, position.

The contrast between philosophy and Gospel, illustrated dramatically in the *Éclaircissement sur les manichéens,* emphasizes the incommensurability of faith and reason. However, this contrast does not need to be made so extreme as to nudge Christian faith into irrationality. In the *Nouvelles de la République des Lettres,* Bayle explains that "it is not easy to find the right middle-point, and nevertheless one must avoid the two opposite extremes. If reason is excluded entirely from the examination of theological positions, one falls into inexplicable difficulties. If one submits all the mysteries that God has revealed to us to the examination of reason, one runs the risk of explaining things in a way other than God would have us do."[33] The same idea can be found in a passage Bayle wrote twenty years later, in the *Entretiens de Maxime et de Thémiste:*

> A famous Protestant theologian [Amyraut] once said that if the majority of the people in the Roman church *made even the smallest efforts to look into and examine their conscience for the reasons that make them hold so strongly to transsubstantiation, they would have to confess that the main reason is the prejudice they have had since their childhood: that to be a good Christian, one must abandon one's intelligence on this point and on a number of others.* But here we find an equivocation that is only too often found in writings of this nature, where what is true in one case is applied indiscriminately to the whole; there have surely been an infinity of theologians who maintained that to be a good Christian, one must submit several maxims of reason to the authority of God; but they have never said that one must submit even this maxim to reason, namely, that *God is to be believed more than men,* and that we must *abandon our intelligence* to the extent that we do not even hold to that which makes us decide nothing is more reasonable than to follow the voice of God as opposed to a number of philosophical maxims.[34]

Many Bayle scholars are quite happy to speak of dissimulation in his rhetorical strategies and of contradictions in his thought. I do not find this convincing and instead suggest that what appears incomprehensible or contradictory should incite one to reflect on the epistemological context in which Bayle works. I do not mean to pretend that he never contradicts himself, but recourse to contradiction as the hermeneutical key still seems the lazy way out. By superimposing several levels of resonance on the question of Protestantism, I have intended to show that if it is difficult to make a coherent whole of Bayle's approach, it is precisely because not everything that Bayle writes should be placed on the same level. Bayle, who is not a system builder but a reactionary writer, is always attentive to logic and to the demands of the discipline which he practices. This observation allows us, for example, to interpret the famous passage from the *Dictionnaire* on the way of examination:

> It is to be feared that a third party will rise up and teach that people are not led to the true religion by way of authority or examination, but some by education, and others by grace. Education without grace and without examination persuades simply. Grace with education, and sometimes without education and without examination, persuades savingly. *Gratia Dei sum quod sum,* each orthodox person ought to say: by the grace of God I am who I am. I am orthodox *by grace, not of myself, it is the gift of God, not by my own works,* by study, by discussion, *so that no one may glory in himself* (16). Whether examination is easy or at least possible, whether it is difficult or even impossible, one thing is sure: no one uses it (17). Most people do not even know how to read; among those who can read, most never read the works of their opponents; they do not know the reasons of the other party except from the fragments they find of them in the writings of their own authors. These fragments represent the claims of the opposing party only imperfectly and very feebly. To be able to see the strength of their objections, one must consider them within the context of their own system, connected to their general principles, their consequences and dependents. It therefore falls far short of an actual examination of an opponent's viewpoints, and is instead a simple comparison of the response of our authors with the objections they themselves report; it is like evaluating the capacities of a gear only by testing what it can do when detached from its machine. That can only improperly be called an "examination." . . . The first thing one would have to do to make a good examination, is to doubt one's own religion: but we fear that it may offend God if we were to form even the smallest

doubts about it; we consider this doubt a dangerous suggestion originating from the Devil himself: and so we never put ourselves in that state in which St. Augustine said that we should put ourselves if we really want to distinguish carefully between orthodoxy and heterodoxy. According to him, we have to distance ourselves from that which we already consider to be the truth.

(16) Cf. the Letter to the Ephesians, chap. II, verses 8 and 9.

(17) Note that this is the argument not of the present author, but of that third party one could fear. This should be noted in several other instances as well.[35]

When Bayle imagines what a third party could teach—"that people are not led to the true religion by way of authority or examination, but some by education, and others by grace"—he does not at all question its defense of the liberty of the conscience as founded on the *possibility* of the *liberty* of examination. The principle of the rights of the erring conscience was valid in the moral sphere and ideally suited to the sociopolitical as well.[36] But when Bayle ridicules the "grotesque" distinction Jurieu drew between the examination of attention and the examination of discussion, when he emphasizes that people appear to be incapable of a proper examination, he reasons as a historian and philosopher.[37] And he reacts all the more strongly, even violently, when this thesis threatens the values he holds and is promoted by one of his own confessional partisans. To base Bayle's supposed "anti-Protestantism," or even "atheism," on the criticism he directs against the Protestants would be to misunderstand completely the principles of conflict—namely, that one is more inclined to attack one's own neighbor, the "enemy brother," than one further removed—as well as Protestantism's propensity to self-criticism. Ethical appropriation, which leads Bayle to explore one path that was to become characteristic of the Protestant position (because it is the persecuted position), is one thing; reflection on the mechanism of faith and conviction, mechanisms from which no one is exempt and that already occupied Bayle's attention in the *Pensées diverses,* is another.[38] In the latter he is doubtlessly led to assimilate belief, faith, and superstition and to consider these phenomena within the context of a methodological atheism. This flexibility leads Bayle to develop within the ethical sphere a "Protestant" intuition so that it corresponds to a precise politico-religious conjunction, accompanied by the general rise of individualism. However, it also leads him to doubt the human capacity to conduct a real examination (and then to act according to the conclusions reached by that process of examination). On this point, Bayle aligns himself with the dark pessimism inherited from Augustine and fiercely defended in a Luthero-Calvinist anthropology. Convinced that people do not adhere to certain ideas or values because of an examination or reasoning they actively carry out but rather because of the education they have received, he cannot conceive of grace as anything but a suspension of the laws of nature.

We finish with a final word on "Protestantism." The currents of thought and confession designated by this term underwent considerable changes in Bayle's time. To the upheavals caused by the Revocation of the Edict of Nantes, and the overturning of the alliance through the Glorious Revolution, we can add the theological crises—notably the one caused by the rise of rationalism and its effects on apologetical issues, as well as the one resulting from the application of historical criticism to the biblical text that overturned the classical order of Scripture as "judge of the controversies" and highlighted the problems in the way of examination. Ernst Troeltsch spoke in this respect of a passage from a paleo-Protestantism to a neo-Protestantism. Bayle is certainly an actor in some of these changes but is in others only a tormented spectator. On the one hand he asks—also himself—questions on several levels; on the other hand, the terms we use to characterize his tendencies are in the process of evolving precisely at this time. This combination of factors explains why a study of Bayle's position is so complex but also so exciting.

Notes

This essay, originally published in French, has here been translated into English by Albert Gootjes. The original piece, "Pierre Bayle, un 'protestant compliqué,'" first appeared in *Pierre Bayle (1647–1706), le philosophe de Rotterdam: Philosophy, Religion and Reception, Selected Papers of the Tercentenary Conference Held at Rotterdam, 7–8 December 2006,* ed. Wiep van Bunge and Hans Bots (Leiden: Brill, 2008), 83–101.

For the purposes of this volume, the editors found it unnecessary to include the opening paragraph of the original essay. This translation is published with permission from Brill.

1. See Roger Zuber, "Bayle protestant français," and Ruth Whelan, "*De Democritus et Heraclitus*: Pierre Bayle et le rire," both in *Les "Éclaircissements" de Pierre Bayle*, ed. Hubert Bost and Antony McKenna (Paris: Honoré Champion, 2010), 235–40 and 459–70, respectively.

2. See Anna Minerbi Belgrado, "Bayle, Jurieu et la théodicée," in Bost and McKenna, *"Éclaircissements" de Pierre Bayle*, 173–92.

3. Elisabeth Labrousse, "Mais qui donc était monsieur Bayle?," in *Pierre Bayle, enfant de l'Ariège, citoyen du monde* (Le Carla-Bayle: Office de Tourisme du Carla-Bayle, 1996), 11: "protestant par choix."

4. Hubert Bost, *Pierre Bayle* (Paris: Fayard, 2006), 39–51.

5. Before leaving Sedan, the Count of Guiscard, governor of Sedan, sought to convert Bayle to Catholicism. As Bayle writes: "[Il] me fit entendre en deux mots qu'il ne tiendrait qu'à moi de faire fortune, et qu'il était temps que j'y songeasse." *La cabale chimérique* 2.10, in *Œuvres diverses de Pierre Bayle, contenant tout ce que cet auteur a publié sur des matières de théologie, de philosophie, de critique, d'histoire, & de littérature, excepté son dictionnaire historique et critique*, 4 vols. (La Haye: P. Husson, 1727–31), hereafter cited as *OD*, 2:674. See Bost, *Pierre Bayle*, 153. On the Paris offers, see Bost, *Pierre Bayle*, 283.

6. See Roger Zuber, "L'écriture comique de *La France toute catholique*," in *La Révocation de l'édit de Nantes et les Provinces Unies*, eds. Hans Bots and G. H. M. Posthumus Meyjes (Amsterdam: Holland University Press, 1986); Hubert Bost, *Un "intellectuel" avant la lettre: Le journaliste Pierre Bayle (1647–1706)* (Amsterdam: APA-Holland University Press, 1994); Hubert Bost, "L'écriture ironique et critique d'un contre-révocationnaire," in *Bayle historien, critique et moraliste* (Turnhout: Brepols, 2006), 189–200.

7. Bayle, *Cabale chimérique* 11, in *OD*, 2:677: "Si quelque autre chose que mon attachement à la religion que j'ai sucée avec le lait, fils et frère de ministres, tous deux des plus zélés qu'il y eut en France, et dont le dernier est mort dans le Château-Trompette où il avait été enfermé pour la Religion, couronnant la piété qu'il avait témoignée toute sa vie par une très belle mort, qui fut admirée de ceux mêmes qui avaient fait tout ce qu'ils avaient pu pour le faire mourir papiste, et des attaques desquels il triompha glorieusement; si, dis-je, quelque autre chose me retenait ici ce serait, selon la nouvelle hypothèse de M. J., le désir de rendre service à ma première divinité Louis XIV."

8. Bayle, *Cabale chimérique* 11, in *OD*, 2:677 n.: "Pour procurer la liberté à un frère qui m'était fort cher, j'aurais sacrifié ma religion si elle ne m'eût été plus chère que toute autre chose."

9. See further Myriam Yardeni, "Langue française et identité 'réfugiée':
Jean Rou et Pierre Bayle," in *Langues et identités culturelles dans l'Europe des XVIe et
XVIIe siècles,* ed. M. S. Ortola and M. Roig Miranda (Nancy: Groupe XVIe et
XVIIe Siècles en Europe, Université Nancy, 2006), 73–84.

10. Erich Haase, *Einführung in die Literatur des Refuge: Der Beitrag der französischen Protestanten zur Entwicklung analytischer Denkformen am Ende des 17. Jahrhunderts* (Berlin: Duncker and Humblot, 1959); Elisabeth Labrousse, *Pierre Bayle,*
vol. 1, *Du Pays de Foix à la cité d'Érasme,* 2nd ed. (Dordrecht: M. Nijhoff, 1985);
Gerald Cerny, *Theology, Politics and Letters at the Crossroads of European Civilisation:
Jacques Basnage and the Baylean Huguenot Refugees in the Dutch Republic* (Dordrecht:
Springer, 1987).

11. Or else the biblical image: to take the plank out of one's own eye before taking the speck of sawdust out of someone else's (cf. Matt. 7:1–5).

12. See Bost, *Pierre Bayle,* and *"L'affaire Bayle": La bataille entre Pierre Bayle et
Pierre Jurieu devant le consistoire de l'Église wallonne de Rotterdam,* ed. Hubert Bost, introd. Antony McKenna (Saint-Étienne: Institut Claude Longeon, 2006).

13. Ruth Whelan, "Images de la Réforme chez Pierre Bayle, ou l'histoire
d'une déception," *Revue de Théologie et de Philosophie* 4 (1990): 85–107; Anna Minerbi Belgrado, "Bayle et la Réforme," in *Pierre Bayle dans la République des Lettres:
Philosophie, religion, critique,* ed. Antony McKenna and Gianni Paganini (Paris:
Honoré Champion, 2004), 97–115; Hubert Bost, "Histoire et critique de l'histoire: La *Critique générale de l'histoire du calvinisme de M. Maimbourg,* 1682–1683"
and "L'histoire des églises réformées de France dans le *Dictionnaire,*" in *Bayle
historien,* 103–34 and 159–76 respectively.

14. See Hubert Bost, "Protestantisme: Une naissance sans faire-part,"
Études Théologiques et Religieuses 67 (1992): 359–73.

15. "L'aversion des religions persécutrices de celle que l'on professe . . . fait
bien souvent plus des trois-quarts de l'amour qu'on a pour sa religion": Pierre
Bayle, "Navarre (Jeanne d'Albret reine de)," in *Dictionnaire historique et critique.*

16. On this topic, see further the studies by Pierre Barthel, "La tolérance
dans le discours de l'orthodoxie 'raisonnée' au petit matin du XVIIIe siècle," in
Naissance et affirmation de l'idée de tolérance, ed. Michel Péronnet (Montpellier: Université Paul-Valéry, 1988), 255–314; "Du salut par la foi, mais non point sans
les œuvres! Notes concernant la naissance de l'orthodoxie 'raisonnée' réformée,
de langue française, au début du XVIIIe siècle," *Zwingliana* 17, no. 6 (1988):
497–512, and 18, no. 3 (1989): 120–42.

17. Pierre Bayle, *Avis aux réfugiés,* ed. Gianluca Mori (Paris: Honoré Champion, 2007).

18. Bayle translated this text into French and had it printed by Leers in October: *Lettre de monsieur H. V. P. à monsieur B*** sur les derniers troubles d'Angleterre, où
il est parlé de la tolérance de ceux qui ne suivent pas la religion dominante.* See Bost, *Pierre
Bayle,* 273–75. On Bayle's place in the Dutch political scene, see Bart Leeuwen-

burgh, "Pierre Bayle in Dutch Politics (1982–93)," in *Protestants, hérétiques, libertins,* Libertinage et philosophie au XVIIe siècle 8 (Saint-Étienne: Honoré Champion, 2004), 91–113, and the introduction by Antony McKenna to Bost, *"L'affaire Bayle."* On his political philosophy, see Hubert Bost, "Entre droit et religion: Obligation de conscience et obéissance civile," in *Bayle historien,* 217–28.

19. Pierre Bayle, *Nouvelles de la République des Lettres,* August 1685, art. 7, in *OD,* 1:352–54.

20. On Bayle's rejection of the prophets in his day, see Hubert Bost, "Les faux prophètes dans le *Dictionnaire*: Fanatiques ou imposteurs?," in *Bayle historien,* 17–27; J. C. Laursen, "L'anti-millénarisme de Bayle: La menace de ceux qui prétendent connaître l'avenir," in McKenna and Paganini, *Pierre Bayle,* 193–209.

21. Pierre Bayle, *Pensées diverses sur la comète,* § 256, in *OD,* 3:155–56: "Les protestants eux-mêmes ne sont pas trop persuadés que Drabicius ait été prophète. Il y en a bien qui se persuadent que c'était un fanatique à qui la lecture des commentaires sur les prophéties du Vieux Testament et sur celles de l'Apocalypse avait bouleversé l'imagination; qu'après s'être rempli de ces idées, il ne concevait les empereurs d'Allemagne que comme des Pharaons, des Sennacheribs, des Nabuchodonosors et des émissaires de la Grande Paillarde, *enivrés du vin de l'ire de sa paillardise*; et qu'il vint enfin jusqu'à se persuader que Dieu le destinait à faire commandement à plusieurs princes d'exterminer ces persécuteurs. Ceux qui avaient souffert ces persécutions et qui s'imaginaient que la providence divine châtierait tôt ou tard les auteurs d'une conduite si barbare devaient apparemment se fier aux visions de Drabicius. Néanmoins, ils en ont fait peu de compte pour la plupart, surtout après avoir éprouvé qu'il s'abusait et qu'il se contredisait assez souvent d'une manière toute visible, et qu'on ne peut excuser qu'en recourant à un grand nombre de gloses qui font plus rire les incrédules que l'aveu sincère que l'on ferait des erreurs de cet homme-là; car avec cette sorte de gloses multipliées selon le besoin, il n'y a point de faux prophète dont on ne puisse faire l'apologie."

22. Bayle, *Cabale chimérique* 2.13, in *OD,* 2:681: "Je prétends avoir une vocation légitime pour m'opposer aux progrès des superstitions, des visions et de la crédulité populaire. À qui appartient-il mieux qu'aux personnes de ma profession de se tenir àà la brèche contre les irruptions de ces désordres?"

23. Bayle's review of Pierre Jurieu's *Jugement sur les méthodes rigides et relâchées d'expliquer la providence et la grâce* (Rotterdam, 1686) is in *Nouvelles,* August 1686, art. 4, in *OD,* 1:620: "M. Jurieu ayant posé cette condition [la conformité à l'idée de l'Être souverainement parfait] la cherche en vain dans tous les autres systèmes, car il trouve que ni la méthode des sociniens, ni le concours indifférent des scotistes, ni la science moyenne des molinistes, ni les lois générales du Malebranche, ni l'hypothèse des remonstrants, ni celle de M. Pajon, ni la grâce des universalistes, ne satisfont pas aux deux choses qu'il demande; l'une, qu'on lui conserve saine et sauve l'idée de l'Être souverainement parfait; l'autre, qu'on lui lève

toutes les difficultés qui l'incommodent dans la doctrine de S. Augustin; c'est pourquoi, ne trouvant personne qui remplisse sa condition, il s'en tient là. C'est agir selon le bon sens et selon ce principe incontestable de la lumière naturelle, *qu'à moins de gagner au change, il ne faut point sortir d'où l'on est*. Parmi les corps, c'est une loi inviolable de la nature qu'ils ne changent jamais d'état si les raisons d'en changer ne sont plus fortes que celles de n'en changer point. Il en doit être de même pour les esprits, de sorte que, quand ce ne serait que le hasard ou le caprice qui nous aurait engagés dans une secte, il y faudrait vivre et mourir si les autres ne valaient pas mieux."

24. The text of the decision of the synod of the Walloon churches held at Rotterdam in April 1686 was edited in "Liste des pasteurs des églises réformées de France réfugiés en Hollande," *Bulletin de la Société de l'Histoire de Protestantisme Français* 7 (1858): 426–28.

25. Isaac Papin, *La foy réduite à ses véritables principes* (Rotterdam, 1687). For the text of Bayle's preface, see *OD,* 5/1:209–10.

26. Pierre Bayle, *Supplément du Commentaire philosophique* 15, in *OD,* 2:526. See Bost, *Pierre Bayle,* 306.

27. Pierre Bayle, "Pauliciens," rem. F, in *Dictionnaire historique et critique.* In a marginal note, Bayle refers to his article on "Nihusius," quotes Jurieu's work, and provides the page references (19, 20, 21, 22, 23). See also the long quotation from Jurieu in *Réponse aux questions d'un provincial* 2:135, in *OD,* 3:774–75. See Bost, *Pierre Bayle,* 648 n. 83.

28. See Bost and McKenna, *"Éclaircissements" de Pierre Bayle.*

29. "Calviniste de la vieille roche" and "théologiens du gros de l'arbre": Bayle, *Réponse* 2:130, in *OD,* 3:765.

30. See especially Bayle, "Pauliciens," rem. F; Bayle, *Réponse* 2.130, in *OD,* 3:764b.

31. I here reverse Leibniz's remark that the "dictionnaire merveilleux de M. Bayle, où la religion et la raison paraissent en combattantes, et où M. Bayle veut faire taire la raison après l'avoir fait trop parler; ce qu'il appelle le triomphe de la foi." Gottfried Leibniz, preface to *Essais de théodicée* (Paris: Garnier-Flammarion, 1969), 39.

32. Bayle, *Réponse* 3.14, in *OD,* 3:937a: "Combien qu'il y ait en l'homme quelque discrétion du bien et du mal, nonobstant nous disons que ce qu'il a de clarté se convertit en ténèbres quand il est question de chercher Dieu, *tellement qu'il n'en peut nullement approcher par son intelligence et raison*." Gallican Confession, art. 9. The italicized words are written in capitals in Bayle's text.

33. Bayle, *Nouvelles,* September 1684, art. 2 (in connection with Wiszowaty's *Religio rationalis*), in *OD,* 1:132: "il n'est pas aisé de trouver juste milieu, et cependant il faut éviter les deux extrémités opposées. Si la raison est entièrement exclue de l'examen des points de théologie, l'on tombe dans des difficultées inexpli-

cables. Si l'on soumet à l'examen de la raison tous les mystères que Dieu nous a révélés, l'on court risque de les expliquer autrement que Dieu ne veut."

34. Pierre Bayle, *Entretiens de Maxime et de Thémiste* 2.9, in *OD,* 4:49–50: "Un fameux théologien protestant [Amyraut] a dit que, si la plupart des peuples de l'Église romaine *avaient quelque peu de soin de rechercher et d'examiner en leurs consciences les raisons pour lesquelles ils retiennent si fermement la créance de la transsubstantiation, ils confesseraient franchement que la principale est ce préjugé dont leurs esprits sont préoccupés dès leur enfance: que pour être bon chrétien, en ce point comme en quelques autres, il faut entièrement renoncer à notre intelligence.* Il y a là une équivoque qui ne se fourre que trop souvent dans les discours de cette nature: on fait glisser le tout pour l'une des parties; il est sûr qu'une infinité de théologiens ont dit que pour être bon chrétien, il faut soumettre plusieurs maximes de la raison à l'autorité de Dieu; mais ils n'ont jamais dit qu'il faut même abandonner cette maxime de la raison, *Dieu est plus croyable que les hommes,* et *renoncer* tellement *à notre intelligence* que nous n'en conservions pas même certaine partie qui nous fait juger qu'il n'y a rien de plus raisonnable que de suivre la voix de Dieu préféérablement à quelques maximes philosophiques." For the questions passages such as this one pose for the issue of faith/reason, I refer to Bost and McKenna, *"Éclaircissements" de Pierre Bayle,* and, particularly, because of their novel character, to the contributions of Todd Ryan, "Évolution et cohérence du fidéisme baylien: le paradoxe du 'fidéisme raisonnable,'" and Kristen Irwin, "Le rejet de la position 'conciliatrice' dans les Éclaircissements de Bayle," 447–57 and 347–56, respectively.

35. Bayle, "Pellisson," rem. D, in *Dictionnaire historique et critique*: "Il est à craindre qu'il ne s'élève un tiers parti qui enseignera que les hommes ne sont conduits à la vraie religion ni par la voie de l'autorité, ni par la voie de l'examen, mais les uns par l'éducation, et les autres par la grâce. L'éducation sans la grâce et sans examen persuade simplement. La grâce avec l'éducation, et quelquefois sans l'éducation et sans examen, persuade salutairement. *Gratia Dei sum quod sum,* doit dire chaque orthodoxe, par la grâce de Dieu je suis ce que je suis. Je suis orthodoxe *par grâce, et cela non point de moi, c'est le don de Dieu, non point par mes œuvres,* par des recherches, par des discussions, *afin que nul ne se glorifie* (16). Que l'examen soit facile, ou du moins possible; qu'il soit malaisé, ou même impossible: une chose est très certaine, c'est que personne ne s'en sert (17). La plupart des gens ne savent point lire; parmi ceux qui savent lire, la plupart ne lisent jamais les ouvrages des adversaires; ils ne connaissent les raisons de l'autre parti que par les morceaux qu'ils en trouvent dans les écrits de leurs auteurs. Ces morceaux ne représentent qu'imparfaitement et très faiblement les droits du parti contraire. Pour connaître la force des objections, il faut les considérer dans leur système, liées avec leurs principes généraux et avec leurs conséquences et leurs dépendances. Ce n'est donc point examiner les sentiments de son adversaire que de comparer simplement la réponse de nos auteurs avec l'objection qu'ils

rapportent; c'est juger de la force d'une roue par les seuls effets qu'elle peut produire étant détachée de sa machine. On ne peut donner à cela le nom d'examen qu'abusivement. . . . La première chose qu'il faudrait faire, si l'on voulait bien examiner, serait de douter de sa religion: mais on croirait offenser Dieu si l'on formait là-dessus le moindre doute; on regarderait ce doute comme une funeste suggestion de l'esprit malin: ainsi l'on ne se met point dans l'état où saint Augustin remarque qu'il faut se mettre quand on veut bien discerner l'orthodoxie d'avec l'hétérodoxie. Il faut, selon lui, se dépouiller de la pensée que l'on tient déjà la vérité. . . .

(16) conférez l'Épître aux Éphésiens, cha II, vers. 8 et 9.

(17) Notez que c'est le discours non pas de l'auteur de ce livre, mais de ce tiers parti qu'on pourrait craindre. Il faut noter cela en plusieurs autres endroits."

36. We are here dealing with a discourse directed to the representatives of power, or to their ideologues. On the other hand, as the development of the affair concerning the *Avis aux réfugiés* would illustrate, Bayle can show himself to be extremely suspicious toward those agitators who manipulate public opinion and can from this perspective defend the idea of a monolithic state. To suggest that there is a contradiction between these two discourses would be to lose sight of the fact that they were directed to different audiences.

37. Pierre Bayle, "Nicolle," rem. C, and "Pellisson," rem. D, in *Dictionnaire historique et critique*.

38. See Bayle, *Pensées diverses* §§ 7, 47, 84, 100.

· *Chapter 8* ·

Leibniz and the Augustinian Tradition

NATHAN A. JACOBS

Although Gottfried Leibniz professes a commitment to historical Christian theism, both the depth and orthodoxy of his commitment have been questioned throughout the past three centuries. Accusations that Leibniz espouses a deistic God-world relationship begin just prior to Leibniz's death and continue through the eighteenth century.[1] In the nineteenth century these charges persist,[2] but they are peppered with suspicions that Leibniz may be a closet Spinozist.[3] By the early 1900s, the suspicion of Spinozism, once tangentially muttered, emerges as a full-blown interpretive theory that accuses Leibniz of privately holding to a virtual Spinozism while hiding behind a facade of theism in his public philosophy.[4] Though more charitable and nuanced readings of Leibniz have emerged since the twentieth century, the charges of deism and Spinozism remain to this day.[5]

Secular readings of Leibniz commonly find their footing on the issue of freedom. How one reads Leibniz on this issue often determines where one places him on the spectrum between Christian theism and Spinozism. Early deistic readings of Leibniz build on a determinist understanding of preestablished harmony. The combination of Leibniz's preferred analogy of synchronized clocks whose harmony requires neither intervention nor mechanical connection (G, 4:498) with his rejection of freedom of equipoise (e.g., C, 25; Grua, 1:384–86), which was the increasingly dominant understanding of libertarian choice in the period, was sufficient to convince most readers in the eighteenth century that Leibniz was a determinist who saw divine decree as monergistic and God-world interaction as impossible.[6] Charges of deism and inklings of Spinozism in the 1800s often built on these same assumptions but added to them a resuscitated belief in Pelagian moral indifference, which casts suspicion on the Augustinian concept of moral necessity. Leibniz's defense of the latter over against the former was thus seen by some as confirmation of the charges of the previous century and as hints of something even more serious.[7] The charge of Spinozism in the early 1900s built on the wealth of resources already used to charge Leibniz with necessitarianism but added to the case Leibniz's talk of possibles pressing themselves toward existence (see G, 7:303). Applying to God the type of necessitarianism already thought to be present in Leibniz's view of the world made the case that, while possibles must go through God to become actual, the fact that they naturally strain for existence makes this process less like voluntarist creation and more like a necessitarian emanation of compossibles that maximize being.[8]

The aim of this essay is to show that Leibniz's pre-1700 thought on free choice, divine decree, and providence sits comfortably within historical Christian orthodoxy and, by extension, that the foundation on which deist and Spinozist interpretations build is faulty. I will argue that Leibniz not only is aware of but embraces without reservation the Augustinian tradition, stretching from Augustine himself on up through the Medievals and into the Protestant scholastics of Leibniz's day.[9] Assuming my inklings are correct, the implications are significant, first, because such Augustinian affinities call into question the efforts to push Leibniz away from Christian theism toward deism or Spinozism, and, second, because, as we will see, the assumptions of the Augustinian tradition often contrast starkly with the assumptions of most Leibniz interpreters of the past three centuries.

Before starting down this road, however, we must address the question: *Do we have good reason to think Leibniz was familiar with, influenced by, and positively disposed toward the Augustinian tradition?* The evidence for an affirmative answer is manifold. Regarding Leibniz's familiarity with

Augustinianism, a mere survey of the names scattered throughout his works, along with the detailed discussions that accompany them, is enough to establish his familiarity with well-known, lesser-known, and completely obscure figures within the Augustinian tradition. Leibniz's corpus is filled with detailed notes on this tradition's theological figures and disputes (e.g., Grua, 1:76–80, 338–46, 347–59; 2:560–61; A, ser. 6, 4b:1680–90; G, 6:49–101), and he displays an unusual mastery of the tradition's history and scholastic minutiae (e.g., Grua, 1:150–55, 380–88; C, 25–27; A, ser. 6, 4c:2355–455).[10] Leibniz penned lengthy, systematic treatments on historical theology, including *Examen religionis Christianae* and *De praedestinatione et gratia dissertatio.* Moreover, unlike some philosophers in his day, such as Pierre Bayle, Leibniz weaves theology into his philosophy as an inextricable component of it.[11] As *Essais de théodicée* shows, Leibniz casts the problem of evil against a uniquely Christian backdrop of God's eternal decrees and the Creation-Fall-Redemption-Consummation story (G, 6:102–5); and he goes to great pains in his opening "Discours preliminaire sur la conformité de la Foy avec la Raison" to show the compatibility of faith and reason in the Christian tradition (G, 6:49–101), a compatibility he takes to be pivotal to his own project.

Though one could try to dismiss these theological forays as the mere by-product of Leibniz's prolific genius, the preeminent Leibniz scholar Leroy E. Loemker argues that one of the main influences on Leibniz's thought was the Herborn encyclopedists. This is significant because, as Loemker points out, "From its foundation in 1584 the old university at Herborn flourished as a center of Reformed theology and philosophy, in close relationship with schools with like convictions in England (particularly Cambridge) and the Protestant Netherlands."[12] Moreover, if we dig down, tracing the roots of this theological influence, we find that they go deep into the soil of Leibniz's early intellectual formation. Leibniz's father, Friedrich, was a professor of moral philosophy at the University of Leipzig. Following Friedrich's death, Leibniz gained access to his father's library, and from age eight onward he gave himself over to Latin classics, Hellenistic philosophy, Patristic works, and scholastic theology (both medieval and post-Reformation).[13] As E. J. Aiton notes, "Alongside the logical exercises performed in school, Leibniz pursued at home, in his father's library, the study of metaphysics, both scholastic and more recent, as well as theology, concentrating especially on the works of the famous Catholic and Protestant controversialists" (cf. P, 168).[14] The significance of the scholastic facet of Leibniz's early studies is testified to by the fact that, when Leibniz agreed to sell off the library to settle his schooling debts, he requested to keep only a handful of books, most of which were from authors of the Ramist tradition.[15] And, as Maria Rosa Antognazza shows, Leibniz's interest in these scholastic Reformed thinkers was no passing phase but was traceable to the earliest days of access to his father's library.[16] Unfortunately, as Loemker points out, Leibniz studies has yet to account fully for such influence.[17]

As for Leibniz's disposition toward the Augustinian tradition, the case for an affirmative embrace of its content will be made throughout the remainder of this essay in an exegetical fashion. However, one biographical consideration is worthy of note at the outset, namely, the personal and professional energy Leibniz devoted to uniting the Christian Church. As an adult, he devoted considerable thought and energy to Protestant-Catholic reunion, including meeting with figures such as Cristóbal de Rojas y Spinola, bishop of Tina, who had received papal permission to negotiate reunion with the princes of Germany. Leibniz was privy to the plan for Catholic-Protestant reunion drafted by Molanus, a plan about which Leibniz wrote with some success to French bishop Jacques Bossuet. Leibniz continued to play a role in Protestant-Catholic negotiations at the behest of Georg Ludwig after the apparent failure of these negotiations in 1691. And Leibniz's later efforts focused on a Protestant reunion of Lutheran and Reformed churches.[18]

Now, all of this could be dismissed as the by-product of Leibniz's public political life. However, such a dismissal ignores the fact that, while Leibniz conceded that theological sects could be reconciled by mere civil union and ecclesiastical tolerance—a strategy advocated by a number of Leibniz's contemporaries—it was Leibniz himself who was emphatic that *theological* reunion should be sought. Moreover, Leibniz not only advocated such reunion but sought to facilitate it himself through writings such as *De praedestinatione et gratia dissertatio*. This is noteworthy because a concern for theological, rather than civil or ec-clesiological, reunion is a peculiar ideal for a closet Spinozist or deist to advocate and personally facilitate. Thus, given the foregoing, we have good reason, when reading Leibniz, to keep an eye open for in-fluences from the theological tradition of which Leibniz professed to be a part, and to which he devoted great energy to reunite.

Now, we could approach Leibniz's writings in either of two ways—globally or locally. In this essay, I have chosen a local treat-ment, focusing on a single essay from 1686, "Vérités necessaries et contingentes."[19] The reasons are two. First, I grant that diverting a three-hundred-year-old stream of interpretation is a task too large for a single essay, especially considering the expansive size of Leibniz's corpus; thus I embrace the idea that this essay is only a modest first step toward recasting Leibniz in light of the Augustinian tradition. Second, as noted above, much of how Leibniz is placed on the spec-trum from Christian theism to Spinozism is rooted in how Leibniz is read on freedom, and "Vérités" has played a significant role in Leib-niz studies on this very topic. In 1902, Louis Couturat used the essay to argue for the Spinozist reading and successfully persuaded Ber-trand Russell of his case, so that Russell went on record admitting the falsehood of his published compatibilist-theist interpretation.[20] In 1992, R. Cranston Paull used "Vérités" to argue for a rare, if not sin-gularly unique, incompatibilist reading of Leibniz.[21] And in 1998, Jack Davidson argued, contra Paull, that "Vérités" demonstrates Leibniz's compatibilism, not incompatibilism.[22] Suffice it to say, the piece has been recognized by Leibniz scholars as singularly significant to how we understand Leibniz's early views on free choice and, by extension, his larger philosophy. Thus, in this piece, I will revisit "Vérités," offer-ing a careful exegetical treatment of it to demonstrate, contra deist and Spinozist readings, that Leibniz's early views are squarely in line with traditional Augustinian theology.

As for my interpretative assumptions, two are worth noting. The first assumption concerns determinism and its relationship (or lack thereof) to the Augustinian tradition. No doubt many readers will take an affinity for Augustinianism generally and Protestant Augustinianism in particular to lead Leibniz only deeper into the woods of determinism.

If this is how one understands the Augustinian tradition, the case made here is helpful, but the ramifications are less radical than if one understands the Augustinian tradition to be libertarian. For a compatibilist reader of this tradition, this essay will simply show that Leibniz is neither a Spinozist nor a deist but a compatibilist theist of like mind with Augustine. Suffice it to say, however, that I am of like mind with the growing number of interpreters who see compatibilist readings of the Augustinian tradition (Patristic, medieval, and post-Reformation) as a contemporary distortion that obscures the libertarian aim and intent of Augustinianism.[23] Moreover, I think good evidence exists to show that both proponents and opponents of the Augustinian tradition in Leibniz's own day recognized this fact—namely, that the Augustinian tradition harbors an incompatibilist commitment entirely contrary to determinism.[24] Hence, for someone such as myself, the ramifications of this essay are more radical. To wit: Leibniz is not only a traditional Augustinian theist but, as such, a libertarian theist in his early philosophy.

The second assumption worth noting concerns Leibniz's intellectual evolution. Leibniz scholars disagree over how many revolutions Leibniz's thought undergoes. All agree to the following: (a) Leibniz parts ways with Aristotle at an early age (G, 3:205, 1:371); (b) following his departure from Aristotle, Leibniz embraces the burgeoning atomism of his day (see G, 4:56–57); (c) Leibniz comes to doubt the adequacy of atomism by 1668, rejecting it outright between 1668 and 1669 (G, 4:108–9, 7:284–88); and (d) by 1671 Leibniz espouses a new metaphysic. The disputed aspects of Leibniz's intellectual development include, first, whether there is a transitional philosophy between 1668 and 1671.[25] Since we will be looking at post-1671 texts, I will forego this question. The second, more relevant question is whether Leibniz's views on free choice and providence change after 1700. Some suggest Leibniz is consistent, while others argue that Leibniz moves from soft determinism (pre-1700) to hard determinism (post-1700).[26] The answer to this question again affects the ramifications of our findings here, as well as the texts on which one draws when exegeting Leibniz. Regarding the former issue, if one holds that Leibniz's views change after 1700, all that this essay will establish is that Leibniz is a traditional Augustinian in his pre-1700 philosophy; the question of his post-1700 philosophy remains open. If, however, one sees consistency in Leibniz's writings, as I do, the implications of this essay are, again, more radical. As for the question of useful texts, though I advocate continuity in Leibniz's writings, I will here seek to limit (though not bar entirely) my use of post-1700 texts, given that the demonstration of continuity goes beyond the confines of this piece.

Divine Versus Human Knowledge of Necessary and Contingent Truths in "Vérités"

"Vérités" opens with Leibniz's peculiar contention that all truths are analytic. That is to say, "An affirmative truth is one whose predicate is in the subject"; and this is true, says Leibniz, whether the particular affirmative truth is necessary or contingent (C, 16; see also 518–23). Therefore, "if anyone were to understand perfectly each of the two notions [i.e., subject and predicate] just as God understands it, he would . . . perceive that the predicate is in the subject" (C, 17). This feature of Leibniz's philosophy has been a serious hurdle for those who would seek to deliver him from necessitarianism. But, as we will see, Leibniz's aim is to defend free contingencies, not deny them.

Despite their common analytic character, Leibniz sees a clear difference between necessary and contingent truths. Necessary truths, says Leibniz, are propositions grounded in the laws of identity and contradiction: "An *absolutely necessary* proposition is one which can be resolved into identical propositions, or *[sive]*, whose opposite implies contradiction" (C, 17).[27] His preferred example is numerical: *every duodenary* (a number divisible by twelve) *is a senary* (a number divisible by six) (C, 17; see also Careil, 183). This type of truth is necessary because, "by the analysis of terms of a proposition, and by substituting for the defined term a definition or part of a definition, one shows a certain equation or coincidence of predicate with subject in a reciprocal proposition, or in other cases at least the inclusion of the predicate in the subject, in such a way that what was latent in the proposition and . . . contained in it virtually is rendered evident and express by the demonstration" (Careil, 182). As (rather imperfect) shorthand, we will refer to such propositions as "demonstrable truths."

Contingent truths, by contrast, lack this demonstrable character. Take, for example, the contingent truth *Caesar crossed the Rubicon in 49 B.C.* According to Leibniz, the relationship between the predicate, *crossed the Rubicon in 49 B.C.,* and the subject, *Caesar,* is such that negating the predicate does not yield contradiction. The opposing proposition, *Caesar did not cross the Rubicon in 49 B.C.,* is possible, and the subject-predicate relationship is therefore contingent.

Now, even though the subject-predicate relationship of contingent truths is not necessary, Leibniz believes contingent truths are analytic. The reason is this. Leibniz defines an affirmative truth as "one whose predicate is in the subject" (C, 16). He maintains that *crossing the Rubicon in 49 B.C.* is part of God's concept of *Caesar* in eternity. Yet because neither Caesar nor the Rubicon nor our world is necessary, this concept does not entail existence. Hence God's concept of Caesar (along with the Rubicon and our world) must logically precede his decree to bring Caesar into existence (cf. C, 23–24), and it therefore follows that God grasps the subject-predicate relationship between *Caesar* and *crossing the Rubicon in 49 B.C.* apart from experience. In short, God understands this subject-predicate relationship to be an affirmative a priori truth (C, 16 and 19). And were we to perceive truth as God does, we too would see that the predicate is in the subject, even though it is in the subject contingently. It is thus Leibniz's theology (i.e., his understanding of divine knowledge and decree) that requires that even contingent truths be analytic.

How Leibniz vindicates this conviction is by a comparison of expressible ratios with surd ratios. Expressible ratios are demonstrable truths—they can be reduced to smaller ratios and given demonstration along lines similar to *Every duodenary is senary.* But surd ratios, such as $\sqrt{2}$, are irrational numbers—their decimal never ends and has no repeating pattern. As such, they cannot be reduced or given demonstration (cf. C, 17–18). This difference is significant because it mirrors the difference between the created mind and the divine mind with regard to contingent truths. In the case of surd ratios, we (creatures) discover these truths by calculation, and even then never fully. For $\sqrt{2}$,

when calculated, yields an infinite decimal. Yet God, "who comprehends the infinite at once," comprehends surd ratios fully, immediately,
and a priori (C, 17)—that is, without calculation. Leibniz is convinced
that the difference between our knowledge of surd ratios and God's
knowledge of surd ratios provides an apt illustration of the difference
between creaturely and divine understanding of contingent truths.

Leibniz's surd ratio analogy is meant to demonstrate that a truth
can be analytic, yet neither reducible nor demonstrable—that it may
be accessible to the created mind in only limited ways that are bound
by temporal deliberation, yet grasped fully, immediately and a priori by
the divine mind. Such is the case with surd ratios, and so it is with contingent truths.[28] While the creaturely mind comes to know contingent
truths a posteriori, the divine mind grasps contingent truths apart from
experience, and this a priori apprehension indicates that these affirmative truths are analytic, not synthetic. Nonetheless, the subject-predicate
relationship is such that it could be otherwise; thus Leibniz insists that
when contingent truths are grasped by the divine mind the subject-
predicate relationship is grasped without necessity. Or, as Leibniz puts
it in *Theodicée*: "In the region of the possibles they are represented as
they are, namely, as free contingencies" (G, 6:126).

Ironically, Leibniz's claim that *all affirmative truths are analytic* is often
a key feature of his thought taken to require necessitarianism.[29] But
Leibniz's own assessment is quite different. After offering his surd-ratio
comparison, he states: "And so I think that I have disentangled a secret which had me perplexed for a long time; for I did not understand
how a predicate could be in a subject, and yet the proposition would
not be a necessary one" (C, 18). Leibniz, unlike many of his interpreters, is confident that he has successfully countered necessitarianism.
And, when his comparison is properly understood, one can see why:
by numerical analogy Leibniz has supplied an example of an analytic
truth that is neither reducible nor demonstrable, yet is (presumably)
grasped by God a priori, while known to created minds in limited
ways only by calculation. He has therefore given analogical reason to
think it is possible for God to grasp future contingents a priori, even
though these truths cannot be reduced to the definition of the subject or be given demonstration or be grasped by the creaturely mind

in advance. His intent is not to show that contingent truths are in fact necessary truths but to show the opposite, namely, that although contingent truths are analytic (as per the doctrines of divine foreknowledge and decree), they retain their contingent character.

Now, as mentioned, Leibniz's theology is what pushes him toward the claim that all affirmative truths are analytic. For Leibniz could concede that an affirmative truth is one whose predicate is in the subject but deny that future contingents are affirmative truths, as did some ancient philosophers, such as Epicurus and Aristotle, and the Socinians of Leibniz's day (G, 6:211–12). Yet Leibniz's theological convictions are far more traditional, and Leibniz offers clues that these convictions are not only generically Christian but in fact Augustinian.

First, Leibniz's terminology is noteworthy. He sets up his discussion of affirmative truth against the backdrop of God's perfect knowledge of propositions. More precisely, he distinguishes God's grasp of true and affirmative propositions by simple intelligence *(simplicis intelligentiae),* as in the case of necessary truths such as mathematics and the essence of things, from divine vision *(visionis)* of a thing or middle conditions concerning its existence *(media circa existentias conditionatas)* (C, 17).[30] The distinction between *scientia simplicis intelligentiae* and *scientia visionis* is an explicitly Thomist one and became commonplace among a number of Protestant scholastics.[31] Whether this means that Leibniz is a Thomist is less clear and is an issue to which we will return later in this essay. For, as Richard A. Muller notes, "In the definitions and explanations of the seventeenth-century Reformed orthodoxy . . . the more Thomistic language of *scientia simplicis intelligentiae/ visionis* is often explained in a voluntaristic manner, yielding the more Scotist model under the Thomistic language."[32] But the fact that Leibniz uses traditional and indeed technical terminology from the Augustinian tradition when establishing his understanding of God's a priori knowledge is significant in its own right.

Second, Leibniz's claim that God has a concept of a given individual that includes his contingent actions logically (as opposed to temporally) prior to God decreeing the existence of that individual is not unique to Leibniz. Augustine himself sets the stage for this type of claim in his characterization of the subject-object relationship between

God and creatures in divine foreknowledge. He states, "It does not follow, then, that there is nothing in our will because God foreknew what was going to be in our will; for if he foreknew this, it was not nothing that he foreknew. Further, if, in foreknowing what would be in our will, he foreknew something, and not nonentity, it follows immediately that there is something in our will."[33] While one could read Augustine as suggesting that God simply foresees what is future, the fact that Augustine separates from foreknowledge the question of divine permission indicates that the *foreknowing* here identified does not entail the existence of the thing foreknown; it is a foreknowing (logically) prior to the decree of permitting.[34] This is in keeping with how the Reformed scholastics understood Augustine on this point, since their concept of predetermination and premotion presumes this as well. We find that Reformed scholastics speak as if God has a (logically) prior understanding of what is in the creature, such that when God predetermines and premoves the creature permissively, that movement harmonizes with the prior concept of the choice that is freely within the creature. To use Voetius's words, "The predetermination turns the will sweetly and nevertheless strongly to that very end, to which it—certainly being moved and premoved by God—would have turned itself."[35] Therefore, while Leibniz's characterization of contingent truths as analytic may seem novel, the premises that ground this characterization have clear theological precedent.

Third, it is noteworthy that, according to Leibniz, God has a priori knowledge of contingent truths because God has perfect knowledge of the subject in whom contingent predicates are found (C, 16). As is evident from the above quotes of Augustine and Voetius, it is common Augustinian fare to suggest that the object known in God's grasp of future contingents is the will of the agent. As Augustine puts it, "God foreknew what was going to be in our will," and again, "If, in foreknowing what would be in our will, he foreknew something . . . it follows immediately that there is something in our will."[36] Likewise, Voetius focuses not on how the individual would turn himself but on how the will would turn itself: "The predetermination turns the will . . . to that very end, to which it . . . would have turned itself."[37] The notion is an extension of Augustine's claim that voluntary causes *(causa voluntaria)* are the efficient cause of free action, and thus that the object known in God's foreknowledge of free choices is the will from which these choices proceed.[38] Augustine's claim would become standard among medieval and Protestant scholastics alike,[39] and a careful examination of Leibniz's talk of God's knowledge of the subject indicates that this is what sits in the background of his claim as well.

In his 1677 essay "Scientia media," Leibniz echoes the point made in "Vérités" that God's knowledge of future contingents is a priori, and argues that such knowledge consists in the knowledge of causes *(cognitione causae)*. As Leibniz continues, it becomes plain that by *causes* Leibniz means *voluntary causes,* given that he goes on to talk of God's knowledge of "the nature of the will of Paul" *(natura voluntatis Pauli),* for example. He then goes on to point out that the perfection of God's knowledge of voluntary or free causes is something understood by "all true philosophers and Augustine" (C, 26), making clear the theological roots of this claim. This very same concept echoes in "Vérités." Just as God knows surd ratios fully, without calculation, and a priori, so with future contingents: "God, who comprehends the infinite at once, . . . can see how the one is in the other, and can understand a priori the perfect reason for contingency" (C, 17). This is why, says Leibniz, God's knowledge of voluntary causes is infallible, not necessary. For God perceives how the predicate is in the subject, and therefore perceives the relationship to be contingent precisely because the subject-predicate relationship is free, or voluntary, and thus could be otherwise (C, 17; also Careil, 178, and G, 6:392).

Fourth and finally, the distinction Leibniz here uses between the *infallible* and the *necessary* adds additional weight to the case for an Augustinian backdrop. This very distinction is used by Augustine himself in his discussion of voluntary causes. In his reply to Cicero's concern that if foreknowledge is real then determinism follows, Augustine is quite clear that, though God knows the will of acting agents and the future is therefore "utterly assured," this does not mean that the will of agents is governed by necessity. To the contrary, God foreknows future contingents as they are: to wit, as free and contingent. Thus future contingents, though certain in God's mind, are not modally necessary.[40] And this insistence on distinguishing the *infallibly certain* from the *modally necessary* would remain standard throughout the Augustinian tradition.[41] We will return to this distinction between the infallible and the necessary shortly, but for now suffice it to say that Leibniz's use of the distinction is not surprising, given that his appeal to voluntary causes credits Augustine.

What we see, then, in the opening remarks of "Vérités" are clues of the Augustinian background of Leibniz's claims. His theological terminology, his understanding of the relationship between divine knowledge and decree, his understanding of voluntary causes and the object of divine foreknowledge, and his distinction between the infallible and the necessary all point in this direction. As Leibniz fleshes out the distinction between the modally necessary and modally contingent, we find only further confirmation of this reading.

Modal Necessity and Contingency in "Vérités"

After distinguishing necessary truths from contingent truths and defending God's a priori knowledge of both, Leibniz moves into a more thorough discussion of the dividing line between the necessary and the contingent. There are propositions, says Leibniz, that are "for the most part true; there are also propositions which are almost always true, so that an exception would be ascribed to a miracle"; there are even "certain propositions which are true with absolute universality, and which cannot be violated even by a miracle" (C, 19). Those propositions that are beyond God's ability to overturn are necessary truths, such as those of mathematics. Here Leibniz echoes the medieval realists who maintain that contradiction is beyond the purview of omnipotence.[42] And with the realists, Leibniz also identifies essences *(essentia)* as among necessary truths. That is, the subject-predicate relationship displayed between a given essence (e.g., *human*) and its essential properties (e.g., *rational*) is such that, like mathematical truths, it "can be demonstrated by the resolution of terms; these are necessary, or virtually identical, and so their opposite is impossible, or virtually contradictory. The truth of these is eternal; not only will they hold whilst the world remains, but they would have held even if God had created the world in another way" (C, 18; cf. G, 6:131–32).[43] Yet all other truths whose negation does not imply contradiction are contingent. Take, for example, the laws of motion. Though typically stable, they could be otherwise, as they are not demonstrable truths. Thus, echoing Augustine, who identifies laws of motion as rooted in a voluntary cause (viz., God's will), Leibniz contends that the stability of such laws is found entirely in the fact that, having decreed them, "by that very act he [God] decreed that he would observe them" (C, 19).[44] But given that such laws have no inherent necessity, a miracle poses no logical difficulty (cf. G, 6:51–54). For example, though unsuspended objects usually tend downward, there is no contradiction in them not tending downward. Were such a miracle to occur, it would simply constitute a rare instance in which God identified a weightier *(potioris)* final cause meriting repeal of his otherwise stable decrees (C, 19). Leibniz's point, in short, is that a great many stable and universal propositions are not necessary in the proper sense, for they depend entirely on God's free decrees *(libero DEI decreto)*.

The implication of Leibniz's claim here is that all existential truths (save *God exists*) are contingent. As such, he suggests they are "hypothetical yet necessary" *(hypotheticè tamen necessarie)* (C, 20), alluding to the scholastic label for such contingencies: *hypothetical necessity*. Leibniz uses this scholastic label in other works with clear awareness of its historical roots and philosophical dynamics (e.g., G, 7:389; A, ser. 6, 4b:1652, 1457–58; cf. A., ser. 6, 4b:1457–58, 4c:2577). The term is linked to medieval developments surrounding Augustine's infallible/ necessary distinction, which Leibniz has already employed and which was utilized by medieval (and later Protestant) scholastics in the context of divine decree on which Leibniz is here focused. As the infallible/ necessary distinction became common in medieval theology, high-medieval theologians, such as Aquinas and John Duns Scotus, among others, formalized the logic of it. Scotus points out that a sentence such as "Everything which is, when it is, is necessary" can be read in two ways. Read in the divided sense, "when it is, is necessary" modifies "Everything which is." On this reading, the sentence indicates a modal necessity, namely, "Everything which is, is necessary when it is." This modal necessity indicates the modal necessity of the consequent thing *(necessitas consequentis)*. Read in the composite sense, however, "is necessary" modifies all that precedes it, indicating only a necessary entailment, or necessity of the consequence *(necessitas consequentiae)*, that "Everything is when it is." The consequence is thus only a hypothetical necessity, not a modal one. The distinction offers a formal way of identifying the difference between that which cannot be otherwise because it is modally necessary (necessity of the consequent) and that which is infallibly certain but could be otherwise (necessity of the consequence).

Now, as already noted above, Leibniz understands hypothetical necessities to include more than just free choices. He admits, as per his discussion of created laws, that a stone tending downward when unsupported "is not a necessary but a contingent proposition" (C, 20). For laws of motion depend upon God's free concurrence, and "[God] alone knows whether he will suspend by a miracle that subordinate law of nature by which heavy things are driven downwards" (C, 20). Hence if the predicate that is in a given rock is *tends downward,* this subject-predicate relationship is contingent because *rock* and *does not tend downward* are compatible, and the rock's tendency downward is due solely to a free choice by God, not to a logical necessity that binds the subject *(rock)* and the predicate *(tends downward)*. Having said this, though creaturely choice and the movement of inanimate objects are both contingent, Leibniz is clear that "free substances" are unique. For free creatures, unlike rocks, are self-moving substances that may interrupt the natural course of efficient causes that act upon them. To use Leibniz's words, "Free or intelligent substances possess something greater and more marvelous, in a kind of imitation of God. For they are not bound by any certain subordinate laws of the universe, but act as it were by a private miracle, on the sole initiative of their own power, and by looking towards a final cause they interrupt the connection and the course of the efficient causes that act on their will" (C, 20).

In this rather remarkable passage, Leibniz indicates that free or intelligent substances are unique precisely because they "act . . . on the sole initiative of their own power." And by this power, they perform a "private miracle," interrupting the course of efficient causes that act upon them. The deeds of free substances, unlike the motion of falling rocks, are therefore grounded in something other than God's monergistic action in typically stable laws of motion. Free substances may in fact interrupt the natural course of physical laws by looking to a final cause. The comparison with God is apt. For, as Leibniz has already pointed out, a miracle is God's suspension of physical laws in view of a final cause he deems worthy of such suspension. Free deeds, in like manner, are those deeds by which free creatures interrupt the natural course of physical laws by looking to a final cause.

The emphasis here on final causality is significant, since it is yet another echo of the medieval and Protestant scholastic understanding of free choice. As Richard Muller points out, traditional theologies and philosophies of the sixteenth and seventeenth centuries "had argued the very nature of free choice as resting on the assignment of final causes by rational agents in their engagement with concatenations of efficient and material causality in the natural order—what could be identified as necessities of the consequence (i.e. contingencies), specifically as 'complex hypothetical necessities.' Final causality, in this view, was intrinsic to the freedom of rational agents—without it, free agency, even in the case of God, might be excluded."[45] Leibniz, as mentioned, employs the connection between free choice and final causality earlier in "Vérités" when discussing the basis on which God might perform a miracle (see C, 19); and final causality is here identified as the grounds on which other free substances also interrupt the concatenation of efficient causes that act upon them. Hence, added to the string of scholastic reverberations already heard in "Vérités" is Leibniz's emphasis on final causality as the foundation for free choice (see also G, 7:389).

One additional feature of this passage worth noting is that Leibniz's description of free substances argues against both psychological and physical determinism. Choice, in both forms of determinism, is itself part of the efficient-cause nexus. While acting agents are more complex than falling rocks, the determinist does not see freedom as dependent on the possibility of doing otherwise (what is sometimes called the Principle of Alternative Possibilities, or PAP).[46] Instead, freedom is uncoerced liberty to act in accord with one's desires, but what one desires is determined by prior causes.[47] By saying that free substances "interrupt the connection and the course of the efficient causes that act on their will," Leibniz makes clear that he is no physical determinist. For the will stands above the efficient-cause nexus. But is Leibniz a psychological determinist? If we look to "Vérités," the answer would seem to be no, since Leibniz goes on to deny that the will is determined by even psychological causes. He argues instead that the will has the power to direct and redirect the mind—that is, the psychological events that precede choice. In particular, Leibniz extends the analogy of miraculous redirection to the "mind's thoughts," indicating that these are included among the efficient causes interrupted by the private miracles performed by the will: "Just as the course of the universe is changed by the free will of God, so the course of the mind's thoughts is changed by its free will" (C, 20).[48] Note that this position is not without precedents in the Augustinian tradition. Bishop Lancelot Andrews, for example, also includes among the free capacities of the soul the power to redirect thought and, for this reason, chastises Eve for not redirecting her thoughts in the hour of temptation from what she could not have toward what she had been given, so as to stir gratitude rather than covetousness.[49]

Now, necessitarian readers are quick to pounce on Leibniz's seemingly epistemic application of these points as a way of countering the libertarian thrust of the passage. In particular, they home in on the following passage: "In the case of minds, no subordinate universal laws can be established (as is possible in the case of bodies) which are sufficient for predicting [*praedicendam*] a mind's choice" (C, 20). Necessitarian readers argue that Leibniz's emphasis on "predicting" indicates that he is saying, not that minds are free from determinative causes, but simply that the number of causes involved is so vast as to be beyond the grasp of finite minds—much like the infinite decimal of surd ratios. If, however, we could perceive the infinite, as God does, we could know all relevant causes acting on the will and thus predict human choice.[50] The difficulty with this reading is twofold. First, Leibniz's point, taken in context, is that the mind is not bound by the order of causes but may redirect it. Hence the necessitarian reading requires that we read Leibniz as saying the mind is not determined by prior causes, only to turn around and grant that the mind is determined by prior causes. Second, such a reading reduces God's knowledge of future contingents to an inductive inference from cause to effect. Yet such a view of divine foreknowledge is the very view Cicero fears in his attack on divination and Augustine rejects in his defense of voluntary causes in reply to Cicero.[51] And, as we have already seen, Leibniz credits Augustine for his position on God's perfect knowledge of future contingents via his understanding of voluntary causes. In this light, the more likely reading is a libertarian one in which the contrast between human inability to predict choice and divine knowledge of future contingents is a reiteration of the contrast established at the opening of "Vérités" between human a posteriori knowledge of contingents and divine a priori knowledge of contingents.

Moral Necessity and Physical Necessity in "Vérités"

Bracketing some passing comments on divine decree to which Leibniz returns at the close of "Vérités," we run headlong into the centerpiece of compatibilist readings, such as Davidson's. After describing various forms of mental deliberation, Leibniz makes the following statement: "This [deliberation] at any rate holds in the case of minds which are not sufficiently confirmed in good or evil; the case of the blessed is different" (C, 21). The difference, Leibniz goes on to explain, is this: "It is in a way a matter of physical necessity that God should do everything in the best way possible. . . . It is also a matter of physical necessity that those who are confirmed in the good—the angels or the blessed—should act in accordance with virtue" (C, 21). This passage Davidson, among others, takes to be clear evidence that the power of contrary choice, possessed by sinful creatures, is, for Leibniz, not freedom at all. For the blessed and God do not have this power. What this passage demonstrates, argues Davidson, is that Leibniz is a compatibilist, since his examples par excellence of freedom (viz., God and the blessed) are psychologically determined: they perceive the good and necessarily do it.[52]

In a very real sense, this reading of Leibniz is right, and in an equally real way, it is far from the mark. Leibniz does hold that our ability to reject the good in favor of evil is an imperfect form of freedom. But, to be sure, two very different issues are at stake here.

The first is the question of whether Leibniz defines freedom as *moral indifference*—that is, as the ability to do good or evil. The second is the question of whether Leibniz understands freedom to require the libertarian power of contrary choice—that is, to satisfy the principle of alternative possibilities. These are two different issues. Yet in the compatibilist reading these issues are conflated. Such readers take Leibniz's affirmation that God and the blessed act by moral necessity to be a denial of the libertarian power of contrary choice and thus an affirmation of psychological determinism. But this is a leap without precedent in the Augustinian tradition. If Leibniz is taking his cues from this tradition, the maneuvre is highly suspect.

The key passage for grasping Leibniz's point comes just before his comments on God and the blessed. It reads: "And although it is most true that the mind never chooses what at present appears the worse, yet it does not always choose what at present appears the better; for it can delay and suspend its judgment until a later deliberation, and turn the mind aside to think of other things. Which of the two it will do is not determined by any adequate sign or prescribed laws" (C, 21). A careful reading of this passage, and of what follows, indicates that the difference between our fallen freedom and the freedom of God and the blessed is the respective moral possibilities that fall to each. When speaking of *which of the two* the mind will choose, the two in view are the perceived "better" *(melius)* and "worse" *(deterius)*. Given that the juxtaposition is between fallen humanity and the blessed, the contrast should be read as a moral one: the better or worse that does not determine fallen humans is a moral better or worse. For we are open to choosing either good or evil; but this is not true of God and the blessed. Note that both *deterius* and *melius* can carry moral connotations—*deterius* meaning degenerate or wicked and *melius* noble or honorable. And such a reading seems inevitable for two reasons. First, Leibniz is clear that what is unique about the blessed is that they always act out of virtue *(ex virtute agant)*. Second, Leibniz identifies our fallen ability to do the better or the worse as "that indifference which accompanies freedom" (C, 21). Given Leibniz's consistent rejection of equipoise—a concept he elsewhere calls an "impossible chimera" *(chimaera impossibilis)* (C, 25)—such a passage makes sense only if read as a reference to moral indifference (i.e., the ability to do good or evil).

On this point, Leibniz sits squarely within the Augustinian tradition. Contrary to Pelagius's contention that freedom requires the ability to do good or evil, Augustine holds that true freedom is the freedom to do only good.[53] This is evidenced in the fact that evil has no being of its own, since existence itself is a good, and thus can be explained only as a corruption of being or a privation of good *(privatio boni)*; thus a will incapable of regressing into evil is not deprived of a perfection but is complete in its perfection, being immune to corrupting regresses from being to nonbeing, just as an eye lacking the ability to be blind is not the lesser for it.[54] This theme continues throughout the Augustinian tradition into medieval theology,[55] and it is prominent in the writings of Reformed scholastics. Common fare in Reformed treatises on free choice is the outlining of various types of freedom, with indication of which types belong to which beings. In such treatises, the freedom to do good or evil (moral indifference) is identified as inferior to the freedom of God and the blessed, which does only good (moral necessity).[56]

Now, the question of whether moral necessity amounts to psychological determinism, as Davidson and others suggest, is another matter entirely. On this point, we may ask whether Augustinian scholasticism understood moral necessity to carry this connotation. The answer is plainly no, in both its medieval and Protestant incarnations. Taking their cues from Patristic writers who recognize that God operates by moral necessity but reject divine determinism, early medieval writers such as Anselm identify God as operating in accord with moral necessity but reject the notion that God's willing displays modal necessity;[57] and high scholastic medieval writers, in both the intellectualist camp and voluntarist camp, recognize the danger of inferring divine determinism from God's moral necessity, but both camps prove committed to avoiding this conclusion, lest they fall into Averroism.[58] The Reformed scholastics echo this conclusion. Franciscus Junius is clear that God is the freest of beings, and, though recognizing that God operates out of moral necessity, notes that God retains freedom of contradiction with regard to singular goods and freedom of contrariety with regard to multiple goods.[59] Franciscus Gomarus is equally clear on this point and makes additionally clear his denial of compatibilism in favor of libertarianism. For he sees a mere lack of coercion as inadequate for true freedom (even falling rocks and dogs are free from coercion) (cf. G, 3:133); freedom of contrariety and contradiction refer to the real possibility of the opposite outcome (PAP), the knowledge of the object remaining the same.[60]

In light of the foregoing, why presume that Leibniz's affirmation of moral necessity implies determinism? Only two features of the passage in question give reason to think this. First, Leibniz has already identified a rock's falling as a physical necessity; and at one point in "Vérités" he suggests that God and the blessed also act out of physical necessity because they always act out of virtue (C, 21). This reading of Leibniz's claim presumes an extremely one-dimensional reading of the term *physical necessity,* however. For a classically minded figure such as Leibniz, *physica* entails more than mechanical laws of motion; it includes the concept of *physis,* or secondary substance, as per book 2 of Aristotle's *Physica* (cf. G, 6:149–51). If, therefore, it is the nature of the thing to be free, one would rightly say it is a matter of physical necessity that the creature acts freely. Likewise, if it is the nature of the thing to be virtuous, it is a matter of physical necessity that the creature act virtuously. This type of necessity is no doubt what is in view when Augustine says the only necessity by which the will is bound is that it will freely, for free is its nature.[61] And some Reformed scholastics use *physical necessity* in precisely this way.[62]

The second feature of this passage that some read as necessitarian is Leibniz's suggestion that moral necessity could enable a prediction with certainty of what the elect angels or blessed would do in certain circumstances. Two points are noteworthy here, however. First, Leibniz qualifies this claim: it holds only "in certain cases" *(in quibusdam).* In light of this qualification, Leibniz is claiming only that there are some situations in which there is only one virtuous option available to a creature and thus that the conduct of those confirmed in righteousness will be certain—unlike the conduct of the morally indifferent (see C, 21–22). This contention is far from a blanket affirmation of compatibilism. Second, such a claim does not in itself negate the prospect of contrary choice, even in these circumstances. Note that Junius too acknowledges that in some instances only one good is available to God, such that what he would do *if* he chose to act would be certain, but Junius insists that God retains freedom of contradiction in such instances, since withholding choice *(non volo)* is always possible.[63] And Leibniz suggests the very same thing elsewhere: though we may be certain that *if* God decrees a world it will be the best (as per the moral necessity by which he operates), nothing necessitates God to decree a world (A, ser. 6, 4b:1652). In this light, Leibniz's claim regarding instances of predictable choice can be read merely as a necessity of the consequence, or hypothetical necessity—*if* the virtuous were to be in this or that circumstance and to choose *(volo)*, then the choice would be *x*—but this is not an absolute necessity, since choice itself is never necessary. Read in this way, the statement hardly amounts to evidence that Leibniz has suddenly lapsed into determinism.

Free Choice and Divine Predetermination in "Vérités"

With the above points established, Leibniz turns to a discussion of the "way contingent things, and especially free substances, depend in their choice and operation on the divine will and predetermination" (C, 22). Leibniz's starting point in the matter is taken unblushingly from Augustine and consistently reiterated throughout his later works: "My opinion is that it must be taken as certain that there is as much dependence of things on God as is possible without infringing on divine justice" (C, 22; cf. G, 6:199–203, 339–40, 344, 347–50, 383–84). As in other contexts, Leibniz has in mind here Augustine's claim that all being is good and comes from God, while evil is a privation of good. Therefore, God, in his extraordinary concourse, produces continually whatever perfection or reality a thing may have *(perfectionis sive realitatis est à DEO continuò produci)* (C, 22; cf. G, 6:347–50). By contrast, evil—whether metaphysical or moral—is a privation; it has no positive reality of its own and adds nothing to the perfections or realities God supplies. Hence "Their limitation or imperfection belongs to them as creatures" (C, 22). That is to say, the creature is the deficient (as opposed to efficient) cause of any and all repugnance to being, whether this repugnance is metaphysical (and derived from finitude) or moral (and derived from free choice) (G, 6:114–15 and 119–21). Such a line of argumentation is precisely the point of Augustine's privation metaphysic, and it would continue to be so applied in medieval and scholastic theology, as Leibniz knows full well (G, 6:119–21).[64]

Leibniz explains this line of argumentation using an analogy of force applied to an object facing limitations based on the body's matter and mass. He uses this same analogy in *Theodicée,* though with a more thorough explanation. There he writes, "Now God is the cause of all perfections, and consequently of all realities, when they are regarded as purely positive. But limitations or privations result from the original imperfection of creatures which restricts their receptivity. It is as with a laden boat, which the river carries along more slowly or less slowly in proportion to the weight that it bears: thus the speed comes from the river, but the retardation which restricts this speed comes from the load" (G, 6:383). In this particular passage, Leibniz goes on to cite Augustine, referring to his privation metaphysic as the background of this insight. But what is particularly remarkable about this analogy is that it has precedents in the writings of Reformed scholastics. An example from Johannes Maccovius should serve to illustrate the point: "The following objection is forwarded: If someone is knowingly and willingly the cause of an action to which deformity is attached, he truly and properly sins: God is knowingly and willingly the cause of actions to which deformity is attached: therefore God is truly and properly the cause of sin. I respond: This is false and this can be shown by an example: for if someone moves a limping horse, the horse limps, but that person is not the cause of its limping."[65] The basic analogy is always the same: motion is provided by an external source (in keeping with divine premotion and concourse), while the object being moved has some defect or trait that determines the character of the resulting movement. And the point is straightforward: though God may supply existence and motion to moral agents, the character of the act itself is rooted in the agent. The parallel with Leibniz is unmistakable, as is his use of proper theological vernacular such as *concursu* and *praedeterminatione* throughout his discussion.[66]

Leibniz's comments that build on this analogy are equally in keeping with Reformed views on predetermination and free choice.

According to Leibniz, the foregoing is all that can be said regarding divine predetermination (C, 22). In other words, the nature of predetermination is that God supplies what is ontologically positive (via his extraordinary concourse), so that the creature is able to act freely, but the character of the free action that follows is predetermined in accord with the free choice God knows to be in the creature. To use Gisbertus Voetius's characterization: "The predetermination turns the will sweetly and nevertheless strongly to that very end *[terminus]*, to which it—certainly being moved and premoved by God—would have turned itself."[67] Or, as Leibniz puts it, "God understands perfectly the notion of this free individual substance, considered as possible, and from this very notion he foresees what its choice will be, and therefore he decides to accommodate to it his predetermination in time" (C, 22–23). It is noteworthy that for Leibniz, as for the Reformed (and others in the Augustinian tradition), God supplies physical predetermination *(physica praedeterminatione),* not moral predetermination. That is, God supplies what is ontologically necessary for the agent to be and to act freely; God does not always approve of the creature's acts—hence, the analogy in which the character of the object, not the source of its motion, determines the character of the object's movements.

Immediately following his statements on predetermination, Leibniz moves into a brief discussion of "determination" *(Determinationem).* Leibniz's point on the matter is open to a good deal of misunderstanding, given contemporary connotations of "determinism." Such terminology, however, was foreign to early modern thought, originating only in the late eighteenth century.[68] In Leibniz's day, determination was tied to final causality, and in free creatures this meant the identification of a *terminus*—hence its literal rendering, "concerning an end" *(de termino).* It was thus linked with the free identification of means to a final cause (i.e., when a free potency is finally determined by a practical judgment), not with the denial of free choice. This background is important for understanding Leibniz's comments on the matter.

Leibniz states, "I understand a determination to be produced when a thing comes into that state in which what it is about to do follows with physical necessity" (C, 22); and he goes on to make clear that there is no metaphysical necessity in contingencies until they have occurred (that is, until they are past events). Nonetheless, the determination from which physical necessity follows is a sufficient grounding for their truth. And such determination never begins, says Leibniz, but is in the eternal notion of the subject and is known perfectly by God, infallibly and without necessity. Determinist readers such as Robert Sleigh Jr. interpret such passages as indicating that Leibniz sees freedom from metaphysical necessity as a sufficient definition of free choice, while physical necessity (by which Sleigh means something akin to physical determinism) is compatible with freedom of a certain kind—to wit, compatibilist determinism.[69] However, taking into account Leibniz's earlier rejection of physical necessity (so defined) in his talk of the private miracle that interrupts the order of causes, Leibniz's comments probably carry a different meaning.

Rather than suggesting that determinations follow from physical necessity, the more likely reading is that Leibniz is saying that physical necessities take hold after an agent is determined—that is, has made a choice in reference to a *terminus*. In other words, even if an agent interrupts the natural course of efficient causes by means of a private miracle (C, 20), physical necessities still take hold following this interruption. This reading fits Leibniz's earlier definition of free choice and accords with the logical order Leibniz gives to determination and physical necessity: physical necessity, says Leibniz, is subsequent to *(consequatur)* the determination (C, 22). In addition, this reading matches another aspect of Leibniz's thought, namely, his stance on equipoise. It will be recalled that Leibniz opposes equipoise as chimerical, and many of Leibniz's interpreters have taken this as proof that he denies libertarian choice.[70] However, we have clear examples among the Reformed scholastics of theologians who oppose compatibilism as heretical, yet also oppose equipoise as chimerical and thus unnecessary to libertarian freedom.[71] One complaint against equipoise by these theologians is not only that the phenomenon of equipoise is chimerical but that equipoise requires the will to be *indeterminate* after being *self-determined.*[72] Unlike proponents of equipoise, theological opponents of equipoise in the sixteenth and seventeenth centuries maintained that *determination* does occur at some point in free creatures, namely, after the creature has made a choice in reference to a judgment of the practical intellect.[73] Given on which side of the equipoise fence Leibniz sits, it should not be surprising to find him speaking of determination occurring at some point in free agents. For the more traditional position (to which Leibniz holds) is that choice does in fact determine the individual. Yet such determination does not negate free choice; it presumes it. If determination is read in this way, we can see why Leibniz would deny that it is necessary prior to its occurrence, and why he identifies it as the contingent predicate eternally within God's concept of the acting agent. In the end, therefore, it would seem a misreading of Leibniz to take his talk of determination to be an affirmation of determinism in the contemporary sense.

Divine Decree and Possible Worlds in "Vérités"

Being satisfied that he has demonstrated the compatibility of free choice and providence, Leibniz raises a lingering issue for divine decree, which occupies the remainder of "Vérités." He introduces the difficulty as follows: "But if one examines the innermost reasons a new difficulty arises. For the choice of a creature is an act which essentially involves divine predetermination, without which it is impossible for that choice to be exercised" (C, 23). Leibniz laid the groundwork for this issue earlier in "Vérités" (C, 18). There he identifies three types of contingent truths known by God: (a) the general possibility of things *(rerum possibilitatem)*; (b) what is in fact actual *(quid actu existat)*; and (c) what would exist contingently, granting certain conditions *(certis positis esset contingenter extiturum)* (C, 18). While the referent of (b) is clear enough, Leibniz's distinction between (a) and (c) echoes the less obvious distinction between logical possibles and real possibles asserted by some scholastic theologians.[74] According to this distinction, while a subject-predicate combination may be free of contradiction and thus possible in a semantic sense (what Leibniz dubs *the general possibility of things*), contingent propositions are ontologically groundless unless somehow upheld by God. For God's decrees are among the necessary conditions for the existence of contingent things, and in the case of free actions the act cannot be conceptually separated from predetermination, premotion, and concourse—hence the distinction between (a) and (c). Yet in what sense can such contingent truths, known a priori by God in eternity, be volitionally upheld by God? This is the problem of the close of "Vérités."

Leibniz's quandary has clear precedent in medieval theology, as does his proposed solution. In the medieval context, the issue is framed relative to faculty psychology. That is, what is the basis for the divine intellect's a priori understanding of contingent truths, and what role, if any, does the will play in the grounding of those contingent truths known by the intellect? This framing is precisely where Leibniz heads in "Vérités." In the medieval discussion, there are several positions on the matter. Aquinas holds that God's knowledge of the effect (i.e., creation) is derived from his knowledge of the cause (i.e., his own essence).[75] Insofar as God's essence is the "first and *per se* object" of God's knowledge, and all other things are seen in his essence (be they necessary or contingent), Aquinas concludes that God's knowledge of possibles is just as much a part of God's necessary knowledge as necessary truths.[76] Hence, Aquinas creates the strict delineation that the actual involves the will, while the possible involves the intellect only.[77] The antithesis of this position is the voluntarist approach of Henry of Ghent. According to this view, contingent truths require a decree on the part of God (as per the very issue Leibniz raises). Therefore, Ghent argues that contingent truths must be rooted in the divine will. If the divine intellect knows a contingent truth to be so, it knows it only because it sees that contingency decreed by the will and knows that the will of God cannot be impeded.[78]

Leibniz's preferred solution in "Vérités" is neither the extreme intellectualist approach of Aquinas nor the extreme voluntarist approach of Ghent. Over against the intellectualist approach, Leibniz maintains that both intellect and will are involved in God's knowledge of contingent truths (C, 23).[79] Yet he does not thereby move to the voluntarist approach of Ghent. For he does not go so far as to suggest that contingent truths are rooted solely in the will. Instead he creates a dynamic relationship between divine vision and voluntarist predetermination.

He grants that God sees contingent truths a priori but suggests that in beholding these contingencies the divine intellect also beholds the predetermination by the will that grounds it as an affirmative truth.

The dynamic relationship between divine vision and predetermination that Leibniz proposes echoes the position of John Duns Scotus, which was later picked up by a number of Protestant scholastics.[80] Scotus's solution combines Aquinas's insistence that the ground of divine knowledge is the divine essence with Henry of Ghent's insistence that the ground of contingent truths is the divine will. Scotus accomplishes this balancing act by separating the question of how contingent truths are grounded from the question of how the divine intellect knows contingent truths. With regard to the former question, Scotus sides with Ghent. He insists that a contingent proposition, considered in itself, has nothing in it to determine its truth-value, since contingents are conceptually inextricable from the First Cause. Hence, a determination of the proposition by the divine will is required. Positing such predetermination, however (which is different from positing a divine decree that this contingency exist), the given proposition has an affirmative truth-value.[81] Yet Scotus goes on to deny Ghent's claim that the intellect thereby knows contingent truths via the will, siding instead with Aquinas. According to Scotus, God knows his essence and subsequently all things according to their being knowable.[82] The ground of divine knowing in reference to contingent truths is thus the same as in reference to necessary truths.[83] Scotus's concern is that we affirm that God knows all truths a priori, regardless of why they are true (i.e., what grounds them); and he fears that Ghent's extreme voluntarist approach runs the risk of ascribing to God discursive knowledge— that is, knowledge that follows inferentially from what the intellect knows of and sees in the divine will.[84] Hence, while the divine will may provide grounding for the truth-value of contingent propositions, the basis on which the divine intellect apprehends truths is always the same, regardless of whether those truths are necessary or contingent, and regardless of how they are grounded.

Leibniz takes this same line of argumentation in "Vérités." Along with Scotus, and indeed the predeterminationists generally (cf. G, 6:125–27), Leibniz identifies predetermination as an essential condition for the very possibility of creaturely action, since "the choice of a creature is an act which essentially involves divine predetermination" (C, 23). This is the very reason why Leibniz, with Scotus, rejects Aquinas's claim that God's knowledge of possibles involves only the intellect. Because predetermination is an essential condition of creaturely action, Leibniz maintains that, whether actual or possible, "contingent truths involve the decrees of the will *[voluntatis decreta]*" (C, 23). Leibniz's rejection of Aquinas in this context may be surprising to some readers, since, as noted in section 1, Leibniz invokes Thomist terminology in reference to divine knowledge at the opening of "Vérités." However, as also pointed out earlier, Muller identifies a number of Reformed scholastics who retain the very same Thomist terminology of *scientia simplicis intelligentiae/visionis* while invoking a more Scotist understanding of divine knowledge.[85] Hence, to find Leibniz doing so should not be surprising, especially given the impact of Reformed scholasticism on his thought.

Leibniz's concern with the intellectualist approach is that it risks the absurdity that God "decree something because he sees that he has already decreed it" (C, 23). The circle Leibniz sees afoot runs something like this. If divine predetermination is essential to the very nature of creaturely action but predetermination concerns the actual only, then the only contingent truths the divine intellect can know as possible are those that God has predetermined to be actual; yet if God's knowledge of possibles logically precedes his decree that they be actual, then God first foresees that he has decreed that these possibles be actual and only then decrees what he has foreseen he decrees. Leibniz's solution follows Scotus. To wit: Leibniz posits two types of predetermination, one by which God determines contingent propositions but only as possible (i.e., *in decernendo*), and a second by which a specific series of contingent truths is granted existence—that is, "by which God decides to render this decree actual" (C, 24). According to Leibniz, it is the former predetermination that the intellect sees in its a priori apprehension of contingent truths. As Leibniz puts it, "I grant that when God decides to predetermine the mind to a certain choice because he has foreseen that it would choose in this way if it were admitted to existence, he foresees also his own predetermination and his own decree of predetermination—but only as possible; he does not decree because he *has* decreed" (C, 23).

Leibniz's uniqueness on this topic is in two areas. The first is relative to the Reformed scholastics who employ Scotus's theory of divine knowledge. Unlike these Reformed thinkers, Leibniz utilizes this
theory to undermine disputes over the order of divine decrees, such
as the infralapsarian/supralapsarian debate. For Leibniz understands
"the series" to be perceived by God in its entirety as a single whole,
and insofar as the divine intellect considers any given world as a whole
relative to competing possible worlds as wholes, Leibniz understands
the decree to grant existence to one world to be a decree in favor of
the entire series. While the series may have a logical, and indeed temporal, order of events, Leibniz takes the decree of existence to embrace all that the given world entails simultaneously. As Leibniz puts it,
when God chooses one such series, "by that very fact also [he] makes
an infinite number of decrees concerning all that is involved in it, and
so concerning his possible decrees or laws which are to be transferred
from possibility to actuality" (C, 24). In other words, if a given series
includes both Adam's sin and the redemption of Christ, the decree to
grant that series existence simultaneously decrees all the particular
decrees that are part of the concept of that series; there is no logical
order in which God first decrees the Fall and then man's redemption
(or vice versa). This peculiar feature of Leibniz's theory of possible
worlds was not intended to remove him from the Protestant scholastic
discussion, however, but was forwarded precisely with a view to solv-
ing the dispute (e.g., G, 6:146–48).

The second area of uniqueness is in a difference between Leibniz
and Scotus, namely, Leibniz utilizes this theory of divine knowledge to
develop an entire theory of possible worlds, while Scotus stops short
of this.[86] As Leibniz goes on to argue, because the first type of divine
predetermination grounds contingent propositions as real possibles
but does not call them into existence—the decree of the actual is a
distinct decree—it takes only one additional step to suggest that not
all propositions predetermined by the divine will are granted existence. Hence, Leibniz conceives of God as first considering the innumerable ways in which he may create the universe (i.e., its creatures
and its laws) and grasps "that a different series of things will come into
existence if he chooses different laws of the series" (C, 23). The im-

plication is that each series constitutes its own discrete world. Yet each world is predetermined in the realm of the possible only; the predicate *exists* is not granted to any of these possible worlds at the outset. The divine intellect thus has before it innumerable possible worlds to judge relative to God's final cause, and in light of this practical judgment, God is free to render actual that series which the intellect judges best (C, 24).

Employing this understanding of divine decree, and using the example of Judas, Leibniz closes "Vérités" by laying the foundation for what will become *Theodicée*. He does so by summarizing how God's decrees simultaneously preserve the freedom of creatures, as per the above discussion of predetermination, while also fulfilling God's own ends. "All that he [God] decrees is that Judas, whom he foresees will be a traitor, must nevertheless exist, since with his infinite wisdom he sees that this evil will be counterbalanced by an immense gain in greater goods, nor can things be better in any way" (C, 24). This decree recognizes that if God decrees the existence of Judas—whose concept includes free choice—and predetermines him according to what is in his will, Judas will freely and contingently betray Christ. Yet God foresees not only the free betrayal by this possible Judas but also how God, in his infinite wisdom, may counterbalance or utilize Judas's evil choice for greater ends. Thus "[God] allows it in his decree that Judas the sinner shall now exist, and in consequence he also makes a decree that when the time of betrayal arrive the concourse of his actual predetermination is to be accommodated to this" (C, 24). Yet divine justice is in no way tainted by this concurrence, since "this decree is limited to what there is of perfection in this evil act; it is the very notion of the creature, in so far as it involves limitation (which is the one thing that it does not have from God) that drags the act towards badness" (C, 24). In other words, Leibniz insists that God provides and approves of only what is ontologically positive in the betrayal of Christ. The limitations in Judas that drag the good into corruption in no way appeal to God. If he permits such evils, it is only because they attach by concomitance to greater goods. These greater goods are what incline God toward the sequence of events, not the evils that attach as a consequence.

In sum, Leibniz returns to the concept of predetermination utilized by the Reformed scholastics. God's decrees and predetermination are in keeping with his understanding and preservation of the choices of free subjects, but God providentially utilizes these choices—be they for good or ill—for his own good ends. Moreover, because God's initial predetermination of contingent propositions grounds multiple possible worlds, he is not bound to any single world, but may decree that world which is best in keeping with his own final cause. In this way, both human freedom and God's ends are preserved.

•   •   •

As stated in the introduction of this essay, the above conclusions are not intended to overturn the whole of Leibniz studies. One could grant the above conclusions and assert that Leibniz changes his views after 1700, for example. Nonetheless, the above exposition of "Vérités" gives good reason to think that Leibniz was strongly influenced by the Augustinian tradition generally and its Protestant manifestation in particular and that this tradition was echoed with positive affirmation in Leibniz's early writings. Moreover, we have seen that the assumptions of this theological tradition on predetermination, physical necessity, moral necessity, and so on are often diametrically opposed to the assumptions of Leibniz's necessitarian interpreters, which raises serious questions over the legitimacy of the more secular readings of Leibniz. The impact of the Augustinian tradition upon Leibniz thus gives reason to rethink the compatibilist and necessitarian portrayal of his thought, or at least the legitimacy of these portraits in reference to Leibniz's early writings. In the end, it must be remembered that whether one believes that those of this tradition succeed in preserving free choice amid their theological commitments is a matter entirely different from whether this tradition aimed at this end and thought itself successful in reaching it. We have seen evidence that those of an Augustinian mind do not see moral necessity or physical necessity, intellective preference or divine foreknowledge, divine predetermination or divine decree as contrary to free choice. And we have seen evidence that Leibniz is of such a mind as well. We therefore have ample reason to question whether Leibniz was in fact a modern necessitarian with deistic or Spinozistic leanings or has merely been labeled so by interpreters at odds with the theological tradition in which Leibniz sits and to which he is indebted.

Notes

Much of the research contained in this essay was originally presented at the symposium "Reformierte Philosophie in der frühen Neuzeit," in Bretten, Germany, in May 2009, under the title "Leibniz and the Reformed Scholastics."

    Abbreviations of Leibniz's works are as follows: A = *Sämtliche Schriften und Briefe,* ed. Deutsche Akademie der Wissenschaften zu Berlin (Darmstadt, 1923–, Leibzig, 1938–, Berlin, 1950–); B = *Die Leibniz-Handschriften der Königlichen öffentlichen Bibliothek zu Hannover,* ed. Eduard Bodemann (Hildesheim: Georg Olms, 1966); C = *Opuscules et fragments inédits de Leibniz,* ed. Louis Couturat (Paris, 1903); Careil = Foucher de Careil, *Nouvelles lettres et opuscules inédits de Leibniz* (Paris, 1857); E = *Opera philosophica quae exstant latina, gallica, germanica omnia,* ed. J. E. Erdmann (Berlin: G. Eichler, 1839–40); G = *Die philosophischen Schriften von Gottfried Wilhelm Leibniz,* ed. C. I. Gerhardt, 7 vols. (Berlin, 1875–90); GP = *G. W. Leibniz, Mathematische Schriften,* 7 vols., ed. C. I. Gerhardt (1849–63; repr., Hildesheim: Georg Olms, 1971); Grua = *G. W. Leibniz: Textes inédits,* ed. G. Grua (Paris, 1948); P = G. H. Pertz, *Leibnizens Gesammelt Werke,* ser. 1, vol. 4 (Hanover, 1847). Citations of Leibniz's writings are embedded in the body of the essay. The following translations are employed throughout: *Leibniz: Philosophical Writings,* ed. G. H. R. Parkinson, trans. Mary Morris and G. H. R. Parkinson (London: J. M. Dent and Sons, 1973); and G. W. Leibniz, *Theodicy: Essays on the Goodness of God and the Freedom of Man and the Origin of Evil,* trans. E. M. Huggard (La Salle, IL: Open Court, 1997). Translations have been modified based on the original Latin/French where necessary.

    1. See, e.g., "An Account of the Book Entitled *Commercium Epistolicum Collinii Aliorum, De Analysipromota*; Published by order of the Royal-Society, in relation to the Dispute between Mr. Leibnitz and Dr. Keill, about the Right of Invention of the Method of Fluxions, by some call'd the Differential Method," *Royal Society of London, Philosophical Transactions (1683–1775)* 29, no. 342 (1714): 224; Thomas Reid, *Essays on the Active Powers of Man* (Edinburgh: printed for John Bell, and G., G., J. & J. Robinson, London, 1788), 338–39; Thomas Reid, *Essays on the Intellectual and Active Powers of Man,* 3 vols. (Dublin: printed for P. Byrne, and J. Milliken, 1790), 1:263–64; and, though less explicit, Julien Offray

de La Mettrie, *Oeuvres philosophiques* (Berlin: Jean Nourse, 1751), 222–26. Note also the exchange between Louis Racine, Le Chevalier De Ramsey, and Alexander Pope, which—though nowhere referencing Leibniz, only fatalism and errors of the Spinozists and the deists or deism (Louis Racine, *La religion, poëme; par Monsieur Racine, de l'Académie Royale des Inscriptions & Belles-Lettres,* 2 vols. [London, 1785], 299, 301, 303, 306)—Pope gathers under the heading, "As some passages in the Essay on Man have been suspected of favouring the schemes of Leibnitz and Spinoza, or of a tendency towards Fate and Naturalism, it is thought proper here to insert the two following Letters, to show how ill-grounded such a suspicion is," in his *Poetical Works,* thus indicating that Leibniz was understood (by at least Pope) to be synonymous with Spinozistic fatalism, deism, or both. See *The Poetical Works of Alexander Pope, with His Last Corrections, Additions, and Improvements. From the Text of Dr. Warburton. With the Life of the Author,* 2 vols. (London: Printed for C. Cooke, No. 17, Paternoster-Row, 1795), 1:243. Exceptions in the 1700s include Johann Jakob Brucker, *The History of Philosophy, from the Earliest Times to the Beginning of the Present Century; Drawn up from Brucker's "Historia Critica Philosophiæ," by William Enfield, LL.D.,* 2 vols. (London: printed for J. Johnason, 1791), 2:563–65; as well as William Jones, who, while not giving an extensive treatment of Leibniz on free choice, recognizes Leibniz's affirmation of divine concourse and leaves the charge of necessitarianism in the conditional. See William Jones, *An Essay on the First Principles of Natural Philosophy: Wherein the Use of Natural means, or Second Causes, in the Oeconomy of the material world, is demonstrated from Reason, Experiments of Various Kinds, and the Testimony of Antiquity* (Oxford, 1762), 21–22.

2. For a linking of preestablished harmony and deism in the 1800s, see Richard Falckenberg, *History of Modern Philosophy,* 3rd English ed. from 2nd German ed., trans. A. C. Armstrong Jr. (New York: Henry Holt, 1897), 270–80 (1888; 2nd ed., 1892). For affirmation of freedom as indifference, see Falckenberg, *History of Modern Philosophy,* 274, 277–78, and Lucien Lévy-Bruhl, *History of Modern Philosophy in France* (Chicago: Open Court, 1899), 118.

3. See, e.g., F. W. J. Schelling, *On the History of Modern Philosophy,* trans. Andrew Bowie (Cambridge: Cambridge University Press, 1994), 77–83 (suggested to have been written either 1833–34 or 1836–37—see ix); Falckenberg, *History of Modern Philosophy,* 277 f.; cf. Arthur Schopenhauer, *Parerga and Paralipomena,* trans. E. F. J. Payne (1851; repr., New York: Oxford University Press, 2001), 1:6–8; and perhaps Friedrich Ueberweg, who, while recognizing that Leibniz's theodicy presumes free choice (113), lumps Leibniz in with the determinism of later Leibnizians, such as Christian Wolff and, without correction or qualification, Johann Joachim Lange (1670–1744), "who was the cause of Wolff's expulsion from Halle, [and] sought . . . to demonstrate the Spinozistic and atheistic character of the Wolffian doctrine and the danger with which it was fraught for religion; he took especial offence at the doctrine of Determinism taught by

Wolff." See Friedrich Ueberweg, *History of Philosophy from Thales to the Present Time* (New York: Scribner, Armstrong, 1876), 2:116, see also 111.

4. See Louis Couturat, "Sur la métaphysique de Leibniz," *Revue de Métaphysique et de Morale* 10 (1902): 1–25; Couturat's Spinozistic reading of Leibniz came in response to Bertrand Russell's *A Critical Exposition of the Philosophy of Leibniz* (London: Allen and Unwin, 1937), which defended the idea that Leibniz's God chooses to create the world, even though Russell understood Leibnizian choice in determinist terms. Russell was eventually persuaded by Couturat, evident in his reviews of Couturat's *La logique de Leibniz d'après des documents inédits* (Paris: Félix Alcan, 1901) and *Opuscules et fragments inédits de Leibniz*. Russell's reviews appeared in *Mind* 12 (1903): 177–201 and *Mind* 13 (1904): 131–32, respectively. Both reviews have been reprinted in *The Collected Papers of Bertrand Russell*, ed. Alasdair Urquhart and Albert C. Lewis (New York: Routledge, 1994), 537–63.

5. For more nuanced readings, see, e.g., Frederick Copleston, *A History of Philosophy* (London: Burns Oates and Washbourne, 1958), vol. 4; Michael J. Murray, "Leibniz on Divine Foreknowledge of Future Contingents and Human Freedom," *Philosophy and Phenomenological Research* 55, no. 1 (March 1995): 75–108; and Michael J. Murray, "Spontaneity and Freedom in Leibniz," in *Leibniz: Nature and Freedom,* ed. Donald Rutherford and J. A. Cover (Oxford: Oxford University Press, 2005). See also the unique essay by R. Cranston Paull, "Leibniz and the Miracle of Freedom," *Noûs* 26, no. 2 (June 1992): 218–35, which defends a libertarian reading of Leibniz. For more contemporary charges of deism and Spinozism, see, e.g., Robert Merrihew Adams, *Leibniz: Determinist, Theist, Idealist* (New York: Oxford University Press, 1994); S. H. Mellone, *The Dawn of Modern Thought: Descartes, Spinoza, Leibniz* (London: Oxford University Press, 1930), 97–115; B. A. G. Fuller, *A History of Modern Philosophy,* 3rd ed. (New York: Holt, Rinehart and Winston, 1960), 118; R. P. Sertillanges, *Le problème du mal,* vol. 1, *L'histoire* (Paris: Aubier, Éditions Montaigne, 1948), 234–35; Samuel Enoch Stumpf, *Socrates to Sartre: A History of Philosophy* (New York: McGraw-Hill, 1966), 273; C. D. Broad, *Leibniz: An Introduction* (New York: Cambridge University Press, 1975); D. W. Hamlyn, *A History of Western Philosophy* (London: Viking Press, 1987), 160–64; R. C. Sleigh Jr., *Leibniz and Arnauld: A Commentary on Their Correspondence* (New Haven: Yale University Press, 1990) and "Leibniz on Freedom and Necessity: Critical Notice of Robert Adams, *Leibniz: Determinist, Theist, and Idealist,*" *Philosophical Review* 108, no. 2 (April 1999): 245–77; and Robert Sleigh Jr., Vere Chappell, and Michael Della Rocca, "Determinism and Human Freedom," in *The Cambridge History of Seventeenth-Century Philosophy,* 2 vols., ed. Daniel Garber and Michael Ayers (New York: Cambridge University Press, 1998), 2:1195–1278.

6. For sources that build the case for Leibnizian deism on preestablished harmony, see note 1 above. On the issue of indifference, see, e.g., Reid, *Essays*

on the Active Powers, 335–37; Voltaire also appears sympathetic to freedom as indifference. See Voltaire, *The Metaphysics of Sir Isaac Newton: or, a Comparison between the Opinions of Sir Isaac Newton and Mr. Leibnitz,* trans. David Erskine Baker (London: printed for R. Dodsley; and sold by M. Cooper, 1747), 19–20, and "Elements of the Newtonian Philosophy," in Voltaire, *Philosophical, Literary, and Historical Pieces,* 2nd ed., trans. W. S. Kenrick (London: printed for Fielding and Walker, 1780), esp. 11–20, although Voltaire offers a more charitable reading of Leibniz in "Dialogue XVII: On Curious Subjects," 411–12, and in "A Short Answer to the Long Discourses of a German Doctor," 171, both in *Philosophical, Literary, and Historical Pieces.*

7. See, e.g., Schelling, *On the History,* 82–83.

8. See Couturat, "Sur la métaphysique," and Russell's reviews of Couturat's *La logique de Leibniz and Opuscules et fragments.*

9. When using the terms *Protestant scholastics, Reformed scholastics,* and *Reformed scholasticism* in this essay, I am affirming the conclusion of Richard Muller (among others) that a specific method of medieval theology was employed by Protestant theologians of the sixteenth and seventeenth centuries. For a full explanation of the term *Reformed scholasticism,* see Richard A. Muller, *Post-Reformation Reformed Dogmatics: The Rise and Development of Reformed Orthodoxy, ca. 1520–1725,* 4 vols. (Grand Rapids, MI: Baker Academic, 2003–), introduction to vol. 1.

10. For an extended treatment of Leibniz's various writings on the doctrines of Trinity and Incarnation, see Maria Rosa Antognazza, *Leibniz on the Trinity and the Incarnation,* trans. Gerald Parks (New Haven: Yale University Press, 2007).

11. On the relationship between philosophy and theology in the works of Pierre Bayle, see Hubert Bost, "Pierre Bayle, un 'protestant compliqué,'" in *Pierre Bayle (1647–1706), le philosophe de Rotterdam: Philosophy, Religion and Reception, Selected Papers of the Tercentenary Conference Held at Rotterdam, 7–8 December 2006,* ed. Wiep van Bunge and Hans Bots (Leiden: Brill, 2008), 83–101 (chap. 7 here).

12. Leroy E. Loemker, "Leibniz and the Herborn Encyclopedists," *Journal of the History of Ideas* 22, no. 3 (1961): 323.

13. E. J. Aiton, *Leibniz: A Biography* (Bristol: Adam Hilger, 1985), 10–12.

14. Aiton, *Leibniz,* 13.

15. Maria Rosa Antognazza, *Leibniz: An Intellectual Biography* (Cambridge: Cambridge University Press, 2009), 41–42.

16. See Antognazza, *Leibniz,* 42–43.

17. One notable exception is Michael Murray, who defends a tempered compatibilist reading via the Thomist tradition. See, e.g., Murray, "Leibniz on Divine Foreknowledge" and "Spontaneity and Freedom."

18. See G. W. Leibniz, *Dissertation on Predestination and Grace,* ed. and trans. Michael J. Murray (New Haven: Yale University Press, 2011), Introduction.

19. "Vérités necessaries et contingentes" is found in C, 16–24. Couturat provides the title by which it has come to be known ("Necessary and Contingent Truths").

20. See note 4 above.

21. See Paull, "Leibniz and the Miracle."

22. See Jack Davidson, "Imitators of God: Leibniz on Human Freedom," *Journal of the History of Philosophy* 36, no. 3 (1998): 387–412.

23. For examples of libertarian readers of Augustine, see Eugene Portalie, *A Guide to the Thought of St. Augustine* (London: Burns and Oates, 1960); Eugene TeSelle, *Augustine the Theologian* (New York: Herder and Herder, 1970); and John M. Rist, "Augustine on Free Will and Predestination," *Journal of Theological Studies* 20, no. 2 (1969): 420–47; for examples of libertarian readers of Aquinas and Scotus, see Eleonore Stump, *Aquinas* (Routledge: London, 2003), 304–5; Norman Kretzmann, "Philosophy of Mind," in *The Cambridge Companion to Aquinas,* ed. Norman Kretzmann and Eleonore Stump (Cambridge: Cambridge University Press, 1993), 147; Hannes Möhle, "Scotus's Theory of Natural Law," in *Cambridge Companion to Duns Scotus,* ed. Thomas Williams (Cambridge: Cambridge University Press, 2003), 326; B. M. Bonansea, *Man and His Approach to God in John Duns Scotus* (Lanham: University Press of America, 1983), 51, 80–81; Thomas Williams, "From Metaethics to Action Theory," in Williams, *Cambridge Companion to Duns Scotus,* 347–48; and Antonie Vos, *The Philosophy of John Duns Scotus* (Edinburgh: Edinburgh University Press, 2006), 413–30; and for libertarian readers of the Reformed scholastics, see, e.g., Antonie Vos, "Always on Time," in *Understanding the Attributes of God,* ed. Gijsbert van den Brink and Marcel Sarot (New York: Peter Lang, 1995); A. J. Beck and Antonie Vos, "Conceptual Patterns Related to Reformed Scholasticism," *Nederlands Theologisch Tijdschrift* 57, no. 3 (July 2003): 223–33; Willem J. van Asselt and Eef Dekker, eds., *Reformation and Scholasticism: An Ecumenical Enterprise* (Grand Rapids, MI: Baker Academic, 2001), esp. Antonie Vos, "Scholasticism and Reformation," 99–119, and A. J. Beck, "Gisbertus Voetius (1589–1676): Basic Features of His Doctrine of God," 205–26; Muller, *Post-Reformation Reformed Dogmatics;* Willem J. van Asselt, "The Theologian's Tool Kit: Johannes Maccovius (1588–1644) and the Development of Reformed Theological Distinctions," *Westminster Theological Journal* 68 (2006): 23–40; and Willem J. van Asselt, J. Martin Bac, and Roelf T. te Velde, *Reformed Thought on Freedom: The Concept of Free Choice in the History of Early-Modern Reformed Theology* (Grand Rapids, MI: Baker, 2010).

24. See, e.g., Richard A. Muller, "Jonathan Edwards and the Absence of Free Choice: A Parting of Ways in the Reformed Tradition," *Jonathan Edwards Studies* (forthcoming).

25. Milič Čapek, in "Leibniz's Thought Prior to the Year 1670: From Atomism to a Geometrical Kinetism," *Revue Internationale de Philosophie* 20 (1966): 249–56, sides with Arthur Hannequin in suggesting that Leibniz's movement

during this three years is toward a "Cartesianisation of Aristotle" (254; cf. Arthur Hannequin, *Études d'histoire des sciences et d'histoire de la philosophie* [Paris, 1908], 2:46) and goes on to defend both the Cartesian flavor of Leibniz's burgeoning ideas (254–56) and a resulting tension that endures throughout Leibniz's thought (256). Others, such as O. Bradley Bassler, argue that a transitional position is found in *Theoria motus abstracti* that, while anticipating, is not yet the fully articulated position of *Specimen demonstrationum de natura rerum corporearum ex phaenomenis* (1671). See O. Bradley Bassler, "Motion and Mind in the Balance: The Transformation of Leibniz's Early Philosophy," *Studia Leibnitiana* 34, no. 2 (2002): 221–31. Bassler contrasts his position to that of Daniel Garber and André Robinet, who do not recognize such nuance in their treatment of *Theoria motus abstracti* (see Daniel Garber, "Motion and Metaphysics in the Young Leibniz," in *Leibniz: Critical and Interpretive Essays,* ed. Michael Hooker [Minneapolis: University of Minnesota Press, 1982], 160–84; and André Robinet, *Architectonique disjunctive, automates systémiques et idéalité transcendantale dans l'œuvre de G. W. Leibniz. Nombreux texts inédits* [Paris: Vrin, 1986], 166.) Other commentators, such as Christia Mercer, focus on the more global transition in Leibniz's thought and thus see commentators such as Bassler (as well as Beeley and Arthur) as too concerned with the minutiae of the transition period; see Christia Mercer, *Leibniz's Metaphysics: Its Origin and Development* (Cambridge: Cambridge University Press, 2001), 261 n. 12 and 414 n. 105.

26. See, e.g., Sleigh, Chappell, and Della Rocca, "Determinism and Human Freedom," esp. 1265–67. These same arguments also appear in Sleigh, "Leibniz on Freedom."

27. *Seu,* or *sive,* is the weakest Latin disjunctive participle, as it "gives a choice between two designations of the same object," suggesting that the designation is a matter of indifference. See B. L. Gildersleeve and Vonzalez Lodge, *A Latin Grammar* (London: Macmillan, 1963), §§ 474–97.

28. Leibniz offers one caveat concerning this analogy: our ability to calculate surd ratios and offer some demonstration thereto is the one point at which the analogy breaks down, for "in the case of contingent truths not even this is conceded to a created mind" (C, 18).

29. See, e.g., David Blumenfeld, "Superessentialism, Counterparts, and Freedom," in *Leibniz: Critical and Interpretive Essays,* ed. Michael Hooker (Manchester: Manchester University Press, 1983), 103. This feature of Leibniz's thought also played a central role in Couturat's case for Leibniz's Spinozism, which ultimately persuaded Bertrand Russell to abandon his compatibilist-theist reading. See note 4 above.

30. Note that "mediating conditions" *(media . . . conditionatas),* which is the likely intent of C, 22 as well, is mistranslated "mediate knowledge" in the Morris-Parkinson translation, giving the misleading impression of Molinistic connotations.

31. See, e.g., Thomas Aquinas, *Summa theologiae,* Ia, q. 14, art. 9. (Bonaventure also discusses the distinction, giving credit to Aquinas: see Bonaventure, *Commentaria in quatuor libros sententiaram,* bk. 1, dist. 39, art. 1, q. 3, scholion.) Cf. Francis Turretin, *Institutio theologiae elencticae* (Geneva, 1688), locus tertius, q. 13.

32. Muller, *Post-Reformation Reformed Dogmatics,* 3:408. Cf. Willem J. van Asselt, "Scholastic Protestant and Catholic: Medieval Sources and Methods in Seventeenth-Century Reformed Thought," in *Religious Identity and the Problem of Historical Foundation: The Foundational Character of Authoritative Sources in the History of Christianity and Judaism,* ed. Judith Frishman, Willemien Otten, and Gerard Rouwhorst (Leiden: Brill, 2004), 457–70 and n. 27, which makes the very same point in reference to Turretin.

33. Augustine, *civ. Dei* 5.10.

34. Augustine, *civ. Dei* 5.10.

35. Gisbertus Voetius, *Disputatio philosophico-theologica, continens quaestiones duas, de Distinctione Attributorum divinorum, & Libertate Voluntatis* 2.4 (as translated in *Reformed Thought on Freedom*). Cf. Augustine, *civ. Dei* 5.10; Turretin, *Institutio* 6.5.11.

36. Augustine, *civ. Dei* 5.10.

37. Voetius, *Disputatio philosophico-theologica* 2.4.

38. Augustine, *civ. Dei* 5.9.

39. See, e.g., Anselm, *De Concordia praescientiae et praedestinationis* 1.1–2, in *Patrologiae cursus completes: sive biblioteca universalis, integra uniformis, commode oeconomica* [. . .], vol. 158, ed. Jacques-Paul Migne et al. (Paris: Apud Garnieri Fratres, 1844–); Aquinas, *Summa theologiae,* Ia, q. 14, art. 13, in *Sancti Thomae Aquinatis, Doctoris Angelici, ordinis praedicatorum opera omnia* (New York: Musurgia, 1948); and Turretin, *Institutio* 6.2.3.

40. See, e.g., Augustine, *civ. Dei* 5.9. Cf. Cicero, *De fato* 10.20 ff. and 17.40.

41. Cf. Anselm, *De concordia* 1.1–3.

42. See Aquinas, *Summa theologiae* I, q. 25, art. 4.

43. There is debate in Leibniz studies over the extent to which Leibniz is a realist and how this plays out in his posture toward hylomorphism versus idealism. See, e.g., Michael K. Shim, "Leibniz on Concept and Substance," *International Philosophical Quarterly* 46, no. 3 (September 2006): 309–25; Justin Erik Halldór Smith, "Christian Platonism and the Metaphysics of Body in Leibniz," *British Journal for the History of Philosophy* 12, no. 1 (2004): 43–59; Jean-Baptiste Rauzy, "An Attempt to Evaluate Leibniz' Nominalism," *Metaphysica* 1 (2004): 43–58; Daniel Garber, "Leibniz on Form and Matter," *Early Science and Medicine* 2, no. 3 (1997): 326–52; Massimo Mugnai, "Leibniz on Substance and Changing Properties," *dialectica* 59, no. 4 (2005): 503–16; Christia Mercer, *Leibniz's Metaphysics: Its Origins and Development* (Cambridge: Cambridge University Press, 2001); Brandon Look, "The Platonic Leibniz," *British Journal for the History of*

Philosophy 11, no. 1 (2003): 129–40. What seems relatively uncontroversial, however, is that Leibniz affirms the Platonic Ideas in the mind of God.

44. Cf. Augustine, *civ. Dei* 5.9.

45. See chapter 4 of this book, Richard Muller's "God and Design in the Thought of Robert Boyle."

46. See, e.g., Robert Kant, "The Contours of the Contemporary Free Will Debate," in *The Oxford Handbook of Free Will,* ed. Robert Kant (New York: Oxford University Press, 2002), 11.

47. See Richard Taylor, "Determinism," in *The Encyclopedia of Philosophy,* 8 vols., ed. Paul Edwards (New York: Macmillan, 1967), 359–68.

48. Cf. Leibniz's letter to Basnage in which Leibniz identifies spontaneous, uncoerced psychological determinism as a view of freedom with which even Spinoza would be pleased (G, 3:133), as well as Leibniz's comments in "On Freedom," in which he identifies the compatibilist view of freedom as his former position (Careil, 178).

49. Lancelot Andrewes, *Apospasmatia sacra, or A Collection of Posthumous and Orphan Lectures: Delivered at St. Pauls and St. Giles his Church, by the Right Honourable and Reverend Father in God Lancelot Andrews, Lord Bishop of Winchester* (London: Printed by R. Hodgkinsonne, for Moseley, [*et al.*], 1657), 95–96 and 259.

50. Cf. Augustine's description of Cicero's fear in *civ. Dei* 5.9.

51. See, e.g., Sleigh, Chappell, and Della Rocca, "Determinism and Human Freedom," 1267. Cf. Davidson, "Imitators of God," 402–3.

52. Davidson, "Imitators of God," 402–5.

53. See, e.g., Pelagius, "To Demetrias," in *The Letters of Pelagius and His Followers,* ed. and trans. B. R. Rees (New York: Boydell Press, 1991).

54. See, e.g., Augustine, *civ. Dei* 14.11.

55. Cf., e.g., Anselm, *De concordia* 3.4.

56. See, e.g., Girolamo Zanchi, "De libero primorum parentum ante lapsum arbitrio" and "De libero arbitrio in homine post ipsum non renato," both in *Omnium operum theologicorum,* 8 vols. (Geneva: Ex typographia Samuelis Crispini, 1619); and Junius, *Theses theologicae Leydenses et Heydelbergenses* 22, "De libero arbitrio," in *Opuscula theologica selecta,* ed. Abraham Kuyper (Amsterdam: F. Muller com soc. et J. H. Kryt, 1882).

57. See Anselm, *De concordia* 1.3 with 3.4. For the early Patristic writers, see, e.g., Irenaeus, *Contra haereses* 2.1.1 and 2.5.4 (PG 7a:709c–710a; 723c–724a); Ambrose, *De fide* 2.3; and Iohannes Damascenus, *De fide orthodoxa,* 1.14 (PG 94:860a–862a). The above patristic references utilizing "PG" or "PL" refer to J. P. Migne, *Patrologiae cursus completes* (Parisiis: Venit apud editorem in vico dicto Montrouge, 1844–66). Citations identify the relevant volume and page numbers.

58. Aquinas identifies the problem of divine determinism in *Summa theologiae,* Ia, q. 19, art. 7, and provides his intellectualist solution in Ia, q. 19. John

Duns Scotus attacks Aquinas's solution as inadequate, providing his own voluntarist solution, in *Lectura* I 39, 5.42–44.

59. See Franciscus Junius, *Theses theologicae Leydenses* 22.

60. See the second definition of a "free act" in Jacchaeus, *Disputatio theologica de libero arbitrio* (1603); see also Gomarus's pupil, Gisbertus Voetius, *Disputatio philosophico-theologica* 2.2–3.

61. Augustine, *civ. Dei* 5.10.

62. See, e.g., John Weemes, *Portraiture of the Image of God in Man,* 3rd ed. (London, 1636), 128. My thanks to David Sytsma for this citation.

63. See Junius, *Theses Leydenses* 22.

64. See Augustine, *civ. Dei* 11.10, 22–23; cf. 3.11–12; *Ench.* 1–14; Anselm, *De concordia* 1.7; and Johannes Maccovius, *Collegia Theologica, quae extant omnia. Tertio ab auctore recognita, emendata, & plurimis locis aucta, in partes duas distributa* (Franekerae: Impensis Vlderici Balck, 1641), 9.120.

65. Maccovius, *Collegia Theologica* 9.120.

66. Cf. Voetius, *Disputatio philosophico-theologica* 2.4; and Turretin, *Institutio* 6.5.11.

67. Voetius, *Disputatio philosophico-theologica* 2.4 (as translated in *Reformed Thought on Freedom*). Cf. Augustine, *civ. Dei* 5.10; Anselm, *De concordia* 2.3; Turretin, *Institutio* 6.5.11.

68. See "Determinisme," in *Vocabulaire technique et critique de la philosophie,* ed. André Lalande, 7th ed. (Paris: P. U. F., 1956), 221–24, esp. 221.

69. See, e.g., Sleigh, Chappell, and Della Rocca, "Determinism and Human Freedom," 1265.

70. See note 6 above.

71. William Hamilton attacks the compatibilism of Jonathan Edwards as heretical in Dugald Stewart, *The Collected Works,* ed. Sir William Hamilton, 10 vols. (Edinburgh: Thomas Constable, 1854–60), 6:402. Hamilton's opposition to equipoise (with his accompanying opposition to compatibilism) can also be found in "Sir William Hamilton's Philosophy," *Eclectic Magazine of Foreign Literature, Science, and Art* 28, no. 1 (January–April 1853): 83. Gisbertius Voetius also opposes equipoise as chimerical in *Disputatio philosophico-theologica* 2.3. His defense of libertarian free choice appears just prior to this in *Disputatio philosophico-theologica* 2.2. For a defense of the libertarian reading of Voetius generally and this passage in specific, see *Reformed Thought on Freedom,* ch. 5.

72. Voetius, *Disputatio philosophico-theologica* 2.3.

73. Voetius, *Disputatio philosophico-theologica* 2.2.

74. See Ria van der Lecq, "Duns Scotus on the Reality of Possible Worlds," in *John Duns Scotus: Renewal of Philosophy,* ed. E. P. Bos (Atlanta, GA: Rodopi, 1998), 89–99. Ria van der Lecq's article is based largely on Scotus's *Lectura* I 39.

75. Aquinas, *Summa contra Gentiles* 1.49.

76. Aquinas, *Summa contra Gentiles* 1.49; *Summa theologica* Ia, q. 14, art. 5, and q. 14, art. 9.

77. See Aquinas, *Summa theologica* Ia, q. 14, art. 9.

78. Henry of Ghent, *Quodlibet VIII* q. 2.

79. Notice that this concession is the heart of what has become known as the grounding objection against Molinism, an objection of which Leibniz is aware (G, 6:125–26), and which casts suspicion on the claim of Michael Murray et al. that Leibniz's possible worlds are Molinistic (see, e.g., Murray, "Leibniz on Divine Foreknowledge"). That said, Leibniz's position appears to be softer on Molinism than that of the Reformed. He holds that the objection is right in claiming that possibles are grounded in God's possible decrees, not in a knowledge between God's necessary and free knowledge (viz., *scientia media*), but Leibniz does not think divine foreknowledge would be without resources apart from this grounding; thus Molinism is not incoherent, as some claim (see G, 6:126–27).

80. See Muller, *Post-Reformation Reformed Dogmatics,* 3:408; Beck, "Gisbertus Voetius," 222–23; Vos, "Conceptual Patterns," 229; and van Asselt, "The Theologian's Tool Kit," 33–34.

81. Scotus, *Ordinatio* 1.39.64–65. To be sure, Scotus understands this predetermination to be an eternal decision by God; hence, propositions do not shift from being open to being affirmative truths. See Scotus, *Ordinatio* 1.39.25 and 1.39.64.

82. Scotus, *Ordinatio* 1.39.23: Tunc autem non sunt vera contingentia, quia nihil est tunc per quod habeant determinatam veritatem. Posita autem determination voluntatis divinae, iam sunt vera *in illo secundo instant,* et idem erit ratio intellectui divino — quod et in primo — intelligendi ista.

83. See Scotus, *Ordinatio* 1.36.22 and 1.39.93.

84. See Scotus's characterization of Ghent's solution in *Ordinatio* 1.39.64.

85. See note 80 above.

86. See Vos, *The Philosophy of John Duns Scotus,* 492 n. 63.

Chapter 9

Hume's Defense of True Religion

LEE HARDY

How is the deity disfigured in our representation of him!
—David Hume, *The Natural History of Religion*

On the back cover of the Oxford World's Classics edition of David Hume's *Dialogues concerning Natural Religion* and *The Natural History of Religion* we read that in these works is to be found "the most formidable attack upon the rationality of religious faith ever mounted by a philosopher."[1] This statement reflects a common view of Hume. But it is the view of many professional philosophers as well. A. J. Ayer maintains that one of the principal aims of Hume's philosophy was the "discrediting not only of the superstitious types of theism but of any form of religious belief."[2] Manfred Kuehn claims that Hume's philosophy of religion implies "the impossibility of any rational religious faith."[3] Sebastian Gardener holds that, in Hume's view, "Religious beliefs, and the whole edifice of metaphysical speculation, have no ground whatsoever."[4] In his book-length study of Hume's philosophy of religion, Keith Yandell states, "Hume is a critic of natural theology and believes that we have no good reason whatever to think that theism is true."[5] J. C. A. Gaskin, British Hume scholar, joins the chorus, claiming that since Hume took himself to have shown that there are no rational grounds for religious belief, such belief must be explained entirely by way of natural causes.[6]

Philosophers looking for antitheistic arguments have found no shortage of ammunition for their assault on religious belief in the pages of Hume's writings. At the same time, philosophers of religious conviction, who, like Nietzsche, understand the value of having enemies, have devoted a great deal of energy and attention to Hume's antitheistic arguments. Typically, both take Hume to represent the unalloyed forces of secular rational criticism against the traditions and propriety of religious belief.

In this essay I intend to challenge this picture of Hume. It represents, in my view, something of a retroactive secularization of the historical record as well as a grave distortion of Hume's position on religious matters. It should be clear from a reading of the *Natural History* that Hume does not reject religion *en bloc*. He is careful to make a distinction between true and false religion. He attacks the latter but endorses the former. The beliefs constituent of true religion are rationally justified, in Hume's professed view, but easily bypassed, overlaid, and perverted by the all-too-human propensities at work in false religion. Thus Hume's criticism of religion is more akin to the prophetic tradition, in which false religion is denounced in favor of true religion, than to the wholesale rejection of religion we should expect to find in the work of an unreserved atheist. Granted, Hume's philosophical theism is much thinner than the robust theism associated with the Judeo-Christian prophetic tradition; granted, too, that much of the positive content of that prophetic tradition will fall, in Hume's view, on the side of false religion. But Hume is still in the business of sorting out true religion from false religion. He is not invested in the project of rejecting all religion as false or irrational, as he is often represented in the philosophical dialectics of the present age.

Hume was well aware of his reputation for irreligion. But he also has his own account of why he is taken for an atheist. It is not because he *is* an atheist; rather, it is because his theism does not match the requirements of the often vulgar and self-serving theism of those who wish to persecute him. Here Hume identifies strongly with Socrates, who, although "the wisest and most religious of the Greek Philosophers," was nonetheless charged with impiety by the citizens of Athens (Letter, *EHU,* 117; see also *NHR,* 186).[7] Hume thought he was experiencing a similar fate, but this time in eighteenth-century Edinburgh, the "Athens of the North."

Given that Hume's philosophy of religion is taken up as tool or target in contemporary debates in the philosophy of religion and is highlighted only for its arguments critical of religious belief, its complexity and richness have almost entirely disappeared from the scene. Obscured is the duality in Hume's account of religious belief; obscured too is the positive role "true religion" played in the thought of this remarkable figure of the Scottish Enlightenment. How is Hume disfigured in our representation of him!

I will begin with a discussion of Hume's account of religion in the *Natural History of Religion* and the *Enquiry concerning Human Understanding,* covering the distinction between true and false religion and the roots of both in the propensities and ethical profile of those who subscribe to them; then I will consider Hume's own explanation of why he is perceived as an atheist. With this material in hand, I shall turn to the vexed issue of Philo's *volte-face* in part 12 of the *Dialogues concerning Natural Religion.* I shall argue that Philo's affirmation of the design argument in the final part of the *Dialogues* is entirely consistent with his rigorous attack on the design argument in the preceding parts. Thus those who are inclined to view Philo as a spokesperson for Hume need not write off Philo's affirmation of the design argument as a lapse on Hume's part, or a piece of irony, or an attempt to placate his potential critics. The affirmation is entirely in keeping with Hume's professed position on the status of the design argument in the *Natural History of Religion*; and it is not in conflict with Philo's earlier attack on the design argument in the *Dialogues concerning Natural Religion.* I conclude with a reference to the distinctive Calvinist stamp of Hume's philosophy of religion.

Throughout this reading of Hume on religion, I will keep to Hume's professed position, taking him at his written word. I will go the extra mile to see consistency in his published writings where others have seen serious conflict. I will keep biographical speculation to a minimum. And I will not apply the magic wand of irony to Hume's positive statements about religion in order to make apparent conflicts in the text simply disappear. I do not claim this is the only possible reading of Hume. But if I am successful in rendering a consistent reading of the professed Hume, then I take it I have thereby increased the burden of proof for those who propose to read Hume as a dissimulator in matters religious.

True Theism

Hume begins the *Natural History of Religion* (1757) by distinguishing between two questions one might ask of religion: one concerns its "foundation in reason," the other its "origin in human nature" (*NHR,* 134). One searches out and assesses the justification of religious belief; the other seeks an explanation of religious belief. "Happily," Hume writes, "the first question, which is the most important, admits of the most obvious, at least, the clearest solution. The whole frame of nature bespeaks an intelligent author; and no rational enquirer can, after serious reflection, suspend his belief a moment with regard to the primary principles of genuine Theism and Religion" (*NHR,* 134). Hume maintains this position consistently and without qualification throughout the work. In the last section he again claims, "A purpose, an intention, a design is evident in every thing; and when our comprehension is so far enlarged as to contemplate the first rise of the visible system, we must adopt, with the strongest conviction, the idea of some intelligent cause or author" (*NHR,* 183). Although Hume does think that we have a natural propensity to believe in an intelligent author of the universe upon the experience of design, here he wishes to emphasize the rationality of the belief according to the rules of evidence and inference. The belief in a deity "infinitely superior of mankind" is, he says, "altogether just" (*NHR,* 163). The basic tenet of theism conforms to "sound reason" (*NHR,* 165). In "A Letter from a Gentleman to His Friend in Edinburgh" (1745), Hume, defending himself against the charge of irreligion, underscores the inferential integrity of the design argument: "Whenever I see order, I infer from experience that *there,* there has been design and contrivance. And the same principle which leads me into this inference, when I contemplate a building, regular and beautiful in its whole frame and structure; the same principle obliges me to infer an infinitely perfect architect, from the infinite art and contrivance which is displayed in the whole fabric of the universe" (Letter, *EHU,* 119). Later I will indicate how Hume, in the *Natural History of Religion,* defends the design argument against Philo's attacks in the *Dialogues concerning Natural Religion.*

Hume's commitment to the design argument for God's existence should be of some assistance in rightly dividing the famous last lines of his *Enquiry concerning Human Understanding* (1748; quotes from the 1777 edition), where he bids us to run through the world's libraries and commit to the flames those books of divinity and school metaphysics that do not contain either abstract reasoning concerning number or experimental reasoning concerning matters of fact (*EHU,* 114). Many have taken this statement as a sign of Hume's militant atheism and a general incitement to theological book burning. But just prior to this great commission Hume states that theology, in its endeavor to prove the existence of God on a posteriori grounds, is based on reasoning concerning matters of fact, both particular and general. Insofar as this theological project is supported by experience, it has, he says, a foundation in reason (*EHU,* 114). So the force of the last lines in the *Enquiry* is not that all books of divinity are mere "sophistry and illusion" but rather only those that do not contain any reasoning concerning matters of fact. The argument for the existence of one wise and powerful Creator God begins with the experience of a matter of fact: the order and design in the universe. Such reasoning is thus supported by experience. It follows that books containing such reasoning should be spared the flames.

The Religious Belief Disposition

Although Hume places the entire weight of rational belief in God on the platform of the design argument, he also thinks that we have a general built-in propensity to believe in an intelligent author of nature upon the experience of design. This propensity works at the level of what Hume sometimes calls "instinctual beliefs" (*EHU,* 30), beliefs that are directly prompted by experience and not based upon an explicit consideration of evidence and its implications. Hume has Cleanthes, in the *Dialogues,* give an example of the triggering circumstance and effect of this remarkable feature of the human mind: "Consider, anatomize the eye: Survey its structure and contrivance; and tell me, for your own feeling, if the idea of a contriver does not immediately flow in upon you with a force like that of sensation" (*DNR,* 56). This propensity, however, is not just a blind fact about human nature; rather, God implanted it in us, Hume claims in the *Natural History,* as a trace or sign of his existence. "The universal propensity to believe in invisible, intelligent power, if not an original instinct, being at least a general attendant of human nature, may be considered as a kind of mark or stamp, which the divine workman has set upon his work; and nothing surely can more dignify mankind, than to be thus selected from all other parts of the creation, and to bear the image or impression of the universal Creator" (*NHR,* 184). Perhaps humanity was not created in the image of God, as the Genesis account has it; even so, Hume insists, it bears the image of God.

The common belief propensities embedded in human nature are powerful and typically outweigh the abstract objections to their doxastic products as advanced by skeptical philosophers. This is why Hume says in the *Enquiry* that we need not fear that his philosophical skepticism will ever undermine the well-entrenched beliefs of common sense, for, "Nature will always maintain her rights, and prevail in the end over any abstract reasoning whatsoever" (*EHU,* 27). This is also true of the propensity to believe in a Creator God upon the perception of order and design in the universe. In fact, the strength of this common belief propensity gives Philo, the notorious philosophical skeptic of the *Dialogues,* the license to explore the full extent of the skeptical point of view on religious matters without the worry that he will have destroyed any religious belief of real value. At the conclusion of the *Dialogues,* in part 12, having unleashed the full force of his skeptical arguments, Philo admits, "I am less cautious on the subject of natural religion than on any other; both because I know that I can never, on that head, corrupt the principles of any man of common sense, and because no one, I am confident, in whose eyes I appear a man of common sense, will ever mistake my intentions" (*DNR*, 116).

Emphasis on the raw power of the belief propensities of common sense may give the impression that on the point of God's existence reason loses and nature wins. The rational discipline of philosophy is simply, in the end, overpowered by the nonrational forces of human nature, thus creating the "whimsical condition of mankind," as Hume famously calls it in the *Enquiry*, where our nature prompts us to believe things that reason can neither certify nor defend (*EHU*, 111). Later I will argue in more detail that this is not the case in connection with the belief in God's existence: as Cleanthes suggests in part 12 of the Dialogues, this belief is both prompted by a "natural propensity" and, despite Philo's prior objections, "supported by strong and obvious reason" (*DNR*, 118).

Vulgar Religion

However powerful the propensity for belief in the existence of the divine may be, Hume ranks it as a secondary rather than a primary principle of human nature. This is both because it can be overridden by other propensities, giving rise to atheism in some cases, and because it is largely indeterminate with respect to the nature of the divine. Here too, other propensities are at work, producing a marked diversity in religious beliefs and in most cases perverting the philosophically inclined belief in a wise, infinite, transcendent Creator God; for the first principles of religion are "easily perverted by various accidents and causes" (*NHR*, 134). Hume takes it that the content of true religion has a foundation in reason as well as our nature. But when he turns to false religion, he seeks an explanation entirely rooted in our nature: "It is chiefly our present business to consider the gross polytheism of the vulgar, and to trace all its various appearances, in the principles of human nature, whence they are derived" (*NHR*, 150).

Polytheism is the "original religion" of humankind in both the historical and existential sense. It is the "first and most ancient religion of mankind" (*NHR*, 135); but it is also a religious tendency rooted in the practical life of finite beings who are not in control of the forces that determine their welfare, a life that rarely admits the occasion for a calm and disinterested awareness of the grand order of the universe. "We may conclude, therefore, that, in all nations, which have embraced polytheism, the first ideas of religion arose not from a contemplation of the works of nature [which would lead to true religion], but from a concern with regard to the events of life, and from the incessant hopes and fears, which actuate the human mind" (*NHR,* 139). Here humanity is moved by "anxious concern for happiness, the dread of future misery, the terror of death, the thirst for revenge, the appetite for food and other necessaries" (*NHR,* 140). Polytheistic deities typically superintend the various passion-filled domains of practical life: marriages, births, agriculture, seafaring, and the like — "and nothing prosperous or adverse can happen in life, which may not be the subject of peculiar prayers or thanksgivings" (*NHR,* 140). Thus the vulgar are led to prayers and sacrifices, rites and ceremonies, as ways of finding favor with the gods (*NHR,* 139). They look upon life "agitated by hopes and fears" (*NHR,* 140). Too little aware of the marvelous order of the universe, "they remain still unacquainted with a first and supreme creator, and with that infinitely perfect spirit, who alone, by his almighty will, bestowed order on the whole frame of nature" (*NHR,* 142). Narrow in their concerns, surrounded by unknown powers on which their tenuous grasp on happiness depends, unable or unwilling to conduct a scientific investigation of these powers, the multitudes exercise their imaginations rather than reason and, under the guidance of certain propensities in human nature, form a religious system. One of the human propensities at work is to conceive of all beings to be like themselves, to transfer familiar qualities in themselves to unfamiliar things, in short, to anthropomorphize the divine (*NHR,* 141). As a result, the deity is often represented as "jealous and revengeful, capricious and partial, and, in short, a wicked and foolish man, in every respect but his superior power and authority" (*NHR,* 141–42).

Vulgar religion is an instrument developed in the search for control over the objects of desire. It is based on a strong attachment to the goods of fortune and is motivated by the fear of losing them or failing to attain them (or, conversely, the hope of attaining them or hanging on to them). The gods of vulgar religion, in the form of polytheism, are there to be placated and persuaded through various actions that possess no positive moral value in themselves. This, according to Hume, was the general condition of religion in "barbarous ages" (*NHR*, 142). Yet progress toward true religion is to be expected on the basis of improvements in government, making life more secure and less fearful, and the development of science, which will acquaint us with the intricate order of the universe, prompting belief in a transcendent and wise Creator God (*NHR*, 142). The full span of this progress would take humanity from "groveling and familiar notions of superior powers" to a "conception of that perfect Being, who bestowed order on the whole frame of nature" (*NHR*, 134–35); from a divine being who is powerful but limited, "with human passions and appetites, limbs and organs," to one who is "pure spirit, omniscient, omnipotent, and omnipresent" (*NHR*, 136). At any point in this process an individual may take a shortcut to the end by way of an "obvious and invincible" design argument that appeals to reason and leads to a pure theism (*NHR*, 137). But the common run of humankind is neither acquainted with nor moved by such arguments. Exceptions are rare, to be found only among the learned.

The kind of religion one has is largely a function of the kind of person one is. Although the propensity to believe in an intelligent author of the world is universally distributed across humankind, it is activated only in those of a more noble and contemplative bent of mind. The vulgar never put themselves before the intricate order of the universe as a whole, or in its parts, and thus are not moved to believe in a supreme intelligence. The "stupidity of men, barbarous and uninstructed [is] so great that they may not see a sovereign author in the more obvious works of nature" (*NHR*, 183). Their vision is narrowed by practical concerns for their own welfare; their attention is keyed only to the immediate but obscure powers "which bestow happiness or misery" (*NHR*, 152). In many ways, the religion of the vulgar is a product of their own vice, their own narrow attachment to the single issue of their own worldly weal and woe. On the other hand, there is a "manly, steady virtue, which either preserves us from disastrous, melancholy accidents, or teaches us to bear them. During such calm sunshine of the mind, these specters of false divinity never make their appearance" (*NHR,* 182). But when we "abandon ourselves to the natural undisciplined suggestions of our timid and anxious hearts, every kind of barbarity is ascribed to the supreme Being, for the terrors with which we are agitated; and every kind of caprice, from the methods which we embrace in order to appease him" (*NHR,* 182). Only the pure in heart will see God.

Clearly, on this point Hume draws from the Stoic tradition, recommending the philosophical life of detachment as a prerequisite for true religion. The Stoics taught that virtue is not only necessary for happiness but sufficient. A concern with the external goods of fortune over which we have, ultimately, no control—a concern with health, wealth, fame, and the like—will only serve to set a person up for a life of disappointment, misery, and vice. "The happy life," counsels Seneca, "is to have a mind that is independent, elevated, fearless, and unshakeable, a mind that exists beyond the reach of fear and of desire."[8] The highest good must find its place beyond hope and beyond fear.[9] This is the way to the best life; it is also the way to true religious devotion. In the *Encheiridion,* Epictetus states that "piety is impossible unless you detach the good and the bad from what is not up to us and attach it exclusively to what is up to us,"[10] that is, unless you detach yourself from the goods of fortune and focus exclusively on the cultivation of virtue within the soul. Hume's sentiments lie in the same direction. Only with the acquisition of Stoic virtue and detachment will a person be delivered from the generation of anxious god-manipulators and enter into the repose of genuine theism. Vulgar religion begins in fear; true religion begins in wonder.

Hume makes no secret of his disdain for polytheism. He associates it with barbarous and vulgar cultures; and he refers more than once to its practitioners as "idolaters" (*NHR,* 134, 152). His more pointed criticism, however, is that polytheism is in fact a form of atheism. The divine beings of polytheism are but denizens of this world, not the transcendent Creator of it (*NHR,* 147). "The gods of all polytheists are not better than the elves or fairies of our ancestors, and merit as little any pious worship or veneration. These pretended religionists are really a kind of superstitious atheists, and acknowledge no being, that corresponds to our idea of a deity. No first principle of mind or thought: No supreme government and administration: No divine contrivance or intention in the fabric of the world" (*NHR*, 145). In words reminiscent of St. Paul's letter to the Romans, Hume identifies the chief defect of polytheism as the worship of the creation rather than the Creator. "Whoever learns by argument, the existence of invisible intelligent power, must reason from the admirable contrivance of natural objects, and must suppose the world to be the workmanship of that divine being, the original cause of all things. But the vulgar polytheist, so far from admitting that idea, deifies every part of the universe, and conceives all the conspicuous productions of nature, to be themselves so many real divinities" (*NHR*, 150). St. Paul put it this way: "Claiming to be wise, they became fools, and exchanged the glory of the immortal God for images resembling mortal man and birds and animals and reptiles . . . and worshiped and served the creature rather than the Creator" (Rom. 1:23, 25).

Vulgar Theism

Hume holds that there are two roads out of polytheism to theism of the monotheistic sort. The high road, which we have already explored, begins with the disinterested experience of design and leads us to the Creator by way of propensity or inference. This road is undergirded by sure and "invincible reasons" (*NHR*, 153). The low road, often taken by the vulgar, has its origins in the irrational side of human nature and the passions that attend it. Starting with the threatening experiences of adversity, death, disease, famine, drought, and the like, travelers on this road ascribe such events to the workings of a particular providence. Modeling the god of particular providence on an earthly king, they then seek to flatter and influence this deity to their advantage. Outdoing each other in flattery in a kind of encomium competition, they eventually form the conception of their god as an infinite, perfect being. This is the vulgar route to the God of the philosophers: "While they confine themselves to the notion of a perfect being, the creator of the world, they coincide, by chance, with the principles of reason and true philosophy; though they are guided to that notion, not by reason, of which they are in a great measure incapable, but by the adulation and fears of the most vulgar superstition" (*NHR*, 155).

The impulse toward the perfect-being theology of the philosophers makes of the divine, however, something cold, abstract, and practically unavailable, a God too distant from human affairs to be of any help in facing the terrors of this life. It therefore spawns within common human nature the opposite impulse: a downward pull by a sentiment that wants to make the divine more familiar, more approachable, more localized, more arbitrary, and therefore more persuadable. This contrary impulse tends to backfill the universe with lesser gods and various intermediaries, infecting the antecedent theism with all manner of idolatry (*NHR*, 159). "Men have a natural tendency," Hume observes, "to rise from idolatry to theism, and to sink again from theism into idolatry" (*NHR*, 158–59). The second idolatry, however, only sets the stage for a renewed theistic impulse. The movement becomes cyclic, giving rise to a constant "flux and reflux" of theism and polytheism, all powered by human anxiety.

The Persecution of Philosophical Theists

Socrates, Hume writes in the "Letter from a Gentleman," was "the wisest and most religious of the Greek Philosophers" (Letter, *EHU*, 117). Yet, in spite of his genuine religious devotion, Socrates was "esteemed impious" because his form of philosophical theism demoted the divine standing of the gods of the ambient polytheism (*NHR*, 186). In effect, Socrates's philosophical theism threatened to deprive the vulgar of those divine beings who, fashioned in their own likeness, could also be persuaded to do their bidding. This was not the only time that philosophical theists have been persecuted by the vulgar. In Hume's day, however, the persecution came not from the camp of vulgar polytheists but from the vulgar theists. Although vulgar theists hold that there is but one God, not many, they drink at the same well as the polytheist: desire and passion more than reason influence their conception of the divine. Their God is much more likely to become an available instrument in the human quest for power and advantage in the domain of earthly goods; and their God is more likely to be in the habit of intervening in the course of the world's affairs in order to honor the requests of those who have learned how to please him. Philosophical theists, on the other hand, believe in a general providence but not a particular. They hold that God established the general and regular order of the universe but deny that God intervenes on particular occasions (or on all occasions). The vulgar equate the denial of particular providence with atheism.[11] Here, Hume avers, they are taught by "superstitious prejudices" to look for God within the workings of the world as the direct cause of particular events. They are thus inclined to identify as atheists all those who limit the explanation of natural events to natural causes. But as science reveals that particular natural events are caused by other natural events within a huge natural system, God disappears from the purview of the vulgar and they are apt to lose their faith, unless by further reflection they see the overall regular order of the universe as evidence of a supreme intelligence and return to belief on a stronger foundation (*NHR*, 154). Here Hume notes, along with Lord Bacon, that a little philosophy makes men atheists, but a great deal reconciles them to religion (*NHR*, 154).

An extreme form of vulgar theism has its philosophical representation in the doctrine of the occasionalists. These philosophers, like the vulgar in the presence of the miraculous, "acknowledge mind and intelligence to be, not only the ultimate and original cause of all things, but the immediate and sole cause of every event, which appears in nature" (*EHU*, 46). Although the occasionalists seek to make God first in all things by their maximal version of particular providence, they actually diminish the deity in Hume's view. "It surely argues more power in the Deity to delegate a certain degree of power to inferior creatures, than to produce every thing by his own immediate volition. It argues more wisdom to contrive at first the fabric of the world with such perfect foresight, that, of itself, and by its proper operation, it may serve all the purposes of providence, than if the great Creator were obliged every moment to adjust its parts, and animate by this breath all the wheels of that stupendous machine" (*EHU*, 47). Greater is the God who had everything figured out at the beginning than a God constantly involved in midcourse corrections.

The philosophical theist (that is, a deist) limits belief in God to only what is licensed by empirical reason—here what can be inferred from the presence and unity of design in the universe. It is skeptical of human reason's ability to make any further determinations on the basis of a priori speculation. In addition, because of their Stoic ethical formation, Humean deists are not overly attached to the desires for earthly goods and the passions that attend them. They are, therefore, under no special motivation to conceive of the divine as an agent of intervention, as a personal assistant in attaining and retaining such goods. This is to say that Hume's brand of deism *cum* skepticism is not aligned with any "disorderly passion" of the mind. In "renouncing all speculations which lie not within the limits of common human practice," it opposes "superstitious credulity" (*EHU,* 26); it cares only about the truth that can be established on the basis of experience. Yet, however innocent, it is the object of much reproach: "By flattering no irregular passion, it gains few partisans: By opposing so many vices and follies, it raises to itself abundance of enemies, who stigmatize it as libertine, profane, and irreligious" (*EHU,* 27). Here Hume exposes the passion of his religious critics as a function of their worldly attachments and anxieties.

Philo's *Volte-Face*

Philo, who plays the role of the skeptic in the *Dialogues concerning Natural Religion* (composed ca. 1750, published 1779), expends a good deal of energy in parts 4 through 8 criticizing the argument from design for God's existence. But in part 12, after the departure of Demea, he confides to his close friend Cleanthes, "Not withstanding the freedom of conversation, and my love of singular arguments, no one has a deeper sense of religion impressed upon his mind, or pays more profound adoration to the divine Being, as he discovers himself to reason, in the inexplicable contrivance of nature. A purpose, an intention, a design strikes everywhere the most careless, the most stupid thinker; and no man can be so hardened in absurd systems as at all times to reject it" (*DNR,* 116). This sudden and seeming reversal in

Philo's estimation of the design argument and religious belief in the concluding part of the *Dialogues* has served as a great stumbling block for interpreters. Jonathan Dancy, in fact, claims that the success of any interpretation of the *Dialogues* hangs on giving a plausible explanation of Philo's mystifying *volte-face*.[12] Many commentators have assumed that Hume is an atheist, that Philo speaks for Hume, and that the affirmation of the design argument in part 12 must therefore be taken as a piece of irony or as a disingenuous sop thrown in the direction of Hume's religious critics. Others have suggested that, after Demea's departure, Philo is no longer doing philosophy; we should take his comments as if they came from one reclining at the backgammon board, having given himself over completely to his nonrational belief propensities.[13] Still others have held that the earlier criticism of the design argument does not represent Philo's actual view of the matter. A lover of argument, he left his own convictions behind in order to score a series of dialectical victories in the presence of the dogmatic Demea. Now that Demea has left the scene, Philo is free to speak his own, considered opinion. After all, Cleanthes, who knows Philo well, says to Philo at this point, "Your spirit of controversy . . . carries you strange lengths, when engaged in an argument; and there is nothing so sacred and venerable, *even in your own eyes,* which you spare on the occasion" (*DNR,* 116, my emphasis). Moreover, Philo himself refers to his pious statements in part 12 as his "unfeigned sentiments on the subject" (*NHR,* 121).[14]

I will not take these interpretive routes. The dismissal of Philo's expression of piety as ironic, the idea that Philo must no longer be doing philosophy, and the notion that he disowns his earlier criticism of the design argument all share a common assumption: that Philo's criticism of the design argument in parts 4 through 8 and his affirmation of it in part 12 are in fact inconsistent with each other. If he were denying and affirming the same argument, of course, they would be inconsistent. They could be consistent, however, if there were at least two ways of construing the design argument. I will argue that this is the case: Philo criticizes a crucial part of the design argument as if it were a deductive argument; but when he later affirms it, he affirms it as an inference to the best explanation.

The overall structure of the design argument is, of course, analogical. Analogical arguments trade on the similarities between two cases, arguing that if something follows in the one case, then something similar follows in the other case. The design argument places the universe in analogical relation to cultural artifacts on the basis of a similarity between the two with respect to apparent design features and then asserts that if we are justified in inferring that a cultural artifact was made by an intelligent agent, then we are also justified in inferring that the universe was made by an intelligent agent. The issue on which Philo's reversal turns is not so much the degree of the analogy between the universe and cultural artifacts as it is the nature of the analogized inferences. In part 5 of the *Dialogues* Philo argues that, given the analogy of design between the human and divine cases, it still does not necessarily follow from the presence of design in the universe that the divine artificer of the universe is one in number. It is possible, for instance, that a designed universe was brought about by a committee of divine beings (*DNR,* 69–70). At this point in the *Dialogues* Cleanthes is asked to "*prove* the unity of the Deity" (*DNR,* 69–70, my emphasis). But clearly he cannot do so, for the conclusion does not necessarily follow from the premises. Here Philo is handing himself an easy point by construing the inference under consideration as deductive in nature and rejecting it as an instance of the fallacy of affirming the consequent (to wit: if one intelligent Creator God exists, then we will detect the presence of design in the universe; we detect the presence of design in the universe, therefore one intelligent Creator God exists). Later, in part 9, Philo reemphasizes the point by saying, "The unity too of the divine nature, it is very difficult, if not absolutely impossible, to *deduce* merely from contemplating the works of nature" (*DNR,* 90, my emphasis).

Interestingly, in the *Natural History of Religion* (1757), Hume himself takes up this very objection to the design argument. "To persons of a certain turn of mind," he writes, "it may not appear altogether absurd, that several independent beings, endowed with superior wisdom, might conspire in the contrivance and execution of one regular plan; yet this is a merely arbitrary supposition, which, even if allowed possible, must be confessed neither to be supported by probability nor necessity" (*NHR*, 138). If we represent the claims that the world was created by a number of divine beings as an explanatory hypothesis (a "supposition"), we will note two things: that it is not necessary and that it is not probable. It is not necessary because other explanations are logically possible (it could have been created by one God). Here Hume, following Philo's cue, construes the claim that the world was created by a committee of gods as the conclusion of a deductive argument, and he rejects it. But when he turns to the question of its probability, he considers it as an explanatory hypothesis and rejects it as well, but for different reasons. It is not probable, Hume argues, because the uniformity of nature—the fact that "one design prevails throughout the whole" (*NHR*, 138)—is better explained by recourse to a unitary divine being. "The uniform maxims, too, which prevail throughout the whole frame of the universe, naturally, if not necessarily, lead us to conceive this intelligence as single and undivided, where the prejudices of education oppose not so reasonable a theory" (*NHR*, 138). The presence of design in the universe does not lead to the conclusion of one Creator God "necessarily," that is, by the inescapable force of deductive logic; but it does lead us to that conclusion "naturally" as the most likely, and hence the most reasonable, explanation of the presence of uniform design. The hypothesis of multiple creators, on the other hand, serves only to "give perplexity to the imagination, without bestowing any satisfaction on the understanding" (*NHR*, 138).

Given Hume's defense of the design argument in the *Natural History*, then, it could be entirely consistent on Philo's part to reject the core of the design argument as a piece of demonstration in part 5, while accepting it in part 12 as the best explanation of data before us, as the most probable hypothesis. Do we have any reason to think that this is in fact what Philo had in mind? We have two hints from the text in part 12 that he did. First, Philo uses the language of reasoning, or inferring, to causes (*DNR*, 119). Reasoning to a cause in the order of deductive logic will typically run afoul of the fallacy of affirming the consequent and will thus be an easy target for criticism. This is the point of Philo's earlier critique of the "one designer" conclusion of the design argument, since the same effect—designedness—could have been brought about by a committee of several designers. But reasoning to a single cause in the hypothetical-deductive order avoids this problem: it looks only for the most probable explanatory hypothesis by comparing the consequences of a hypothesis with observed data and its plausibility against competing hypotheses. This leads us to the second hint. Noting the intricacies of order in the discoveries of the natural sciences in the opening passages of part 12, Philo claims that although a design argument launched from any one of these examples of order is not "forcible" (which I read as "not deductively necessary"), it is nonetheless fitting. That is, Philo says, "according to all rules of just reasoning" it is well adapted to the nature of the fact it is attempting to establish, and the cumulative force of the argument upon case after case of interlocking design becomes virtually irresistible to all those but a philosopher who suffers from a serious case of "pertinacious obstinacy" (*DNR*, 117–18). Given the empirical evidence before us, it is the most likely and hence the most reasonable explanation.

In an earlier statement, "Letter from a Gentleman" (1745), Hume states that, in criticizing the notion that reason can prove the existence of God through intuition and demonstration, he was not claiming there was no evidence for God's existence. Rather, he was claiming that there was just not that kind of evidence. There is such a thing as moral certainty, as well as a mathematical or "rational" certainty. The certainty that attends the design argument is not the rational certainty gained through intuition and demonstration; it is, rather, a certainty based on moral evidence, that is, on matters of fact plus a high degree of probability. "It would be no difficult matter to show, that the arguments *a posteriori* from the order and course of nature, these arguments so sensible, so convincing, and so obvious, remain still in full force," since the critique of natural theology he proposed was focused only on the a priori arguments that depend on deductive reason alone (Letter, *EHU*, 118). Here Hume is not denying that there is evidence for the existence of the Deity but only trying to identify which kind of evidence is relevant (Letter, *EHU*, 118). Assigning one kind of evidence to a proposition instead of another is not the same as denying the proposition in question. Hume is against only one kind of argument for God's existence, not all the arguments (Letter, *EHU*, 119).

Hume's Calvinism

Norman Kemp Smith claims that a good part of Hume's philosophical trajectory can be explained as a reaction to the Calvinism of his Scottish Presbyterian upbringing.[15] No doubt this is in some sense true. And yet the Calvinist approach left an unmistakable mark on Hume's philosophy of religion. If we turn to the founding text of the Calvinist movement, John Calvin's *Institutes of Christian Religion* (final edition, 1559), we find themes strikingly familiar to any student of Hume's work. I will highlight four of them.

First, like Hume, Calvin claims that humans carry within them a built-in awareness of the divine. In book 1 of the *Institutes,* on the "Knowledge of God the Creator," Calvin writes: "There is within the human mind, and indeed by natural instinct, an awareness of divinity"; for God "has implanted in all men a certain understanding of his divine majesty."[16] Indeed, "a sense of divinity is engraven on human hearts" (1:51). This sense is triggered by the presence of design in creation, through which God "daily discloses himself." Because of the "workmanship of the universe . . . men cannot open their eyes without being compelled to see him" (1:52). This awareness, however, in Calvin's book does not count as a complete and sufficient knowledge of God; it remains but a vague premonition of divine power and wisdom— about as far as Hume's empirical reason will take us.

Second, we find the world over that this natural awareness of the divine has been corrupted by ignorance and vice (*Institutes,* 1:47). Left to their own devices, human beings wind up worshipping a "figment and a dream of their own heart" rather than the true God (1:48). "Scarcely a single person has ever been found who did not fashion for himself an idol or specter in place of God" (1:65). The tendency toward idolatry is nothing adventitious in human life and history; it is rooted in our nature (for Calvin, our fallen nature). "Man's nature, so to speak, is a perpetual factory of idols" (1:50). Moreover, the motivational fuel of this factory, Calvin claims, is fear. "That saying of Statius' that fear first made gods in the world corresponds well to this kind of irreligion [idolatry], and to this alone" (1:50). We recall that for Hume an "anxious fear of future events" gives rise to "primary religion [the idolatry of polytheism]" (*NHR,* 176).

Third, one will also find a resonance between Hume and Calvin in their rejection of superstition—the attempt to influence divine powers through morally irrelevant means. In every religion, no matter how noble, Hume writes, many of its followers "will seek the divine favor, not by virtue and good morals, which alone can be acceptable to a perfect being, but either by frivolous observances, by intemperate zeal, by rapturous ecstasies, or by belief of mysterious and absurd opinions" (*NHR,* 179). True religion is corrupted apart from the view that "nothing but morality could gain the divine favor" (*NHR,* 180). Those given over to superstition typically degrade their deity into a likeness of themselves, only slightly more powerful and intelligent than human beings (*NHR,* 180), and then seek to flatter that deity through a variety of superstitious acts. Morality is of little interest to the superstitious because it gives them no bargaining chips they can use in their negotiations with divine powers. "Moral obligation, in our apprehension, removes all pretension to religious merit; and the virtuous conduct is deemed no more than what we owe to society and to ourselves. In all this, a superstitious man finds nothing, which he has properly performed for the sake of his deity, or which can peculiarly recommend him to the divine favor and protection. . . . He still looks out for some more immediate service of the supreme Being, in order to allay those terrors, with which he is haunted" (*NHR,* 181). Likewise, Calvin claims that we should seek to please God with an upright life, not ceremonies, rites, and sacrifices. Referring to those as "hypocrites" who pretend to approach God even as they flee him, he writes: "They boldly rebel against him in almost all their deeds, and are zealous to placate him merely with a few paltry sacrifices. Where they ought to serve him in sanctity of life and integrity of heart, they trump up frivolous titles and worthless little observances with which to win his favor" (*Institutes* 1:51).

Fourth and finally is the weakness of human reason. In his "Letter from a Gentleman," Hume states that the Fathers of the Church as well as the Reformers "were copious in representing the weakness and uncertainty of *mere* human reason" (Letter, *EHU,* 117). Later Hume has Philo point out in the *Dialogues* that the Reformers, unlike the Scholastics, were skeptical about the ability of human reason alone to discern the nature of God in the project of natural theology (*DNR,*

40). Skepticism need not always be opposed to the interests of religion; a certain amount of skepticism can be a sign of genuine religious humility (see *EHU,* 111, 116). Calvin especially was aware of the weakness and limitations of the human mind and the consequent need for a revelation received in faith, for a self-manifestation of the divine in the words of a religiously authoritative scripture. "The human mind because of its feebleness can in no way attain to God unless it be aided and assisted by his Sacred Word" (*Institutes,* 1:74). It is only by recourse to Scripture, in fact, "that God, the Creator of the universe, can by sure marks be distinguished from all the throng of feigned gods" (1:71). The need for a turn from reason to revelation is echoed in the last statement Philo makes in the *Dialogues* (added to the *Dialogues,* poignantly, by Hume in the last year of his life):

> The most natural sentiment, which a well-disposed mind will feel on this occasion, is a longing desire and expectation, that Heaven would be pleased to dissipate, at least alleviate, this profound ignorance, by affording some more particular revelation to mankind, and making discoveries of the nature, attributes, and operations of the divine object of our Faith. A person seasoned with a just sense of the imperfections of natural reason, will fly to revealed truth with the greatest avidity: While the haughty dogmatist, persuaded that he can erect a complete system of theology by the mere help of philosophy, disdains any farther aid, and rejects this adventitious instructor. To be a philosophical skeptic is, in a man of letters, the first and most essential step towards being a sound, believing Christian. (*DNR,* 130)

We have no reason to believe that Hume himself took this last step in the Calvinist program for the acquisition of the knowledge of God and thus became a sound, believing Christian. But the echoes of that program resound in the texts he left behind.

Notes

1. See David Hume, *Dialogues and Natural History of Religion,* ed. J. C. A. Gaskin (Oxford: Oxford University Press, 1993).

2. A. J. Ayer, *Hume* (Oxford: Oxford University Press, 1980), 23.

3. Manfred Kuehn, "Kant's Critique of Hume's Theory of Faith," in *Hume and Hume's Connexions,* ed. M. A. Stewart and John P. Wright (University Park: Pennsylvania State University Press, 1995), 240.

4. Sebastian Gardener, *Kant's Critique of Pure Reason* (London: Routledge, 1999), 6.

5. Keith Yandell, *Hume's "Inexplicable Mystery"* (Philadelphia: Temple University Press, 1990), 33.

6. J. A. C. Gaskin, "Hume on Religion," in *The Cambridge Companion to Hume,* ed. David Fate Norton (Cambridge: Cambridge University Press, 1993), 319.

7. I will use the following abbreviations for the titles of Hume's works cited in text: "Letter" for "A Letter from a Gentleman to His Friend in Edinburgh"; *EHU* for *An Enquiry concerning Human Understanding* (Indianapolis: Hackett, 1993); *NHR* for the *Natural History of Religion* (Oxford: Oxford University Press, 1993; and *DNR* for *Dialogues concerning Natural Religion* (Oxford: Oxford University Press, 1993). In some of the Hume quotes I have slightly, and silently, modernized the spelling and orthography.

8. Seneca, *Dialogues and Essays* (Oxford: Oxford University Press, 2007), 88.

9. Seneca, *Dialogues and Essays,* 99.

10. Epictetus, *Encheiridion* (Indianapolis: Hackett, 1983), 21.

11. At the time, the General Assembly of the Scottish Presbyterian Kirk considered deism to be a form of atheism, as evidenced by its 1696 statement against Thomas Aikenhead in an "Act against the Atheistical Opinions of the Deists." See M. A. Stewart, "Religion and Rational Theology," in *The Cambridge Companion to the Scottish Enlightenment* (Cambridge: Cambridge University Press, 2003), 34.

12. Jonathan Dancey, "'For Here the Author Is Annihilated': Reflections on Philosophical Aspects of the Use of the Dialogue Form in Hume's *Dialogues concerning Natural Religion,*" in *Philosophical Dialogues: Plato, Hume, Wittgenstein,* ed. Timothy J. Smiley (Oxford: Oxford University Press, 1995), 30.

13. See Yandell, *Hume's "Inexplicable Mystery,"* 38–39.

14. For more on this interpretation, see William Lad Sessions, *Reading Hume's Dialogues* (Bloomington: University of Indiana Press, 2002), 184–85.

15. Norman Kemp Smith, introduction to *Dialogues concerning Natural Religion* (Indianapolis: Bobbs Merill, 1947), 1–8.

16. John Calvin, *Institutes of the Christian Religion* (Philadelphia: Westminster Press, 1960), 1:43 (hereafter cited parenthetically in the text as *Institutes,* with volume and page number).

Chapter 10

The Illegitimate Son

Kant and Theological Nonrealism

CHRIS L. FIRESTONE

*Get rid of that slave woman and her son, for that slave woman's
son will never share in the inheritance with my son Isaac.*
—Genesis 21:10

Two interpretive bloodlines flow from the philosophy of Immanuel
Kant. The theologically positive bloodline, as Gordon Michalson characterizes it, "veer[s] off in the direction of constructive theological
efforts to accommodate Christian faith and critical thinking."[1] The
theologically negative bloodline portrays Kant as advocating the "aban-
donment of theism." This stream contends that Kant's "efforts to ameliorate the theologically destructive effects of the *Critique of Pure Reason*
implicitly make things worse for Christian theism, not better."[2] The
theologically positive bloodline includes deists and theists who take
Kant to be a theological realist; the theologically negative bloodline
consists of atheists and nonrealists.[3] Neither positive nor negative Kant
interpreters dispute the fact that atheists, even when speaking of Kant
as their proverbial "father," bear little family resemblance to Kant. In
other words, there is uniformed agreement that atheism has no real

blood relation to Kant and thus cannot be a legitimate heir of Kant's estate. The question of this essay is whether theological nonrealism is a legitimate heir of Kant or merely another illegitimate son.

The structure of the argument to follow is straightforward, consisting of two parts. In the first part, I trace the birth and biography of a prominent strand of theological nonrealism extending from P. F. Strawson, through Keith Ward and Peter Byrne, to Don Cupitt. Taking my cues from Cupitt, I examine how nonrealism understands itself to be within the lineage of Kant. On one level, Cupitt's philosophy of religion is the logical extension of an influential British strand of Kant interpretation, gaining traction for theological nonrealism by an implicit relationship to the work of these Kant scholars. On another level, Cupitt focuses his argument on the history of ideas and the reception and development of Kant's philosophy. As we will see, by Cupitt's lights, Ludwig Feuerbach is the one who finally birthed theological nonrealism after it had been conceived by Kant and had gestated throughout the period of the objective idealists. In examining these two levels, I make plain the grounds on which theological nonrealism supports its claim to have a direct relationship to Kant's philosophy and thus to be Kant's "truest" theological heir. In the second part, I turn to Kant's texts in order to contest this claim, indeed to cut it off at the root. Examining cognition and faith against the backdrop of Kant's critical strictures on knowledge, I show that Kant's philosophy, in particular its transcendental constituents and perspectival character, does not entail, or support, theological nonrealism. Instead, it moves so decisively in the direction of rational religious faith and theological realism that any claim by theological nonrealists to Kant's legacy is simply not credible.

Kant and the Genealogy of Theological Nonrealism

In Kant studies today, debate continues between those who hold that Kant's critical writings and writings on religion amount to deism and those who believe these writings entail a more vibrant form of theism. Allen Wood's career as the preeminent scholar of Kant's philosophy of religion in the English-speaking world is an excellent example of both sides of this dispute. In his groundbreaking early work on Kant, Wood defended the position that Kant's philosophy of religion supports faith in "a living God."[4] In recent years, he has backpedaled from this position, suggesting that Kant's philosophy edges toward deism.[5] It is not important for the purpose of this essay to decide which Wood is right. The fact is that neither theism nor deism sits comfortably within the confines of theological nonrealism.

For an interpretation of Kant amenable to theological nonrealism, we must steer our attention down an altogether different interpretive stream, namely, one composed principally of influential British interpreters of Kant. P. F. Strawson's book *The Bounds of Sense* (1966) caused a surge of dissent in Kant scholarship away from Kant the theist-deist and toward Kant the theological nonrealist. For Strawson, talk and thought of God cannot be grounded in empirical observation, so theology must find other transcendental resources for its grounds. Strawson points to the moral dimension of reason as the place where Kant attempts to provide theology with firm footing. The moral philosophy is, in this sense, the ready-made, formal launching pad for theology. Grounding God-talk and God-thought in morality, however, strictly separates God from "knowable" objects within human experience and permanently relegates the idea of God to a formal kind of subjectivity. As the story goes, the robust and real God was kicked out the front door of Kant's theoretical philosophy, only to be let back in the back door of Kant's moral philosophy as merely a subjective and formal shadow of God's former self. In *The Bounds of Sense,* Strawson shows an awareness of these entailments but sees no way out of them.[6]

Perhaps the most influential book to draw out this close connection between Kant's ethics and Kant's philosophy of religion was Keith Ward's *The Development of Kant's View of Ethics* (1972).[7] Ward contends that "[Kant] holds open the future possibility of a final synthesis of human knowledge under necessary principles" and grants that Kant's motives behind completing the system are never far removed from Kant's religious convictions.[8] Despite these positive leanings toward theism in the critical philosophy, Ward determines that Kant was never able to get beyond the purely formal expansion of his ethical theory.

In agreement with Strawson, Ward contends that Kant rejects traditional theistic metaphysics in the first *Critique* and does not allow any form of it back into his critical philosophy until the moral theology of the second *Critique*. This new, "critical" form of theistic metaphysics, he contends, no longer has noumenal implications but is radically subjective: that is, it erases virtually all of the robust realism of Kant's precritical work on theology in favor of a kind of moral formalism, conducive to the transcendental nature of reason but limited by the theoretical strictures of the first *Critique*.

The issue for Ward is not that Kant openly endorses theological nonrealism. For Kant's language, on the contrary, appears to favor realism. Ward finds a fundamental and irresolvable tension, however, between Kant's moral formalism and the theological realism implied in much of Kant's language.[9] Given the structural limitations of the theoretical philosophy, Kant's critical philosophy as a whole, in its effort to ground theology critically, begins to tilt under the weight of moral formalism. According to Ward, Kant's transcendental philosophy turns principally to the practical for its rational justification of God-talk and God-thought. In other words, it roots God merely in the formal-moral dimension of reason, with no trace whatsoever of God in the objective-theoretical dimension of human experience. Without acknowledging that, for Kant, the proper object of moral belief must first be furnished by theoretical reason if any God-talk or God-thought is even to be possible, Kant's philosophical program begins to list in the direction of theological nonrealism. On Ward's view, the idea of God attains no ontological status whatsoever and becomes merely a formal figment of the human imagination.

Ward's development of the Strawsonian position on Kant proved highly influential in Britain and received further affirmation and elaboration in similar studies of Kant later that decade. Peter Byrne's 1979 essay "Kant's Moral Proof of the Existence of God" is a good example.[10] Employing a crisp analytic analysis of Kant's philosophy in the first and second *Critiques,* Byrne presses the logical entailments of Kant's position on knowledge and faith in such a way that the whole discussion of philosophy and theology in Kant is forced in the direction of theological nonrealism. Kant's clear intention is to make room for faith in practical reason in spite of the fact that he has rigidly denied knowledge of God in theoretical reason. Following the work of Strawson and Ward, Byrne determines that Kant's rational grounds for faith, if they exist at all, are formal, moral, and subjective in nature. The problem, however, is that "practical considerations [that] fully justify his faith that God exists" are not possible.[11] For Byrne, Kant's philosophy can support faith in God, but only in a nonrealist sense. There are no rational grounds for claims of God's existence.

Don Cupitt's interpretation of Kant is in accord with these developments in Britain. However, we need to do more than simply locate this connection in order to make a proper assessment of Cupitt's Kantian heritage; we also need to understand something of Cupitt's personal intellectual pilgrimage and the perceived association of this pilgrimage to the flow of Western thought after Kant. Kant's philosophy becomes pivotal for Cupitt, both in the wide sense of being the watershed of Enlightenment philosophy leading to theological nonrealism of the nineteenth century and in the narrow sense of being the main intellectual influence on Cupitt as he studied Kant and Kant's interpreters at the formative stage of his academic development. Put simply, Cupitt's understanding of philosophy is deeply personal, as embedded in his own academic biography as it is in his arguments about Kant and the history of ideas. Any exposition of Cupitt's work on Kant and assessment of theological nonrealism based on it must therefore move carefully between these various modes of argumentation and presentation.

Cupitt's career has two phases. In 1977, Cupitt contributed to the well-known collection of essays entitled *The Myth of God Incarnate*.[12] This marked the symbolic turning point in his theological development. Having achieved tenure the year before, Cupitt speaks of the freeing effects of his new teaching post and the fresh frontiers this essay represented: "Until then, it was not safe to speak; but thereafter I came out quickly."[13] Not much later, in his self-described "boundary period," Cupitt wrote three pieces laying out his understanding of Kant's philosophy and constituting in very clear terms the philosophical grounds for his turn to theological nonrealism. Setting the stage for this period, Cupitt wrote "God and the World in Post-Kantian

Thought" (1972), and then, soon after his "coming-out" contribution in *The Myth of God Incarnate, The Nature of Man* (1979) and "Kant and the Negative Theology" (published in 1982 but written in 1979).[14] So that we do not get sidetracked in the array of ideas and materials Cupitt forwards in support of his theology, our attention will remain fixed on this trio of writings. They constitute the Kantian pivot point in Cupitt's career toward theological nonrealism. Much of Cupitt's work from this point forward, which is prolific and can be only mentioned here in passing, is a frontal assault on the theological realism of classical Christian thought. In this regard, Cupitt calls *Taking Leave of God* (1980) and *The World to Come* (1982) his "breakout" books and everything else that follows them an elaboration of these positions.

In "God and the World in Post-Kantian Thought," Cupitt outlines two streams of Kant interpretation in the nineteenth century. One stream, traceable through the German idealists, saw Kant "as the harbinger of Idealist metaphysics." The other stream saw "a quite different picture of Kant, . . . the Kant who, by pressing some basically simple criticisms, finally showed dogmatic metaphysics to be impossible, and brought about the critical revolution in philosophy."[15] Over the course of several pages, Cupitt affirms aspects of both interpretative streams but finally favors the latter. The latter stream, for Cupitt, recognizes the inevitable consequences of the various dualisms in Kant's philosophy and, in this sense, is more like the mainstream flowing forth from Kant than any kind of subsidiary.

In working out the details of this interpretation, Cupitt highlights several points that are typical of the British interpretation of Kant outlined earlier. First, "This Kant, the critical Kant, argued that ways of thinking which apply within the realm of experience cannot be used in an attempt to go beyond the range of possible experience."[16] There is a strict boundary line between the phenomenal and noumenal realms that makes phenomenally based language ineffective in reference to noumenal realities. Cupitt puts the problem even more acutely in *The Nature of Man*: "Since God is not given in sense-experience, and since there is no objective knowledge except by the process of sense experience, there is no objective knowledge of God. God's existence cannot be proved either by pure abstract argument, or by inference from facts about the world. The traditional ideas of God and the cosmos are kept as no more than useful fictions ('ideals of reason') which inspire us to move towards a complete understanding of the world. In practice man has taken over from God the traditional function of creating the world from primal chaos."[17] Common to what I have labeled the "British interpretation" of Kant is the problem of grounding God-talk and God-thought in Kant's theoretical philosophy. The problem is not that God is not a viable idea for reason, all things considered, but that the idea of God simply cannot refer to a phenomenal thing. If existence in this sense cannot be predicated of God, then interpreters such as Cupitt, Byrne, and Ward aver that God can never be shown to be more than a formal-moral figment of the human mind.

Cupitt, second, separates the theoretical and practical realms of Kant's philosophy and applies this strict separation to theology. Cupitt points out that Kant distinguishes between "two types of cognition"—theoretical cognition, which deals with objects of nature on purely objective terms, and practical cognition, which deals with "objects of religious and moral belief . . . [as] transcendental conditions of our moral experience."[18] Because Cupitt limits the designation of "realism" to things that can, in principle, be objects of immediate experience concerning facts (theoretical cognition), objects of moral experience—things like the human moral disposition and God—must be relegated to human mental activity concerning values (practical cognition). For Cupitt, "Moral and religious beliefs are not the same sort of thing as empirical beliefs."[19] Empirical beliefs are beliefs about reality that could in theory be verified (i.e., the number of craters on the dark side of the moon), while moral beliefs, when they concern matters like God and the eternal destiny of the soul, do not admit to such verification. They do not "stand out" as facts and are thus not real.

Sometimes theological realists contend that belief in the existence of God is warranted by the pure force or act of the human will. For example, in response to Byrne's interpretations of Kant, Don Wiebe argues that practical faith fills in the need or gap at the apex of human understanding and thus becomes a species of theoretical knowledge.[20] If we admit that morality matters, so much so that human dignity and identity depend on it, Cupitt contends that we still cannot gain rational support for anything other than theological nonrealism. Cupitt writes, "There is nothing moral in mere obedience to commands issued by someone else. To be moral I must formulate moral principles for myself, recognize their authority for myself, and freely adopt them as my own. God again appears as a humanly postulated ideal limit, but God does not formulate the moral law or lay it upon us as binding. Only we can do that."[21] Moral and religious beliefs are products of human transcendental subjectivity; they are formal and postulated beliefs, not empirical and referential beliefs. They may fill in a gap or need in the transcendental nature of reason, but they do so with beliefs formulated in the formal confines of the moral philosophy.

Despite the restrictive way in which Cupitt relates knowledge and belief in Kant's philosophy, Cupitt's writings show an awareness of the efforts of post-Kantian philosophers of religion who avow theological realism (i.e., Friedrich Schleiermacher and Rudolf Otto). Such philosophers emphasize the objects of religion in Kant's later writings, the openness of Kant's transcendental philosophy to further refinement and advancement, and the lack of awareness on Kant's part of the distinctive and pervasive nature of religious experience in humanity. Their work makes it seem plausible, at least initially, to hold that Kant's philosophy might be developed according to a transcendental analysis of religious experience. Cupitt dismisses such a notion, however, because of the problem of religious diversity. He remarks, "In our period, that of Christian thought since Kant, the nearest we get to [a transcendental analysis of religious experience] is the common, but dubious claim that beneath local diversity all religions are in essence one, and all religious feeling is basically the same structure."[22] Such a claim runs counter to the nonrealist understanding of the flow of Western thought, and Cupitt summarily dismisses it, calling it "the post-Kantian form of a well-known Deist doctrine."[23]

Since the theoretical and practical divide in Kant's philosophy is, for Cupitt, patently self-evident and no options occur to Cupitt's mind for resolving this apparent bifurcation in reason from within Kant's corpus, the resources left for explaining the existence and nature of religious experience are minimal. Put bluntly, they are traceable entirely to the conventions of Kant's moral philosophy and their subsequent manifestations in art and religion. Cupitt writes, "Critical philosophy may take a psychological form, as the critique of *thought*, or it may take a linguistic form, as the critique of *language*." In either their psychological or linguistic form, God-thought and God-talk have no ready referent in experience, nor could they have, because the epistemic strictures on such knowledge set up in the first *Critique* simply preclude this possibility. This "leaves morality, art and religion in an odd position . . . [and displays] a close analogy here between Kant and Wittgenstein."[24] According to Cupitt, both of these philosophers are in agreement that "the map of knowledge is made up of two elements. There are the things represented on the map, the subject matter of the various sciences; and there are the various cartographical conventions—the system of projection and so forth—for philosophy to study."[25]

This twofold understanding of reason as addressing scientific matters (factual or propositional knowledge) and the transcendental conditions for morality (practical or duty-based knowledge) outlines the content of rationality without remainder. These two aspects of Kant's philosophy not only constitute distinct areas of human inquiry but also exhaust its possibilities. According to Cupitt, "Kant and Wittgenstein are agreed, religion, art and morality are not additional territories on the map of factual knowledge. They are something quite different. What then are they?"[26] Cupitt thinks we are basically left with two post-Kantian options for explaining moral, aesthetic, and religious diversity, both of which appeal to positivist philosophy. "The straightforward positivist proposes to treat the discourse of religion, morality and art as having no cognitive significance at all, but merely serving to express our feelings."[27] This option is not viable for Cupitt because of its tendency to reduce in an eliminative way the universal phenomenon of religious experience without offering a viable thesis regarding its nature and origin. For a more potent thesis, Cupitt turns to "more subtle positivists [who] found religion and morality upon human nature."[28] It is at this point in Cupitt's narrative that we first begin hearing echoes of Hegel, Feuerbach, and Marx.

Cupitt describes the period immediately after Kant as "a brilliant flowering of speculative philosophy in Germany."[29] During this period, atheism emerged as a viable philosophical alternative to traditional Christian metaphysics and required only "a plausible explanation of why virtually the whole human race throughout history has had a religious view of the world and man's place in it."[30] Cupitt does not examine the entire period but instead focuses on a few themes that connect Kant's philosophy with atheistic humanism. Hegel, thinks Cupitt, sought to unify Kant's bifurcation of theory and practice with religious and theological resources. Early religious persons like the Patriarchs had struggled to overcome nature and had "imagined a God who was wholly sovereign over Nature. Obeying this God, they might gradually win some power over Nature."[31] Hegel understood religious belief to have developed, suggests Cupitt, as "a way of coping with the harsh facts of experience."[32] God becomes the great Absolute for Hegel and is identifiably equivalent in the human understanding to reality as a whole. As Hegel famously put it, "The real is the rational and the rational is the real." The unifying effects of Hegel's philosophy, at least for Hegel's most zealous followers, the Young Hegelians, were to complete and emancipate humanity in such a way that "God becomes an empty husk and withers away."[33]

The essential thrust of Kant and Hegel regarding religion, according to Cupitt, was to achieve its deepest penetration in Western thought in Feuerbach's *The Essence of Christianity*. For Feuerbach, "Religion was fundamentally human, and religious objects expressions of human psychology. So he set out to dissolve the whole of Christian doctrine into statements about man. He sets aside God's metaphysical existence and negative attributes (like God's infinity, simplicity, impassability, incomprehensibility and so on) because he thinks them unimportant, and concentrates entirely on God's positive, anthropomorphic attributes."[34] Cupitt highlights the fact that, for Feuerbach, "man is a social being . . . a 'species-being' who becomes conscious of himself as a member of the species."[35] From the anthropomorphic insight of man being at the center of Christian thought and man being a social being, Feuerbach's argument is simple: "Religion is distinctly human, consciousness of the species is distinctly human, and therefore religion is consciousness of man's own infinite nature; the religious object is Man with a capital M, Man the species."[36] Although Cupitt characterizes Feuerbach's work as "bad philosophy," he believes it contains a historical truth directly indebted to Kant's philosophy—"The classic Christian doctrine of God had largely been lost by Feuerbach's time and the man-centred piety of his day invited just the kind of treatment he gave it."[37]

This mix of Kant interpretation and philosophical appropriation comes to a head in the essay Cupitt describes as being "On the Brink" of his personal conversion to and public explication of theological nonrealism. In "Kant and the Negative Theology," Cupitt compares Kant's philosophy on the topic of God and religious belief with that of past theists from various religious traditions, including Platonists, Christians, Jews, and Muslims, but with specific reference to the Greek Orthodox tradition. He concludes that, while structural similarities exist between Kant and the thinkers in the tradition of negative theology in general, their conceptions of God's existence and nature and our cognitive access to these aspects of the divine are vastly different. Negative theology has consistently asserted, argues Cupitt, that "it is certain that God exists, but the nature or essence of God is unknowable."[38] Kant, on the other hand, holds that "God's existence is problematic, but God's nature *as the Ideal of Reason* is explicable."[39] For Cupitt, "What Kant is saying is strikingly different from older negative theology. . . . [Whereas its] language is designed to *attract*, . . . Kant's language is designed to *repel*."[40] The upshot of this line of reasoning, for Cupitt, is decidedly nonrealist: "Kant wants us to renounce impossible and futile aspirations and be content with doing our duty. Do not aspire after the real God, he says, for that will only end in anthropomorphism and fantasy. Be content with the available God postulated by practical reason—fully recognizing his non-descriptive character—for that is sufficient."[41]

Kant on Cognition of God and Rational Religious Faith

Cupitt's theological nonrealism gains its appeal from the fact that, rather than venturing deep into Kant's transcendental philosophy in an effort to understand its inner workings on their own terms, it interprets

Kant's writings superficially and with exclusive reference to what the British stream of Kant interpretation holds to be true about them. Adopting this procedure, Cupitt latches hold of a perceived disconnect between the theoretical philosophy and the practical philosophy concerning the idea of God. God is relegated to the practical philosophy and altogether removed from the theoretical philosophy. Cupitt privileges this insight as though it were standard in the field of Kant studies and the primary influence of Kant on the history of ideas. When Cupitt combines his analysis of the historical situation with what others in the British stream hold to be true about Kant, a foundation for theological nonrealism is thereby established. Cupitt's personal academic pilgrimage serves as a testimony to the profound impact this Kantian narrative can have on a life.

One strategy for demonstrating the shortcomings of Cupitt's approach would be to provide a detailed examination of the history of Kant interpretation and to compare that with Cupitt's interpretation of Kant and Kant's influence. I undertake the first part of this task in the "Editors' Introduction" to *Kant and the New Philosophy of Religion*.[42] Interested readers can compare that account of Kant interpretation with Cupitt's interpretation of Kant to get a sense of the immensity of the gap between Cupitt and the main interpretations inhabiting the landscape of Kant studies in the twentieth century. Undertaking such a task here would take us beyond the limitations of this essay and, in the end, steer us toward the secondary literature rather than toward Kant's writings. Instead, I will focus my criticism of Cupitt on one specific misunderstanding of Kant that his work exhibits, namely, Kant on theoretical and practical cognition, and will show how this misunderstanding becomes a series of false accounts and outright mistakes. It should be noted that these misrepresentations and mistakes are not all original to Cupitt; we find them first in the British strand of Kant interpretation mentioned earlier and only then worked out in the more widely disseminated works of Cupitt.

Before proceeding, I think it appropriate first to take a moment here to identify those places where Cupitt hits the mark on Kant. Clearly, he is right in affirming Kant's epistemic limits. Knowledge, for Kant, amounts to a synthesis of intuitions and concepts. No intuition, avers Kant, is synthetically sufficient to the concept of God. We cannot know, for example, the reality of God in the same way that we know the reality of tables and chairs. The concept of God admits no limitations, and thus perceiving God through one or more of the five senses is, in fact, impossible. Using a biblical example, Thomas, upon seeing the risen Jesus, declares, "My Lord, and my God!" Thomas did not "know" God in the Kantian sense of knowledge. As Allen Wood puts it, "But though divine revelation itself is not impossible, it is impossible for any man to know through experience that God has in any instance actually revealed himself."[43] All competent interpretations of Kant are in agreement—it is impossible to "know" God—and no one, by Kant's lights, is exempt from this theoretical stricture.

Likewise, Cupitt is right to trace the focus of Kant's theological efforts to the moral philosophy. Without a doubt, God is a postulate of morality, and the moral philosophy is the place where faith in God finds its most complete and compelling foundation. When considering the question "What ought I to do?" the critical philosopher must, thinks Kant, postulate God and immortality to support and maintain the stability of the moral law. We must *act* on the presuppositions of God's existence and the immortality of human life; otherwise morality gives way to purely prudential decision making, which, according to the transcendental strictures of practical reason, cannot be the ultimate outcome of the reciprocal relationship between freedom and the moral law. To act out of one's own self-interest—that is, to act prudentially—is to act as if God did not exist and human life had no final end. For Kant, this is tantamount to "moral unbelief" and is a monstrosity to the essential interests of reason.

The problem with Cupitt's interpretation is thus not that it recognizes limits to human knowledge, or that it emphasizes the singular importance of God to morality for Kant's philosophy. Rather, the problem is that it insists on strictly bifurcating reason into theoretical cognition and practical cognition and draws out the implications of this division in a way antithetical to Kant's philosophy. For Cupitt, *theoretical cognition* refers to the objectivity of facts, while *practical cognition* refers to the subjectivity of values. Cupitt interprets Kant's philosophy as holding that theoretical cognition is to be identified in all instances with knowledge (viz., a synthesis of intuitions and concepts) and practical cognition is to be identified in all instances with moral subjectivity (viz., ideas postulated to regulate moral activity). According to this paradigm, God is merely a formal idea of practical cognition, not a possible object of theoretical cognition. This enforced bifurcation of cognition into theory and practice is the single most important misstep in Cupitt's interpretation. For it ignores the common thread of "pure cognition" running between the *Critiques* (and culminating in Kant's writings on religion) and leads Cupitt to conclude that all talk of God in Kant's philosophy is empty of ontological significance and thus is nonrealist in orientation.

In the first *Critique*, Kant refers to God as the *"ens realissimum,"* "the *original being,"* "the *highest being,"* and "the *being of all beings"* (A576–79/B604–7).[44] One cannot read the second half of the "Transcendental Doctrine of the Elements" in the first *Critique* without being struck by the detail and persistence of Kant's arguments on this point. The idea of God is an ontologically robust one; it is not a figment or creation but the transcendental idea of the unconditioned totality. According to Kant, "Reason does not presuppose the existence of a being conforming to the ideal, but only the idea of such a being, in order to derive from an unconditioned totality of thoroughgoing determination the conditioned totality" (A577–78/B605–6). Kant's point, of course, is not that God is a possible object of immediate experience or knowledge; God does not "stand out" or exist in this theoretical sense but is present to the understanding nevertheless as the being of all beings, the highest being, the original being, or the transcendental idea of the unconditioned totality. In contemporary terms, God is the ultimate reality.

Even though we cannot place God within the phenomenal sphere of human experience or think of God as a noumenal reality somehow "out there," we can and do get God in mind in a transcendental sense. Referring to this feature of Kant's thought, Allen Wood writes, "These strictures, however, do not really apply to some predicates, such as those based on the categories, or on the 'pure derivative concepts,' such as duration and change. For although such concepts are 'empty' ones in their application to noumena, they are nevertheless available to us a priori as formal elements of our concept of a thing or object in general. Kant gives the name 'ontological predicates' to these 'a priori realities' which belong to God in virtue of the fact that they 'refer to the universal attributes of a thing in general.'"[45] For Kant, God is "the concept of an individual being, because of all possible opposed predicates, one, namely that which belongs absolutely to being, is encountered in its determination" (A577–79/B605–7). Elaborating on this point, Wood writes, "The most proper idea of God, as a supremely perfect being or *ens realissimum*, . . . comes about in the course of our attempt to conceive the conditions for the 'thorough determination' of things, that is, the unconditionally complete knowledge of them, or the thoroughgoing specification of the properties belonging to them."[46] This insight leads to Wood's general thesis that "Kant's argument for the rational inevitability of the idea of an *ens realissimum* is an original and well thought out one, making use of concepts that belong to the metaphysical tradition."[47]

Kant summarizes the various conceptions of God's ultimate reality under the concept of the "transcendental *ideal*." God is the cognitional wellspring from which all that is determinable is determined. It is wrong, says Kant, to think of an ideal as "the objective relation of an actual object to other things"; it is the idea that grounds our concepts, and "the existence of a being of such preeminent excellence . . . leaves us in complete ignorance" (A579/B607). The hypostatizing of this transcendental ideal, Kant argues, gives rise to the notion of a critical metaphysic or transcendental theology. Hypostatization yields the attributes of singularity, simplicity, all-sufficiency, eternality, and more (A580/B608). "The concept of such a being is that of *God* thought of in a transcendental sense, and thus the ideal of pure reason is the object of a transcendental *theology*" (A580/B608). It should be noted, of course, that Kant thinks of the hypostatizing of God as a temptation to be resisted, but, just as clearly, the very notion of transcendental theology (as an enterprise that emerges along with the ongoing critical excavation of reason) requires it.

Because reason has a clear and compelling idea of God present to its understanding, a critical doorway for the transcendental excavation of reason in its other employments is open. Kant, on this point, is worth quoting at length:

For if in some other, perhaps practical relation, the *presupposition* of a highest and all-sufficient being, as supreme intelligence, were to assert its validity without any objection, then it would be of the greatest importance to determine this concept precisely on its transcendental side, as the concept of a necessary and most-real being, to get rid of what is incompatible with the highest reality, what belongs to mere appearance (anthropomorphism broadly understood), and at the same time to get out of the way all opposed assertions, whether they be *atheistic, deistic* or *anthropomorphic;* all this is very easy to do in such a critical treatment, since the same grounds for considering human reason incapable of asserting the existence of such a being, when laid before our eyes, also suffice to prove the unsuitability of all counter-assertions. (A640–41/B668–69)

Kant writes directly against atheistic, deistic, and anthropomorphic forms of transcendental theology as positions every bit as problematic as those positions claiming knowledge of God's existence. When Kant balances the theological scales in the first *Critique,* arguing that knowledge of God's existence and nonexistence are equally impossible, what Kant is essentially doing is clearing the way for faith in God as present to reason transcendentally in its theoretical employment. This faith is not to be supported with arguments based on empirical considerations (those, by Kant's lights, are always open to counterarguments and, as such, are contingent); rather, Kant asserts that faith in God must be based on rational considerations that are rooted in the theoretical but that go beyond it to the practical.

Because the idea of God is established in the theoretical philosophy, moral reason has a clear and compelling object with which to regulate and uphold freedom and the moral law. Likewise, teleological judgment, as Kant explains in the third *Critique,* can appeal to God when reflecting on the supersensible substrate that grounds the unity of nature and freedom in experiences of beauty and sublimity. The theoretical cognition of God is thus a key transcendental resource for other dimensions of Kant's thought. By the time we have walked our way through Kant's philosophical program and have arrived at *Reli-*

gion within the Boundaries of Mere Reason, faith in God is utterly crucial to making sense out of Kant's philosophy of religion and transcendental quest to understand the meaning and purpose of human existence.[48] Contrary to this synopsis of Kant's program, Cupitt would have us believe that God is a product of moral subjectivity alone. However, so many aspects of Kant's philosophy of religion would be unintelligible if it were not for the presentation of God to reason via pure theoretical cognition that on this point Cupitt's thesis simply does not survive close scrutiny.

A question may arise in the mind of an astute reader: How can theoretical cognition present the idea of God to reason if knowledge of God is ruled out as utterly impossible? The answer is simple. For Kant, knowledge is a subset of theoretical cognition, not an exhaustive determination of its full range of meaning. Rolf George makes this important clarification regarding Kant's use of the term *Erkenntnis* (cognition) relative to the term *Wissen* (knowledge) in his essay entitled "*Vorstellung* and *Erkenntnis* in Kant."[49] He points out that Johann Christoph Adelung's dictionary of 1793 lists ten senses for the root *erkennen* and highlights two senses of particular interest to the study of Kant. The first sense of "the word may be translated as 'to come to know,' or 'to know.'"[50] This sense of the term *erkennen* "has become very much more common during the nineteenth and twentieth centuries."[51] For this reason, the common mistake when interpreting Kant is to assume that *cognition* means knowledge without significant variances.

The second sense of *Erkenntnis* that George finds significant to the study of Kant "requires the direct object construction; in this sense the word means 'to represent it to ourselves clearly or obscurely, distinctly or indistinctly.'"[52] Unlike the way in which most today use *Erkenntnis* to mean knowledge of empirical objects, "To have *Erkenntnis* of a thing [in the time of Kant] was to have in one's mind a presentation, an idea, an image, a token referring to that thing."[53] Cognition, in Kant's writings, is a bigger and more flexible concept than merely knowledge in the sense of *Wissen*. George argues persuasively that Kant's use of the term *Erkenntnis* is, in many cases, more closely associated with its definition as a kind of mental representation than with its use as a synonym for knowledge. One can have a meaningful mental representation or idea without the need for a corresponding intuition.

It is imperative that readers of Kant understand that theoretical cognition comes in two forms. These two forms are "empirical cognition" and what Kant calls variously "the cognition of reason" or "pure cognition." The latter of these two forms serves as the transcendental bridge between theory and practice. Rather than bifurcate Kant's philosophy into theoretical and practical cognition in order to ground theology solely in the practical, Kant's modus operandi is first to ground theology in theoretical cognition when *theoretical cognition* is understood to refer to the cognition of reason rather than empirical cognition. As Kant puts it, "The principles <*principia*> or grounds of cognition are so constituted that one connects the necessity of what one cognizes with the cognition itself, and the concepts are directed at objects that are not only cognized independently of all experience, but that also can never *possibly* become an object of experience. E.g., God, freedom, immortality."[54] These objects of cognition are far from human creations, mere figments, or idle speculation; they emerge naturally in the course of reason's deliberations. "Metaphysics thus has no *a posteriori* principles <*principia*>," writes Kant, "but rather only *a priori*: they are given and are cognized through reason alone, but are not made."[55]

Kant makes plain in his *Lectures on Metaphysics* that we can and do cognize God, freedom, and immortality and that these cognitions are neither empirical objects nor mere opinions or objects of wishful thinking; they are gotten in mind and rooted in the transcendental nature of pure reason. In other words, they are transcendental ideas whose objective reality cannot be determined by empirical observation but that are nevertheless objectively valid and thus open to subjective support and conviction. When Cupitt uses the term *theoretical cognition,* he implies an equation of cognition and knowledge in all cases. This identification of theoretical cognition with knowledge in effect relegates all theology in Kant to moral subjectivity without a clear and compelling theoretical object. The moral philosophy must be understood to manufacture an anthropomorphic conception of God ex nihilo out of resources that have no relation whatsoever to theoretical reason. Such a conception must be nonrealist in orientation, for it has not even a rudimentary understanding of God with which to work. This rendition of Kant's program yields a theologically vicious form of circularity that acts as a hedge against theological realism.

If the foregoing comparison of Kant and Cupitt is accurate, Cupitt's bold thesis is nothing less than a complete inversion of Kant's method. Throughout the critical philosophy, Kant uses pure cognition to move between (and indeed beyond) knowledge and opinion to establish rational religious faith. Admittedly, putting together the pieces of this grand puzzle is not easy, but the basics are clear enough. In the "Canon of Pure Reason" (a well-known section of the first *Critique*), Kant draws out the distinctions between knowledge, faith, and opinion. Each of these concepts identifies a form of truth assertion in the economy of Kant's philosophy. However, Kant lumps faith and knowledge together as properly rational truth assertions, leaving opinion as the product of idle speculation closely related to what Kant calls "persuasion."[56] Opinions deal with objectively valid concepts that have precious little in the way of empirical or rational support for their truth. They are thus the lowest level of truth assertion, since the one asserting an opinion is conscious, or at least should be conscious, of the assertion's objective and subjective insufficiency.

Faith is somewhat like opinion in that it too is rooted in pure cognition and thus deals with objects of thought that have objective validity without decisive empirical support. Unlike opinion, however, faith has a subjective sufficiency that opinion lacks—objects of faith are grounded in the transcendental nature of theoretical reason *and* glean support from reason's nontheoretical employments. According to Kant, "In judging from pure reason, *to have an opinion* is not allowed at all" (A822/B850). Faith, however, finds rational grounds not only from being rooted in the pure cognition of theoretical reason but also as an indispensible element of the practical philosophy. With faith, "it is absolutely necessary that something must happen, namely, that I fulfill the moral law at all points. The end here is inescapably fixed, and according to all my insight there is possible only a single condition under which this end is consistent with all the ends together and thereby has practical validity, namely, that there be a God and a future world" (A828/B856).

For Kant, faith in God and immortality is inextricably linked with the systematic nature of human cognition and the needs of practical reason. So sure of this point is Kant, even at this earliest stage of the critical philosophy, that he confidently writes, "I also know with complete certainty that no one else knows of any other conditions that lead to this same unity of ends under the moral law" (A828/B856). In one of his most famous statements on this topic, Kant goes on to drive the point home: "I will inexorably believe in the existence of God and a future life, and I am sure that nothing can make these beliefs unstable, since my moral principles themselves, which I cannot renounce without becoming contemptible in my own eyes, would thereby be subverted" (A828/B856). Kant makes clear in the "Canon" that God and immortality are not just possible objects of faith but morally mandated principles of any critical understanding of reason. Kant's faith is likewise not merely faith in a practically postulated idea of God but faith in God because theoretical reason presents us with a clear object whose existence is presupposed and practical reason lays hold of and expounds on this object in faith.

Leslie Stevenson probes Kant's definition of faith in an essay entitled "Opinion, Belief or Faith, and Knowledge." He defends the notion that faith *(Glaube),* along with the gerund "believing" *(glauben),* has a critical role in the transcendental development of Kant's philosophical theology. Faith, for Stevenson, "is holding something to be true, and being practically but not theoretically justified in doing so."[57] The faith that Kant understands to be involved here is of a special kind: "The conviction is not *logical* but *moral* certainty, and, since it depends on subjective grounds (of moral disposition) I must not even say '*It is* morally certain that there is a God', etc., but rather '*I am* morally certain' etc." (A829/B857). Referring to this passage from the first *Critique,* Stevenson writes, "Here Kant strikes an existentialist note, giving us a sneak preview of his practical philosophy. It seems that the distinction between moral beliefs and theoretical beliefs about the supersensible is not between different propositions, but different styles of believing the same propositions: firmly believe in a moral way, unstably believe in the doctrinal way."[58] What Stevenson's discussion highlights is that faith is a legitimate category of rational conviction in which certain metaphysical propositions are believed for rationally warranted practical reasons. These practical reasons, together with the idea of God present in pure cognition, constitute Kant's conception of rational religious faith and realist theology.

Kant thus provides two criteria governing subjectively sufficient reasons for belief in an object of pure cognition: (1) the criteria of cognition itself, which ground faith in the universal validity of concepts required of all human reasoning; and (2) the criteria of practical reason, which provide decisive reasons for believing in the existence of God and human immortality. While the criteria of practical reason apply only to faith, the criteria of cognition apply to reasoning about knowledge and faith alike. Stevenson concludes,

> As Wood has pointed out, Kant holds that both *wissen* and *glauben* are based on grounds that are *universally* valid—that is, reasons that appeal to the judgement of any rational person. They both involve conviction rather than mere opinion or persuasion, but the degrees of conviction are different—*wissen* must be based either on logical proof (deduction) or such strong empirical evidence (induction) as to amount to knowledge beyond all reasonable doubt, whereas *glauben* is based on inner faith or moral commitment. (*Glauben* can be even stronger than *wissen* in another way, for as Kant remarked in his lectures, people have sometimes been ready to die for their moral or religious beliefs but not for mathematical theorems.)[59]

Pure cognition and moral faith thus concern themselves with ideas that have objective validity (i.e., logical possibility). We are justified in holding to these cognitions as objects of rational faith with a conviction of their truth even if their intuitional status is empty, provided we have sufficient practical grounds for doing so.

Kant famously denied knowledge to make room for faith, and what we now know is that pure cognition is the room—the transcendental room—that Kant was talking about. Pure cognition is the room at the boundaries of reason when those boundaries are operating from moral, aesthetic, teleological, and religious considerations *in addition to* theoretical ones. As these critically significant rational resources are unearthed through a more complete excavation of reason's synthetic a priori constituents, they tip the scales of faith immediately and decisively in favor of God. This faith is more than merely assent to a theoretical conception of God as the highest being; it is what Stevenson calls an "existential faith," or what Wood, following Kant, calls faith in a "living God."[60]

Admittedly, this existential faith in the living God does not ascend to the lofty level of knowledge of God's existence, but how could it? God is the being of all beings or highest reality. No intuition is sufficient to such a concept of God. This is precisely Kant's point, for example, in his essay "What Does It Mean to Orient Oneself in Thinking?" Kant, speaking of the manifold of ideas one could cognize as pure possibilities and why no reason exists for presupposing the existence of these ideas, singles out God as being uniquely important to the economy of reason. He writes,

> It is quite otherwise with the concept of a first *original being* as a supreme intelligence and at the same time as the highest good. For not only does our reason already feel a need to take the *concept* of the unlimited as the ground of the concept of all limited beings— hence of all other things—, but this need even goes so far as the presupposition of its *existence,* without which one can provide no satisfactory ground at all for the contingency of the existence of things in the world, let alone for the purposiveness and order which is encountered everywhere in such a wondrous degree.[61]

The existential status of the idea of God is an open question in the first *Critique,* not because God does not exist, but because existence speaks first and foremost of finitude. Tables and chairs, in this sense, have an advantage over God in that they admit finite determinability. Unlike tables and chairs, God does not admit to actual or possible finite determination or empirical confirmation. Nevertheless, God has an infinite "existential" advantage over tables and chairs in the area of pure cognition and rational faith. People are sometimes willing to die for their belief in God, but not for tables and chairs. Why is this? Because God is not only an objectively valid pure cognition but also the most significant, real, and high object of rational religious faith.

.   .   .

In the first section above, we unpacked the arguments behind Cupitt's claim that theological nonrealism lies within the lineage of Kant's philosophy. Seizing on a theme common in a British strand of Kant interpretation—namely, that God is not a possible object of knowledge, and that therefore faith in the existence of God is not possible—Cupitt maintains that God is merely a formal-moral figment of the human mind. In defense of this claim, he argues that theoretical and practical cognition are strictly separated in Kant's philosophy. Theology, for Kant, is rooted in practical reason, not theoretical reason. This strict bifurcation means that Kant's philosophy must be understood to promote theological nonrealism. In the second section, we saw that an examination of cognition and faith against the backdrop of Kant's critical strictures on knowledge shows that Kant's philosophy does not establish a bifurcation of cognition into the theoretical and practical. Instead, it distinguishes between empirical and pure forms of cognition. Where empirical cognition is merely theoretical in nature, pure cognition is both theoretical and practical. In this sense, pure cognition is a transcendental and linguistic bridge between theory and practice. This way of understanding Kant not only makes sense of Kant's critical writings but also puts Kant neatly on the map of the rationalist tradition extending back to Descartes that understood God to be the highest being of reality or the *ens realissimum*.

No doubt, thinks Kant, we cannot have empirical knowledge of God; the boundaries of theoretical reason preclude this possibility. These very same boundaries, however, have a thickness that goes undetected by Cupitt. They have not only the negative function of limiting our knowledge so as to silence the dogmatist and the skeptic (or, in this case, the dogmatic nonrealist, who builds on a form of atheism) but also the positive function of providing reason with a storehouse

296 Chris L. Firestone

of ideas a priori via pure cognition. Among the ideas we have is God as the highest being, and pure cognition of God, when combined with a transcendental analysis of reason in its various employments, yields robust transcendental theology. The fruit of this endeavor, for Kant, is rational religious faith. Contrary to Cupitt, Kant's appeal to rational religious faith is not ontologically vacant but transcendentally full. This essay has shown that theological nonrealism is not very far removed from mainstream aspects of Kant interpretation but is nonetheless far removed from Kant. Although it employs many of Kant's terms and texts, theological nonrealism has no genuine blood relationship to Kant's philosophy. We must surely conclude, then, that any and all claims by the theological nonrealist to be the true heir of Kant's estate are best denied as fraudulent.

Notes

1. Gordon Michalson, *Kant and the Problem of God* (Oxford: Blackwell, 1999), 4–5.

2. Michalson, *Kant and the Problem*, 5.

3. In *Kant and the New Philosophy of Religion,* interpretations that read Kant as a strict deist were lumped into the theologically negative camp, while here these interpretations are understood to be theologically positive. To a large extent, framing the debate well will depend on where one stands. In the context of Kant studies proper, deism slides into the theologically negative camp insofar as it tends to truncate Kant's program of rational religious faith; while, in the context of recent disputes between metaphysical realism and nonrealism, deism moves squarely into the affirmative camp. See Chris L. Firestone and Stephen R. Palmquist, "Editors' Introduction," in *Kant and the New Philosophy of Religion,* ed. Chris L. Firestone and Stephen R. Palmquist (Bloomington: Indiana University Press, 2006).

4. Allen W. Wood, *Kant's Moral Religion* (Ithaca: Cornell University Press, 1970), 161.

5. See Allen W. Wood, "Kant's Deism," in *Kant's Philosophy of Religion Reconsidered,* ed. Philip J. Rossi and Michael Wreen (Bloomington: Indiana University Press, 1991), 2. It is not the purpose of this essay to argue this issue, but, for readers interested in views contrary to the deistic trends in Kant studies today, see John Hare, *The Moral Gap: Kantian Ethics, Human Limits, and God's Assistance* (New York: Oxford University Press, 1997), and Christopher McCammon,

"Overcoming Deism: Hope Incarnate in Kant's Rational Religion," in Firestone and Palmquist, *Kant and the New Philosophy of Religion.*

6. Strawson, in his most recent work on Kant, backpedals on these conclusions, suggesting that a more positive portrayal of Kant on metaphysics may be possible. He writes, "The curtain of sense cuts us empirical beings irrevocably off from *knowledge* of things as they are in themselves. . . . The curtain is not, according to Kant, in every respect impenetrable. From behind it reality, as it were, speaks." P. F. Strawson, *Entity and Identity* (Oxford: Clarendon Press, 1997), 251.

7. Keith Ward, *The Development of Kant's View of Ethics* (Oxford: Basil Blackwell, 1972).

8. Ward, *Development,* 28.

9. Ward, *Development,* 154.

10. Peter Byrne, "Kant's Moral Proof for the Existence of God," *Scottish Journal of Theology* 32 (1979): 333–43.

11. Byrne, "Kant's Moral Proof," 335.

12. Don Cupitt, "The Christ of Christendom," in *The Myth of God Incarnate,* ed. John Hick (Philadelphia: Westminster Press, 1977), 133–47.

13. Don Cupitt, *Nothing Sacred? The Non-Realist Philosophy of Religion* (New York: Fordham University Press, 2002), xv.

14. Don Cupitt, "God and the World in Post-Kantian Thought," *Theology* 75 (1972): 343–54, *The Nature of Man* (London: Sheldon Press, 1979), and "Kant and the Negative Theology," in *The Philosophical Frontiers of Christian Theology,* ed. B. Hebblethwaite and S. Sutherland (London: Cambridge University Press, 1982), 55–67.

15. Cupitt, "God and the World," 350.

16. Cupitt, "God and the World," 352.

17. Cupitt, *Nature of Man,* 52.

18. Cupitt, "God and the World," 352.

19. Cupitt, "God and the World," 352.

20. Don Wiebe, "The Ambiguous Revolution: Kant on the Nature of Faith," *Scottish Journal of Theology* 33 (1983): 519. For a detailed analysis of the Byrne-Wiebe debate, see Chris L. Firestone, *Kant and Theology at the Boundaries of Reason* (Aldershot: Ashgate, 2009), ch. 3.

21. Cupitt, *Nature of Man,* 52–53. As Cupitt later puts it, "Kant had argued that in morality mere obedience to authority is not morally commendable: my action is only truly moral when I myself have freely chosen the moral principles on which I act" (90).

22. Cupitt, "God and the World," 353.

23. Cupitt, "God and the World," 353.

24. Cupitt, "God and the World," 351.

25. Cupitt, "God and the World," 351.

26. Cupitt, "God and the World," 351.

27. Cupitt, "God and the World," 352.

28. Cupitt, "God and the World," 352.

29. Cupitt, *Nature of Man,* 53.

30. Cupitt, *Nature of Man,* 53.

31. Cupitt, *Nature of Man,* 55.

32. Cupitt, *Nature of Man,* 55.

33. Cupitt, *Nature of Man,* 55.

34. Cupitt, *Nature of Man,* 55.

35. Cupitt, *Nature of Man,* 55.

36. Cupitt, *Nature of Man,* 55–56.

37. Cupitt, *Nature of Man,* 56.

38. Cupitt, "Kant and the Negative Theology," 57.

39. Cupitt, "Kant and the Negative Theology," 59.

40. Cupitt, "Kant and the Negative Theology," 63.

41. Cupitt, "Kant and the Negative Theology," 63.

42. See Firestone and Palmquist, "Editors' Introduction."

43. Wood, *Kant's Moral Religion,* 204.

44. In all page citations to this work, "A" refers to the first edition (Riga: J. F. Hartknoch, 1781) and "B" to the second (Riga: J. F. Hartknoch, 1787) of *Kritik der reinen Vernunft,* and the translation is from *Critique of Pure Reason,* trans. Paul Guyer and Allen W. Wood (Cambridge: Cambridge University Press, 1997).

45. Wood, *Kant's Rational Theology* (Ithaca: Cornell University Press, 2009), 80–81.

46. Wood, *Kant's Rational Theology,* 18–19.

47. Wood, *Kant's Rational Theology,* 147. "Kant's conception of God and his theory of the rational origin of the conception both depend heavily on ontological views which are part of a tradition which goes back at least to Plato" (28).

48. See Chris L. Firestone and Nathan Jacobs, *In Defense of Kant's "Religion"* (Bloomington: Indiana University Press, 2008), ch. 4.

49. Rolf George, "*Vorstellung* and *Erkenntnis* in Kant," in *Interpreting Kant,* ed. Moltke S. Gram (Iowa City: University of Iowa Press, 1982), 31–39.

50. George, "*Vorstellung* and *Erkenntnis,*" 34.

51. George, "*Vorstellung* and *Erkenntnis,*" 34.

52. George, "*Vorstellung* and *Erkenntnis,*" 34.

53. George, "*Vorstellung* and *Erkenntnis,*" 35.

54. Immanuel Kant, "Metaphysik Vigilantius" (1794–95), in *Kant's Gesammelte Schriften,* ed. Gerhard Lehmann (Berlin: Walter de Gruyter, 1900–), 29:945. This edition is hereafter cited as Ak [Akademie edition] with volume and page number. Translation here is from Kant's *Lectures on Metaphysics,* trans. Karl Americks and Steve Naragon (Cambridge: Cambridge University Press, 1997), 417–506.

55. Kant, "Metaphysik Vigilantius," 29:945.

56. Friedrich Paulsen, *Immanuel Kant: His Life and Doctrine* (New York: Charles Scribner's Sons, 1902), 110.

57. Leslie Stevenson, "Opinion, Belief or Faith, and Knowledge," *Kantian Review* 7 (2003): 88.

58. Stevenson, "Opinion, Belief or Faith," 95.

59. Stevenson, "Opinion, Belief or Faith," 85.

60. Wood, *Kant's Moral Religion,* 161. The term appears in Kant's description of the "theist" in the first *Critique* (A633/B661).

61. Immanuel Kant, "What Does It Mean to Orient Oneself in Thinking?," in Ak 8:137; translation in *Religion and Rational Theology,* ed. Allen W. Wood and George di Giovanni (Cambridge: Cambridge University Press, 1996), 7–18.

Chapter 11

The Reception and Legacy of
J. G. Fichte's *Religionslehre*

YOLANDA ESTES

Fichte, Philosophy, and Religion

The philosophy of religion [is that part of the philosophy of the
postulates that deals with] the postulate that practical philosophy
addresses to the theoretical realm, to nature, which, by means
of a supersensible law, is supposed to accommodate itself to the
goal of morality. . . . The Wissenschaftslehre *has to derive*
and explain this postulate {as such}. But it is not the task of
the Wissenschaftslehre *to apply this postulate within life,*
{to generate religious sentiments within ourselves and, through us,
within other rational beings outside of us}.
    —Fichte, *Foundations of Transcendental Philosophy*

Johann Gottlieb Fichte (1762–1814) was an autumn child of the German Enlightenment, or *Aufklärung*. Educated to be a moderate theologian, persuaded to be a material determinist, and inclined to be a
firebrand moralist, he became a transcendental idealist after deciding that Immanuel Kant's critical philosophy reconciled the naturalism of his "head" with the moralism of his "heart."[1] Fichte's philoso-

phy, *Wissenschaftslehre*—and the religious theory, or *Religionslehre,* it contained—would reflect an abiding commitment to rational faith, scientific rigor, and ethical responsibility.

Fichte's first book, *Attempt at a Critique of All Revelation* (1792), defended his claim that moral consciousness was the sole religious miracle and helped him to gain a position at the University of Jena, where he showed himself to be a beloved educator and luminous mind, but also a divisive personality.[2] Various foes hounded Fichte with allegations, which ranged from violating the Sabbath to corrupting youth, based on misinterpretations of his idea that genuine religiosity involved steadfast pursuit of moral perfection rather than concern for worldly or otherworldly consequences. Eventually, Fichte lost his position because of accusations of atheism leveled at his essay "On the Basis of Our Belief in a Divine Governance of the World" (1798).[3] After fleeing to Berlin, he published *Vocation of Man* (1800) and *The Way toward a Blessed Life, or the Religionslehre* (1812), where he developed his nascent religious theory.[4] Although he anticipated that his later *Wissenschaftslehre*—and specifically his later *Religionslehre*—would be construed as a rapprochement with orthodox theology, he explicitly denied such an interpretation.[5]

Fichte's *Wissenschaftslehre* provides a transcendental account of the world—experience in general—by showing how it must be theoretically known by rational beings and by showing how it ought to be practically constructed by rational beings.[6] In addition to its theoretical and practical parts, the *Wissenschaftslehre* contains a philosophy of the postulates, a mixed theoretical-practical branch of philosophy that includes the *Religionslehre,* which provides a transcendental account of the spiritual world—religious experience in particular—by showing how the theoretical realm, or nature, must conform itself to the practical goal of morality.[7]

The *Wissenschaftslehre* requires that the transcendental philosopher abstract from the object (the thing) and reflect on the subject (the I) of consciousness. The philosopher postulates the concept of the I, or the philosophical intellectual intuition, as the ground of experience, but this concept must be thought according to the law of reflective opposition, which requires that every object of thought be conceived as something determinate in opposition to something determinable.[8]

This law drives the central argument of the *Wissenschaftslehre* to produce increasingly refined concepts of the I until the philosopher discovers that intellectual intuition depends on the hypothesis of a single act of consciousness wherein a rational individual, a rational world, a material object, and a material world are synthetically connected by a principle of unity.[9] The *Wissenschaftslehre* would be purely speculative except that this fivefold synthesis occurs in experience as a real intellectual intuition of the moral law and a concomitant intuition of the conditions necessary to fulfill its command: an individual will, an object (the body) affected by the will, a sensible world order where willing becomes deed, and an intelligible world order where willing accomplishes its supersensible goal.[10]

According to Fichte, the real intellectual intuition provides an extraphilosophical sanction of the theoretical portion of the *Wissenschaftslehre* that explains objective experience, an extraphilosophical sanction of the practical portion of the *Wissenschaftslehre* that explains ethical experience, and an extraphilosophical sanction of the *Religionslehre* that explains religious experience.[11] Hence, the entire project of the *Wissenschaftslehre* presupposes that philosophical knowledge—the standpoint of philosophy—rests on an extraphilosophical belief, or faith, produced by real intellectual intuition in experience—the standpoint of life.[12] In this regard, the *Religionslehre*—like the *Wissenschaftslehre* as a whole—is revealed as an odd fruit of the *Aufklärung*. Fichte rejects the overweening confidence in knowledge that characterized that era without disallowing the aspiration for a reconciliation of faith and reason that characterized its champions, the *Aufklärer*.

Comprehending the *Religionslehre* presumes some cognizance of the tension between faith and knowledge that ran through the *Aufklärung*.[13] The *Aufklärer* embraced the notion that enlightenment would foster human well-being, manifest as unlimited intellectual, moral, and spiritual progress, but many disagreed about how to promote that goal. Ultimately, conflict over the nature of knowledge and the authority of reason divided them into myriad factions: the empiricists argued that knowledge depended on experience, while the rationalists claimed it consisted in analysis; the skeptics and mystics identified "reason" with faith, while the transcendental idealists, or critical philosophers, defined "faith" as rational. Conflict and controversy distinguished the Age of Enlightenment.

Enlightenment, Conflict, and Controversy

What comes to be in and through knowledge is only knowledge. But all knowledge is only a depicting, and in it something is always demanded which could correspond to the image. This demand can be satisfied by no knowledge, and a system of knowledge is necessarily a system of mere images, without any reality, meaning, or purpose.
—Fichte, *Vocation of Man*

Originally, the *Aufklärer* had hoped that reason would replace — or at least support — tradition and revelation as a justification of religion, morality, and society, but many began to suspect that reason, *qua* scientific mechanism and philosophical criticism, led to atheism, egoism, and, in due course, nihilism. Predictably, some offspring of the *Aufklärung* began to question the ultimate compatibility of human welfare and enlightenment and, indeed, of faith and knowledge. So the initial confidence in reason that typified the *Aufklärung* provoked a battle between practical belief and theoretical knowledge, the former generating a seemingly illogical fideism and the latter a seemingly logical skepticism. This dichotomy incited a series of philosophical-*cum*-religious controversies regarding faith and reason.[14]

In 1753, the Berlin Academy of Science hosted a competition, posing a question on Leibniz's optimism, or more generally, on the possibility of divine providence in the face of manifest evil.[15] During the ensuing quarrel, Kant argued that reason compels rational faith in a divine providence, whereas the mystic Hamann claimed that reason compels acknowledgment of the absurdity of human existence. However, the essential concern was the priority of reason vis-à-vis faith within human life.[16] The death of the *Aufklärer* G. E. Lessing initiated the Spinozism Controversy, or *Spinozismusstreit* (1783–87).[17] Ostensibly, the fray, led by Mendelssohn and Jacobi, concerned the theological implications of Lessing's alleged Spinozism; but actually the controversy involved the precedence of reason—*qua* abstract ratiocination—in opposition to faith—*qua* naive belief.[18] Whereas Mendelssohn insisted that reason—moderated by common sense—could justify religious and ethical beliefs, Jacobi maintained that speculation undermined trust in God and freedom, which required a *salto mortale,* or mortal leap, of faith.

After Mendelssohn's death, Kant and Reinhold's critical philosophy eclipsed optimism and pantheism, but the battle over the authority of reason continued as a triangular attack on transcendental idealism. The Lockean *Popularphilosophen* argued that the critical philosophy treated experience as illusory. Touting a return to natural religion, common sense, and eudaemonism, they disparaged the emptiness of the categorical imperative. Meanwhile, the Leibnizian-Wolffian *Popularphilosophen* claimed that Leibniz had already provided a critique of reason and that the critical philosophy merely reiterated Hume's idealism, which led to solipsism. Nonetheless, the new, critically informed skepticism of Schulze and Maimon posed the most serious challenge to transcendental idealism. The critical skeptics charged that Kant and Reinhold failed to answer Hume and that the critical philosophy generated nihilistic results. This latter accusation would reappear during the Atheism Controversy, or *Atheismusstreit* (1798–99).

The *Atheismusstreit* involved the religious, moral, and social implications of transcendental idealism.[19] It began with the publication of Fichte's "On the Basis of Our Belief in a Divine Governance of the World" and F. K. Forberg's "Development of the Concept of Religion" in the *Philosophisches Journal einer Gesellschaft Teutscher Gelehrter.*[20] The articles received little attention until a mawkish anonymous brief, "A Father's Letter to his Son," initiated a pamphlet war—during which Kant and Jacobi repudiated Fichte—between friends and foes of the *Wissenschaftslehre.*[21] When the fray drew the attention of several German courts, including the Weimar court of Duke Karl-August, who sponsored the University of Jena, confiscation orders, noble rescripts, and formal investigations followed. Eventually, Fichte launched a passionate—and injudicious—public self-defense that resulted in his estrangement from Weimar and his expulsion from Jena.[22]

The *Atheismusstreit* hinged on the question of whether transcendental idealism entailed social anarchy and moral despair. As a former

supporter of the French Revolution and author of the "first philosophy of freedom," Fichte tested the social and political order.[23] By
vesting ultimate moral authority in the individual, he wrested it from
the hallowed powers of church and state. Moreover, his vision of personal moral revelation foisted tremendous responsibilities on the frail
human conscience. Jacobi, who believed that Fichte's "inverted Spinozism" implied atheism and nihilism, was not alone in doubting the
average individual's ability to support those burdens without the rein-
forcement of some temporal or eternal consequences.[24]

In addition to the genuine ethical and religious questions at the core
of the *Atheismusstreit,* egotistical social and political interests helped fuel
the dispute. Fichte's apparent impertinence toward Weimar endangered
the lenience that his colleagues enjoyed under their relatively enlightened ruler, Karl-August. His active support of student groups devoted
to "free-thinking" and his direct mediation of the violent conflicts between the student fraternities lent credence to the suspicion that he intended to put his theories into immediate and immoderate practice, so
he became an easy scapegoat for powerful courtiers, such as Goethe,
who had adopted a lackadaisical approach to their own responsibilities in Jena.[25] Moreover, even prior to the secretly funded mass cir-
culation of the "Father's Letter," Fichte had been the victim of an in-
sidious campaign to malign his character and undermine his influence
led by various reactionary parties, including (often anonymous) contributors to the journal *Eudämonia.*

The Reception of Fichte's Early *Religionslehre*

This is the only possible confession of faith: joyfully and innocently
to accomplish whatever duty commands in every circumstance,
without doubting and without pettifogging over the consequences.
—Fichte, "On the Basis of Our Belief in
a Divine Governance of the World"

During the *Atheismusstreit,* many misconceived criticisms were directed
toward Fichte's early *Religionslehre.* Kant claimed that the *Wissenschaftslehre*

lacked religious and philosophical significance.[26] Jacobi described it as a thoroughgoing idealistic determinism that reduced freedom to formal egoism and God to an abstract moral principle. He coined the term *nihilismus* to describe the amoral egoism that he believed Fichte's "inverted Spinozism" implied. According to Jacobi's precepts, any philosophy, but Fichte's in particular, must necessarily be secular and thus godless and irreligious. Some less informed readers were shocked by Fichte's seeming iconoclastic disregard for many tenets of traditional religion, such as belief in a personal, creative deity, the revealed texts, and an afterlife. Others perceived Fichte's philosophy as essentially pantheistic or skeptical.[27]

Although the amount of vitriol inspired by "Divine Governance" remains inscrutable, it is easy to understand why the early *Religionslehre* generated debate. In "Divine Governance," Fichte identifies God with the concept of an intelligible providence—the moral world order—and denies that the notion of a personal deity contributes any theoretical or practical force to that concept. Not only does he regard individual moral consciousness as the only legitimate source of religious authority and treat general utility and personal immortality as irrelevant, but he also condemns any action performed for the sake of temporal or eternal consequences. Nonetheless, Fichte was no iconoclast. Far from hoping to undermine or replace traditional organized religion, Fichte supported it as a means to spiritual development, abhorring the possibility of professors sermonizing from the lecterns or of parsons philosophizing from the pulpits. He was certainly no pantheist, for he explicitly distinguished between moral subjects, moral activity, and the moral world order; and he was certainly no skeptic or agnostic, for he explicitly affirmed the reality of the moral world order (and explicitly denied the existence of a divine personal creator).[28] During the *Atheismusstreit,* Fichte's critics showed a rather obtuse indifference to the task of a *Religionslehre* as well as of the "Divine Governance" essay, which was a preliminary investigation of the ground of religious belief.

Since transcendental philosophy does not confirm beliefs but rather explains how convictions arise in human consciousness, Fichte does not attempt to prove that God exists but rather to show how the concept of God originates.[29] Although different religions include various beliefs, all religious people believe in God; and whatever features their idea of God involves, it includes the concept of divine governance, or a moral world order, whereby good prevails over evil. Many traditional arguments try to infer God's existence from the sensible world. Such arguments claim that the nature or existence of the sensible world implies an intelligible cause or designer, but none of these arguments yields ground for belief in a moral, and hence, intelligible, world order.

Considered from the standpoint of life, the world is a matter of fact, in which particular events are causally governed, but it permits no causal explanation of itself because any such explanation would violate the boundary of experience; considered from the standpoint of philosophy, the general features of the world, or experience, can be derived from the I, which also permits no explanation, because any such explanation would violate its status as a philosophical ground, or first principle.[30] A moral world order can be derived only from the concept of an intelligible world, which cannot be generated by empirical observation or philosophical speculation but rather arises in moral experience through a conjoined immediate consciousness of the moral law and freedom. Acknowledging the moral law entails recognizing the conditions necessary to discharge its commands. These conditions include a sensible order whereby the moral subject performs its deed—the determination of its body as a material thing in the sensible world—and an intelligible order whereby it fulfills its intended goal—the determination of its will as a spiritual individual in the intelligible world.[31]

Moral consciousness includes both sensible and intelligible experience that the human being *qua* moral subject regards as based on intuitions admitting no explanation. The moral subject simply perceives itself as limited by certain sensible and intelligible boundaries, which it interprets as delineating its individual duties, or moral vocation. These spiritual, physical, and social parameters define each subject's individuality, which is revealed gradually as a series of particular, immediately perceived moral imperatives.[32]

The moral subject first discovers itself through its particular duties, so its individual moral vocation provides the "absolute starting point" of all subjective consciousness; likewise, it first discovers the

sensible and intelligible worlds through the moral law, so the moral
world order provides the "absolute starting point" of all objective consciousness.[33] The transcendental philosopher arrives at the concept
of this starting point, or intellectual intuition, by abstraction and simply
postulates it as the explanatory ground of consciousness, but since
the philosopher is also a moral subject, and thus has prephilosophical
access to this concept as a real intellectual intuition, it provides an extraphilosophical sanction for the *Religionslehre* and for the *Wissenschaftslehre* as a whole. Neither the moral subject nor the philosopher can
question this foundation without damaging its status as the ultimate
conviction underpinning morality and religion. To presume that this
conviction requires an author or creator subordinates the moral law
to an extramoral justifying force or causal power, thus undermining
morality.[34]

For Fichte, the concept of God is simply equivalent to the concept of the moral world order, which is not questionable but rather
the ultimate ground of all other beliefs and knowledge: "We require
no other God, nor can we grasp any other."[35] Religion consists in pursuing one's moral vocation without regard for consequences. To do
otherwise involves subjecting morality to one's own finite intellect
and thereby assuming the status of God. Atheism is any type of moral
consequentialism—whether the anticipated results exist in the present world or another—whereas agnosticism, or religious skepticism,
is any type of despair of a moral world order—whether motivated by
theoretical or practical concerns. Considered morally, atheism and agnosticism are indistinguishable because each subordinates duty to the
tribunals of sensible utility and finite intellect.

Fichte responded to the *Atheismusstreit* in the *Vocation of Man,* which
offers a poignant description of the alleged conflict between faith and
knowledge, a satirical portrait of Fichte's critics, and a sophisticated
clarification of the standpoints of philosophy and life.[36] In the final
chapter, "Faith," he reiterates his claim that moral consciousness is
not only the extraphilosophical ground of philosophical knowledge
but also the practical basis of religious belief. Accordingly: "There is
nothing truly real, lasting, imperishable in me except these two parts:
the voice of my conscience and my free obedience. Through the first,

the spiritual world bends down to me and embraces me as one of its members; through the second, I raise myself into this world, grasp it, and act in it."[37]

The Reception of Fichte's Later *Religionslehre*

Show me what you truly love — what you search and strive for with
all your heart in hope of finding true self-satisfaction — and you
have exposed your life to me. As you love, so you live. This very
love is simply the root, the seat, and the middle point of your life.
— Fichte, *Die Anweisung zum seligen Leben,*
oder auch der Religionslehre

Although Fichte explains the origin of religious belief in "Divine Governance" and clarifies the relation between philosophy and life in the *Vocation of Man,* his complete description of religious consciousness and its connection to the *Wissenschaftslehre* appears in *The Way to the Blessed Life, or the Religionslehre,* which contains a popular description of human spiritual development, or a *Seligkeitslehre,* and a philosophical deduction of human religious consciousness, or *Religionslehre.*[38] In the *Way to the Blessed Life,* Fichte depicts human existence, or *Dasein,* in terms of desire, or love, through which human beings perceive themselves and reality. Love seeks concord, so yearning for communion with an infinite, eternal unity — God, or *Sein* — characterizes *Dasein.*

The popular *Seligkeitslehre* traces human existence through five standpoints of consciousness: sensibility, stoicism or legality, morality, religion, and knowledge or philosophy.[39] At each lower standpoint of consciousness, misdirected desire results in despair, which leads the human subject to reflect, thereby clarifying its true desire and impelling it toward its final goal of blessedness where goodness, wisdom, and fulfillment coincide.[40] The moral subject recognizes that blessedness consists in pursuing its individual moral vocation, but it perceives the world — and, particularly, other individuals in the world — as thwarting its endeavors. If the moral subject realizes that its ultimate task consists in cultivating freedom in itself and others, it reaches the standpoint of religion. The moral-religious subject wills a sensible result only conditionally as a temporal manifestation of the intelligible world where each individual's moral contribution is eternally preserved.[41] Thus love generates the intelligible world order, or God.[42] To experience a relationship with God, human beings need only act morally, but to understand the relation between *Sein* and *Dasein,* they must reach the standpoint of philosophy.[43]

The philosophical *Religionslehre* derives *Dasein* from *Sein.* The law of reflective opposition drives the argument to an ultimate synthesis whereby a law of unity joins the rational individual, the rational world, the material object, and the material world within a single act of consciousness.[44] In thinking about *Sein,* the knowing subject posits it as a determinate self-consciousness in opposition to a determinable, and insofar as thinking is unlimited, infinitely divisible, manifold, or world.[45] In thinking about *Dasein,* the knowing subject posits it as a determinate consciousness opposed to five determinable standpoints of consciousness.[46] Each aspect of the determinable quintuple form is connected to the free activity of a determinate subject, or I, that is characterized by duality, or the desire for unity. Insofar as the I obtains a complete self-comprehension, it recognizes its desire as love of a unifying, moral law. So conceived, the five standpoints of consciousness become elements of a synthesis where the moral law unites an individual will, an object (the body) affected by the will, a sensible world order, and an intelligible world order as a single act of consciousness.[47]

Although Fichte claimed explicitly in his introduction to *The Way to the Blessed Life* that his theory differed in no manner from the theory aborted by the *Atheismusstreit,* no confiscations were issued, no rescripts were signed, and no investigations were initiated. Fichte had been invited to present his *Religionslehre* to an assembly of burghers in a local home. It was received amiably and quietly, with nary an accusation of sacrilege or anarchy. To be sure, apart from that genial congregation of upright citizens and their virtuous wives (and apart from Fichte's students in Berlin), none cared to discuss the latest and final presentation of Fichte's *Religionslehre.* The mature version of the fearsome doctrine that had raised the specter of nihilism thirteen years prior garnered neither fame nor infamy. It waited, preserved in the published notes, for later generations to debate.

The Legacy of Fichte's *Religionslehre*

These lectures . . . are entirely the result of my unremitting development—during the past six or seven years of more leisure and greater maturity—of a philosophical view that came to me thirteen years ago. Although I hope a good many things might have changed in me, no part of this view itself has changed since that time.

—Fichte, *Die Anweisung zum seligen Leben, oder auch der Religionslehre*

Fichte's *Religionslehre* remains a source of controversy. Current scholars often misunderstand either the practical significance of the *Religionslehre* as a *Seligkeitslehre* or its theoretical importance as a part of the *Wissenschaftslehre*. The *Atheismusstreit* is sometimes reduced to political or personal issues and the later *Religionslehre* to a transition toward absolute idealism or to a compromise with religious orthodoxy or state authority. Other scholars would treat the *Religionslehre* as an unusually, but intrinsically, Christian doctrine. Either approach oversimplifies the profundity of the *Religionslehre* and distorts the continuity of the *Wissenschaftslehre*.

The inclination to disregard the genuine issues at stake in the *Atheismusstreit* is understandable in light of the vicious polemics, factional maneuvers, and private vendettas surrounding Fichte's tenure in Jena. Nonetheless, personality and politics ought not to diminish the central religious and philosophical concerns of the controversy. Fichte's stubborn refusal to alter his position during the *Atheismusstreit* suggests that he viewed the religious elements as significant. Moreover, his steadfast persistence in developing this position long after the debate ended indicates that he believed the *Religionslehre* occupied a crucial place in his philosophy.

It might seem tempting to construe Fichte's later *Religionslehre* as mending his reputation as an educator or as making his introduction as a proto-Hegelian philosopher, but any such allegations should be considered in light of Fichte's nonconciliatory behavior in Jena and Berlin and of his own arguments regarding the overall consistency of his *Religionslehre.* Had Fichte desired to reconcile with religious orthodoxy, he might have taken advantage of his opportunities to do so rather than engaging in an ardent self-defense. Had he hoped to repair his standing, he might have shown contrition in Berlin rather than attempting to reform the Masonic orders.[48] Leaving these psychological speculations aside, had Fichte made a turnabout, he might have acknowledged it rather than explicitly denying it; and had he made a turnabout, there might be textual evidence to support it. However, Fichte explicitly denied altering his position, and textual evidence supports the overall consistency of Fichte's early and later *Wissenschaftslehre.*[49]

Many current scholars regard Fichte as an atheist and thus as necessarily a secularist; others regard him as genuinely concerned by religious and spiritual issues and thus as necessarily a theist. Either position oversimplifies the *Religionslehre.* By and large, anglophone scholars have downplayed Fichte's work on religion as an inconsequential, albeit contentious, part of his systematic corpus. Their disregard is regrettable, for the *Religionslehre* was not a fleeting metaphysical folly but an integral part of Fichte's philosophy, which he anticipated in the *Wissenschaftslehre nova methodo.*[50] If some current scholars have overlooked the philosophical and spiritual import of Fichte's *Religionslehre,* others have overemphasized its place in the *Wissenschaftslehre* or its connection to specific Christian doctrines.[51] Although the position of both the early and the later *Religionslehre* may be consistent with Christian morals—as with all of the great world religions—binding it to the tenets of any particular religious dogma undercuts the priority of the moral world order as the sole ground of religious belief.

Finding the proper label for Fichte's religious views is problematic, for the most common titles (*atheist, theist,* or even *deist*) all carry connotations contrary to his position. The theist understands God anthropomorphically, as a personal being, while Fichte thinks of God as the moral order itself, which is impersonal. Yet to label this deism is equally problematic, for the deist denies God's relationality, but Fichte believes that the moral order is by nature relational, even if not personal. One could label Fichte's view atheistic, as he denies the traditional understanding of God, but Fichte himself abhorred the title and lost his faculty position denying it. The atheist denies that there is any objective reality to which the word *God* refers, while Fichte understands the moral order itself as the proper referent for the word *God.*

The *Religionslehre* was neither a perfunctory religious avowal to mollify ecclesiastical authorities nor an injudicious skeptical irreverence to titillate enlightened colleagues but rather, seamlessly and simultaneously, a philosophical and profoundly spiritual religious doctrine. Fichte denied the existence of a personal deity in his Jena writings, then reiterated this denial in his public defense during the atheism dispute, and finally reaffirmed it in his last lectures on the philosophy of religion. In Jena and Berlin, he argued that the *Religionslehre* was a crucial and integral part of the entire *Wissenschaftslehre* in that the ground of religious belief, the ground of ethical belief, and the ground of theoretical belief involved the same intellectual intuition of freedom obtained through practical activity.

The real intellectual intuition provides the basis for Fichte's account of spiritual life and its development, which is reciprocally bound to sensible life and its development, and thus allows for a philosophical concept of religion as a system of spiritual beliefs and moral values that guides practical activity. His account of the relation between philosophy, philosophy of religion, and religion must be considered in light of the distinction between the transcendental standpoint of philosophy and the practical standpoint of life. Life, the sphere of practice, allows an intuition of freedom that grounds moral-religious belief and activity, which require no theoretical justification. This same intuition also grounds philosophy, the sphere of theory, which describes life, including religion, and demonstrates the origin of its beliefs in intellectual intuition. Consequently, neither philosophy nor philosophy of religion, which are theoretical, should be confused with religion, which is practical; but philosophy, philosophy of religion, and religion share a common ground in life: the intellectual intuition of the moral law.

In whatever the holy man does, lives, and loves, God appears: no longer hidden in shadows or cloaked in garb but rather in his own, immediate, and efficacious life. The question, which the empty, obscure notion of God cannot answer—What is God?—is answered here. He is whatever his devoted and inspired follower does. Do you want to see God, as he is in himself, face to face? Do not search for him in the clouds. You can find him wherever you are. Just look at his followers' lives and you see him. Give yourself to him and you find him in your own breast.[52]

Notes

The first section epigraph, from Fichte, *Foundations of Transcendental Philosophy*, is taken from the edition edited and translated by Daniel Breazeale (Ithaca: Cornell University Press, 1992), 471. The second section epigraph, from Fichte's *Vocation of Man*, is taken from the edition translated by Peter Preuss (Indianapolis: Hackett, 1987), 64–65. The third section epigraph, from Fichte's "On the Basis of Our Belief in a Divine Governance of the World," can be found in *Introductions to the Wissenschaftslehre and Other Writings*, ed. and trans. Daniel Breazeale (Indianapolis: Hackett, 1994), 150 (see also 150–51). The fourth and fifth epigraphs, from *Die Anweisung zum seligen Leben, oder auch der Religionslehre*, are drawn from the edition edited by Fritz Medicus (Hamburg: Felix Meiner, 1910), 13 and 5 respectively (my translation).

1. Johann Gottlieb Fichte, *Early Philosophical Writings*, ed. and trans. Daniel Breazeale (Ithaca: Cornell University Press, 1988), 357–58, hereafter cited as *EPW*, and *Vocation of Man*, trans. Peter Preuss (Indianapolis: Hackett, 1987), 24–25, hereafter cited as *VM*.

2. J. G. Fichte, *Attempt at a Critique of All Revelation*, trans. Garrett Green (Cambridge: Cambridge University Press, 1978).

3. "On the Basis of Our Belief in a Divine Governance of the World" can be found in J. G. Fichte, *Introductions to the Wissenschaftslehre and Other Writings*, ed. and trans. Daniel Breazeale (Indianapolis: Hackett, 1994), hereafter cited as *IWL*. For excellent accounts of Fichte's life in Jena, see *EPW*, 1–49; see also Anthony La Vopa, *Fichte: The Self and the Calling of Philosophy (1762–1799)* (Cambridge: Cambridge University Press, 2001).

4. "The Way towards a Blessed Life, or the *Religionslehre*" can be found in *The Popular Works of Johann Gottlieb Fichte*, trans. William Smith (London: Trübner, 1889). However, I shall cite *Die Anweisung zum seligen Leben, oder auch der Religionslehre* (1806), ed. Fritz Medicus (Hamburg: Felix Meiner, 1910); hereafter cited as *RL*. This work was originally presented as a series of lectures, but Fichte later published the transcriptions of them.

5. In 1800, Fichte anticipated this interpretation in "From a Private Letter," which can be found in *IWL*. In 1812, he reiterated his denial in his introduction to "The Way toward a Blessed Life."

6. Johann Gottlieb Fichte, *Foundations of Transcendental Philosophy*, ed. and trans. Daniel Breazeale (Ithaca: Cornell University Press, 1992), 467–74, hereafter cited as *FTP*.

7. *FTP*, 467–74. The philosophy of the postulates also includes the theory of right, or *Rechtslehre*, which deals with the postulate that theoretical philosophy addresses to the practical realm, namely, that free, rational beings ought to enter into relations of mutual influence. See also *RL*, 124; and *Fichte: The System of Ethics*, ed. and trans. Daniel Breazeale and Günter Zöller (Cambridge: Cambridge University Press, 2005), 197–201; hereafter cited as *SE*.

8. *FTP*, 119–20 and 122.

9. *IWL*, 10–11; *FTP*, 108–11 and 444; *SE*, 197–201.

10. *FTP*, 293–94, 337–38, and 437. See also J. G. Fichte, *The Science of Knowing: J. G. Fichte's 1804 Lectures on the "Wissenschaftslehre,"* trans. Walter E. Wright (Albany: SUNY Press, 2005), 71 and 157, hereafter cited as *SK;* and Yolanda Estes, "Intellectual Intuition, the Pure Will, and the Categorical Imperative," in *New Essays on Fichte's Later Jena Wissenschaftslehre*, ed. Daniel Breazeale and Tom Rockmore (Evanston: Northwestern University Press, 2002), 212–19. For a discussion of the various senses in which Fichte used the term *intellectual intuition,* see Daniel Breazeale, "Fichte's Nova methodo phenomenologica: On the Methodological Role of 'Intellectual Intuition' in the Later Jena Wissenschaftslehre," *Revue International de Philosophie* 206 (1998): 587–616; Alain Perrinjaquet, "'Wirkliche' und 'Philosophiche' Anschauung: Formen der intellektuellen Anschauung in Fichtes System der Sittenlehre," *Fichte-Studien* 5 (1993): 7–82; and Estes, "Intellectual Intuition."

11. The real intellectual intuition also provides an extraphilosophical sanction for the other part of the philosophy of the postulates, the philosophy of right, or the *Rechtslehre*. For a discussion of this extraphilosophical sanction and of the relation between the theoretical and practical portions of the *Wissenschaftslehre*, see Ives Radrizanni, "The Place of the Vocation of Man in Fichte's Work," in Breazeale and Rockmore, *New Essays*, 317–44; Estes, "Intellectual Intuition"; Yolanda Estes, "Fichte's Hypothetical Imperative: Morality, Right, and Philosophy in the Jena Wissenschaftslehre," in *Rights, Bodies, and Recognition: New Essays on Fichte's Foundations of Natural Right*, ed. Tom Rockmore and Daniel Breazeale (Hampshire: Ashgate, 2006), 59–70.

12. *EPW*, 411–12, 428–29, and 432–35.

13. For excellent accounts of the tensions at work within the *Aufklärung*, see Frederick C. Beiser, *The Fate of Reason: German Philosophy from Kant to Fichte* (Cambridge, MA: Harvard University Press, 1987); and George di Giovanni, introduction to *Friedrich Heinrich Jacobi: The Main Philosophical Writings and the*

Novel Allwill, trans. George di Giovanni (Montreal: McGill-Queen's University Press, 1994), 3–167.

14. These controversies are discussed in detail in Beiser, *Fate of Reason.*

15. The subsequent debate, which involved Voltaire, Rousseau, Lessing, Mendelssohn, Kant, and Hamann, intensified after the Lisbon earthquake of 1755.

16. The luminaries collided again over the production of an introductory physics text for children, or a *Kinderphysik.* Kant, who aspired to provide an accessible account of Newton's physics, was taken aback when Hamann insisted that the text should approach the subject from the position of childlike innocence by beginning with Genesis. Again, the crux of the debacle was not the question of pedagogy but of whether reason or faith should have priority in the education of human beings.

17. Lessing's intimate of many years, the rational theist Moses Mendelssohn, intended to write a tribute to Lessing's character, but the fideist F. H. Jacobi revealed that Lessing—on his "deathbed"—confessed to following Spinoza.

18. Among others, Kant, Herder, Wizenmann, and Goethe participated in this debate.

19. For two insightful discussions of the dispute, see di Giovanni, "From Jacobi's Philosophical Novel to Fichte's Idealism: Some Comments on the 1798–99 'Atheism Dispute,'" *Journal of the History of Philosophy* 27 (1989): 75–100; and Curtis Bowman, "Fichte, Jacobi, and the Atheism Controversy," in Breazeale and Rockmore, *New Essays,* 279–98.

20. Fichte and Niethammer edited the *Philosophisches Journal.* "The Development of the Concept of Religion" (1798), trans. Paul Edwards, can be found in *Nineteenth-Century Philosophy,* ed. Patrick L. Gardiner (New York: Free Press, 1969).

21. This pamphlet was mass produced and widely distributed at some great expense by the author or his supporters. It can be found in *J. G. Fichte and the Atheism Dispute (1798–1800): Selected Writings,* ed. Yolanda Estes, trans. Curtis Bowman (Hampshire: Ashgate, 2009).

22. Fichte threatened to resign if censured for publishing the essays, and his resignation was "accepted" in a postscript to the rescript censuring him.

23. *EPW,* 358 and 385–86.

24. Jacobi, *Friedrich Heinrich Jacobi,* 497–536.

25. La Vopa, *Fichte,* 368–424.

26. Kant's "Declaration" can be found in *J. G. Fichte and the Atheism Dispute.* It is likely that Kant never read any of Fichte's work, including "Divine Governance." His "Declaration" attacks a wounded—and indeed, professionally disabled—man, who revered him enough to name his sole child after him.

27. The allusion of pantheism generally resulted from errors about Fichte's concept of an immanent God. Some accusations of agnosticism or skepticism followed from a widespread conflation of Fichte's "Divine Governance" and

F. G. Forberg's "Development of the Concept of Religion." Fichte offered substantial replies to many of these criticisms and defamations in his "From a Private Letter" and "Concluding Remarks from the Editor," which can be found in *IWL,* and in "Appeal to the Public" and "Juridical Defense," which can be found in *J. G. Fichte and the Atheism Dispute.*

28. *IWL,* 160–61.

29. *IWL,* 143–44.

30. *IWL,* 144–46.

31. According to Fichte, "Once one has resolved to obey the [ethical] law within oneself, then the assumption that this goal can be accomplished is utterly necessary. It is immediately contained within this very resolve. It is identical to it." *IWL,* 145–48.

32. Fichte argues that this immediate consciousness is the only possible religious revelation. *IWL,* 150.

33. *IWL,* 151.

34. Moreover, doing so would subordinate the moral law to an intellect, which—however powerful—would be limited by the constraints that the *Wissenschaftslehre* shows determine any possible personality. In short, Fichte offers a more refined and sophisticated version of Plato's Euthyphro argument. *IWL,* 151–52.

35. *IWL,* 151–52.

36. *VM,* 61–65, 67–123. For quite possibly the best account of Fichte's goals in the *Vocation of Man,* see Radrizanni, "Place of the Vocation," 317–44.

37. *VM,* 107.

38. "Popular" here does not refer to the commonsense philosophy of the *Popularphilosophen* but rather to an account that provides the conclusions of philosophical arguments without requiring the reader or listener to actually reconstruct those arguments.

39. *RL,* 72–86, 104–5, 126. See also *VM,* 73, 84–85.

40. From the standpoint of morality, the moral subject regards itself as a means for executing the moral law, which it loves as its own will insofar as morality, desire, and personality coincide in individual moral vocation (*RL,* 112–18). In connecting feeling and morality, Fichte differs markedly from Kant, who regards feeling as a moral-religious temptation. Moreover, unlike Kant, he locates the "kingdom of ends" within human experience, arguing that the empirical subject enjoys peace and contentment in exact proportion to its level of spiritual development.

41. This is Fichte's postulate of immortality. See also *RL,* 131–35, 146, and *VM,* 90.

42. *RL,* 136–47, 162; *VM,* 75 and 80–81; *IWL,* 146–47.

43. Fichte claims that philosophy serves two main practical purposes. First, it reconciles the seeming conflicts between faith and knowledge that distress

many individuals. Second, it is a vocation for (and thus necessary for the blessedness of) a few individuals who have an unusually strong drive for knowledge. *RL,* 28 and 61–62; *FTP,* 81 and 83; *VM,* 26–27, 99, and 114–15.

44. In philosophical reflection, this requirement is felt as an inexplicable limitation of consciousness (which appears in ordinary consciousness as an "ought" or command from being). *RL,* 66–67.

45. *RL,* 58–71.

46. *RL,* 72–86.

47. *RL,* 119–35. See also *FTP,* 444. This synthesis is expressed in the later *Wissenschaftslehre* in terms of a union of "reason as self-making, being as made, being as not made, making as primordial, and making as copied." *SK,* 197–201 and 217.

48. While in Berlin, Fichte attempted to make the *Wissenschaftslehre* accessible to members of the Masonic orders in hopes of having a practical effect in the world.

49. For a discussion of the continuity of Fichte's *Religionslehre,* see Yolanda Estes, "After Jena: Fichte's *Religionslehre,*" in *After Jena: New Essays on Fichte's Later Philosophy,* ed. Daniel Breazeale and Tom Rockmore (Evanston: Northwestern University Press, 2008), 99–114, and "Fichte," in *Nineteenth Century Philosophy and Religion,* vol. 4 of *History of the Philosophy of Religion,* ed. Graham Oppy and Nick Trakakis (Middlesex: Acumen, 2008), ch. 1.

50. *FTP,* 471.

51. Some scholars have misunderstood the spiritual aspects of the *Religionslehre,* portraying Fichte as a mystic, a Christologist, a Trinitarian, or some form of Christian theist. Despite my claim that the textual evidence supports a different interpretation, many of these interpretations are insightful and respectful to the texts. Some examples include Anthony N. Perovich, "Fichte and the Typology of Mysticism," in *Fichte: Historical Contexts/Contemporary Controversies,* ed. Daniel Breazeale and Tom Rockmore (Atlantic Highlands, NJ: Humanities Press, 1994), 128–41; George Seidel, "The Atheism Controversy of 1799 and the Christology of Fichte's Anweisung zum seligen Leben of 1806," in *New Perspectives on Fichte,* ed. Daniel Breazeale and Tom Rockmore (Atlantic Highlands, NJ: Humanities Press, 1996), 143–52; and Jeffery Kinlaw, "The Being of Appearance: Absolute, Image, and the Trinitarian Structure of the 1813 Wissenschaftslehre," in Breazeale and Rockmore, *New Perspectives on Fichte,* 127–42.

52. *RL,* 83; cf. *IWL,* 150.

Chapter 12

Metaphysical Realism and Epistemological Modesty in Schleiermacher's Method

JACQUELINE MARIÑA

How are we to understand religion? It is undeniable that religion, and religious motivations, have played a very large role in shaping world events. As such, the question of how to understand religion has become increasingly urgent. At one extreme are those who adopt a comprehensive scientific naturalism. They approach religious beliefs and practices in such a way as to reduce them to nonreligious social or psychological factors; for them religion is part of an ideology or an infantile wish projection that must be outgrown. At the other extreme are many of the religious believers themselves, who take their own religion as absolute truth and take themselves to be in a privileged epistemic position to apprehend it. Both extremes are dangerous: the first because it fails to take both religion and the religious drive seriously, and so ignores an integral facet of human life; the second because it is exemplary of the dangers of religion itself, which can take absolutist and Manichean forms. When religion does take such a form, it degenerates into idolatry, for it mistakes what must always remain a finite and conditioned apprehension of the transcendent for the transcendent ground itself. Often coupled with such a mistake comes a failure to recognize the validity of other perspectives, as well as a violent exclusion of everything that is other or unfamiliar.

Schleiermacher's theory of religion charts a third course allowing us to avoid the pitfalls of these two unappealing alternatives. Against reductionism, it takes religion and the object of religion seriously: this I will call its *realism*. Religion cannot be reduced to psychology, anthropology, or ideology. It is not a "mass of metaphysical and ethical crumbs."[1] It demands understanding on its own terms because it is directed to the Absolute, or, as John Hick would put it, to the Real as such. However, Schleiermacher also recognized that the only access we have to this Absolute is through *experience*. Yet it cannot be stressed enough that this focus on human experience does not amount to a mere speaking about humanity, as it were, "in a loud voice."[2] Schleiermacher's emphasis on experience does not ignore the fact that religious experience is always experience *of* the Absolute, and that it is *to* the Absolute that religious symbols point. Moreover, from the standpoint of Schleiermacher's metaphysics, the Absolute is that which establishes and preserves everything that is; it is that which ultimately works in and through history to transform human beings into Godlike persons. Schleiermacher's theory of religion decidedly does not reduce religion to mere anthropology; to claim that it does is to misunderstand him on a grand scale.

Nevertheless, Schleiermacher is quite attentive to the *conditions* of human knowing and experiencing. Concern with these conditions was not new to theology; Thomas Aquinas had already noted, "The thing known is in the knower according to the mode of the knower."[3] What was new to theology was the comprehensive character of Schleiermacher's account of human subjectivity, an account that both recognized and stressed the finite and conditioned character of all human apprehensions. This account, heavily influenced by Kant's metaphysics and epistemology, went beyond even Kant in recognizing not only the contribution of the human subject to all knowing and experiencing, but the contribution of human communities—themselves historically conditioned—to human knowing as well. These insights were especially applied to religious experience. Because Schleiermacher's theory begins with a comprehensive account of human subjectivity, it is theoretically equipped to recognize the validity of different religious experiences without degenerating into relativism. This I will call its *perspectivalism*. This paper will be a discussion of these two themes—Schleiermacher's realism and his perspectivalism—and their significance for a theory of religion.

Realism

Schleiermacher called his own brand of realism a "higher realism." The later Schleiermacher contrasted his own position with the idealism of Fichte, in which the I knows only itself. Fichte, famously, eliminated Kant's thing in itself and all of Kant's dualisms: for him there is nothing distinct and "outside" the self with which the self interacts. There is nothing that is *in itself*, that is, apart from its relation to the subject, unknowable by the subject. For knowledge to be possible, Fichte argued, there must be a subject-object identity, and hence, in any act of knowledge, the self really knows only itself. For the mature Schleiermacher, on the other hand, the Absolute really does transcend consciousness: it is distinct from the self, while at the same time remaining the ground of the self.[4] Moreover, other finite individuals are also genuinely distinct from the I. Hence, for Schleiermacher, there are *real* relations between the self and others, and between the self and the Absolute. Even in the earliest edition of the *Speeches* (1799) Schleiermacher recognizes these real relations.[5] While certainly there are Spinozistic tendencies in his earlier works, the mature Schleiermacher leaves these behind, becoming more consistent in thinking through the necessary conditions for real relations between individual substances.[6]

Famously, in *The Christian Faith* Schleiermacher grounds genuine religion in "the feeling of absolute dependence" or what he also calls the "God-consciousness."[7] This "feeling" is not one feeling among others that can be made an object *of* consciousness; rather, it is given at the very ground of consciousness itself, in what Schleiermacher calls the immediate self-consciousness. In self-consciousness, the self makes itself its own object and can thereby distinguish between itself and the world. However, the relation between self and world, between the spontaneity and receptivity of the self, presupposes an original unity of consciousness, a moment given in pure immediacy, where the two are one. This original unity of consciousness makes possible the transition between the moments of spontaneity and receptivity. The consciousness of absolute dependence is given in this moment of pure immediacy; it is "the self consciousness accompanying the whole of our spontaneity, and because this is never zero, accompanying the whole of our existence, and negating absolute freedom" (*CF* 4.3; *KGA* I/13/1, 38; MS, 16). God is the "Whence of our active and receptive existence" (*CF* 4.4; *KGA* I/13/1, 39; MS, 16). However, while the Absolute must accompany all moments of consciousness since it grounds the self, consciousness of God is not directly given in the immediate self-consciousness.[8] What is given, rather, is a consciousness of the self as absolutely dependent, in particular in regard to its own spontaneous action in relation to the world. The consciousness of absolute dependence is the consciousness that "the whole of our spontaneous activity comes from a source outside us" (*CF* 4.3; *KGA* I/13/1, 38; MS, 16). Consciousness of the self as dependent arises from the consciousness of a "missing unity" in the river of the soul's life as it flickers from spontaneity to receptivity. One of the most insightful analyses of Scheiermacher's understanding of the feeling of absolute dependence is that of Manfred Frank, which is worth quoting at length here:

> Consciousness feels itself to be *absolutely* dependent on Being, and this dependence is indirectly represented as the dependence on the Absolute. When immediate self-consciousness (or feeling) flickers from one to the other pole of the reflexive rift, this does not shed light on the positive fullness of a supra-reflexive identity, but rather on its lack. Schleiermacher notes that in the moment of "transition" (286) from object to subject of reflection, self-consciousness always traverses the space of a "missing unity" (C 290, §li). Since the self cannot attribute this lack to its own activity, it must recognize this lack as the effect of a "determining power transcending it, that is, one that lies outside its own power" (C 290). The self can

only ascribe to itself the ground of *knowledge* of this dependence. Schleiermacher can thereby say that the cause of this feeling of dependence is not "effected by the subject, but only arises in the subject" (CF §3.3). However, in feeling, the activity of the self is "never zero," for "without any feeling of freedom a feeling of absolute dependence would not be possible" (CF §4.3).[9]

We can think of this "missing unity" as the horizon or backdrop of consciousness. This horizon comprehends both self and world and is the condition of the possibility of both their difference from one another *and* their relation. It is traversed by consciousness itself insofar as consciousness must move between itself as the subject of reflection and the world that is given to it to know. As such, consciousness comes to awareness of this missing unity only in reflecting upon the transcendental conditions of the possibility of the moments of self-consciousness, in which there is an antithesis between self and world. Both the immediate self-consciousness and the feeling of absolute dependence are given only along *with* the sensuous self-consciousness: only insofar as the self distinguishes between itself and its world can it arrive at an awareness of the underlying unity conditioning the possibility of its making this distinction.

In the *Dialektik,* Schleiermacher asks, "How does it [the immediate self-consciousness] relate to the transcendental ground?" And he answers, "We consider the latter to be the ground of the thinking being in regards to the identity of willing and thinking. The transcendental ground precedes and succeeds all actual thinking, but does not come to an appearance at any time. This transcendental ground of thought accompanies the actual thinking in an atemporal manner, but never itself becomes thought."[10] The Absolute transcends consciousness so thoroughly that it "does not come to an appearance at any time." For Schleiermacher, consciousness of God is not given directly in the immediate self-consciousness. As noted above, what is directly given is a consciousness of the self *as* absolutely dependent. Co-posited along with this consciousness is the Absolute itself.

Some Schleiermacher scholars have insisted that Schleiermacher is self-consciously aware that all he has arrived at is a *consciousness* of the

Absolute, leaving the skeptical question of whether there actually *is* an Absolute completely untouched.[11] On such a reading, one never moves past consciousness and its objects: on the one hand, there is the *feeling* of absolute dependence given in the immediate self-consciousness, and on the other, its correlate, the consciousness of God or the Absolute, which must be posited along with it. But both the feeling and its correlate are, so to speak, mere elements of consciousness carrying no metaphysical implications beyond themselves.[12]

There are several reasons to be highly suspicious of such an anti-metaphysical reading. First is the fact that Schleiermacher clearly posits a transcendental ground and its effects throughout his theological and philosophical works: for instance, in the passage just quoted Schleiermacher clearly tells us that the "transcendental ground precedes and succeeds all actual thinking." Second, the antimetaphysical reading ignores much of the work that Schleiermacher is doing in positing both the immediate self-consciousness and the feeling of absolute dependence. And third, one cannot make sense of the whole of Schleiermacher's theology without assuming his metaphysical realism. It is to the second and third of these reasons that I now turn.

Can Schleiermacher legitimately move past mere reports concerning states of human consciousness? The answer lies in the nature of his analysis of "the consciousness of absolute dependence." Is this a mere phenomenological report, analogous to, let us say, the phenomenological report of the person in a fever who is conscious of feeling cold? If so, then of course Schleiermacher cannot move beyond a report on consciousness and its objects, since in both cases there is no guarantee that the mind actually reflects the real. However, Schleiermacher does not arrive at his description of the immediate self-consciousness and the feeling of absolute dependence through any kind of phenomenological introspection. He arrives at them through an *analysis of the conditions of the possibility of consciousness itself*. And this means that both his analysis of the immediate self-consciousness and his analysis of the consciousness of absolute dependence have significant metaphysical implications. As I have argued above, Schleiermacher's analysis of the consciousness of absolute dependence is grounded in the immediate awareness of the rift that consciousness must cross as it transitions from the subject to the object of reflection. If we can grant Schleiermacher that this rift is a real one, that is, that there *is* a genuine distinction between self and world, then we can also grant him the dependent character of both self and world: both presuppose a horizon conditioning the consciousness of both. But this means the self is conscious of its absolute dependence because it *is* absolutely dependent. And once we posit the self as absolutely dependent, it follows that we can also posit *that* upon which the radically conditioned self depends. We don't just arrive at a *consciousness* of the Absolute but come to the Absolute as the condition of the possibility of consciousness itself. And the latter, as the ground of consciousness, must be real. To summarize: if it can be shown that *a condition of the possibility of self-consciousness* is a consciousness of absolute dependence (which is itself based on the reality of the absolute dependence of consciousness), then the Absolute is a condition of the possibility of consciousness itself. And this is a metaphysical claim.

It seems to me that this reading of Schleiermacher is fundamentally sound, and that Schleiermacher can legitimately move from his "thick" description of the feeling of absolute dependence to the positing of a metaphysical Absolute. What, of course, still remains problematic — certainly at this stage — is the identification of this Absolute with God. A much less robust understanding of this Absolute, for instance, an identification of it with Being, would still do the required work. Nevertheless, it is important to point out that Schleiermacher understands the "God-consciousness" he describes at the beginning of *Christian Faith* as an abstraction from the Christian God consciousness that he is presupposing as the primary data for his theology.

I now briefly turn to my third point: Schleiermacher's theology makes no sense if we do not attribute to him the conviction that God, and not just the consciousness of God, is real and genuinely effective. Schleiermacher's theology, like that of Albert Magnus and Aquinas before him, is based on the way of causality. He claims in the *Christian Faith* that "all the divine attributes to be dealt with in the *Glaubenslehre* must go back in some way to the divine causality since they are only meant to explain the feeling of absolute dependence" (*CF* 50.3; *KGA* I/13/1; MS, 198). This, of course, means that Schleiermacher does not claim to have any knowledge of God as God is *in se*. Nevertheless, we do have knowledge of God in relation to us. Of particular importance for this knowledge is the redemption that God effects in us through Christ. This redemption is powerful and transformative not only of persons but of whole communities as well. What is the source of this redemption? Schleiermacher is clear that it is not something we effect in ourselves; it has its basis in a source outside ourselves, namely, the communicated perfection and blessedness of Christ. And as I have argued elsewhere, Schleiermacher conceived of all the moments of Jesus's sensuous self-consciousness as utterly conditioned by the divine influence.[13] This influence is the source of Jesus's transformative power on human consciousness. While Schleiermacher is careful not to make any claims concerning God's nature as God is *in se,* he clearly posits God as the ultimate author of our salvation in Christ. Once again, this transformation is the result of a very real power whose source lies beyond what we ourselves are capable of as radically conditioned and finite subjects.

Insofar as Schleiermacher affirms the existence of the Absolute, and acknowledges that what is real is independent of our conceptions of it, he is a metaphysical *realist.* His realism can be contrasted with contemporary antirealism in religion, which affirms that all existence claims concerning God should simply be reunderstood as commitments to a certain way of life.[14] For Schleiermacher, on the other hand, all religious expressions point past themselves to the "Whence of our active and receptive existence" (*CF* 4.4; *KGA* I/13/1, 39; MS, 16). While for Schleiermacher religious expressions are reflective of human experience, they do not merely refer to human ways of being in the world or to human experience, but also point to the transcendent ground of all human experience. Hence, while the disciplines of psychology, sociology, and anthropology might shed light on religion, religion can in no way be reduced to a study of the objects of those disciplines. Moreover, crucial to Schleiermacher's enterprise is the claim that God not only exists but is also continuously *active* in the providential direction and care of humanity. This is a key point to keep in mind, especially given the high premium that Schleiermacher places on human transformation, which is effected in us by the loving source of all existence.

Perspectivalism

It is, of course, important to keep in mind that this "Whence" is apprehended *through* human experience. What is revealed is never a proposition mirroring the structure of what is known, but an experience *of* the transcendent ground. Schleiermacher tells us that revelation does not "operate on man as a cognitive being," for that "would make the revelation to be originally and essentially doctrine" (*CF* 10.3; *KGA* I/13/1; MS, 50). Furthermore, this experience is completely different in kind from the experience we have of finite objects in the world. It occurs at the level of the immediate self-consciousness grounding our awareness of both self and world. As such, the original religious experience is never of anything *in* the world but is rather given in pure immediacy, at that fleeting moment prior to reflection of the self as distinct from the world. Religious doctrines, beliefs, and practices arise from a culturally conditioned reflection upon this experience, which is always one of finite subjects. Hence, the religious experience of other persons may be different from one's own, and yet just as valid. As Schleiermacher notes: "Each person must be conscious that his religion is only part of the whole, that regarding the same objects that affect him religiously there are views just as pious and, nevertheless, completely different from his own, and that from other elements of religion intuitions and feelings flow, the sense for which he may be completely lacking."[15] Hence, while Schleiermacher is a *metaphysical realist,* epistemologically he is a *perspectivalist.* God is real, but our cognitive access to God is always finite and conditioned. Not only does our state influence how we perceive and how we can be affected, but our historical and cultural standpoint influences the range of how religious experience can be *interpreted* and its significance expressed.

This range of how religious experience is interpreted can nonetheless be quite broad, since key to the task of interpretation is the imagination. In Kant's system, which clearly influenced Schleiermacher, the imagination mediates between sense and understanding, synthesizing the data of perception and readying them for the application of concepts. But experience can be imagined and reimagined in different ways. This is especially true the broader the implications of an experience, which can then be connected with other aspects of human experience in myriad ways. The religious experience, occurring as it does at the level of the immediate self-consciousness, is not the experience of an object existing over against a subject. As such, what is experienced transcends all of our cognitive capacities, and our concepts are never adequate to it. Occurring, as it does, at the level of the immediate self-consciousness, the genuine religious experience is one with global implications. It affects every aspect of the subject's life, particularly how the subject understands herself and her relation to the world. Here, in particular, the role of the imagination is paramount. In *On Religion,* Schleiermacher makes the bold statement that "belief in God depends on the direction of the imagination." He continues:

> You will know that imagination is the highest and most original element in us, and that everything besides it is merely reflection upon it; you will know that it is our imagination that creates the world for you, and that you can have no God without the world. Moreover, God will not thereby become less certain to anyone, nor will individuals be better able to emancipate themselves from the nearly immutable necessity of accepting a deity because of knowing whence this necessity comes. In religion, therefore, the idea of God does not rank as high as you think. Among truly religious persons there have never been zealots, enthusiasts, or fanatics for the existence of God; with great equanimity they were always aware of what one calls atheism alongside themselves, for there has always been something that seemed to them more irreligious than this.[16]

A person who has a genuine religious experience must continually strive to understand its significance for his or her life. Interpretation of such experience, as well as a grasp of its implications for life as a whole, involves both the imagination and the use of concepts. If the religious experience is revelatory of that which is of ultimate concern, then it must also be capable of transforming priorities in what is worth valuing. Genuine religion thereby implies a comprehensive integration of one's view of oneself and of the world with the understanding of this religious experience itself; in both, imagination and concepts are involved.

Nevertheless, Schleiermacher stresses that in religion "the idea of God does not rank as high as you think." So, while Schleiermacher praises the importance of the imagination in integrating and understanding religious experience, at the same time he claims that the concepts used to make sense of that experience *are not* of the highest importance. Why is this? Important here is Schleiermacher's observation that among the truly religious there have never been zealots and enthusiasts. In fact, one of the principal points of the second speech in *On Religion* is that the persecution and spitefulness that "wrecks society and makes blood flow like water" often associated with religion does not arise from genuine or true religion. It arises only when religious experience is systematized in such a way that it is fettered. Those who "inundate religion with philosophy and fetter it to a system" are the corrupters of religion,[17] and it is they, Schleiermacher claims, who are responsible for the perversion of the religious drive. It is, of course, true that some degree of "systematization" is involved in any attempt to take the religious experience seriously and to thereby understand it. Schleiermacher himself wrote *The Christian Faith,* a fine piece of systematic theology. There are, however, two important dangers associated with systems. First, a system can become so comprehensive that it ceases to allow the religious experience to break *through* it. Elements of the system can encompass so many aspects and can be so tightly interwoven so as not to allow any room for anything foreign to these ideas (such as a transformative experience) to break in. Second, closely related with this first danger is the mistaking of this system for ultimate reality itself. Here something finite and conditioned, something human, is taken as absolute. But this is nothing less than idolatry, and from it spring the zealotry and enthusiasm at the bottom of the religious intolerance that can so easily degenerate into religious warfare.

Persons who are truly religious have faith in *God,* that is, in the love and wisdom of ultimate reality. They recognize that God remains God regardless of what ideas one—or others—may have of God. God does not need to be defended, for the Absolute cannot be assailed. It is only all-too-human ideas that can be threatened and need defense. This is what Schleiermacher means when he says: "God will not thereby become less certain to anyone, nor will individuals be better able to emancipate themselves from the nearly immutable necessity of accepting a deity because of knowing whence this necessity comes." Accepting a deity, that is, standing in relation to the Absolute, is an immutable necessity. Yet the religious experience is one that each person must have for him- or herself in the inner sanctuary of the soul; the Absolute is always experienced *from* a particular perspective. Religious systems, and the enthusiasm and zealotry of the system builders who take themselves to have a privileged access to the Absolute, can only get in the way of this genuine experience. A truly transformative religious experience thereby carries with it *epistemological modesty*. This epistemological modesty goes hand in hand with Schleiermacher's *metaphysical realism*. What is real is independent of our conceptions of it, which are always limited and partial. The object of true religion is "the great, ever-continuous redemptive work of eternal love,"[18] not *our* ideas of the real.

An Objection to Epistemological Modesty, and a Rejoinder

What good is Schleiermacher's realism when whatever conceptual access we have to the Absolute is always partial and conditioned? Does this position not leave us in a quandary, since we can never really know God, but only our ideas of God, which are radically historically conditioned? Is not Schleiermacher's perspectivalism, for all practical purposes, little better than sheer relativism? With one hand Schleiermacher seems to take away what he gives with the other. His realism offers only a false sense of security: given his emphasis on the conditioned character of our subjectivity and all our acts of knowledge, we really cannot know anything about the Absolute as it is *in itself*. While there are important differences, some may be inclined to argue that his position has much in common with John Hick's. Famously, Hick claims that "we cannot apply to the Real *an sich* the characteristics encountered in its *personae* and *impersonae*. Thus it cannot be said to be one or many, person or thing, substance or process, good or evil, purposive or non-purposive. None of the concrete descriptions that apply within the realm of human experience can apply literally to the unexperienceable ground of that realm. For whereas the phenomenal world is structured by our own conceptual frameworks, its noumenal ground is not. We cannot even speak of this as a thing or an entity."[19] And this seems to leave us simply adrift, without any real sense of direction. If we cannot even legitimately say that the object of religion is good or evil, purposive or nonpurposive, then religion loses its point. This is an important objection that is not easy to overcome. Nevertheless, a correct understanding of Schleiermacher's position shows that he has the resources to answer it.

It is important to keep in mind that Schleiermacher's perspectivalism is a consequence of his realism. In *On Religion* he tells us:

> All intuition proceeds from the influence of the intuited on the one who intuits, from an original and independent action of the former, which is then grasped, apprehended, and conceived by the latter according to one's own nature. If the emanations of light—which happen completely without your efforts—did not affect your sense, if the smallest parts of the body, the tips of your fingers, were not mechanically or chemically affected, if the pressure of weight did not reveal to you an opposition and a limit to your power, you would intuit nothing and perceive nothing, and what you thus intuit and perceive is not the nature of things, but their action upon you.[20]

That is, Schleiermacher posits real relations between ourselves and others, and between ourselves and the Absolute. This means that our access to others and to the Absolute arises from their influence upon us. But what this influence is depends on two things: first, the powers of that which influences us, and second, our *capacities* to be affected in certain ways (our own "nature"). It is only because we are capable of being affected in certain ways that we can perceive, but these very capacities play an important role in shaping the content of perception. As such, this very realism and the positing of real relations imply that we do not have access to things as they are *an sich*, but only to how they affect us. Furthermore, how we are affected by things is then interpreted by us through our own culturally conditioned categories.

At this point, it is important to keep in mind a key feature of realism, allowing us to distinguish it from idealism and antirealism. In a short paper on realism and antirealism in religion, Roger Trigg defines realism in the following way: "What we have beliefs about is not meant to be *logically* related to them."[21] That is, *what* we have beliefs about is distinct from our ideas about it, and we cannot make inferences from our ideas about something to the actuality of the thing. We can only make inferences from one idea to another. But if beliefs are not logically related to what they are about, then what is our relation to things? Such a relation is a *real* relation, that is, a relation of *influence* where one thing affects another.

How might such realism allay the qualms mentioned above? In *The Christian Faith,* Schleiermacher affirms that piety is "the consciousness of being absolutely dependent, or, which is the same thing, of being in relation with God" (§4). God is the "Whence of our active and receptive existence" (4.4); faith then, is the consciousness of being absolutely dependent upon God. It cannot be stressed enough, however, that for Schleiermacher the object of faith is not the consciousness of being absolutely dependent (for then the object of faith would be something human) but rather this real relation of absolute dependence itself. As creatures, we stand in absolute dependence on God. Moreover, as Schleiermacher would develop in later sections of *The Christian Faith,* God's absolute causality is qualitatively different from finite causality. In finite causality, one thing influences another, and the influence of one thing upon another is always conditioned by the capacities of that thing to be affected by the other. In God's absolute causality, on the other hand, God establishes the very existence of that which receives the divine influence. Hence, nothing is left outside God's power with respect to how the divine influence is to be received. For Schleiermacher, the process of the complete divinization of the cosmos is only a matter of time, and is assured in virtue of God's absolute causality. Given this stress on real relations, Schleiermacher's emphasis is ultimately not on what *we* can know about God, but on God's relation to us, which has real effects on us, namely, our transformation and divinization. This transformation is dependent, not upon our ideas of God, but rather on God's direct influence upon us.

Notes

1. In the third edition of the *Speeches,* Schleiermacher claims that "piety cannot be an instinct craving for a mess of metaphysical and ethical crumbs." Friedrich Schleiermacher, *On Religion,* trans. John Oman (New York: Harper and Row, 1958).

2. This is Karl Barth's famous criticism of liberal Protestant theology. See Karl Barth, *The Word of God and the Word of Man* (Boston: Pilgrim Press, 1928), 195–96.

3. Thomas Aquinas, *Summa theologica* II-II, q. 1, art. 2, in *Basic Writings of Saint Thomas Aquinas,* vol. 2, English Dominican trans., ed. Anton Pegis (New York: Random House, 1945), 1057.

4. Schleiermacher differs significantly from Fichte on this point. Günter Zöller has correctly noted that Fichte "insists on the presence of the absolute in the I. It is the absolute itself that manifests itself under the form of the thinking and willing I." Günter Zöller, "German Realism: The Self-Limitation of Idealist Thinking in Fichte, Schelling, and Schopenhauer," in *The Cambridge Companion to German Idealism,* ed. Karl Ameriks (Cambridge: Cambridge University Press, 2000), 206.

5. In *On Religion* Schleiermacher notes, "All intuition proceeds from an influence of the intuited on the one who intuits." Friedrich Schleiermacher, *On Religion: Speeches to Its Cultured Despisers,* ed. and trans. Richard Crouter (Cambridge: Cambridge University Press, 1996), 24. I discuss this passage at length below. Subsequent citations of *On Religion* refer to this Cambridge edition.

6. I discuss this issue at length in my book *Transformation of the Self in the Thought of Friedrich Schleiermacher* (Oxford: Oxford University Press, 2008), esp. chs. 3, 4, and 6.

7. Citations to *The Christian Faith (CF)* are to the 1830–31 edition and will be indicated first by section and paragraph numbers, then by section/volume/part and page numbers in *Die Kritische Schleiermacher-Gesamtausgabe,* ed. Hermann Fischer et al. (Berlin: De Gruyter, 1980–) (*KGA;* Friedrich Schleiermacher's *Der christliche Glaube nach den Grundsätzen der evangelischen Kirche im Zusammenhange dargestellt [1830–31],* ed. Rolf Schäfer [Berlin: De Gruyter, 2003], is sec. I, vol. 13, pts. 1 and 2 of the *KGA*) (*KGA* I/13/1 and 2); and finally by pagination in Friedrich Schleiermacher, *The Christian Faith,* trans. H. R. Mackintosh and James Stewart (1928; repr., Edinburgh: T. and T. Clark, 1999), cited in text as MS.

8. This has been argued by both Manfred Frank and Robert Adams. See Robert Adams, "Faith and Religious Knowledge," and Manfred Frank, "Metaphysical Foundations: A Look at Schleiermacher's *Dialectic,*" both in *The Cambridge Companion to Friedrich Schleiermacher,* ed. Jacqueline Mariña (Cambridge: Cambridge University Press, 2005).

9. Frank, "Metaphysical Foundations," 31.

10. Friedrich Schleiermacher, *Vorlesungen über die Dialektik, KGA,* II/10/2, 568.

11. This antirealist reading was expressed by several of the Schleiermacher scholars participating in the conference "Schleiermacher, the Study of Religion, and the Future of Theology."

12. Robert Adams recognizes a related problem when he asks, "Can we say then that according to the *Christian Faith* God is not the intentional object of the essential religious consciousness, the feeling of absolute dependence, but only of thoughts that reflect that feeling?" His answer to this particular problem differs from the one I offer below in that it does not rely on the "thick" description of the feeling of absolute dependence that I analyze. However, Adams is certainly correct in insisting that "Schleiermacher is plainly committed to the *correctness* of his interpretative description of piety as a feeling *of* absolute dependence. He gives us no reason to think that this feeling can be specified or identified except in terms of religious concepts expressing such intentionality, as Proudfoot rightly points out. And Schleiermacher seems equally committed to the correctness of the inference from absolute dependence to a whence that can be called 'God.'" Adams, "Faith and Religious Knowledge," 38.

13. See my "Transformation of the Self through Christ," ch. 7 of my book *Transformation of the Self.*

14. One example of such antirealism is the position put forward by Don Cupitt, who emphasizes the human world "bounded by language, time and narrativity and radically outsideless." For Cupitt, there just is nothing outside our linguistic practices that constrains them in any way, and thus we must return "science into its own theories, religion into its own stories and rituals—and history into its own varied narratives." Don Cupitt, *After All* (London: SMC Press, 1994), 17. For a discussion of realism and antirealism in religion, see Roger Trigg, "Theological Realism and Antirealism," in *A Companion to Philosophy of Religion,* ed. Philip L. Quinn and Charles Taliaferro (Cambridge, MA: Blackwell, 1999), 213–22.

15. Schleiermacher, *On Religion,* 27.

16. Schleiermacher, *On Religion,* 53.

17. Schleiermacher, *On Religion,* 28.

18. Schleiermacher, *On Religion,* 43.

19. John Hick, *An Interpretation of Religion* (New York: Palgrave, 2004), 246.

20. Schleiermacher, *On Religion,* 24–25.

21. Trigg, "Theological Realism and Antirealism," 213–22.

Chapter 13

Schelling's Turn to Scripture

NICHOLAS ADAMS

F. W. J. Schelling (1775–1851) is an unusual figure in this volume. He is significantly less well known and less read than his contemporaries Fichte and Hegel; there are thus fewer signs of the tendency, identified by Firestone and Jacobs, to treat theological questions as of secondary importance in interpretations of Schelling's work. More importantly, Schelling wrote extensively and explicitly on topics such as divine creativity and the relation between evil and human freedom in *An Essay on Human Freedom* (hereafter, "the *Freedom* essay") and *The Ages of the World,* as well as on the relation of philosophy to revelation *(Philosophy of Revelation).*[1] Few commentators claim that Schelling's interests in theology are matters of passing concern or mere pretence. I will suggest, nonetheless, that Schelling certainly belongs in a volume whose purpose is to rethink the theological dimension of Enlightenment philosophy.

The three most useful recent monographs on Schelling in English, which are indispensable for understanding the relationship between philosophy and theology in Schelling's work, are Andrew Bowie's *Schelling and Modern European Philosophy* (1993), Edward Allen Beach's *The Potencies of God(s)* (1994), and Dale Snow's *Schelling and the End of Idealism* (1996). Snow's study of Schelling's earlier works up to the *Freedom* essay, Beach's account of Schelling's later philosophy of mythology,

335

and Bowie's correlation of Schelling with contemporary philosophical questions of language and ontology all acknowledge the role that theological themes play in Schelling's work. Until recently, the principal shortcoming in readings of Schelling was not the soft-pedaling of theological topics but the failure to see how Schelling's treatment of theological topics involved radical challenges to post-Kantian philosophical thought, challenges that are of enduring interest to philosophers today. Such failure is much rarer since the appearance of Bowie's and Snow's studies and the two volumes of essays devoted to Schelling's contemporary significance, *The New Schelling* (edited by Judith Norman and Alistair Welchman, 2004) and *Schelling Now* (edited by Jason Wirth, 2005), and especially since the publication of translations of some of the major works by SUNY Press, some of which contain outstanding introductory essays and notes. In Germany, because of the strong influence of Dieter Henrich and Manfred Frank's pioneering *Konstellationsforschung,* Schelling has, since the 1970s, been appreciated as a major figure who challenged and transformed the questions and answers offered by Hegel. In French, Miklos Vetö's impressive two-volume *De Kant à Schelling* (1998, 2000) traces the paths that lead to Schelling's late philosophy in a way that comprehensively displays Schelling's alternatives to certain Hegelian problems. It is less usual today to hear Schelling described as a mere waypoint on the grand intellectual pilgrimage from Kant to Hegel.[2]

These bibliographical remarks indicate that commentaries on Schelling stand in less urgent need of theological repair than those on many other figures treated in this volume. There is, however, good reason to include him, for there is a deeper issue. There are relatively few commentaries on Schelling at all, and very few by theologians interested in philosophy.[3] Why is this? I wonder if it is, in part, precisely because of the overt theological interest he shows in his philosophy: philosophers who are otherwise skilled in wrangling idealist argumentation may be intimidated by the breadth and density of his theological references. Lacking the knowledge that would enable confident judgments as to when Schelling's theology is mere rehearsal of commonplaces and when it displays radical rethinking, philosophers working in English tend to tread cautiously. This leads to Schelling being read mostly by specialists, much as Suárez is mostly read by experts on the history of natural law, or Peirce is mostly read by experts on pragmatism.[4] This analogy can be pressed a little further. Consider Suárez's relation to Descartes, Schelling's relation to Hegel, and Peirce's relation to James and Dewey. Schelling, like his Spanish and American analogues, rarely shows up on survey courses despite making major fundamental contributions to philosophy that are better known through their rehearsal and development by later thinkers who are explicitly dependent on him.

This leads to a reason theologians may tend to neglect Schelling (along with Suárez and Peirce), despite the intricate and fascinating entanglement of theology and philosophy in his thinking: theologians tend to learn their philosophy from philosophers. If philosophers avoid certain thinkers, because of the need to learn enough theology to understand them, theologians in turn tend not to encounter them during their formative study and thus fail to investigate them at all. It is tempting to form the hypothesis that as a result of the excessive separation of the studies of philosophy and theology in modern universities, those thinkers who entangle philosophy and theology are understudied precisely by theologians. To Suárez and Peirce one might add the earlier names of Nicholas of Cusa, Francisco de Vitoria, and Hugo Grotius and the later names of Walter Benjamin, Ernst Bloch, and Karl Jaspers. Such a hypothesis would need to account for the surprisingly (on this account) broad appeal of Kierkegaard and Nietzsche, whose works, despite a healthy entanglement of philosophy and theology, are often better known to undergraduate students than those of Kant and Hegel. One might point to the fact that Kierkegaard and Nietzsche tend to appear in literature courses as often as in philosophy courses: this would partly explain their popularity. One might also notice, quite separately, the fact that many of the leading English-speaking scholars of German idealism entered their fields via study of German literature: perhaps in the study of literature there is not the same tendency to play down the significance of religious thinking compared with the study of philosophy.

These brief speculations are intended to suggest that the separation of philosophy from theology in the Enlightenment—now institutionalized in the modern university—leads to an endemic failure to equip students to study certain figures, of which Schelling is a preeminent example. For this reason it is appropriate to include Schelling in this volume. It is not the commentaries that need repairing because they play down the significance of theology; it is the lack of commentaries that needs repairing. To repeat: English-speaking philosophers tend to be underequipped to treat forms of thought that (quite properly) entangle philosophy and theology, and theologians tend to learn their philosophy from such philosophers. To consider Schelling is to consider this sorry state of affairs. Rethinking the Enlightenment surely means rethinking the modern university, but as this carries us far outside the scope of this volume, I shall leave these remarks vague and introductory.

My task in this essay is to show the entanglement of theology and philosophy in two of Schelling's shortest and most difficult works from the middle of his life: the *Freedom* essay and *The Ages of the World*. Considering them will afford ample opportunity to see what kind of formation in theology and philosophy a commentator needs to do justice to them and to appreciate how rethinking the Enlightenment means rethinking the relationship between theology and philosophy in our own time.

It is important to note the position in Schelling's work occupied by *On the Essence of Human Freedom* (1809) and *The Ages of the World* (1811–15). The *Freedom* essay was Schelling's last published book, and it marks a departure from the drier, more systematic, approach that characterizes his transcendental philosophy, his philosophy of nature, and his identity philosophy. *The Ages of the World* is his first major unfinished and unpublished work, to be followed by several others. Some of the latter are available to us now as manuscripts or editions of his lecture series, such as those on mythology and on revelation and those that elaborate his "positive" philosophy; others were destroyed by Allied bombing of Munich in 1944. Both of the works considered here are marked by a noticeable shift away from stepwise chains of propositions toward a more fluid, vague, and allusive style, characterized by reliance on metaphor as well as direct reference, and association of ideas alongside deductive reasoning.

To understand Schelling's entanglement of theology and philosophy requires identifying the questions he asks and forming a sense of the kind of answers he gives, as well as reporting on the views he elaborates. Schelling is a deeply reparative thinker who identifies significant weaknesses in the philosophical reasonings he inherits. His mode of repair is not merely to think better with the existing tools at hand in order to solve problems but in many cases to recognize that the tools themselves need repairing. It is this that gives rise to Schelling's many reflections on what kinds of habit best serve philosophy, alongside his displays of the philosophical habits of his day. Most significant for this essay is his use of theological tools to repair philosophical ones, especially his discussions of divine action, creativity, and evil.

Schelling is concerned with questions of freedom, necessity, and rationality in the *Freedom* essay. He is concerned with the relation of life and thinking in *The Ages of the World*. He is concerned with grounds in both. Schelling tries to soften the brittle accounts of freedom and necessity that he inherits by offering different modes of freedom and different modes of necessity. There are many ways in which something can be said to be necessary. Some of them force a choice: freedom *or* necessity. Others permit more subtle approaches: freedom in relation to necessity in various ways. Schelling wants to show that one needs a more nuanced account of necessity—and of God's action—if one is to do justice to human freedom. It is thus not a binary opposition for him—freedom *or* necessity—but a question of finding the right relation between them. This right relation then permits an inclusive, but corrective, account of previous versions of the opposition. Schelling does not want to destroy previous ways of framing the issue but to incorporate them within his own account and so repair them. He thus has some surprisingly positive things to say about Spinoza and Leibniz—surprising given their strong emphases on necessity.

The *Freedom* essay confronts directly an impasse in then-contemporary philosophy regarding how best to account for human freedom. The impasse concerns a series of problems. First, there is, in the then-recent tradition, a strong emphasis on divine necessity. Things are as they must be. This, for Schelling, is not wrong; it rightly avoids attributing to God any hint of irrational arbitrariness. On the other hand, there is a strong emphasis on divine freedom. God acts as he wills and is not subject to any external force. This is not wrong either: it rightly avoids attributing to God any hint of subordination to a greater power. But the impasse emerges nicely: things are as they must be, but at the same time God acts freely. Human action, or rather any philosophical account of that action, is caught up in this impasse. When we act, are we free? If I simply act and have no reasons for that action, this seems not to be *human* action. "To be able to decide for A or -A without any compelling reasons would be, to tell the truth, only a prerogative to act entirely irrationally" (*Freedom,* 48). The key word here is *compelling.* To act reasonably is not merely to weigh up reasons for action and then act; it is to experience a strange compulsion exerted by reasons and to yield to it. Schelling suggests there is something inhuman about some-one who does not experience such compulsion. So the impasse strikes at the heart of human action too. In what sense are we compelled, and in what sense free?

If Schelling had been a fourteenth-century Dominican, he might have begun by following Thomas Aquinas in suggesting that "no name is predicated univocally of God and of creatures. . . . Neither . . . are names applied to God and creatures in a purely equivocal sense."[5] In more informal English: the closer language gets to God, the stranger it gets. Thus words like *necessity* and *freedom* can be used to describe God's action, but they will not have the same sense as when they are used to describe human action. One would thus avoid thinking that *necessity* and *freedom* have univocal application. Schelling, like most of his con-temporaries, is no scholar of the angelic doctor. But his account has some family resemblances to the latter's invocation of analogy, in two respects. First, like Aquinas, it is brief, vague, and generatively sugges-tive. Second, it takes words/names that appear to have a certain univo-cal stability (here *necessity* and *freedom*) and performs their being made strange. It does so by putting the terms *necessary* and *free* in all sorts of awkward and puzzling contexts and by yanking the reader to and fro. In the excellent introduction to their edition and translation of the *Freedom* essay, Jeff Love and Johannes Schmidt summarize their analy-sis of this performance: "Schelling's attempt to reconcile God's neces-sary nature with his freedom is beset with fundamental conflict and re-veals one of the central ambiguities in Schelling's thought: God seems to play a delicate balancing act in his own self-revelation, which both *may* (as conditioned by the ground) *and must not* (as somehow overcoming this condition) end in a disastrous contraction back into the ground."[6]

Love and Schmidt argue persuasively that Schelling's account of nature is of a life whose character is marked by contradictions; the whole must be inhabited in a kind of drama. This insight seems to me sound and can be taken further. Something can be said about language itself: not just the language Schelling uses but language as such. It is not true that language is stable and that Schelling has problems getting his account straight. Language itself is unstable when it approaches God, yet must still be used if there is to be any relation to God. Schelling's account of nature is most fruitfully viewed as an analogy of language. Schelling's description of creation is a performance of language unfolding analogically. Schelling's account of the ground of God's freedom upsets the familiar paths that the central terms usually take, while refusing to abandon their core usages. It is no more a "theory" of analogy than Aquinas's skeletal remarks in the *Summa theologica;* like its medieval predecessor it is a brief performance of analogical thinking, and it leads the reader on a wild, but not wholly unintelligible, journey.

Schelling's genius is displayed in his commentary on those "familiar paths," especially of Spinoza and Leibniz. Schelling could have made things easy for himself by portraying his forebears as rigid determinists for whom necessity always trumps freedom and by describing himself as a radical thinker who seeks to rescue freedom from such a prison. He does not. Of Spinoza, he says that there are two different ways of taking his determinism. One can say, as most people do, that it is a consequence of his pantheism: human freedom is "unable to maintain itself in opposition to God" (*Freedom,* 17). Or one can say, as Schelling does, that Spinoza's insistence that human freedom depends on God is quite proper and that the problem lies elsewhere: Spinoza (in Schelling's account) treats the human will as a thing and then shows that all things are determined. "The error of his system lies by no means in his placing things *in God,* but in the fact that they are *things*" (*Freedom,* 20). Schelling's task is thus of avoiding what he calls an "abstract" description characterized by "severe" definitions, in favor of a "dynamic notion of nature," an account that is "brought to life."

Of Leibniz, Schelling says that his accounts of freedom are indeed highly deterministic and that Leibniz's attempts to "improve" it (i.e., reduce the harshness of the determinism) by saying that the motivating causes "incline" but do not "determine" the will are unconvincing (*Freedom,* 49). But he also draws attention to Leibniz's fascinating claim that the laws of nature are not "geometrically necessary," which is what one might expect him (Leibniz) to say. Leibniz attributes the regularities of nature neither to "absolute necessity" nor to complete arbitrariness but to God's perfect wisdom. For Schelling, this dimension of Leibniz's thinking "is one of its most pleasing aspects" (*Freedom,* 60). This too has echoes of medieval theological reasoning, which, when considering whether something is "necessary" for God, often prefers to answer that it is "fitting."

What, then, of human freedom? On this matter, things are at some remove from the Dominican world. If Schelling's account of divine freedom has some family resemblances with orthodox theology, his account of human freedom is much more experimental. It is here that Schelling's adventures with the notion of evil develop in surprising ways.[7] Evil is one of the topics through which Schelling elaborates his dynamic notions and brings to life the drama of human action. There are thus two jobs for the theologically minded reader. One is to understand the account of evil and to compare it with other more obviously orthodox accounts. The other is to understand how this account, whatever the integrity of its orthodoxy—and even if it is to be robustly rejected on dogmatic grounds—serves the attempt to bring nature to life and to place human action uncompromisingly in the middle of it.

For Schelling, freedom means "the capacity for good and evil" (*Freedom,* 23). He rehearses three common chains of argument, in opposing pairs, that he views as defective: in each case either the attributes of God are thrown into question or human freedom is abolished. (1) One can say that evil is in God, in which case God is not God. Or one can say evil is not real, in which case freedom is not real either (given Schelling's account of freedom). (2) One can say that humans are dependent on God and that God "participates" in human action, in which case God shares responsibility for evil. Or, once again, one can deny the reality of evil. (3) One can say that whatever is positive in evil, in so far as it "has being," is good, in which case the "basis" for evil (what "constitutes" evil) is obscure. Or one can say that evil is just "less good" or a "deficiency," in which case one is playing with words, he says, because there is no such being as a deficiency in nature: there are only existing beings. (Schelling implies that even in this argument, therefore, evil must exist somehow *as evil,* and not merely as "less good.")

One can attempt a quick comparison with orthodox accounts. The third of these arguments is the most interesting. Schelling objects to any account that says that the basis of evil is inexplicable: "The first capacity for an act striving against God always remains inexplicable in all the previous systems" (*Freedom,* 25). Most of the profoundest orthodox reflections on evil do indeed claim that it is inexplicable and that this is one of the marks of evil. Schelling also objects to any account of *privatio boni* because it confuses the "more or less" grammar of deficiency with the "yes or no" grammar of beings/nonbeings. Again, orthodox accounts of evil insist on complex ways of holding "more or less" with "yes or no" grammars (the sheep will be "separated" from the goats, but the goats are those who do "less" than the sheep). Schelling's refusal of obscurity and his insistence on separating "more or less" from "yes or no" grammars are, I think, signs of a rationalism that itself stands in need of repair.

Nonetheless, Schelling's aim is to bring nature to life and to plant human action dramatically in the middle of it. Schelling sets this up with two explicitly reparative moves. (1) "God is something more real than a merely moral world order and has entirely different and more vital motive forces in himself than the desolate subtlety attributed to him by abstract idealists."[8] (2) "The entire new European philosophy since its beginning (with Descartes) has the common defect that nature is not available for it and that it lacks a living ground" (*Freedom,* 26). There are thus two problems in then-contemporary philosophy that need repairing. The first is an inadequate account of God and the second is an inadequate account of nature. This is a comprehensive complaint. The *Freedom* essay is an attempt at repair. It thus has to find resources outside philosophy for its repair. What are these resources?

Material from *The Ages of the World* becomes especially relevant here.[9] The problem with contemporary philosophy and with what he calls "modern philosophy" in general is its reduction of life to what can be stated in concepts—not only stated but systematized (one might say tidied up) in various ways. Schelling is no enemy of conceptual thinking or of idealism, in the broad sense of an attempt to display how the ways we think the world produce a world for ourselves. His objection is to a satisfaction with such a "represented" world. He wishes to acknowledge the relation between the represented world and something altogether unmanageable by us, which is at the same time the ground (i.e., the possibility) of the represented world. One might say that his goal is not a correspondence between representation and reality but an account of reality in which representations play a part but are, in significant ways, overwhelmed by the reality that makes them possible.

The Ages of the World employs a number of strategies in presentation, as well as in trains of reasoning, to accomplish this goal. Most striking is the concern with suffering and pain, which intensifies toward the end, accompanied by evocations of the wildness and uncontrollability of the cosmos. People of a certain kind of rationalizing disposition are happy to look at flowers and animals, Schelling wryly observes: they find in them signs of a gentle and benevolent divine creativity. But they can cure themselves of these comforting theological investigations by doing two things. First, they should look to the stars. Consider these massive, dangerous, ancient hulks of unimaginably monstrous conflicts of forces: echoing Böhme, he declaims, "They are works of wrath, of the paternal and most ancient force" (*AW*, 98). Schelling complains that one of the trends in modern theology is an analogous taming of human action. The wildness and madness that bring our imaginations to life, rather than merely recording facts like accountants completing a ledger, are leaching out of modern discourse. That discourse produces a mere image of the world, rather than a world to live in. "What was the endeavor of all modern theology other than a gradual idealization and emptying of Christianity?" (*AW*, 106). The cure for this is a willingness to overcome, but emphatically not entirely to get rid of, the "barbarism" that is the root of greatness and beauty. Second, theologians should read Scripture more carefully. Schelling, like Hegel, is fascinated by Genesis. Indeed, it is striking that both *The*

Ages of the World and the *Freedom* essay are illustrated, at key points, by references to parts of the Old Testament. We will return to this shortly.

It is important to note that all this is accomplished in a very short space. This version of *The Ages of the World* is just over 137 pages in the German (and barely over a hundred pages in translation)—and this is the longest version. Even this is much longer than the *Freedom* essay: 80 pages of German (68 in translation). Ideas are introduced, variations are briefly explored, and the discussion moves on. It is easy to see that, compared with more monumental works like the *Phenomenology of Spirit* or the *Science of Logic,* Schelling's works might seem somehow less authoritative. It is thus worth reflecting briefly on the style employed. Both *The Ages of the World* and the *Freedom* essay not only argue that there is a need to acknowledge the role of ungraspable and uncontrollable reality vis-à-vis philosophy; they perform it. They are composed narratively—each tells a story—rather than in an exclusively claim-follows-claim structure. More significantly, they are evocatively and self-consciously metaphorical. Both draw heavily on scriptural metaphors, elaborate a tale of the struggle of darkness and light, illustrate themes with images from the major works of late antiquity, and rehearse a strong account of the yearning of creation. *The Ages of the World* is insistently and explicitly sexual, particularly toward the end. The ideal reader of these works is someone with a secure classical education who appreciates the subtleties of Latin and Hebrew, is familiar with the long Western tradition of theology and philosophy—and appreciates the dynamics of healthy sexual relationships. The modern university still manages to produce such people, who, in any case, were never numerous, but this is clearly not the formation of the contemporary philosopher.

I asked earlier: What are the resources with which to repair a philosophy that has inadequate accounts of God and inadequate accounts of nature, and which thus fails to give persuasive or sufficiently rich accounts of human freedom? Part of the answer is the attempt to develop a new genre of philosophical writing. The *Freedom* essay and *The Ages of the World* are responses to problems in Kantian and post-Kantian philosophy but do not resemble the forms that this philosophy takes. Another part of the answer is a turn to Scripture. Schelling writes commentary on Scripture in order to repair philosophy.

Sometimes Schelling's use of Scripture resembles that of Kant in *Religion within the Boundaries of Mere Reason*. That is, he rehearses a series of claims, often using terms from Greek philosophy (*being, change, idea, virtue,* etc.), and attaches biblical illustrations. It is not clear, in this style of presentation, which gives rise to which. Is the author so steeped in reflection on Scripture that a particular mode of reasoning offers itself, and then the author becomes self-conscious of that origin and attaches the biblical text as illustration? Or is the author dominated by Greek philosophy, and does he add the biblical illustration afterwards, as acknowledgment of a happy coincidence between them? (This is, of course, a false choice, as the reception of Greek philosophy is refracted through the lens of biblical reasoning in the medieval period. But there is still a distinction between the author inheriting biblically refracted Greek philosophy and reasonings explicitly arising from meditation by the author on Scripture.) There is no way to be sure, in either case.

Yet in two places in *The Ages of the World* explicit meditation by Schelling on Scripture gives rise to forms of reasoning whose purpose is to repair modern philosophy. These are fascinating attempts to re-think the Enlightenment. Each is brief. The first is a section entitled "Short Episode on the Importance of the Old Testament for Tracing the Concept of God," which comes at the end of the first major part (of three). The second is the commentary on Genesis 1:1–16. It is worth investigating these a little to discover the ways in which Schelling turns to Scripture in order to repair philosophy.

First are the remarks on Genesis. Schelling devotes several pages to a philosophical commentary on the opening chapters, in which he finds in that text a distinction between "God created" (Gen. 1:1) and "God said" (Gen. 1:3–15) or "God made" (Gen 1:16). The first act happens only once. God created the heaven and the earth. Schelling explores various shades of meaning of the Hebrew *bara*. For Schelling, it indicates a production of a ground out of which all else is formed; it also indicates the possibility of time, in which all else is an unfolding. Speaking and making, by contrast, produce things from this ground and—as is clear from the discussion of human action that follows this—is something humans participate in, to a lesser but meaningful degree. Humans do not create, in the sense of *bara*. The philosophy of Schelling's contemporaries fails, he thinks, to make distinctions of this kind: turning to Scripture requires a more nuanced ontology if proper commentary is to be attempted and at the same time teaches the philosopher what that ontology is.

The "short episode" opens with a summary of the work thus far (sixty-two pages into the work). Schelling's goal has been "a complete construction of the idea of God which does not let itself be grasped in a short explanation nor circumscribed with limits like a geometrical figure" (*AW*, 49). This is surely a reference to forms of philosophy that reproduce Descartes's famously short definition of God in *Meditations* and Spinoza's even shorter definition of God at the opening of *Ethics*. This "complete construction" is an account of the "eternal life of the Godhead"; what follows in the second major part will be the "actual history" of God's self-revealing. Schelling reminds the reader that his task is to show how God is a unity that is a duality, or a duality that is a unity. The duality in question is that of necessity and freedom, darkness and light, outpouring and retreating, unconscious and conscious. This task is needed because of the deep-seated habit among philosophers to think that God is most honored when descriptions of God remove all living forces and all nature. This is not just an observation about his contemporaries: it is, he believes, a mark of philosophy since the 1600s:

> How utterly modern this manner of representation is could be easily shown. For the entirety of our modern philosophy only dates as if it were from yesterday. For its originator, Descartes, completely rent the living interrelation with earlier developments and wanted to construct philosophy all over from the beginning, exclusively in accordance with the concepts of his time, as if no one before him had thought or philosophized. Since then, there is only a coherent and logically consistent further development of one and the same fundamental error that has spun itself forth into all of the various systems up to and including the contemporary ones. It is in itself backward to apply this utterly modern standard to what has broken itself from all interrelation to the past in order to reconnect oneself again with the truly ancient and the truly most ancient. (*AW*, 50)

It is the last sentence that signals Schelling's reparative aims most clearly. Modern philosophy is damaged, and the resources for repairing it cannot come from that same modern philosophy. We can again ask: Where then do the resources come from? Schelling is quite self-conscious about his method: he intends "to connect to something or other venerable from time immemorial, to some kind of higher, attested tradition upon which human thought rests" (*AW*, 50). The characteristic resource for repairing philosophy in the late twentieth century tends to be common sense: the cure for confusion is supposed to be clearer, more purified thinking. But Schelling already indicates that it is precisely the purification of thinking in modern philosophy that leads to an inability to do justice to living forces and nature. Schelling offers a critique of analytic philosophy long before it was dreamed of. Or, more plausibly, he gives the reader a strong indication that the roots of analytic philosophy—the kinds that show no interest in life, in Schelling's sense—lie recognizably in certain forms of philosophy in the time leading up to 1811, when he began *The Ages of the World*. Schelling's method is not to purify thinking, or to strip nature from thought, but explicitly to reach deep into the tradition.

To the philosophical reader today, Schelling seems to begin waffling at this point, with lots of hot air about how previous philosophers—including Plato—have often felt the need to turn to the venerable prior tradition when dealing with particularly weighty matters. But this throat-clearing is better interpreted as a sign that Schelling is defensive about his resort to tradition. Such a resort is not unknown at that time: as one would expect, he is familiar with the works of Hamann ("the excellent J. G. Hamann," as he calls him in the *Freedom* essay). But it is certainly unusual. Even more unusual is his claim that he finds this tradition in the Old Testament. Schelling tries to explain why the Old Testament is his primary source, and his reasonings are instructively strange. He praises it as containing a complete world history; he notes that the Old Testament requires for its interpretation all the erudition of the world. This is an uncharacteristically (for Schelling) flimsy explanation: the Old Testament offers a cosmic vision and is difficult to interpret. So do, and are, many other classic texts. Strangest of all, however, is this claim: Schelling notes that no one has yet found an interpretation of Scripture that brings everything into harmony and that many difficult passages defy clear exposition. He also observes that, as a consequence of this, his contemporaries' work contains many fine "points of teaching" but these are isolated and lack the kinds of connection that would render them a comprehensible whole. "In a word, the interior (esoteric) system, whose consecration the teachers should especially have, is lacking" (*AW,* 51). This should sharply attract the attention of theologically trained readers and lead them to look far beyond the usual criticism that Schelling slumps into a woolly and cryptic esotericism. Schelling is suggesting, rather, that there is a shape to theology. He claims that current doctrinal thinking is disconnected and fails to conform to the true shape of theology. That true shape, when grasped by those who have studied deeply in the tradition, has the character of an esoteric system. It is esoteric because it requires deep study of the tradition; if it did not require such study, its shape and meaning would be quite plain. This is not Gnosticism but a complaint about lack of study of Scripture.

Schelling insists, in a way that is quite surprising in the early 1800s, that an adequate repair of philosophy can be undertaken only by someone who has deeply studied Scripture and who thus has a sense of the "esoteric system," that is, of its deepest shape. To a degree, he himself is uncertain about this. He also says that the Old Testament offers lightning flashes that "illuminate the darkness of primordial times, the first and the oldest relationships with the divine essence itself" (*AW,* 51). This kind of claim occupies Schelling extensively in his much later *Philosophy of Mythology* and *Philosophy of Revelation.* Schelling tends sometimes to claim that Scripture offers an insight into the origin of everything on account of its great age. But this is surely not the only source of its authority for him: if it were, then it would be merely a description of certain phenomena, quickly displaced by any substantial earlier text that might be discovered. It is enough for our purposes to note two tendencies in Schelling's reasons for turning to the Old Testament: first, one's study of the Old Testament leads to a sense of the shape of Scripture, which in turn enables one to connect the different points of doctrine; second, it narrates the primordial relation of humanity to God. I think it is the first reason that most significantly informs his method. It is a focal point of a tradition into which one must reach deeply if one is to find resources for repairing philosophy.

The repair needed is one that enables philosophy to offer an account that does justice to the unity in duality or duality in unity of God. Schelling finds the resources for such a repair in Genesis and in Exodus, especially in the relation between Elohim and Jehovah/YHWH. Schelling speculates that the intertwining and "frequent liaison" of YHWH, in the singular, and Elohim, in the plural, model "the duality in the unity" that he seeks in his account of God. His speculations also offer, he claims, a much better model of the relation between philosophy and theology. The problem with philosophers, he thinks, is that they have a quite empty concept of God. And the problem with theologians is that they are bewitched by and dependent on the philosophy of their own time. If they paid more attention to Scripture, Schelling observes caustically, they might discover much richer indications of God's individuality "than they imagine in their so-called theism" (*AW*, 53). It is thus not only philosophy but also theology that needs repair.

What lessons can we learn from reading Schelling in this way? Certainly one can learn from the particular repairs of philosophy that Schelling attempts. To the extent that in our own time we still struggle to find the right way to ask questions about human freedom, or to pursue the most fruitful investigations into questions about evil, or to do justice to the ways in which reality exceeds what can be captured by our representations, Schelling is an instructive teacher. These are certainly good reasons to read Schelling. But that is not primarily why he belongs in a volume dedicated to rethinking the Enlightenment. The tools he uses for that repair, and the entanglement of philosophy with theology that characterize those tools, make him instructive for those who wish to do justice to the concern with religious life displayed by thinkers from the seventeenth to the early nineteenth centuries. Schelling does not merely show an interest in religious life in his philosophy. He mounts a radical critique of modern philosophy and uses not only philosophical theology but also detailed meditations on Scripture to repair it. Schelling does not merely try to rethink the Enlightenment. His aim, like Hegel's, is to transform it by thinking about God.

Notes

1. Citations to the *Freedom* essay are drawn from F. W. J. Schelling, *Philosophical Investigations into the Essence of Human Freedom,* ed. and trans. Jeff Love and Johannes Schmidt (New York: SUNY Press, 2006). References to *Ages of the World* (hereafter *AW*) are to F. W. J. Schelling, *The Ages of the World from the Handwritten Remains Third Version (c. 1815),* trans. Jason Wirth (New York: SUNY Press, 2000).

2. Andrew Bowie, *Schelling and Modern European Philosophy* (London: Routledge, 1993); Edward Allen Beach, *The Potencies of God(s): Schelling's Philosophy of Mythology* (New York: SUNY Press, 1994); Dale Snow, *Schelling and the End of Idealism* (New York: SUNY Press, 1996); *The New Schelling,* ed. Judith Norman and Alan Welchman (London: Continuum, 2004); *Schelling Now,* ed. Jason Wirth (Bloomington: Indiana University Press, 2005). For a translation in the SUNY series with good introductions, in addition to those detailed in note 1, see esp. F. W. J. Schelling, *The Grounding of Positive Philosophy: The Berlin Lectures,* ed. and trans. Bruce Matthews (New York: SUNY Press, 2008). See also F. W. J. Schelling, *On the History of Modern Philosophy,* ed. and trans. Andrew Bowie (Cambridge: Cambridge University Press, 1994); Dieter Henrich, *Selbstverhältnisse* (Stuttgart: Reclam: 1982); Manfred Frank, *Der unendliche Mangel an Sein* (Frankfurt: Suhrkamp, 1975) and *Selbstbewußtsein und Selbsterkenntnis* (Stuttgart, Reclam, 1991); and Miklos Vetö, *De Kant à Schelling: Les deus voies de l'Idéalisme allemand,* 2 vols. (Grenoble: Millon, 1998, 2000).

3. My remarks here concern work in English. Schelling's reception in German scholarship is more nuanced.

4. On Suárez in relation to Descartes, see esp. Jorge Secada, *Cartesian Metaphysics: The Scholastic Origins of Modern Philosophy* (Cambridge: Cambridge University Press, 2000). On Peirce in relation to philosophy and theology, see Peter Ochs, *Peirce, Pragmatism and the Logic of Scripture* (Cambridge: Cambridge University Press, 1998).

5. Thomas Aquinas, *Summa theologica* Ia, q. 13, art. 5.

6. *Freedom,* xxi.

7. For a deeper and richer engagement with the theme of evil in Schelling, see Peter Dews, *The Idea of Evil* (Oxford: Blackwell, 2008), 61–80.

8. I have reworked this sentence so that it reads more easily.

9. For reasons of space, and because there is a readily available, excellent translation and introduction by Jason Wirth, I will restrict my remarks to the third version of 1815.

Chapter 14

Hegel and Secularization

PETER C. HODGSON

*Wise, I may not call them, for that is a great name which belongs
to God alone — lovers of wisdom is their fitting title.*
—Plato, *Phaedrus*

The Disappearance of the God Question
in Contemporary Philosophy

Secularizing interpretations of Hegel have arisen largely as a consequence of the professionalization of philosophy as a secular academic
discipline and the concomitant rejection of metaphysics, including
metaphysical interpretations of Hegel. It is assumed by most philosophers today that Hegel can be retrieved and discussed only if his
thought is stripped of its metaphysical dimension. Theology is identified with metaphysics, or, more precisely, precritical metaphysics. It
is simply passé. There is no need to bother with Hegel's philosophy of
religion, which would be like attacking a dead horse; but other aspects
of his thought, with their attention to nature, anthropology, ethics,
history, logic, and so on, are retrievable. In this way, Hegel can be made
intelligible to a secularist mentality; and—despite his forthright indications to the contrary—it has been argued that Hegel himself was at

heart a secularist who regarded the language of religion to be passing away. In any event, the God question has all but disappeared from mainstream philosophical discussion, and anyone who talks about God today is under suspicion. This consensus within the philosophical guild is enforced in various ways, subtle and not so subtle—ironically so, since philosophy as critical thinking is supposed to reject settled orthodoxies.

Hegel himself offers an interesting comment that bears on this situation. In a passage in the *Lectures on the Philosophy of Religion* to which I shall return later, he summarizes his entire philosophical vision as one for which absolute spirit is exhibited as the truth of all things; first, it "unlocks itself in the resolve" to go forth into nature and finite spirit, then it returns to itself through the journey of the finite to its infinite source and goal. Two moments or movements together—God creating the world, and the world betaking itself back to God—make up the activity of God. This process shows itself first outside religion, then within religion itself. Outside religion, there is an "innocence" with respect to God; within religion, it is God who is strictly the first and the last (*LPR* 1:320–24). In other words, while the divine *exitus et reditus* transpires and even shows itself outside religion, in the natural and human worlds, there the awareness of God is often inchoate and confused; only within religion is the God concept thematized on its own account. Speculative philosophy shares with theology a recognition of God (or absolute spirit) as the ultimate object of all thought; but its accounts of the various domains of natural and human experience reflect the unthematized nature of God that is present in these domains. In this respect, it is phenomenologically faithful to the world's "innocence" with respect to God. If Hegel's explicit treatment of religion is set aside or read simply in the light of his treatment of other topics, then it might seem that he himself endorsed this innocence, this nonknowing of or resistance to God, and fixed his attention solely on finitude. Insofar as he continues to attend to something that transcends finitude, this attention, so it is thought, can be regarded from today's perspective only as incredulous and out of sync with his writings about nature, history, humanity, ethics, art, logic, and philosophy.

Such a perspective is illustrated by Charles Taylor in his influential book on Hegel. Taylor acknowledges that Hegel refers to God and offers an interpretation of Christianity. But, in what from my point of view is a careless and idiosyncratic reading of the philosophy of religion lectures, he argues that Hegel's God is simply a pantheistic cosmic spirit whose essence is rational necessity. Such a God is not a free personal creator and a source of grace but is dependent on the world, and thus Hegel utterly destroys orthodox Christianity by his demythologized version of it. The Christian dogmas, though presumably saved, are in fact destroyed. Taylor cannot envision the possibility of a postcritical reconstruction of theology along the lines of liberal Protestantism. The only legitimate alternatives are Christian orthodoxy or post-Christian rationalism and humanism.[1] Hegel's alternative, the central thesis of his system, as Taylor interprets it, is "quite dead," no longer believed by anyone. Hegel's ontology has been abandoned because modern civilization has developed in an industrial, technological, rationalized direction and has suppressed or privatized romantic sensibilities about the unity of nature and spirit that are essential for Hegel. His synthesis is built on an expressive Spinozistic pantheism, whereas modern civilization focuses on humanity. Thus the left-Hegelians, notably Ludwig Feuerbach and Karl Marx, anthropologize the synthesis, transferring it from *Geist* to man—to man not as an individual but as a species essence *(Gattungswesen)*. With this accomplished, quite a bit of Hegel's philosophy, especially his ethics and anthropology, proves still to be relevant because Hegel thinks deeply about the situatedness of human subjectivity, showing how thought and freedom emerge from the stream of life and find expression in social existence.[2]

Suspicious of Taylor's interpretation of the religious themes, Robert Pippin finds it incredible that Hegel could have been "a post-Kantian philosopher with a precritical metaphysics" that actually makes claims about God as a transcendent reality. In arguing that Hegel's theory of the absolute idea can be interpreted "in a way that is not committed to a philosophically problematic theological metaphysics," Pippin simply ignores Hegel's writings on religion or statements to the effect that logic is "metaphysical theology" because it "treats of the evolution of the idea of God in the aether of pure thought, and thus it properly attends only to this idea, which is utterly independent in and for itself" (*Proofs,* 99). Pippin does not recognize the validity of Hegel's attempt to construct a postcritical speculative ontology but rather, following Klaus Hartmann, reads him as a transcendental philosopher along Kantian lines whose idealist categories are simply conditions of possibility for empirical experience. There is no true infinite, only self-knowing and self-affirming finitude.[3]

It is one thing to question whether Hegel's ontotheology is intellectually credible or religiously persuasive but quite another to question whether he is a metaphysical thinker with a God concept at all. Robert Williams suggests that Hegel himself diagnoses the problem represented by such interpretations. It is the problem of the "stubbornness" and "sadness" of finitude. According to Hegel, finitude is the most stubborn category of the understanding *(Verstand),* since the latter takes its stand on the absoluteness of finitude and human experience, which overwhelms it. This fixation is not simply a psychological but a metaphysical illusion that arises when philosophy believes that it has disposed of and liberated itself from metaphysics. "A denial of God seems so much more intelligible than a denial of the world." The stubbornness of finitude also expresses a sadness, not unlike that of the unhappy consciousness; it is both self-sufficient and self-stultifying, a complacency that conceals both hubris and despair. The understanding's claim that nothing can be known of God is, Hegel remarks, an arrogant degradation of humanity and directly opposed to the whole of the Christian religion and much of classical philosophy.[4] Philosophers who fix their vision on finitude alone do not rise to their title, "lovers of wisdom." For as Plato avers, and Hegel agrees, God alone is true wisdom.

The Reduction of Theology to Anthropology in Recent Interpretations of Hegel

Faced with Hegel's somewhat embarrassing ontotheology, the prevailing tendency of recent interpreters of his thought has been to convert his theological statements into anthropological ones. In this respect, they are heirs of Feuerbach and Marx, who made sense of Hegel's God-talk by regarding it as simply the projection of the human species essence onto the screen of transcendence. Stephen Houlgate, in a popular introduction to Hegel's philosophy, argues that the essence of the human species is reason. As such, reason is not identical with individual human beings; indeed, it is present initially in nature. But it is not a transcendent idea that subsists on its own apart from the world; it is simply the essence of nature and humanity. Houlgate's explanation of why Hegel makes it appear that reason exists before nature as its creator is that he is trying to say that nature is self-generating rationality, not brute contingency. Reason becomes self-conscious for the first time in human consciousness. At this point it assumes the shape of spirit, *Geist.* Absolute spirit is not a mysterious cosmic entity to which we are subject; rather it is self-conscious, rational existence, and we humans are its "head." To be sure, we do not create ourselves; nature brings us into being. But to the question "What creates nature?" there is no answer other than nature itself. So all the theological predicates really refer to human beings as products of nature in which nature's rationality becomes self-conscious. Christianity expresses this truth in the form of images and representations *(Vorstellungen).* According to Houlgate, Hegel does not believe that the *Vorstellung* of divine creation is to be taken literally, any more than that of an immanent Trinity. Houlgate overlooks Hegel's speculative reconstruction of these doctrines, arguing that his emphasis falls rather on incarnation, love, spirit, and worship as the union of the believer with his or her true self. He insists that Hegel's Christianity is genuine, as opposed to critics like Robert Solomon who regard it as a subterfuge to protect his professional ambitions, but he believes that Hegel's intention is to interpret Christian doctrines nontheologically.[5]

In a more recent book on Hegel's logic, Houlgate attends to the concept of the "true infinite." The true infinite is not a separated beyond but rather a product of finitude as it relates to itself, of human consciousness affirming its own true infinitude.[6] Robert Wallace offers a similar interpretation. The true infinite is a thesis about human freedom and self-transcendence. The starting point of Hegel's system is not God but human self-determination. God's freedom is simply human freedom's self-superseding and self-realization; God is the self-surpassing of human beings.[7] In the view of Robert Williams, which I share, these are fundamental misinterpretations of what Hegel means by the true infinite, a reversal of his doctrine and every bit as reductive as Feuerbach's projectionist thesis.[8] Thomas Lewis argues that Hegel's anthropology, as found in his philosophy of subjective spirit, is the interpretative key to his other texts. Viewing the philosophy of religion through this lens reduces religion to an anthropological project. God is simply the religious name for spirit, which constitutes the essence of human beings.[9]

Whereas Houlgate, Wallace, and Lewis all endorse what they regard to be Hegel's anthropological project, William Desmond criticizes Hegel from a different angle, that of orthodox theism. Hegel's "monism" can be viewed as either an acosmic pantheism or an atheistic humanism. These are essentially the same and are incompatible with what Søren Kierkegaard insisted must be for Christian faith an infinite qualitative difference between divinity and humanity.[10]

What all these interpreters have in common is an overlooking of Hegel's dialectical way of thinking about God and the world that preserves difference as well as unity. Either God and the world must be related paradoxically and disjunctively, so that God's absolute transcendence is protected, or all of reality reduces to naturalism and humanism. The breakdown in mediation is what principally characterizes the post-Hegelian period right down to our own time, and the ongoing question is whether Hegelian mediation is possible without damaging the mediated elements. The alternative to mediation, however, is some form of either theological supernaturalism or secular naturalism. Theological critics of Hegel endorse the former, while philosophical critics embrace the latter.

Hegel's Speculative Theology of God

Hegel faced the challenge of developing a new philosophical theology as the basis for determining the reality status of God. The alternative would have been either to conclude that such a basis does not exist, in which case religion is nothing other than a specifically human expression of life, or to return to the classical metaphysics that had been discredited by Kant. Kant's rational theology, in which God becomes a postulate of practical reason, and Schleiermacher's experiential theology, in which God becomes the source of the feeling of utter dependence, did not, in Hegel's view, provide cognitive knowledge of God and were inadequate as a foundation for theology. In their stead, Hegel set forth a postcritical speculative theology of his own. It is indeed a form of ontotheology, but one in which the terms are fundamentally redefined.[11] The being of God *(ho ontos tou theou)* discloses itself to be not pure immediacy or abstract substance or supreme being (a highest entity) but rather "spirit" *(Geist)* in the sense of energy, movement, life, revelation, differentiation, and reconciliation. *Spirit* designates a God who is intrinsically self-revelatory, self-manifesting; God is not locked up within godself but is knowable and related to the world. Spirit is not an aspect or person of the divine Trinity but the Trinity as such and as a whole, considered as an encompassing act or process of creating, communicating, consummating—an act by which God's own being is accomplished as well as that of the world. While God is not an otherworldly supreme being (the traditional metaphysical view), God is the most actual of subjects—absolute subjectivity and absolute spirit—rather than a human projection or a religious feeling or an ethical postulate.[12] Such a concept of God is not orthodox theism, but neither is it atheism or pantheism. It is closest to what has come to be called panentheism.

Hegel's doctrine of the true or genuine infinite provides an account of the "in" of panentheism. An infinite that is simply the opposite of the finite shows by this opposition that it is itself finite, that is, a leveled or false infinite. The true infinite must suspend such opposition and include finitude within itself; it overrreaches the difference between finite and infinite and is the unity (not the identity) of finite and infinite. In this process the finite is shown to be the negative, the non-self-sustaining, and the infinite is shown to be the affirmative, the negation of negation. The truth of the finite is its *ideality,* which means that it is an essential moment in a holistic process that encompasses it. "This ideality of the finite," says Hegel, "is the most important proposition of philosophy. . . . Everything depends on not mistaking for the infinite that which is at once reduced in its determination to what is particular and finite. . . . The basic concept of philosophy, the genuine infinite, depends on [this distinction]."[13]

These formulations indicate that the true infinite cannot be a product of the finite and that indeed the reverse is true. If the infinite were produced by the finite, then it would be the infinite that was ideal in the Kantian sense of a transcendental condition of knowledge and experience. Instead, it is the finite that is ideal; its ideality means that it finds its truth not in its empirical existence, its reality, but in the absolute idea, which is both independent, in and for itself, and the universal substance or principle of the real. Hegel's doctrine of the triple syllogism means that each of the three main elements of philosophy—the logical idea, nature, and finite spirit—stands out from the other two and is mediated by them.[14] In his philosophy, the logical idea—the categories and relations of rational thought—functions as the universal principle or ontological foundation of nature and spirit; nature is identified with the particular qualities or determinate modifications of the universal; and spirit is the individuality or subjectivity that emerges from the union of the universal and the particular. This transcendence of the idea yields Hegel's speculative or absolute idealism by contrast with the subjective idealism of Kant and the naturalism of Hume or Feuerbach. God is the religious name for the absolute idea, which is also absolute spirit. God is both beginning and end, *alpha* and *omega*—the whole that encompasses every part and every moment within itself.

God does not simply become spirit through human consciousness, as Houlgate claims; rather, human consciousness is also already the self-consciousness of absolute spirit. Hegel expresses this idea as a "speculative reversal" that overcomes subjectivism and anthropocentrism. *Speculative* derives from the Latin word for mirror, *speculum,* and for Hegel it involves a relationship of double mirroring—of consciousness by the object, but also of the object by consciousness. "Absolute spirit is itself that which connects itself with what we have put on the other side to distinguish it. Thus, on a higher plane, religion is this idea, the idea of spirit that relates itself to itself, *the self-consciousness of absolute spirit.* Within this its *self-consciousness,* there falls also its *consciousness,* which was previously defined as relationship. Thus in the highest idea, religion is not the affair of the single human being; rather it is essentially the highest determination of the absolute idea itself " (*LPR* 1:318).[15] Hegel employs images of reversal to describe this situation. The progression of consciousness to the absolute "is a stream *flowing in opposite directions,* leading forward to the other, but at the same time working backward, so that what appears to be the *last,* founded on what precedes, appears rather to be the *first*—the foundation" (*LPR* 1:227 n. 115). "Absolute truth cannot be a result; it is what is purely and simply first, unique. It is what takes up simply everything into itself—the absolute plenitude in which everything is but a moment. . . . It is in this result itself that the one-sidedness is abolished: the result casts off its position as result and develops a *counterthrust [Gegenstoß],* so to speak, against this movement. . . . Absolute spirit, conscious of itself, is the first and alone true" (*LPR* 1:322).[16] The counterthrust cancels the overreaching of finite consciousness; it discloses that the true nature of finitude is self-negation, while the negation of negation or affirmation is the work solely of the infinite. The finite is properly related, not affirmatively to itself and negatively to the infinite (thus reducing the infinite to an extension or projection of consciousness), but rather negatively to itself and affirmatively to the infinite (thus recognizing the being of the infinite to be the only true being). It is the *infinite* that overreaches the finite, both encompassing and transcending it as an "affirmative infinitude" (*LPR* 1:288–310).

   Contra the secularizing interpretations, Hegel's God is not reducible to cosmic reason or human self-consciousness. There is, to be sure, an essential connection between God and the world, but also a real difference; and the two are related asymmetrically in the sense that God is the Creator and the world the creation. This asymmetry is articulated in Hegel's speculative reconstruction of the doctrines of the Trinity and creation—precisely those doctrines that are passed over lightly by the modern interpreters. As to the first, Hegel does not simply empty the immanent or logical Trinity into the economic or worldly Trinity. God does have an inner and abstract self-relatedness, a process of inward differentiation and return by which God is both subject and object to godself and in this sense utterly independent in and for godself. Precisely this independence is the condition of possibility for God's going out from godself freely and creating a world that in its empirical otherness corresponds to and completes God's logical otherness. The economic Trinity outwardly reenacts the dialectical relationships of the immanent Trinity. Hegel does not really speak of two Trinities but rather of what is more properly called an inclusive or holistic Trinity, the first moment of which is God's immanent self-relatedness (symbolized by the figure of the "Father"), and the second and third moments of which represent God's self-externalization in the world (the figure of the "Son") and God's self-reunification through the elevation of the world into communion with God (the figure of the "Holy Spirit"). All three moments are essential and co-constitutive: God is God in relation both to godself and to what is not-God, the world; the world as not-God is a moment within the divine life to which it contributes materiality and finitude; and the union of God and the world engenders spirituality, a living, dynamic, recognitive process. God is a holistic community of recognition in which differences are honored and communion is accomplished.[17]

Hegel does not abandon the doctrine of creation but interprets and reconstructs it, articulating the truth preserved in the *Vorstellung*. He does so by introducing two sets of metaphorical concepts: creation entails on the one hand a *positing (Setzen)* or a *primal judgment (Urteil)* and on the other hand a *release (Entlassen)* or an *unlocking (Entschließen)*. Positing and judging suggest that the divine creativity is exercised by a primordial saying or decree, a calling into being, a verbal shaping, a discriminating judgment. Creation is not so much a physical as an intellectual act: God creates by speaking a word (*LPR* 3:86–88). This is certainly how the Hebrew Bible describes it (Gen. 1:3 ff.). The description underscores the nonobjectifiability of the creative act and the insubstantiality of the created result. Creation hovers on the brink of nonbeing and is sustained solely by the divine word and goodness. While from the standpoint of eternity the world is a "disappearing moment of appearance," it is nonetheless an essential moment. Without it, "we have a relationship of God, of the idea, merely to godself. The act of differentiation is only a movement, a play of love with itself, which does not arrive at the seriousness of other-being, of separation and rupture." However, continues Hegel, "it belongs to the absolute freedom of the idea that, in its act of determining and dividing, it *releases* the other to exist as a free and independent being. This other, released as something free and independent, is the world as such" (*LPR* 3:292).

Here, the other set of metaphors used by Hegel to describe the act of creation, "release," "letting exist," or "unlocking," comes into play. Only an utterly free being can do this. God is able to create the world without any threat to God's own radical freedom, which is complete in and for itself, and which gratuitously overflows into the world without any self-diminishment. Here Hegel is drawing upon mystical rather than Jewish tradition (e.g., Meister Eckhart, Jacob Boehme). God is an inexhaustible fount that releases its fecundity into that which is not God. In this way, the nonserious play of love with itself becomes deadly serious, subject to the ruptures, conflicts, and suffering of the finite world. God is not thereby diminished but enlarged, for the world (precisely in its otherness from God) remains a moment within the divine life. God does not abandon this world but preserves and saves it, and indeed is enriched and completed by it; but this is an existential, not a logical, completion. Both truths must be maintained: that God is complete apart from the world and that God achieves completion through the world.[18]

I shall pass over the interpretations of Hegel's anthropology, Christology, and Pneumatology on the part of the secularizing interpreters to focus on an area of his religious thought that they totally ignore, namely, his treatment of the proofs of the existence of God. Hegel attended to the proofs not only in the *Lectures on the Philosophy of Religion* but also in the *Lectures on the Proofs of the Existence of God,* which he delivered as a separate course in 1829. His lecture manuscript was a partial first draft of a book that he intended to publish and for which he signed a contract only a few days before his death in the autumn of 1831. These plans indicate the urgency he attributed to the tasks of establishing the reality status of God over against secular and agnostic tendencies with which he was concerned and of distancing his own thought from charges of pantheism and atheism.[19]

Hegel views the proofs as the rational expression of the elevation of the human spirit to God. This "elevation" is essentially what religion is about, its *Sache* or content, knowledge of which is not a subjective operation but an exposition of an objective movement. The elevation is "the driving power within us" and is not our own self-projecting power but a negative power that is generated by the affirmative, overreaching power of the absolute (*Proofs,* 43–44, 63, 127–31).

Related to this concept of religious elevation is what Hegel describes in these lectures too as a "speculative" discussion of "the self-consciousness of God and of the relationship of God's self-knowing to God's knowing in and through the human spirit," or of "God's self-knowing in humanity and humanity's self-knowing in God." This discussion is properly a topic for theology, which is not part of a philosophical treatment of the proofs. Yet Hegel offers a theological excursus to make the point that it is God's very nature to communicate godself to humanity (*Proofs,* 64–68). Christianity "teaches that God brought godself down to humanity, even to the form of a servant, that God revealed godself to humans; and that, consequently, far from *grudging* humanity what is . . . highest, God laid upon humans with that very revelation the highest duty that they should *know* God" (*Proofs,* 67). A related philosophical principle is that "it is the nature of spirit to remain fully in possession of itself while giving another a share of its possession." The hindrance in knowing God is not on God's part but on ours, owing to caprice and false humility, an arbitrary insistence that the limits of human reason prevent knowledge of the infinite. "The more precise point is that it is not the so-called human reason with its limits that knows God, but rather the Spirit of God in humanity; . . . it is God's self-consciousness that knows itself in the knowing of humanity" (*Proofs,* 68). Thus the human elevation is generated by the divine descent; it is God's self-revelation or self-communication that is at work in humanity's knowledge of God. This is the speculative insight. Hegel returns to it at the end of the lectures where he speaks of "the community and communion of God and humanity with each other," which is "a communion of spirit with spirit." "The spirit of humanity—to know God—is simply God's Spirit itself" (*Proofs,* 126). This is an "is" of relationship, not identity. "Identity is . . . a misleading expression, for what is essentially involved is organic life within God" (*LPR* 3:351). God's Spirit does not displace or possess the human spirit but indwells and empowers it. A cognitive and communal relationship between God and humanity is possible because both are spirit.

While there exists an empirical multiplicity of proofs, they reduce to three major forms that arise from a reciprocal movement between finite and infinite. The *cosmological* proof starts out from a *contingent*, non-self-supporting being and reasons to a true, intrinsically necessary being. The *teleological* proof starts out from the *purposive relations* found in finite being and reasons to a wise author of this being. The *ontological* proof makes the *concept of God* its starting point and reasons to the being or reality of God (*Proofs*, 92). The unique contribution of Hegel's *Lectures on the Proofs of the Existence of God* is to show the logical progression from one proof to the next. A contingent thing can exist only if it has the ground of its being in an absolutely necessary being (the cosmological proof). Necessity, in turn, finds its truth in freedom, and freedom entails purposive relations. Given the ambiguity of good and evil in the world, finite purposiveness is true only if it has its ground in universal, divine purposiveness (the teleological proof). But the latter is not simply submerged in objectivity, as it is when, as end or purpose, it is merely the teleological determination of things (the objective concept). Rather, it is for itself, self-mediating, the unity of objectivity and subjectivity, and, as such, it is the living idea, including within itself the transition into reality, becoming thereby spirit (the ontological proof) (*Proofs*, 98–100). In this way the cosmological proof passes into the teleological, and the teleological into the ontological; but then the ontological proof returns to the reality from which the first two proofs arise. A dialectical spiral (not merely a circle) inscribes itself between contingency/necessity, purpose/freedom, and concept/idea; and God is progressively disclosed as necessary being, wise author, and free spirit.

Hegel's detailed treatment of the cosmological and teleological proofs shows how their traditional deductive logic is subverted into a truer meaning. The challenge is to show how the infinite and absolutely necessary being starts from an other—the finite and contingent—and yet in doing so starts only from itself. Absolute necessity cannot be a result that follows from contingency. In fact, finite, contingent being does not possess its own being but only that of its other, the infinite.

It is not because the contingent *is,* but because it *is not,* is nonbeing—
the very meaning of finitude—that absolute necessity is. The finite
passes over to the infinite, not by its self-affirmation or self-projection,
but by its self-negation and by the affirmative relating of the infinite
(*Proofs,* 111–18, 127–32, 159–65). Similarly, with the teleological proof,
the evidence adduced for worldly purposiveness is highly ambiguous. "There is much good in the world, but also an infinite amount of
evil" (*LPR* 2:718). The universal divine purpose cannot be demonstrated from experience; nonetheless it is fulfilled in the world by
its own power and against private human purposes. The universal at
which the teleological proof arrives is best described as *nous,* world
soul, or *logos,* life principle; it does not attain to subjectivity and spirit
(*LPR* 2:713–19). For the latter a further step is needed.

In the ontological proof, the reversal in ontological/epistemologi-
cal flow between finite and infinite that is already implicit in the cosmological and teleological proofs becomes explicit, and for this reason it is the "only genuine" proof (*LPR* 3:352). The logical form of
the argument is very simple: the concept of God must include being
or reality within itself, otherwise it is not the concept of God; thus
God as the most perfect being must also be the most real being. Hegel
concedes to Kant that being is not a predicate that adds something to a
concept. "What is required, however, is not indeed to add anything to
the concept . . . but to remove from it rather the shortcoming of being
only subjective, of not being the idea. The concept that is only something subjective, separate from being, is a nullity" (*LPR* 3:352–54).
The identity of concept and being cannot, however, simply be assumed;
it must be demonstrated. Hegel's demonstration unfolds in three steps.
First, the concept contains being implicitly because it is that in which
all distinction has been sublated and thus it is sheer self-presence. Second, just as when human beings realize their purposes what was at
first only ideal becomes real, so "the concept objectifies itself, makes
itself reality and thus becomes the truth, the unity of subject and object." The concept is alive and active, it has *drives,* and every satisfaction of a drive is a sublation of the subjective and a positing of
the objective (*LPR* 1:438–39, 3:355–56). Third, in Christianity we
find a concrete representation of this logical insight. Here the unity of

concept and being is to be grasped "as an absolute process, as the living activity of God." The Christian God is self-differentiating, self-revealing, and self-incarnating spirit (*LPR* 1:437, 3:356–57). Incarnation is the "speculative midpoint of religion" (*LPR* 1:245), and God, as incarnate, takes on finite, worldly existence *(Dasein)* in the form of a human being.

The proofs taken together provide an adequate conception of God as absolute necessity, absolute wisdom, and absolute spirit. They are philosophical ways of thinking about God; they probe and purify the meaning and truth of God-talk. In them, a two-way passage is occurring: from nature and finite spirit to God, and from God to nature and finite spirit. The two passages form a single whole, a totality that is both foundation and result. The result of one movement becomes the foundation of the other. By its own dialectical nature each movement drives itself over to the other, shows itself to be transient (*Proofs*, 89–92; *LPR* 3:174–75). There is no abstract and fixed foundation but a dialectical mirroring of elements that are always in play. The proposition of the cosmological proof is that the being of the finite is not its own being but rather that of its other, the infinite. Likewise, the proposition of the ontological proof is not simply that "the infinite *is*" but that "the infinite is finite." "For the infinite, in resolving to become *being*, determines itself to what is *other* than itself; but the other of the infinite is just the finite." By contrast with a "silly idealism" that maintains that if anything is thought it ceases to be, a serious idealism "contains with itself the counterstroke *[Gegenschlag]* that is the nature of the absolute unification into one of the two previously separated sides, and that is the nature of the concept itself" (*Proofs*, 164–65). The "counterstroke" is the ontological transition from infinite to finite, from concept to being, that balances and incorporates the cosmo-teleological transition from finite to infinite, from being to concept. It is another image of the speculative reversal that lies at the heart of Hegel's thought: the rise of finite consciousness to the absolute is at the same time the return of absolute spirit to itself from its materialization and externalization in finitude.[20] The infinite is the ground of the whole process in the sense of being the energy or power that pulses through it in a twofold direction.

Hegel's Conception of Secularization

The pulsation, the *Schlag,* that drives the infinite into the finite moves through the religious realm into the secular world. This is the basis for Hegel's conception of secularization, which differs profoundly from that of his secularizing interpreters. For the latter, nothing of divinity remains, whereas for Hegel divinity perseveres and returns to itself enriched by the occurrence of redemption in a tragically conflicted world. Social and political ethics represent an extension and realization of the religious cultus. Indeed, ethical life *(Sittlichkeit)* is "the most genuine cultus," but "consciousness of the true, of the divine, of God, must be directly bound up with it" *(LPR* 1:446). In the *Lectures on the Philosophy of Religion* Hegel describes the process by which the infinite love and glorious freedom that characterize the community of the Spirit must assume structured form, first in a church that has offices, doctrines, and cultic practices, then in the institutions of ethical life— law, family, civil society, and state. What is needed is that "out of the womb of the church there be formed a free life, a civil and political life, stemming from eternal principles, a rational, worldly kingdom in accord with the idea of freedom and the absolute character of rights" *(LPR* 3:151–52). The church plays an essential role in the formation of the body politic; it is the provider of ideals, goals, frames of reference. But on its own it is unable to transform the world into an image of the kingdom of freedom. For that a process of secularization must occur, a "realization of the spirituality of the community in universal actuality."[21]

In the 1831 lectures on religion, Hegel develops the role of the state in ethical life in an especially forceful way. He uses a strong image, similar to that of the *Gegenschlag,* when he says that it is in the organization of the state that "the divine has broken through *[eingeschlagen]* into the sphere of actuality." The foundation of the worldly realm is "the divine will, the law of right and freedom. The true reconciliation, whereby the divine realizes itself in the domain of actuality, consists in the ethical and juridical life of the state: this is the authentic discipline of worldliness" *(LPR* 3:342 n. 250). Worldliness must be disciplined, made to serve divine purposes, rather than be allowed to pursue self-gratifying desires and idolatrous ends. The state properly governed accomplishes this discipline. The alternative to the state is anarchy and barbarism. Religion does not wither away into the state for Hegel, as it does for Marx and other left-Hegelians (nor does the state wither away into a proletarian utopia). Hegel devotes considerable attention to the relations between religion and state, regarding them as both essential but leaving the question of their right relationship unresolved. Should they be separated so as to avoid theocratic abuses? Or related in such a way that political principles have their ultimate ground in God? (*LPR* 1:451–60).

Employing again the image of the pulse or stroke *(Schlag)*, Hegel suggests that the divine idea is like the weft *(Einschlag)* that drives back and forth across the warp of human passions, weaving the fabric of world history.[22] The fabric gradually takes on the pattern of ethical freedom *(sittliche Freiheit)*, the creation of which is the goal of God in history. Of course the pattern remains flawed and unfinished, given the power of the passions and the terrible tenacity of evil. The divine idea has to employ the "cunning of reason" to achieve its goal even partially and fragmentarily.[23] Hegel is not optimistic about the present state of the secular world. At the end of the 1821 philosophy of religion lectures, he enumerates signs of modern decadence and concludes that philosophers can do little to ameliorate them (*LPR* 3:158–62). His reserve seems to allow space for a prophetic role to be played by the church and theology, but he has little confidence in them either. Such a conclusion may seem unsatisfactory. But it reminds us that, while Hegel stresses the "now" of reconciliation in the life of the spiritual community, he also allows for a "not yet" that manifests itself in the never-finished struggles of history—not in a suprahistorical beyond or personal immortality. History is the place where God is at work, but the divine work is often hidden and never triumphant. Its predominant symbol is the anguished, suffering love of the cross. This is not an eschatology of sheer presence but one that arises out of the experience of loss and death; yet there is a reversal of the loss, a rebirth of life, and a broken presence of the Spirit.

Is such a conclusion something that no longer is believed by anyone? Does it reflect a romantic sensibility that has no place in the empirical and technological orientation of postmodernity? Does it express an optimism that is wholly out of touch with the realities of the human condition? Is it simply a relic of a long-discarded metaphysical worldview? Is it instead a mutilation of Christian orthodoxy? Or does it articulate a wisdom, realistic yet hopeful, about how God's wisdom works in the world and how the world lives into God? If so, let us, with Hegel, be lovers of this wisdom.

Notes

In this contribution I depend in various ways on the work of Robert R. Williams, especially his essay "Hegel's Concept of the True Infinite," *Owl of Minerva* 42 (2010–11): 89–122. I also draw on my book *Hegel and Christian Theology: A Reading of the Lectures on the Philosophy of Religion* (Oxford: University Press, 2005), and my essay "Hegel's Proofs of the Existence of God," in *A Companion to Hegel,* ed. Stephen Houlgate and Michael Baur (Oxford: Blackwell, 2111), 414–29. The principal texts on which I rely are Hegel's *Lectures on the Philosophy of Religion,* ed. and trans. Peter C. Hodgson et al., 3 vols. (1984–87; repr., Oxford: Oxford University Press, 2007; cited in text as *LPR*), and the *Lectures on the Proofs of the Existence of God,* ed. and trans. Peter C. Hodgson (Oxford: Oxford University Press, 2007; cited in text as *Proofs*). To avoid cluttering the text, the in-text citations often cover several preceding, related quotations.

1. Charles Taylor, *Hegel* (Cambridge: Cambridge University Press, 1975), ch. 18, esp. 492–95.

2. Taylor, *Hegel,* ch. 20, esp. 538–52 and 560–71.

3. Robert B. Pippin, *Hegel's Idealism: The Satisfactions of Self-Consciousness* (New York: Cambridge University Press, 1989), 5, 7, 180, and 198. Frederick Beiser, in his introduction to *The Cambridge Companion to Hegel and Nineteenth Century Philosophy,* ed. Frederick C. Beiser (New York: Cambridge University Press, 2008), sides with Taylor against Pippin and others in acknowledging that the "real historical Hegel" has genuine metaphysical and religious interests that cannot simply be bypassed or converted into something else. However, to avoid the dilemma between an antiquarian interest in Hegel and an anachronistic philosophical stance, Beiser proposes that we can "reconstruct Hegel's position as a contribution to a past conversation" ("Introduction: The Puzzling Hegel Renaissance," 1–14, quotation from 9). By contrast, I argue that the conversation is far from past and that Hegel's reconstruction of traditional doctrines holds promise for the future of theology and philosophy.

4. Robert Williams, "Hegel's Concept of the True Infinite," 101–15. His references are to G. W. F. Hegel, *Science of Logic*, trans. A.V. Miller (London: George Allen and Unwin, 1969), 129–30; *Encyclopedia of the Philosophical Sciences*, § 50 remark, from which the above quotation derives (G. W. F. Hegel, *The Encyclopaedia Logic*, trans. T. F. Geraets, W. A. Suchting, and H. S. Harris [Indianapolis: Hackett, 1991], 95–98; G. W. F. Hegel, *The Logic of Hegel*, trans. William Wallace [Oxford: Oxford University Press, 1892], 102–6); and *LPR* 1:87–88.

5. Stephen Houlgate, *Freedom, Truth and History: An Introduction to Hegel's Philosophy* (London: Routledge, 1991), ch. 5. See Robert Solomon, *From Hegel to Existentialism* (Oxford: Oxford University Press, 1987), 57–58, 61, and 66.

6. Stephen Houlgate, *The Opening of Hegel's Logic: From Being to Infinity* (West Lafayette: Purdue University Press, 2006), 424–25 and 434.

7. Robert M. Wallace, *Hegel's Philosophy of Reality, Freedom, and God* (New York: Cambridge University Press, 2005), 8, 52, 77–78, 96–102, 208, and 309.

8. Williams, "Hegel's Concept of the True Infinite," 94–101.

9. Thomas A. Lewis, *Freedom and Tradition in Hegel: Reconsidering Anthropology, Ethics, and Religion* (Notre Dame: University of Notre Dame Press, 2005), ch. 8, esp. 189–90.

10. William Desmond, *Hegel's God: A Counterfeit Double?* (Aldershot: Ashgate, 2003). I offer an evaluation of Desmond's critique in *Hegel and Christian Theology: A Reading of the Lectures on the Philosophy of Religion* (Oxford: Oxford University Press, 2005), 248–58.

11. Right-Hegelian theologians fail to recognize this redefinition. I am proposing a middle-Hegelian interpretation that affirms Hegel's reconstruction of the God concept.

12. See Hodgson, *Hegel and Christian Theology*, 13 and 16–17.

13. Hegel, *Encyclopedia of the Philosophical Sciences*, § 95 remark (*The Encyclopaedia Logic*, 152).

14. Hegel, *Encyclopedia of the Philosophical Sciences*, §§ 183–89 (*Encyclopaedia Logic*, 259–64). See Hodgson, *Hegel and Christian Theology*, 9–11.

15. See Hodgson, *Hegel and Christian Theology*, 81–82, where Hotho's freely edited version of this passage is quoted in a footnote.

16. See Hodgson, *Hegel and Christian Theology*, 83–84. See also Hegel, *Encyclopedia of the Philosophical Sciences*, § 36 addition (Hegel, *Encyclopaedia Logic*, 75).

17. I cannot do justice to Hegel's complex trinitarian thought in this brief account. See Hodgson, *Hegel and Christian Theology*, ch. 6. The key texts are in *LPR* 3:77–86, 189–98, and 275–90.

18. See Hodgson, *Hegel and Christian Theology*, ch. 7. Hegel's discussion of creation is found in *LPR* 3:86–90, 198–201, and 290–95. He also takes up the doctrine of creation in his treatment of Judaism (*LPR* 2:426–40 and 671–82). Here he stresses that it is an absolute creation, ex nihilo, an inner, "intuitive," eternal activity on God's part. For Hegel this means a nonemanationist *creatio ex*

Deo, a creation out of nothing other than God. God's creative activity not only discloses God's sublimity and subjectivity but also manifests the divine goodness and wisdom in the world. This Jewish doctrine is an essential part of Christian faith.

19. See my editorial introduction to the *Lectures on the Proofs of the Existence of God,* 1–4, 21, and 25. Hegel's manuscript on the proofs covers only introductory matters and the cosmological proof. For the teleological and ontological proofs it must be supplemented by materials from the *Lectures on the Philosophy of Religion.*

20. See the discussion above of the counterthrust *(Gegenstoß)* and the bidirectional stream.

21. For a discussion of these matters, see Hodgson, *Hegel and Christian Theology,* ch. 9. The key texts are found in *LPR* 3:149–62, 233–47, and 333–47.

22. G. W. F. Hegel, *Lectures on the Philosophy of World History,* vol. 1, ed. and trans. Robert F. Brown and Peter C. Hodgson, with William G. Geuss (Oxford: Clarendon Press, 2011), 147. In the introduction to these lectures, Hegel discusses quite explicitly matters relating to divine providence and knowledge of God. He says that he does so to allay suspicions that philosophy should shy away from considering religious truths or have an uneasy conscience about them (85). This is the very attitude that the secularizing interpreters attempt to foist on Hegel and that they assume to be normative for philosophy.

23. Hegel, *Lectures on the Philosophy of World History,* 96 n. 44. The cunning of reason means that divinity cannot be identified with any specific ethical or political agenda. Human actions are used against their own intended ends (worthy or unworthy) to achieve the divinely intended end, the actualization of freedom in history. Here again we encounter an image of negation and reversal.

Chapter 15

Kierkegaard's Critique of Secular Reason

MYRON B. PENNER

The deification of the established order is the secularization of everything.

—Anti-Climacus, *Practice in Christianity*

One stubborn perception among philosophers is that there is little of value in the explicitly Christian character of Søren Kierkegaard's thinking.[1] Those embarrassed by a Kierkegaardian view of Christian faith can be divided roughly into two camps:[2] those who interpret him along irrationalist-existentialist lines as an emotivist or subjectivist, and those who see him as a sort of literary ironist whose goal is to defer endlessly the advancement of any positive philosophical position. The key to both readings of Kierkegaard depends upon viewing him as more a *child* of Enlightenment than its critic, as one who accepts the basic philosophical account of reason and faith in modernity and remains within it. More to the point, these readings tend to view him through the lens of secular modernity as a kind of hyper- or ultra-modernist,[3] rather than as someone who offers a penetrating analysis of, and corrective to, the basic assumptions of modern secular philosophical culture. In this case, Kierkegaard, with all his talk of subjectivity as truth, inwardness, and passion, the objective uncertainty and absolute paradox of faith, and the teleological suspension of the ethical, along with his emphasis on indirect communication and the use of pseudonyms, is understood merely to perpetuate the modern dualisms between secular and sacred, public and private, object and subject, reason and faith—only as having opted out of the first half of each disjunction in favor of the second. Kierkegaard's views on faith are seen as giving either too much or too little to secular modernity, and, in any case, Kierkegaard is dubbed a noncognitivist, irrationalist antiphilosopher.

Against this position, I argue that it is precisely the failure to grasp Kierkegaard's dialectical opposition to secular modernity that results in a distortion of, and failure to appreciate, the overtly Christian character of Kierkegaard's thought and its resources for Christian theology. Kierkegaard's critique of reason is at the same time, and even more importantly, a critique of secular modernity. To do full justice to Kierkegaard's critique of reason, we must also see it as a critique of modernity's secularity. Simply to note that Kierkegaard's account leaves room for reason and that he has a fallibilist epistemology misses the crucial role that the concept of authority plays in his critique of reason. In particular, my thesis here is that Kierkegaard's objections to reason stem from his conviction that modern philosophy leaves no basis for rational warrant and has no authority to authorize belief in anything. The Kierkegaardian texts offer us a perspectival view of reason whose normativity has a kind of *potential* universality to it, rather than a self-grounding metaphysical necessity.[4]

This essay consists of three sections. In the first I summarize the irrationalist, existentialist reading of Kierkegaard, focusing primarily, though not exclusively, on the work of Alasdair MacIntyre and Caleb Miller. In the second I offer an overview of the literary-ironist interpretation of Kierkegaard, defended by Louis Mackey and Roger Poole. Finally, in the third I outline a series of recent criticisms of these positions and, building on these criticisms, advance the case for the unsecular Kierkegaard.

Rumors of Irrationality

Caleb Miller articulates an all-too-common (mis)reading of Kierkegaard when he writes: "Chief among those who have defended the view that reason undermines faith, and that Christian faith should spurn reason, is surely the nineteenth-century Danish philosopher, Søren Kierkegaard."[5] There are several versions of the charge that Kierkegaard is an irrationalist and/or subjectivist protoexistentialist who prefigures the atheistic existentialisms of Sartre and Camus, but the general character of these objections asserts that Kierkegaard believed truth, meaning, and value (whether moral or religious) are ultimately a matter of the will and that rational inquiry is (or should be) thereby excluded from the proper domain of religious belief; one should, as Cyril Connolly is reported to have said, just select the illusion that appeals to one's temperament and embrace it with passion. The problem, of course, is that if Kierkegaard's account of Christian faith is fundamentally irrational, subjectivist, and emotivist, it presents itself as a kind of anti- or nonphilosophy that isolates faith not only from secular (non-Christian) sources of rational critique but also from rational articulation and intelligibility. Kierkegaard has found a way to "save" Christian faith from the rational assault of secular reason but has done so at the price of jettisoning rational inquiry *tout court.* It also follows (or so the argument goes), first, that Christian belief cannot be known to be true in ways that are universal, objective, and public, and second, that theology has little positive value, as it consists in a set of arbitrary and ungrounded propositions. Either corollary, it is supposed, is sufficient motivation to set aside Kierkegaardian thought.

Alasdair MacIntyre's *After Virtue* presents a particularly influential version of this argument in its account of Kierkegaard's "emotivism."[6] The objection comes from Kierkegaard's account of "existence spheres" or "stages" of a person's life and specifically the movement between or transition from one sphere to another.[7] Under the pseudonym Frater Taciturnis, Kierkegaard summarizes these "stages" in *Stages on Life's Way* as (1) the aesthetic, (2) the ethical, and (3) the religious.[8] Under another pseudonym, Johannes Climacus, he splits the religious sphere into religiousness A, which is a generic sort of religiousness, and religiousness B, which is a distinctively Christian religiousness based on faith (or belief) in the "Absolute Paradox"—the God-man.[9] The existence spheres demarcate relatively autonomous life-views or points of view that delineate sets of rational criteria exhaustive of the possible modes of historical existence available to a human self. The term most often used to describe these transitions from one qualitative form of existence to another is "the leap" *(Spring),*[10] and sometimes the Kierkegaardian texts use the Greek construction *meta-basis eis allo genos* (change or shift from one genus to another).[11] The charge of irrationalism typically finds its basis in Kierkegaard's account of the "leap," or transition, between spheres in terms of faith or belief *(Tro).* Certain of Kierkegaard's detractors infer from this that Christian belief is, for him, a "blind leap of faith," implying that the leap *to* faith is also made *by* faith.[12]

MacIntyre does not focus so much on the "leap" language as on the specific nature of the transitions between existence spheres, particularly as portrayed in Kierkegaard's first major pseudonymous work, *Either/Or. Either/Or* is a two-volume work that presents, in Part 1, a series of aesthetic papers (aphorisms, critical essays, etc.) of A, the aesthete, which display an exclusively aesthetic perspective, and, in Part 2, a series of personal letters from B, Judge William, which embody the ethical perspective. William's letters to A urge him to make the shift to the ethical sphere. "Rather than designating the choice between good and evil," the judge writes, "my Either/Or designates the choice by which one chooses good and evil or rules them out. Here the question is under what qualifications one will view all existence and personally live."[13] Both the ethical and the aesthetic points of view are presented in the two volumes of *Either/Or* with little or no editorial commentary. We are left in the dark as to Kierkegaard's personal view, as the ethical and aesthetic are represented by pseudonymously authored papers of A and B, which are then edited under yet another pseudonym (Victor Eremita). MacIntyre describes Kierkegaard's work as "at once the outcome and the epitaph of the Enlightenment's systematic attempt to discover a rational justification for morality."[14] According to MacIntyre, *Either/Or* offers us with "a criterionless choice" between the ethical and aesthetic points of view that is completely arbitrary—and MacIntyre extends this analysis to include Climacus's account of Christian belief too.[15] Thus MacIntyre concludes that Kierkegaard's texts indicate that the authority and justification for any normative choice or belief are derived from principles that are themselves rationally ungrounded.

376 • *Myron B. Penner*

The key to understanding MacIntyre's reading lies in his implicit assumption that Kierkegaard's existence spheres are entirely incommensurate with each other, so that one *either* is completely and totally immersed within (or defines themselves entirely within or views all life according to the categories within) one sphere and its norms of rational evaluation, *or* has made a (blind and irrational—"emotivist") leap to some other sphere and defines oneself entirely within that one. The main point for MacIntyre is that on Kierkegaard's view one is never able to inhabit the overlap or interstices between spheres, imaginatively or otherwise. Existence spheres are epistemologically and rationally isolated from each other. This being the case, there can be no effective rational communication or evaluation of beliefs across the spheres.[16] According to MacIntyre, Kierkegaard suggests that because judgments or normative evaluations are always made from within one particular sphere of a person's existence, those judgments and evaluations can have no rational claim on the range of choices that belong to some other sphere of existence.

Caleb Miller and Robert Adams also find in Kierkegaard's Climacean writings an irrationalist position on faith and reason in the form of "the approximation argument," which, they tell us, concludes that one cannot or should not use objective reasons to bolster or support the truth of Christianity.[17] On Climacus's account, Christianity demands that we base our eternal happiness on a historical phenomenon— God's incarnation in the historical person of Jesus of Nazareth. However, Climacus notes, the most epistemic certainty one can have with respect to any historical phenomenon is mere "approximation."[18] An approximation cannot operate as a sufficient basis for eternal happiness insofar as the infinite interest an individual has in her eternal happiness demands absolute certainty. Or, as Climacus puts it, "An approximation is too little to build an eternal happiness on and is so unlike an eternal happiness that no result can ensue."[19] Therefore, Miller summarizes, Climacus believes that "we should not have a faith that is based on, or supported by, objective reasoning."[20] Miller counters Climacus's so-called approximation argument by observing that it does not really demonstrate that objective reasoning is of no value to the religious believer. Climacus mistakenly apportions existential commitment to objective evidence (or lack thereof). Miller understands Climacus to assume "that the only degree of commitment that can be supported by objective reasoning is exactly equal to the degree of support from objective reasoning, for the truth of the belief."[21] Miller responds by noting that "relatively low probabilities can rationally support very high degrees of commitment and very high probabilities can support very low degrees of commitment."[22] For example, suppose the probability of my four-year-old daughter being struck by a car in our neighborhood is relatively low (we live on a back street with an exceptionally low rate of traffic, and it is unpaved and narrow, so cars are unlikely to speed). This low probability does not change the fact that I have a fairly strong commitment to not letting her play on the street. Miller is right to note this. Conversely, the evidence that there are craters on the backside of the moon might make that probability very high, but still I am not deeply committed to this truth and could easily revise it. The upshot of Miller's charge is that Kierkegaard sets rational inquiry in opposition to Christian faith insofar as he disconnects objective reasons, such as evidence or probabilities, from Christian commitments. Miller believes Kierkegaard to hold that, because of the incommensurability between the infinite passion of Christian faith and the finitude of human reason, Christians cannot and should not use evidence or probabilities to support or establish the validity and/or truth of their propositional claims or to apportion their doxastic commitments accordingly. Once again, on this account the Kierkegaardian position isolates faith from public, rational critique. Having stared rational criticism in the face, Kierkegaard sequesters faith to the private, subjective sphere whose justifications can only be personal and absurd to others.

Ironic Indirection

Some secularizing commentators are not at all concerned with or bothered by Kierkegaard's alleged irrationalism but nonetheless find the efficacy of Christian faith or theological inquiry to have been effectively nullified by Kierkegaard's literary performance. Roger Poole's

contribution to *The Cambridge Companion to Kierkegaard* (1998) heralds
the "deconstructive turn" in Kierkegaard interpretation as a form of
reading that takes seriously a "literary approach" to Kierkegaard's
works begun by Louis Mackey's *Kierkegaard: A Kind of Poet* (1971).[23]

"Indirect communication" figures prominently in Kierkegaard's
authorship as his primary mode of address,[24] so one cannot avoid the
conclusion that his texts exhibit what one may at least call "deconstructive" tendencies. That is, Kierkegaard undeniably uses a host of literary
techniques, all of which may be collected under the rubric of indirect
communication, to "deconstruct" certain ways of reading his texts. For
example, in Johannes Climacus's *Concluding Unscientific Postscript to Philosophical Fragments,* Kierkegaard (under his own name) adds "A First and
Last Explanation" in which he divests himself of any authorial rights to
interpret the pseudonymous authorship, declaring that "in the pseudonymous books there is not a single word by me. I have no opinion
about them except as a reader."[25] Kierkegaard goes on to declare it
his wish and prayer that, should anyone want to quote from the pseudonymous books, the appropriate pseudonym, and not Kierkegaard's
own name, should be used.[26] In *The Point of View,* Kierkegaard explains
further: "If I were to begin *qua* author to protest [that his foregoing interpretation of his authorship was the right one], I might easily bring
confusion to the whole work, which from first to last is dialectical."[27]

Rather than understanding Kierkegaard's indirect communication
to deconstruct a *way* or cluster of *ways* of reading his texts as merely
abstract communications, Poole interprets Kierkegaard's refusal of authorial rights as severing the text from any "serious" philosophical or
theological intention, in something akin to a precognition of the death
of the author.[28] Kierkegaard, Poole argues, is a literary ironist who
avoids making any philosophical pronouncements or holding any theological positions and, like the so-called "death of God" theologians, realizes that all we may do is theorize and theologize within the sphere
of immanence.

Poole's thesis is that Kierkegaard's use of pseudonyms, irony,
humor, and alternative literary forms (e.g., sermons or "edifying discourses")—all aspects of indirect communication—are part of his
commitment to a view of language and authorship that deliberately

subverts the "objective" philosophical and theological content of his own texts. Kierkegaard's ironic stance does not pose a problem, however. Poole believes Kierkegaard has done us a service by freeing moral and religious thought from theoretical dogmatism.[29] As a matter of fact, Poole reasons, it is precisely theological and religious concerns that have occluded Kierkegaard's significance and caused a wealth of bad readings (and translations) of his texts.[30] Poole labels any attempt to read Kierkegaard's works for their philosophical (or theological) content as "blunt reading."[31] The trouble with so-called blunt reading is that "the Kierkegaardian text does not *tell* us something, it *asks* us something."[32] To think the text tells us something is to look "180 degrees in the wrong direction," and unless the reader recognizes that one derives from Kierkegaard's (or *any*) text only what one puts into it in the first place, then "the hermeneutic adventure will never begin."[33] In the end, Poole deems all "blunt" attempts to read Kierkegaard's diverse literature for its philosophical or theological content to be overly imbued with "fundamentalist and literalist assumptions" about "readerly intentionality."[34] Poole (among others) not only understands Kierkegaard to isolate faith from rational inquiry but sees *all* discourse on meaning, value, and truth to be ironically subverted by the Kierkegaardian texts in order to make space for authentic literary performance. Kierkegaard's engagement with Christian concepts and categories is purely ironical; they are merely instruments of parody and means to coax the reader to existential engagement. On Poole's reading, Kierkegaard advocates nothing like "serious" or "edifying" Christianity, as this has nothing whatever to do with one's private self-relation.

The (Un)Secular Kierkegaard

The irrationalist-existentialist Kierkegaard of MacIntyre and Miller and the literary-ironist Kierkegaard of Mackey and Poole have both been countered on textual and philosophical grounds in recent journal articles and book-length studies. Contra MacIntyre, Edward Mooney argues that Kierkegaard's texts actually *exhibit* the possibility of rational dialogue across existence spheres;[35] what is more, Anthony Rudd contends that Kierkegaard's texts assume that a form of practical reason is always operative—even for the aesthete—in the choices through which one ratifies one's existential comportment within one sphere or another.[36] Similar rejoinders have been offered for Miller's approximation argument. The target of Climacus's invective against objective reason is not reason giving per se but a specific *type* of rationality coupled with a particular notion of objectivity that excludes subjective interests from rational considerations.[37] Climacus's main contention, so the argument runs, is that objective reason (for humans) is not self-grounding and, as such, is always fallibilist and defeasible—subject to further review. Climacus's favorite terms for objective fallibility are *approximation* and *objective uncertainty*. And it is just this defeasible character of objective reasoning that is incommensurate with the infinite passion one has over eternal happiness or salvation. C. Stephen Evans has further argued that literary-ironist readings of Kierkegaard's such as Poole's are wrong to think that this rules out the possibility of Kierkegaard's texts containing theological and philosophical claims and arguments.[38] It makes better sense to understand Kierkegaard's irony as a form of "stable irony," to use Wayne Booth's distinction, as Kierkegaard deploys irony to further his ethical and Christian ideals.[39] Evans goes on to describe an alternate view of Kierkegaardian irony that allows for this positive stance. One might add that Poole's position is mired in self-referential incoherence, as Poole tries to counter so-called blunt reading on the grounds that it perpetuates a fascination with authorial intentionality, but then does so by claiming to have discerned Kierkegaard's true intentions!

All this is well and good; it appears that careful readings of Kierkegaard's texts and serious philosophical reflection on his ideas bolster the claim that Kierkegaard is not a noncognitivist or irrationalist. However, it is a mistake to think that Kierkegaard's critique of reason can be framed in terms consistent with modernity's secularized concept of reason. The concept of "secular" used here has in mind the Kierkegaardian contrast between Christianity and "the world," which parallels several other contrasts made in Kierkegaard's texts, such as that between the eternal and the temporal, the infinite and the finite, transcendence and immanence, and the religious and the aesthetic. For example, Anti-Climacus, in *The Sickness unto Death,* describes "the secular mentality" in terms of mortgaging oneself to "the world" and later correlates secularity with finitude, culture, and civic justice.[40] In this case, *secular* indicates a this-worldly, immanental sphere of mundane, material reality and relations, in contrast to an immaterial, transcendent sphere of spiritual reality and relations. Secularity, in this sense, involves a lack of openness to extrahuman transcendence rather than denoting the mere denigration of religion.[41] To speak of modern philosophy's view of reason as secular, then, is to say that its rational norms will be those that are governed by the terms of immanence—such as universal access, objectivity, neutrality—so that human reason may dissolve every paradox, unify each difference, and (potentially) provide an overarching explanation whose intelligibility and justification depend exclusively on factors within its immanental purview.

Thus the Kierkegaardian charge is not that modern philosophy is explicitly atheistic or that it denies religious transcendence or God-talk altogether.[42] Some of Kierkegaard's favorite targets, such as Descartes, Kant, and Hegel, attempt to rescue Christian theology rather than deny or destroy it, and Kierkegaard regularly assumes that the edifice he refers to as "modern speculation" understands itself to be explicitly "Christian." Therein is precisely Kierkegaard's trouble with modern philosophy—that modern philosophy unwittingly produces a pseudo-Christianity[43]—and the Kierkegaardian critique of reason and modern philosophy will be incoherent if one does not recognize his fundamentally religious diagnosis of modernity.[44] This account of modern secularity does not ignore or downplay, for example, Hegel's view that the world is more than just the world of nature and ultimately is the world of human spirit, and further that Christianity is the supreme religion and the church an indispensable social institution; Hegel's approbation of Christianity is based on the fact that he sees it as the highest expression of philosophical reason. But what this Kierkegaardian charge of secularity does say is that modern philosophy views any legitimate religious transcendence or talk of God as immanentally available to human reason.

Kierkegaard, then, does not simply challenge modern philosophy's version of the Greek *logos,* although he does that as well. More importantly, Kierkegaard's writings attempt to articulate a distinctly

382 • Myron B. Penner

Christian account of belief, in the wake of the Enlightenment project of Descartes, Kant, Hegel, and others, that does not collapse epistemic justification of belief into the categories of immanental human reason but remains faithful to the Christian categories of revelation, incarnation, sin, conversion, repentance, faith, hope, love, and so on— that is, the categories that structure distinctively Christian forms of transcendence.[45]

The Kierkegaardian challenge to modern philosophy is to be mindful of Socrates' principal lesson—that we are not rationally autonomous. The temptation for modern philosophy, because of its method and assumptions, is to rule out a genuinely Christian account of reason and belief that appeals to a transcendent revelation as the warrant for its assertions. Kierkegaard's critique of reason is not of reason *simpliciter,* but specifically *modern* reason, which, in the end, appeals to some form of human rational autonomy as the basis for its rational accounts. In *Philosophical Fragments,* Johannes Climacus contrasts the modern shift to human rational autonomy with the premodern, Socratic recognition of rational dependence (on God, the universe, preexistence) and shows how modernity's alleged philosophical progress is a chimera. Socrates refuses to ground his access to the truth in himself, his own rational resources, and appeals to the doctrine of anamnesis— of preexistence, transcendence, the eternal, and "the god"—in order to account for rational justification. Subsequently, Climacus argues, Socrates acknowledged human rational dependence on a transcendent source for truth and did not presume to teach others or offer them his wisdom. Instead, Socrates had the humility and equanimity "to be merely an occasion" for others.[46] Climacus places this in sharp relief to the modern age: "What rare magnanimity—rare in our day . . . when every second person is an authority, while all these distinctions and all this considerable authority are mediated in a common lunacy and in a *commune naufragium* [common shipwreck], because, since no human being has ever truly been an authority or has benefitted anyone else by being that . . . there is better success in another way, for it never fails that one fool going his way takes several others along with him."[47]

Here Climacus articulates the heart of the Kierkegaardian critique of reason and modern philosophy in general.[48] Kierkegaard at once sees how the modern shift to the rational autonomy of the self has at least two ramifications. First, the modern understanding of reason as rational autonomy produces a crisis of authority that, in the end, undercuts the very claims of reason—what Climacus calls here the "common shipwreck." As Kierkegaard develops it, modern philosophy advances a secularized view of reason that, despite its protestations to the contrary, deconstructs (i.e., ends in aporia) in the exact same manner as the Socratic *logos*. Here the problem is one of authority. When rational thought (as the universal or immanental) becomes the basis of authority, authority is effectively abolished because, *ex hypothesi*, all humans are equal.[49]

Second, Kierkegaard recognizes that this modern, secularized view of reason rules out a priori the possibility of incarnation—or at least rules out incarnation as an intelligible, rational, normative phenomenon for doxastic practice—which, as the breaking through of transcendence into immanence (without thereby losing its character as transcendence), Climacus labels "the ultimate paradox of thought" because it is "something that thought itself cannot think."[50] Kierkegaard produces an account (a *logos*) of Christian belief that appears as foolishness to the Greeks and is a stumbling block to modern philosophers. Climacus therefore uses terms such as *offense, the absurd, contradiction,* and *paradox* to describe the relation of Christian belief/truth to modern reason. Nevertheless, this constitutes, for Climacus, belief for *the best possible reason,* as the new sphere of Christian faith constitutes, for him, the *fulfillment* of reason.[51] What Climacus and Kierkegaard leave us with is a perspectival view of reason in which the existential and religious commitments circumscribe the parameters of rational discourse for particular rational agents. Kierkegaard does not close off Christian belief, grounded as it is in transcendence, to rational discourse, objectivity, or public inquiry. The Christian account of reason presented in Kierkegaard's writing persists in the general task of human reason, which is to make human experience (and our beliefs about it) intelligible.[52] Thus Christian belief has the quality of being *potentially* universal—as all may encounter the god-in-time by faith and receive the condition for the possibility of acquiring the truth—while at the same time Christian belief has a kind of objectivity insofar as it

384 · *Myron B. Penner*

is not simply a subjective passion or fantastic projection of inwardness but a belief that has been won *through* one's subjective commitments and inward appropriations. There is, then, also the ability to
determine the "superiority" of perspectives, but this can never be determined in an algorithm or set of procedures.

We are now in a position to understand how the irrationalist-
existentialist and literary-ironist interpretations of Kierkegaard are
secularist (in the above sense) and why this is the source of their fail-
ings. Readings like MacIntyre's, in which Kierkegaard is an irrationalist fideist, interpret Kierkegaard as the proponent of the modern
conception of autonomy, which recognizes no binding authority
or transcendent values that might limit the freedom of the self. Mac-
Intyre thus believes that the Kierkegaardian insistence on a distinctly
religious sphere, unassimilated by human reason, amounts to the assertion that the highest authority for human belief is criterionless
self-choice. This, however, could be true only if Kierkegaard believes
reason to be inherently secular. Similarly, when Kierkegaard protests
against the modern emphasis on objective reason, Miller and Adams
assume he must thereby view the scope and *telos* of reason as exhausted
on the horizon of human immanence, without recourse to a transcendent revelation. On their view, Kierkegaard is forced to choose between transcendence and faith, on the one hand, and immanence and
reason, on the other. They thus interpret him as a fideist who opts for
transcendence and spurns the use of reason altogether in religious belief. On my account, the Kierkegaardian opposition to objectivity is
a by-product of his refusal to grant human reason the autonomy required to ground itself in secular immanence. Furthermore, literary-
ironic interpreters such as Poole, who deny Kierkegaard any substantial voice, also present a Kierkegaard who stands at the crossroads of
immanence and transcendence and chooses to travel the well-worn
modern path of immanence. Their Kierkegaard sees through the modern game and understands that the jig is up; there is nothing left to
affirm or deny, leaving only the play of difference and the attempt to
find meaning in mundane performance. However, as I have argued,
Kierkegaard's reticence regarding the self-grounding nature of secular reason does not mean, for him, that there can be no truth or meaning or rational discourse whatsoever.

Ultimately, the problem for all these views is that they conflate any meaningful sense of reason with the modern, secular view of reason, so that when Kierkegaard objects to reason he is understood to take a stand against *all* forms and uses of reason altogether. I have argued that this is not the case and that the Kierkegaardian texts present Christian belief, reason, and its attendant norms through explicitly Christian categories and in a manner that preserves the possibility of a normative, transcendent revelation.

.   .   .

The Kierkegaardian critique of reason is launched, not against reason per se, but against *modern* reason. In modern philosophy, the ground of rational inquiry and truth is the autonomy of the human self. The key issue for Kierkegaard is authority—the fact that modern philosophy invests authority entirely in human reason while denying authority to a transcendent source of revelation outside itself. The distinction between immanence and transcendence is not erased in the Kierkegaardian texts; Kierkegaard leaves it squarely in play, but he does not think that this relegates us to a fanatical irrationalism, a helpless relativism, or a malevolent nihilism. What Kierkegaard does mean is that the uses of human reason are limited and contextual, requiring faith to ground them in a wider (transcendent) frame of reference. Once we understand this, Kierkegaard's Christianity is not an unqualified rejection of philosophical and rational discourse and does not reduce Christian belief to an arbitrary, subjective whim or leave theology any rational account.

Kierkegaard was and remains a child of the Enlightenment, if by this one means that his project is set within the context of Enlightenment concerns and that he is not a reactionary thinker who hearkens back to a pre-Enlightenment, premodern worldview. Insofar as Kierkegaard accepted that modernity posited a new situation for human thought and human being that had to be reckoned with on its own terms, he was irremediably modern. What he attempted to do, however, was to point the way forward by insisting that modern thought must not and cannot simply wipe the slate clean and start from scratch but must be careful to listen to ancient wisdom and resituate it in this new, modern context. As Climacus remarks in his "Moral" at the end

of *Philosophical Fragments,* "To go beyond Socrates when one nevertheless says essentially the same thing as he, only not nearly so well—
that, at least, is not Socratic."[53]

Notes

The epigraph from Kierkegaard's *Practice in Christianity* is taken from the edition edited and translated by Howard V. Hong and Edna H. Hong (Princeton:
Princeton University Press, 1991), 91.

1. George Pattison, *The Philosophy of Kierkegaard* (Montreal: McGill-Queen's
University Press, 2005), 5. This perception is not as commonplace as it once
was, and I am referring more to a general philosophical appraisal of Kierkegaard that exists largely outside the circle of those who take Kierkegaard's philosophical thought seriously and actually specialize in his work. For just a few of
the recent philosophical overviews of Kierkegaard's thought, in addition to Pattison's, that are appreciative of his religious commitments, see C. Stephen Evans,
"Kierkegaard as Christian Thinker," in C. Stephen Evans, *Kierkegaard on Faith and
the Self: Collected Essays* (Waco: Baylor University Press, 2006), 3–26; David E.
Cooper, "Søren Kierkegaard," in *The Blackwell Guide to Continental Philosophy,* ed.
Robert C. Solomon and David Sherman (Oxford: Blackwell, 2003), 43–61; and
Merold Westphal, "Kierkegaard," in *A Companion to Continental Philosophy,* ed.
Simon Critchley and William R. Schroeder (Oxford: Blackwell, 1998), 128–38.
It goes almost without saying, of course, that there is indeed a rich history of
taking Kierkegaard's Christianity seriously within theological discourse since the
mid-twentieth century. For two excellent examples of recent theological appre-
ciations of Kierkegaard, see Sylvia Walsh, *Living Christianly: Kierkegaard's Dialectic
of Christian Existence* (University Park: Pennsylvania State University Press, 2005);
and David J. Gouwens, *Kierkegaard as Religious Thinker* (Cambridge: Cambridge
University Press, 1996).

2. I am keenly aware of the imprudence of describing "Kierkegaard's
view" of anything, thus my use of the locution "a Kierkegaardian view." In light
of Kierkegaard's request for us to distance his own views from those of his
pseudonyms, and because of his use of indirect communication, I follow Merold Westphal's lead and use the term *Kierkegaard* to represent a body of texts
rather than Kierkegaard's personal beliefs or opinions. See Westphal, "Kierkegaard," 129.

3. For more on my use of this term, see Myron B. Penner, "Christianity
and the Postmodern Turn: Some Preliminary Considerations," in *Christianity*

and the Postmodern Turn: Six Views, ed. Myron B. Penner (Grand Rapids, MI: Brazos, 2005), 18.

4. As Merold Westphal has argued in "Kierkegaard," 132–35, and in his *Overcoming Onto-Theology: Toward a Postmodern Christian Faith* (New York: Fordham University Press, 2001), 6–8, 143–47, when Kierkegaard's critique of Christendom is combined with his critique of reason, a space is opened up for a "positive postmodernism" in which Christian faith may "overcome onto-theology." For more on this theme, see also Merold Westphal's *Kierkegaard's Critique of Reason and Society* (University Park: Pennsylvania State University Press, 1987), 29–59, and *Becoming a Self: A Reading of Kierkegaard's "Concluding Unscientific Postscript"* (West Lafayette: Purdue University Press, 1996), 114–43.

5. Caleb Miller, "Faith and Reason," in *Reason for the Hope Within,* ed. Michael J. Murray (Grand Rapids, MI: Eerdmans, 1999), 139.

6. Alasdair MacIntyre, *After Virtue* (Notre Dame: University of Notre Dame Press, 1981), 39–50. MacIntyre's reading of Kierkegaard is carefully examined in *Kierkegaard after MacIntyre: Essays on Freedom, Narrative and Virtue,* ed. J. J. Davenport and A. Rudd (Chicago: Open Court, 2001), and MacIntyre's replies to the essays are included. See especially Marilyn Gaye Piety, "Kierkegaard on Rationality," 59–74; Anthony Rudd, "Reason in Ethics: MacIntyre and Kierkegaard," 131–50; and Edward F. Mooney, "The Perils of Polarity: Kierkegaard and MacIntyre in Search of Moral Truth," 233–64.

7. The terms *stage* and *existence sphere* are used alternately in Kierkegaard's writings to denote his concept of the possible modes of existence for a human being. However, the term that occurs most often is *sphere,* especially in the more mature writing of Johannes Climacus's *Postscript.*

8. Søren Kierkegaard, *Stages on Life's Way,* ed. and trans. H. V. Hong and E. H. Hong (Princeton: Princeton University Press, 1988), 476.

9. Søren Kierkegaard, *Concluding Unscientific Postscript to Philosophical Fragments* 1.555–1.616; here and subsequently I draw from the two-volume edition edited and translated by H. V. Hong and E. H. Hong (Princeton: Princeton University Press, 1992).

10. The term occurs first in Kierkegaard's published authorship in Søren Kierkegaard, *Philosophical Fragments* (I draw here and subsequently on the edition *Philosophical Fragments, Johannes Climacus,* ed. and trans. by Howard V. Hong and Edna H. Hong [Princeton: Princeton University Press, 1985]), 43, and occurs throughout *Søren Kierkegaard's Journals and Papers,* 7 vols., ed. and trans. H. V. Hong and E. H. Hong (Princeton: Princeton University Press, 1967); see vol. 1, §§ 26, 385, 653, 808, and 972; vol. 2, §§ 1248, 1603, and 1607; vol. 3, §§ 2704, 2807, 3247, and 3598; and vol. 4, § 4421.

11. Kierkegaard, *Philosophical Fragments,* 73, and *Concluding Unscientific Postscript* 1.98.

12. E.g., Francis A. Schaeffer, *Escape from Reason* (London: Inter-Varsity Fellowship, 1968), 46, 51.

13. Søren Kierkegaard, *Either/Or,* pt. 2, ed. and trans. Howard V. Hong and Edna H. Hong (Princeton: Princeton University Press, 1987), 169.

14. MacIntyre, *After Virtue,* 39.

15. MacIntyre, *After Virtue,* 37, 41.

16. Cf. Mooney, "Perils of Polarity," 240–41.

17. See Miller, "Faith and Reason," 139–42, and Robert M. Adams, "Kierkegaard's Arguments against Objective Reasoning in Religion," in *The Virtue of Faith and Other Essays in Philosophical Theology* (New York: Oxford University Press, 1987), 25–41. C. Stephen Evans has already argued in *Faith and Reason: A Kierkegaardian Account* (Grand Rapids, MI: Eerdmans, 1998), 107, that Adams's version of the so-called approximation argument is not even a challenge to Kierkegaard's Climacus, since it stems from a fundamental misunderstanding as to what Climacus means by objectivity.

18. Kierkegaard, *Concluding Unscientific Postscript* 1.23. Miller, following Adams, who wrote before the advent of the new Hong and Hong translation, uses the older Swenson-Lowrie translation. I am citing from the Hong and Hong translation, but I follow the passages Miller uses to support his thesis.

19. Thus Evans, in *Faith and Reason,* 11, 107, justly renames this argument of Climacus the "incommensurability argument," as the basic idea is that there is an incommensurability between the sort of beliefs required by an infinite passion for eternal blessedness and the sort of certainty granted by historical evidence.

20. Miller, "Faith and Reason," 140.

21. Miller, "Faith and Reason," 141.

22. Miller, "Faith and Reason," 141.

23. Roger Poole, "The Unknown Kierkegaard: Twentieth Century Receptions," in *The Cambridge Companion to Kierkegaard,* ed. A. Hannay and G. Marino (New York: Cambridge University Press, 1998), 66 ff.; Poole's analysis here is a continuation of his earlier work *Kierkegaard: The Indirect Communication* (Charlottesville: University of Virginia Press, 1993). Louis Mackey, *Kierkegaard: A Kind of Poet* (University Park: Pennsylvania State University Press, 1971). Other works that receive honorable mention in this interpretive tradition are Louis Mackey, *Points of View: Readings of Kierkegaard* (Tallahassee: Florida State University Press, 1986); Pat Bigelow, *Kierkegaard and the Problem of Writing* (Tallahassee: Florida State University Press, 1987); John Vignaux Smyth, *A Question of Eros: Irony in Sterne, Kierkegaard and Barthes* (Tallahassee: Florida State University Press, 1989); and Mark C. Taylor, *Altarity* (Chicago: University of Chicago Press, 1987).

24. Itself a rather complex concept, Kierkegaard's indirect communication, for Poole, involves five things: (1) the use of pseudonyms, (2) the use of irony, (3) the publication of edifying discourses (under his own name), (4) a

"lived presence" that undermines public perception of Kierkegaard's published works, and in the end (5) a shift in his daily routine. Poole, "Unknown Kierkegaard," 59. See Kierkegaard's unpublished and incomplete set of lecture notes on communication in Kierkegaard, *Søren Kierkegaard's Journals,* vol. 1, §§ 617–81; and *Concluding Unscientific Postscript* 1.274–77.

25. Kierkegaard, *Concluding Unscientific Postscript* 1.626.

26. Kierkegaard, *Concluding Unscientific Postscript* 1.627. This is most likely the passage Poole has in mind when he states that blunt readers miss "the entire dialectical structure" of Kierkegaard's work (see above). It is also, in fact, the very passage Poole cites (perhaps a little strangely) to support his thesis that blunt readers have missed Kierkegaard's intentions by looking to him for philosophical and theological content. See Poole, "Unknown Kierkegaard," 62. Cf. Poole, *Kierkegaard,* 160–64.

27. Søren Kierkegaard, *The Point of View for My Work as an Author,* trans. Howard V. Hong and Edna H. Hong (Princeton: Princeton University Press, 1998), 33.

28. Poole states that "the tradition of 'blunt reading' insists on interpreting [Kierkegaard] as a 'serious' writer who is didactic, soluble, and at bottom, 'edifying.'" Poole, "Unknown Kierkegaard," 61. See below for more on Poole's concept of blunt reading.

29. Interestingly, despite his disavowals of any positive conceptual content in the Kierkegaardian texts, Poole also is very careful in the end to distance himself from both the laissez-faire subjectivism of one such as Mark C. Taylor and "the naïve consumerism of Richard Rorty." Instead, Poole sees the deconstructive way of reading Kierkegaard as creating the conceptual space for Kierkegaard to emerge "after Rorty, after [Jürgen] Habermas, after [Charles] Taylor, after . . . 'Derrida,' as a thinker who would enable us to reopen the question of justice in a mood of new optimism." Poole, "Unknown Kierkegaard," 71, 72, cf. 68–69.

30. Poole, "Unknown Kierkegaard," 59.

31. Poole, "Unknown Kierkegaard," 58–66 and esp. 62–64, where Poole runs through a list of rather impressive Kierkegaardian scholarship in philosophy and theology and manages to dismiss each scholar's work as rubbish in just a sentence or two.

32. Poole, "Unknown Kierkegaard," 61 (italics mine).

33. Poole, "Unknown Kierkegaard," 62.

34. Poole, "Unknown Kierkegaard," 62.

35. Mooney, "Perils of Polarity," 240–45.

36. Rudd, "Reason in Ethics," 139; and Myron Bradley Penner, *Subjectivity and Knowledge: Self and Belief in Kierkegaard's Thought* (Cheltenham: Paternoster, forthcoming), chs. 6 and 7.

37. Evans, *Faith and Reason,* 107.

38. Evans, *Kierkegaard on Faith*, 67–80. Sylvia Walsh develops a similar view of Kierkegaardian irony in "Kierkegaard and Postmodernism," *International Journal for Philosophy of Religion* 29 (1991): 113–22.

39. Evans, *Kierkegaard on Faith*, 11.

40. Søren Kierkegaard, *The Sickness unto Death*, ed. and trans. Howard V. Hong and Edna H. Hong (Princeton: Princeton University Press, 1980), 35 and 33–35, and *Practice in Christianity*, ed. and trans. Howard V. Hong and Edna H. Hong (Princeton: Princeton University Press, 1991), 112.

41. Cf. Johannes de Silentio's commentary in Søren Kierkegaard, *Fear and Trembling*, ed. and trans. Howard V. Hong and Edna H. Hong (Princeton: Princeton University Press, 1983), 186: "Modern philosophy makes no movement; as a rule it makes only a commotion [the word used here is the Danish equivalent of the German term *aufhebung*, so important in Hegel's writings], and if it makes any movement at all, it is always within immanence, whereas repetition is and remains a transcendence."

42. For an excellent exposition of both Hegel and Kierkegaard on the issue of transcendence, see Merold Westphal, *Transcendence and Self-Transcendence: On God and the Soul* (Bloomington: Indiana University Press, 2004), 66–90, 201–26.

43. An excellent account of Kierkegaard's critique of the Christianity of his day, though not with specific reference to modern philosophy, is found in Walsh, *Living Christianly*, esp. 1–16.

44. One could read the religious diagnosis of modernity as the entire point of *Philosophical Fragments*. See also Søren Kierkegaard, *The Book on Adler*, ed. and trans. Howard V. Hong and Edna H. Hong (Princeton: Princeton University Press, 1998), 173 ff., *Practice in Christianity*, 81 n., 91, 111–12, and *Two Ages, The Age of Revolution and the Present Age: A Literary Review*, ed. and trans. Howard V. Hong and Edna H. Hong (Princeton: University of Princeton Press, 1978), 106–7.

45. Cf. Kierkegaard, *Book on Adler*, 112 ff. Kierkegaard writes that "not every outpouring of religious emotion is a Christian outpouring. In other words, emotion that is Christian is controlled by conceptual definitions . . . *in connection with all inwardness in the sphere of immanence.* . . . The transformation in feeling and imagination takes place within such concepts and definitions of which it can be said that every human being discovers them in using them. . . . A Christian awakening . . . *lies in the sphere of transcendence.* . . . Proficiency and schooling in the Christian conceptual definitions are . . . required" (113–14, his emphasis).

46. Kierkegaard, *Philosophical Fragments*, 10–11.

47. Kierkegaard, *Practice in Christianity*, 91.

48. The advantage of this reading of Kierkegaard's critique of reason is that it makes sense of, and furthers, Merold Westphal's insight that Kierkegaard's critique is at once social and political, as well as epistemological. See Westphal, *Kierkegaard's Critique*, passim.

49. Kierkegaard believes that authority essentially depends on a qualitative difference between the authority and that over which the authority is exercised. See Kierkegaard, *Book on Adler,* 179 ff.

50. Kierkegaard, *Philosophical Fragments,* 37. Climacus also calls this "a metaphysical caprice" (37).

51. Climacus speaks of "the unknown" of "faith" or "the paradox" as "the self-ironizing of the understanding" in which the understanding "wills its own downfall," in Kierkegaard, *Philosophical Fragments,* 44–48, 59. Cf. John Milbank, "The Sublime in Kierkegaard," in *Post-Secular Philosophy: Between Philosophy and Theology,* ed. Phillip Blond (New York: Routledge, 1998), 139.

52. Milbank, "Sublime in Kierkegaard," 139.

53. Kierkegaard, *Philosophical Fragments,* 111.

Contributors

Nicholas Adams teaches theology and ethics at the University of Edinburgh. He works on German philosophy in relation to twentieth-century theology, especially the thought of Hegel and Kant. His principal interest is "reparative reasoning" or the practice of repairing philosophy. His recent publications include *Habermas and Theology* (Cambridge University Press, 2006); "Making Deep Reasoning Public" (*Modern Theology*, 2006); and "Rahner's Reception in Twentieth Century Protestant Theology," in *The Cambridge Companion to Rahner*, ed. Declan Marmion and Mary Hines (Cambridge University Press, 2005).

Hubert Bost is director of research for the Religious Studies section at the École Pratique des Hautes Études (Paris-Sorbonne), where he holds the chair in Protestantism and Culture in Modern Europe, Sixteenth to Eighteenth Century. His publications include, as editor, *Le consistoire de l'Eglise wallonne de Rotterdam, 1681–1706* (Champion, 2008); and as author, *Pierre Bayle* (Fayard, 2006), and *Pierre Bayle historien, critique et moraliste* (Brepols, 2006).

Philip Clayton is dean of faculty at Claremont School of Theology and provost of Claremont Lincoln University. He also holds the Ingraham Chair in Theology. He has been a guest professor at Harvard University, Humboldt Professor at the University of Munich, and Senior Fulbright Fellow also at Munich. He is a past winner of the Templeton Book Prize and the Templeton Research Prize. He is author or editor of over a dozen books, including *Practicing Science, Practicing Faith: Twelve Scientists in the Quest for Integration*

(Columbia, 2007); *In Whom We Live and Move and Have Our Being: Panentheistic Reflections on God's Presence in a Scientific World* (Eerdmans, 2004); and *The Problem of God in Modern Thought* (Eerdmans, 2004).

John Cottingham is professor emeritus of philosophy at the University of Reading, professorial research fellow at Heythrop College, University of London, and an honorary fellow of St. John's College, Oxford. He is an authority on early modern philosophy, co-translator of *The Philosophical Writings of Descartes*, and editor of *The Cambridge Companion to Descartes*. His recent titles include *The Spiritual Dimension* (Cambridge University Press, 2005); *Cartesian Reflections* (Oxford University Press, 2008); and *Why Believe?* (Continuum, 2009). He is editor of the international philosophical journal *Ratio*.

Yolanda Estes is associate professor in philosophy and religion at Mississippi State University. Her areas of specialization are the history of modern philosophy, German Idealism, and feminist social and political philosophy. Her publications include *J. G. Fichte and the Atheism Dispute* (1798–1800), ed. Yolanda Estes and Curtis Bowman (Ashgate, 2010); "The Pure Will and the Categorical Imperative in the Later Jena *Wissenschaftslehre*," in *New Essays on Fichte's Later Jena* Wissenschaftslehre, ed. Daniel Breazeale and Tom Rockmore (Northwestern University Press, 2002); and, as co-editor, *Marginal Groups and Mainstream American Society* (University Press of Kansas, 2000).

Chris L. Firestone is associate professor of philosophy at Trinity International University. He has published numerous articles in the field of Kant studies and on the interpretation and reception of Kant in philosophy of religion and theology in the nineteenth and twentieth centuries. His research interests include modernity, Continental philosophy, and philosophy of religion. He is co-editor, with Stephen Palmquist, of *Kant and the New Philosophy of Religion* (Indiana University Press, 2006); co-author, with Nathan Jacobs, of *In Defense of Kant's* Religion (Indiana University Press, 2008); and author of *Kant and Theology at the Boundaries of Reason* (Ashgate Publishers, 2009).

Lee Hardy is professor of philosophy at Calvin College in Grand Rapids, Michigan, and part-time professor at Calvin Theological Seminary. His publications include "Kant's Reidianism: The Role of Common Sense in Kant's

Epistemology of Religious Belief," in *Kant's Moral Metaphysics: God, Freedom, and Immortality*, ed. Benjamin Bruxvoort Lipscomb and James Krueger (Berlin: Walter De Gruyter, 2010); "Context and Temporality: Heidegger's View of the Person," in *Human Nature in Chinese and Western Culture*, ed. Kelly James Clark and Chen Xia (Sichuan University Press, 2005); and "Postmodernism as a Kind of Modernism: Nietzsche's Critique of Knowledge," in *Christian Philosophy and Postmodern Thought*, ed. Merold Westphal (Indiana University Press, 1999).

Peter C. Hodgson is the Charles G. Finney Professor of Theology, Emeritus, at Vanderbilt University. Hodgson's research and teaching focus on theology, both historical and constructive. He is a leading translator of the works of G. W. F. Hegel and the author of numerous essays and books, including *Shapes of Freedom: Hegel's Philosophy of World History in Theological Perspective* (Oxford University Press, 2012); *Liberal Theology: A Radical Vision* (Fortress Press, 2007); and *Hegel and Christian Theology: A Reading of the Lectures on the Philosophy of Religion* (Oxford University Press, 2005).

Nathan A. Jacobs is assistant professor of religion and philosophy at John Brown University. He has taught at Trinity International University and Calvin College and Seminary. His research interests include patristic theology, medieval and post-Reformation scholasticism, and modern philosophy of religion. He has published numerous journal articles on these subjects. He is a contributor to *Kant and the New Philosophy of Religion*, ed. Chris L. Firestone and Stephen Palmquist (Indiana University Press, 2006), and co-author, with Chris L. Firestone, of *In Defense of Kant's Religion* (Indiana University Press, 2008).

Jacqueline Mariña is professor of philosophy at Purdue University. In addition to many articles, she is the author of *Transformation of the Self in the Thought of Friedrich Schleiermacher* (Oxford University Press, 2008) and editor of *The Cambridge Companion to Friedrich Schleiermacher* (Cambridge University Press, 2005). She is currently working on a book on personal identity in Kant.

A. P. Martinch is Roy Allison Vaughan Centennial Professor in Philosophy and professor of history and government at the University of Texas at Austin.

He is the author of *The Two Gods of Leviathan* (Cambridge University Press, 1992), and *Hobbes: A Biography* (Cambridge University Press, 1999), which won the Robert W. Hamilton Book Award. He is the editor of *The Philosophy of Language*, 5th ed. (Oxford University Press, 2006), and co-editor, with Kinch Hoekstra, of *The Oxford Handbook of Hobbes* (Oxford University Press, forthcoming 2012).

Richard A. Muller is P. J. Zondervan Professor of Historical Theology at Calvin Theological Seminary. His major teaching fields are Reformation and early modern studies, and the history of Christian thought. His works include *After Calvin: Studies in the Development of a Theological Tradition* (Oxford University Press, 2003); *Post-Reformation Reformed Dogmatics*, 4 vols. (Baker Book House, 1984–2003); and *The Unaccommodated Calvin* (Oxford University Press, 2000).

Myron B. Penner is former director of the Graduate M.A. Program in Philosophy of Religion and Religious Studies at Liberty University Graduate School. He is the editor of *Christianity and the Postmodern Turn* (Brazos Press, 2007). His other publications include *Against Apologetics: A Postmodern Critique* (Baker Academic, forthcoming 2012); *Living Reasonably, Loving Well: Conversing with Frankfurt and Kierkegaard*, co-edited with Søren Landkildehus (Indiana University Press, forthcoming 2012); and "The Moral Interpretation of Religion" (*European Journal of Theology*, 2001).

Stephen D. Snobelen teaches at the University of King's College, Halifax, Nova Scotia. He specialises in the history of the interaction between science and religion. His current research focus is on the theological and prophetic views of Isaac Newton. Snobelen is one of the founders of the Newton Project and Director of the Newton Project Canada. His work on Newton's theology has been featured in documentaries produced by the BBC, Nova, Vision TV, and the History Channel. He has published more than twenty-five academic papers on Newton, theology, and science and religion. He has also edited a special issue of *Enlightenment and Dissent* entitled "Isaac Newton in the Eighteenth Century" (2009).

Nicholas Wolterstorff is Noah Porter Professor of Philosophical Theology at Yale University and Senior Fellow at the University of Virgina. He taught for thirty years at his alma mater, Calvin College. He delivered the Wilde Lectures at Oxford University in fall 1993 and the Gifford Lectures at St. Andrews University in spring 1995. He has been president of the American Philosophical Association (Central Division) and of the Society of Christian Philosophers. His many works include *Justice: Rights and Wrongs* (Princeton University Press, 2007); *Thomas Reid and the Story of Epistemology* (Cambridge University Press, 2001); and *John Locke and the Ethics of Belief* (Cambridge University Press, 1996).

Index